Extreme Methods

Extreme Methods

Innovative Approaches to Social Science Research

J. Mitchell Miller
University of South Carolina

Richard Tewksbury
University of Louisville

Allyn and Bacon
Boston • London • Toronto • Sydney • Tokyo • Singapore

Editor in Chief, Social Sciences: Karen Hanson
Editorial Assistant: Karen Corday
Executive Marketing Manager: Lisa Kimball
Editorial Production Service: Marbern House
Manufacturing Buyer: Julie McNeill
Cover Administrator: Jennifer Hart
Electronic Composition: Omegatype Typography, Inc.

Copyright © 2001 by Allyn & Bacon
A Pearson Education Company
160 Gould Street
Needham Heights, MA 02494

Internet: www.abacon.com

Library of Congress Cataloging-in-Publication Data

Miller, J. Mitchell.
    Extreme methods : innovative approaches to social science research /
J. Mitchell Miller, Richard Tewksbury.
       p.   cm.
    Includes bibliographical references.
    ISBN 0-321-05487-3
    1. Sociology—Field work.   2. Social sciences—Field work.
I. Tewksbury, Richard A.   II. Title.
HM517.M56   2000
301'.07'23—dc21

                           99-054990

Printed in the United States of America

10 9 8 7 6 5 4 3 2 1   05 04 03 02 01 00

Contents

Preface

Extreme Methods: Innovative Approaches to Social Science Research promotes the "criminological ethnographic enterprise," which is the use of alternative qualitative research methods to study crime and deviance. This type of ethnography is vital to our understanding of crime and deviance and has a rich tradition in the history of social science dating to the 1920s and the Chicago school of fieldwork. It has since been so discredited and dismissed that, until very recently, ethnography on criminological, deviant, and criminal justice topics was deemed inferior social science and thus infrequently conducted. This book argues otherwise. To better understand the readings (i.e., the research strategies advocated), we offer the following observations for consideration of alternative fieldwork relative to traditional methods and in the context of academic paradigmatic politics.

It is ironic that fieldwork on crime and deviance is discouraged and considered secondary to variable analysis-based research methods. The methodological tradition of sociology in the United States associated with the Chicago school in the inter-war years featured firsthand observation, participation, and interaction with subjects in their natural environments. Many of the pioneering social science works were conducted within this tradition (Anderson 1923; Thrasher 1927; Shaw 1930; Cressey 1932), and fieldwork was the leading paradigm (model) of research.

The rise of positivism (1950s) as the leading philosophy of science, coupled with the popularity of functionalist theorizing, bode the dawn of a dark period that witnessed the demise of ethnography as standard science. Positivism advocates causality as determined by the statistical analysis of the relationship between variables representing reduced social realities. Emulation of the natural science research approach fostered quasi-experimental designs with which ethnographers were out of sync. The philosophy of positivism and the strategy of variable analysis has held dominion since its rise, rendering qualitative research a second-tier alternative.

The paradigmatic shift to positivism as the preferred research style has been supported because of the attack on competing approaches. Fieldwork on crime and deviance, for example, has been successfully suppressed largely on grounds of ethical impropriety. As some of the following selections demonstrate, beliefs over the misuse of human subjects, exposure to danger, and the controversies associated with secrecy and legality—although often erroneous—taint criminological ethnography. These ethical/legal objections have raised eyebrows within our universities that have, through institutional review boards, consistently objected to and frequently disapproved of ethnographic proposals in the name of "proper" science and the avoidance of liability. Unable to secure approval at the university level, ethnographers have seldom secured research funding from state and federal agencies because proposals either are not forwarded for consideration or are denied for the same objections.

The result has been the widespread observation that fieldwork on criminals is not rewarded and is best avoided, in turn generating a strong methodological training bias wherein new generations of researchers never seriously consider the germane philosophical, methodological, and practical issues. It is ironic that social science has forsaken fieldwork for a quasi-laboratory approach. Our subject matter is *in* society and that is where we should engage it; however, much social science research is conducted through surveys and statistical analysis altogether detached from any social/human interaction. In the case of crime and deviance this is particularly problematic.

A long-standing issue in criminology centers on the fact that much of the knowledge base is derived from known criminals and identified crime. This information is pieced together after-the-fact in a variety of ways, both quantitatively (e.g., self-reported delinquency surveys) and qualitatively (e.g., interviews with offenders in incarcerated settings). Such strategies rely on memory and place faith that reports are not selectively biased. Criminals and deviants resist inspection from outsiders, be they criminal justice system representatives or researchers. Prisoners have vested interests in minimizing and altering shared versions of their experiences as research outcomes carry perceived, if not real, ramifications. So, in order to understand the realities of crime and the behaviors of criminals we must study *active* criminals in their *natural* settings. To know about crime, we must be willing to observe its occurrence for that is where the real action and truth is to be found.

Despite the obstacles to conducting alternative fieldwork, a growing cadre of social scientists have resisted the mainstream. Most are critical or conflict criminologists whose ideologies are in sync with subjective philosophies of science. Methodology is, in a very real sense, political. A recent resurgence of fieldwork on crime and deviance, be it "edge ethnography," "criminological *verstehen*" (seeing something from the point of view of those involved) (Ferrell and Hamm 1998) or simply radical ethnography, involves researchers willing to go to *extreme* measures in pursuit of the truth, which is, after all, the goal of science.

The authors thank the following reviewers: Tod Burke, Radford University; Richard Anson, Albany State University; Phyllis Coontz, University of Pittsburgh; Jill Gordon, Virginia Commonwealth University; and Kathryn Feltey, University of Akron.

J. Mitchell Miller
Richard Tewksbury

References

Anderson, Nels. 1923. *The Hobo: The Sociology of the Homeless Man.* Chicago: University of Chicago Press.

Cressey, Paul G. 1932. *The Taxi Dance Hall.* Chicago: University of Chicago Press.

Ferrell, Jeff and Mark S. Hamm. 1998. *Ethnography at the Edge.* Boston: Northeastern University Press.

Shaw, Clifford. 1930. *The Jack Roller.* Chicago: University of Chicago Press.

Thrasher, Frederic. 1927. *The Gang.* Chicago: University of Chicago Press.

Extreme Methods

Section 1

Beyond Convention: Extreme Methods of Fieldwork

The title of this book is *Extreme Methods*. What exactly is meant when researchers say that the ways they conduct their research are "extreme methods"? What is it that makes a particular approach to doing research *extreme?* How does the topic of a research project influence whether a researcher needs to use extreme methods? These are some of the questions that are addressed in this book and introduced in this first section.

When saying that a particular research project utilizes an extreme method, we mean that some combination of 1. the approach to conceptualizing a project, 2. gaining access to research subjects and settings, and 3. gathering data is outside the boundaries of traditional, standard, and typical approaches. Extreme research methods are those that involve either highly unusual or creative approaches to finding answers to difficult-to-answer questions. Researchers using extreme methods are thus usually thought of as individuals (or teams) that go about their work in ways that many other researchers would see as dangerous, innovative, and sometimes unethical.

Extreme research methods are, usually by necessity, qualitative approaches to social science. Extreme methods involve researchers' immersing themselves in the lives and social settings of those whom they study and doing so in creative ways that involve either a great amount of interaction with people or accessing people and activities through unique materials or products created by those being studied.

The five articles in this first section highlight some of the creative ways that social science researchers, especially those studying deviance and crime, obtain access to information. The articles emphasize ways of gaining access to difficult-to-reach groups and aspects of people's lives that are usually kept hidden and secret.

In the first two articles, Tewksbury and Miller discuss ways in which researchers can study highly secretive communities that usually have strict barriers that prohibit outsiders from knowing about the members, their activities, and how such communities are structured. Both of these articles discuss observational research techniques that allow a researcher to get inside a community and see people and their activities, as they are actually experienced. Both consider how a researcher presents him/herself so that those being studied believe the researcher is a real member of the community. Tewksbury's article discusses how a researcher can interact in a setting (adult bookstores) and can appear to be a real participant. By presenting oneself as someone who may potentially engage in all the activities within a setting, the researcher can see and experience the full set of activities while maintaining objectivity and safety. Building on the suggestions in this first article, Miller's discussion of covert participant observation examines why researchers find it important (and sometimes necessary) to gather data through observation but do so in ways that do not include announcing one's research to those being studied. Miller's article also outlines the long-standing debate among social scientists about whether it is ethical to conduct research from a disguised vantage point. In the end, Miller concludes that covert participant observation can be conducted as ethical social science, although researchers need to be careful how they interact with those they are studying and always need to keep their research goals in mind.

Covert participant observation approaches are also the focus of the third article in this section. In this paper, Hilbert outlines how a covert observational role can actually be blended into some roles and activities so that the research and the actual involvement in the setting can become one and the same. The focus of Hilbert's article, however, is not on how to conduct covert participant observation, but rather on how maintaining a sense of "secrecy" and one's own "real" identity can be time- and energy-consuming activities. Extreme methods researchers who immerse themselves in the settings and communities they study will often find that their self-perceived identities may come into conflict with each other, and, at times, the identities attributed to a researcher by those being studied will be different from what the researcher knows to be his/her own identity, also. Maintaining a sense of self and being able to juggle research goals with the necessary activities for passing in a research setting are problems and obstacles unique to extreme methods researchers.

A more explicit discussion of how an extreme methods researcher can approach studying a community is presented in Marquart's discussion of his research working as a correctional officer. Taking the idea of full participation literally, Marquart worked as a guard in a maximum security Texas prison. In this article he discusses how he managed the dual (and sometimes competing) demands of his job and his research. The difficulties in maintaining his separate roles and how these demands were both anticipated and unanticipated are addressed. In the end, the difficulties on a practical as well as an ethical/moral level are seen as stresses that a full participant researcher must contend with and must learn to manage if his/her research is to be successful.

In the final article in this section, Barker, Fong, Grossman, Quin, and Reid look at how researchers can combine traditional survey approaches with creative observational methods of collecting data. By comparing the data obtained from surveying and observing college students (without the students' knowing they were being watched), Barker et al. show how extreme methods can provide more informative data than many traditional approaches to research can provide.

These five articles provide an introduction to several of the approaches to social science research that are outside the boundaries of traditional data collection and research designs. What is stressed throughout these articles is the need for researchers to think creatively and to identify ways to overcome obstacles that would prevent researchers' using common approaches from seeing what it is "really like" in certain settings and communities.

Seeing what it is "really like" includes firsthand examination of crime in its immediate context, rather than observing it "after the fact." While reading these articles, it will be helpful to keep in mind questions about why these research approaches are encouraged. What is it about the research, the topics, and the people being studied, that makes these researchers believe these approaches are necessary? Or, would there be other ways to do these types of research projects that could also answer questions about these topics?

Discussion Questions

1. What makes a particular research approach *extreme?*

2. How do researchers define *ethical* and *unethical* strategies? Where do we draw the line on acceptable ways of conducting research?

3. At the core, what makes an extreme method approach to research different from a traditional approach?

Acting Like an Insider:
Studying Hidden Environments
as a Potential Participant

RICHARD TEWKSBURY

Abstract

Studies of hidden environments traditionally draw on some form of observational or participant observation research but have been hampered by researchers' methods of gaining access to such settings. This paper outlines an alternative approach to covert participant observation: the potential participant role. This approach emphasizes data collection through observation in an apparently complete membership role but with self-imposed limitations on participation so as to maintain ethical standards. Such an approach to qualitative research emphasizes observational and experiential data. Issues of implementation and ethical considerations for such practices are discussed.

Research of behaviors and interactional processes in sexualized settings is a uniquely challenging form of social science. Such research, in seeking descriptive and analytic insights, typically relies on qualitative research methodologies, as these provide greater opportunities to access depth and breadth of understandings. However, the specific methodologies employed in studying "hidden" or "marginalized" sexual environments may require unique modifications and may present potential ethical dilemmas. This paper presents one methodological approach that can be successfully employed in studies of sexual environments: the observational role of the *potential participant.*

The potential participant is a distinct role available to participant observation researchers that is especially suited for the study of interactants in sexual environments. Whereas others have differentiated between membership roles that are peripheral, active, or complete (Adler and Adler, 1987) or complete participant, participant as observer, observer as participant, and complete observer (Gold, 1969), these characterizations can be restrictive and can guide researchers into mistakenly believing that some forms of understanding can be accessed, which in fact may not be possible with such approaches. The potential participant can and does access otherwise inaccessible aspects of the experience and can provide first-hand understandings of the culture and persons under study.

As a clear outgrowth of the legacy of the Chicago school of sociology, potential participation is a way for researchers to gain a depth of understanding not otherwise accessible. However, the break from the Chicago school is most obviously seen in the fact that the majority of research produced by these pioneers relied on overt observational roles (Adler and Adler, 1987; Lofland and Lofland, 1995). The Chicago school believed that, with the researcher himself as the primary instrument, an intense involvement with those being studied would distort the observations and research. Although as the Chicago sociologists clearly demonstrated, and is continued herein, researcher roles in observational work are fluid and ever changing.

The potential participant is a covert (or, unknown) observational role and offers researchers all of the opportunities and advantages of covert observation, but it establishes limits on participation. In some ways, this is a call for entrance to sexualized worlds similar to Freilich's (1970) "marginal native." However, even here, the original idea called for being able to "observe the essence of ongoing activity while inconspicuously fading into the background" (Adler and Adler, 1987:19). A potential participant does not "fade into the background" but, rather, is a recognized member of the community being studied.

The potential participant approach also draws on the existential approach of experiencing a setting as a true participant and feeling as true participants feel. However, limits are recognized here on *what* is fully experienced. While recognized as, in some ways, a contradiction to the Chicago school's concern with the dilemmas of "going native," the existential approach nonetheless emphasizes depth and insider involvement in gaining understandings (Adler and Adler, 1987). In this way, the presently proposed role bridges the gaps between these apparently divergent approaches to investigation.

In addition, a potential participant role draws on ethnomethodological approaches in which researchers become members of their communities of study. Here the Chicago school's dilemma of going native is actually established as a goal. Only through becoming what one studies, or "mak[ing] a total commitment to becoming the phenomenon in order to study it" (Adler and Adler, 1987:32) can one know the world from the perspective of those being researched. However, the ethical difficulties in such an approach to the study of sexuality are clear.

A major obstacle to qualitative research in sexuality research is found in the opportunities for violating ethical standards and intruding upon the rights of the participants. Qualitative social science, especially sexuality research, is often stigmatized as unethical, due mostly to attacks upon a few unique works (Humphreys, 1975; Horowitz, 1967; Styles, 1979). However, not only can qualitative methodologies yield a vast amount of rich data, but they can do so while remaining within the parameters of ethical considerations. The discussion below outlines both the parameters and utilization of the potential participant role and the ethical considerations in using such an approach.

This paper draws on applications of a potential participant role in two sexualized, subcultural, homosocial environments: an adult bookstore video peep-show and a public park frequented by men seeking sexual liaisons with other men. As such, it focuses on the utilization and inherent obstacles to such work, efforts at overcoming obstacles, and questions of maintaining professional, scientific ethics in such research.

The Research Settings

The adult bookstore and accompanying video peep-show area presents some unique challenges and obstacles to conducting research. The most important of these is the complete maintenance of anonymity and secrecy among location participants. Whereas one purpose for visiting such locales may be to participate in impersonal and anonymous sex, patrons exhibit a high degree of wariness of inquisitive others. Hence, any attempts to discover and elaborate on participants and their activities are presented with a variety of obstacles (see Sundholm, 1973; Tewksbury, 1990, 1993; Weatherford, 1986).

Public parks known for "cruising" have rarely been studied (Ponte, 1974; Tewksbury, 1995, 1996), as have similar meeting places (Corzine and Kirby, 1977; Delph, 1978; Donnelly, 1981; Gray, 1988; Humphreys, 1970). In part, this lack of scholarly investigation can be attributed to the difficulties social scientists encounter. Whereas public park cruising is not an entirely silent behavior, the level of anonymity among participants is high, and the "public" nature of the setting presents both special challenges and opportunities for observational research.

The Potential Participant Role

The potential participant role combines aspects of complete observation, complete participation, and covert observational research designs. Whereas the researcher adopting a potential participant role seeks to appear to those being researched as a "real" setting member, the "science" activities are conducted in covert manners. To anyone noticing the potential participant, the researcher is a real member of the setting being studied. To the scientific community, the potential participant is a complete observer, acting in a covert manner *inside* the research environment. By maintaining such a scientific distance, the potential participant actively avoids "going native," and losing an analytical perspective (Adler and Adler, 1987; Hammersley and Atkinson, 1983). In sexualized settings this means that there is a side-stepping of the potential ethical dilemmas involved in becoming sexually involved with research subjects.

However, this is not to say that some who have researched sexual environments have not used the ethnomethodological approach. Especially in sexual environments, the temptation for some to "learn by doing" can be quite great. As explained by one researcher of gay bathhouses,

> For a month or so I continued to separate my research and my sexual activity by conducting them in different bathhouses. Gradually, however, the asexual observation became more and more tiresome, more tedious, and more frustrating until I simply gave up observing without sexual intent and plunged fully into the sex life of the baths. (Styles, 1979:142)

As a result of his complete immersion in the activities of the bathhouse, not only does Styles (1979) report that "my important objects of inquiry changed dramatically" (p. 142), but also " my sexual participation allowed me to move closer to an ideal typical insider researcher strategy" (p. 152). Importantly, there is an acknowledgment that "there are many issues that can be raised about my research. There are ethical and moral issues", including whether or how protection of human subjects was achieved, the political rights of gay men, issues regarding the effect of such disclosures on an academic career, and "substantive issues concerning my research findings" (p. 147). (Also, see Myers, 1992; Palson and Palson, 1974; Rambo-Ronai & Ellis, 1989 for additional examples of researchers who have utilized full participation in studying sexual environments.)

Covert research designs are not without their dilemmas, however (see Miller, 1995). In large part because of the difficulties posed to the actual conduct of covert participant observation and the personal stresses such methodologies may induce, this is an approach that has been often described as our least-used method of research.

> It is unfortunate that covert research is so rarely conducted because a veiled identity can enable the examination of certain remote and closed spheres of social life, particularly criminal and deviant ones, that simply cannot be inspected in an overt fashion. . . . Clearly, complicated ethical issues inherent to secret investigations have created a methodological training bias that has suppressed their application. (Miller, 1995:97).

What is it, then, about a potential participant role that can overcome these biases? Clearly, the more weighty advantage offered by a form of covert observational investigation is the insight and depth of data that can be uncovered, especially when incorporating experiential aspects of sexualized setting investigations with straightforward observational data. Covert research, though, "means full participation in various group and individual activities, many of which contain risks" (Miller, 1995:99).

Typically, covert research is conducted by investigators who are true ("complete") members of the settings in which they work (Adler and Adler, 1987). However, when membership in a subculture precedes investigative undertakings, the likelihood of biases and skewed interpretations of derived data are great (despite the ethnomethodologists' belief that this is the "only" way to get valid data). The possibilities of skewed interpretations may be especially true when the subculture being investigated is a stigmatized, or hidden, population and/or a population that is built around "deviant" (i.e., sexual) activities.

Whereas much of the specifics of using the potential participant method is patterned (at least in part) on Humphreys' (1970) classic work in tearooms, many specifics of his approach must be modified. Humphreys' oft' criticized approach to securing interviews subsequent to observation is not replicated. Rather than using Humphreys' method of covertly recording license plate numbers of vehicles at tearooms and later tracing these so as to identify the participants and, at a later date, in disguise, conducting "public health surveys," the interviews that have been used to supplement public park observations are openly solicited from setting participants. However, the focus in this discussion is on the observational data collection methods.

Both Humphreys and Delph (1978) conducted observations while inside tearooms, functioning as either a lookout during sexual encounters or as a naïve intruder. My modification of the functional role is to present myself as a potential participant, in setting activities, not as a lookout, accidental intruder, or sexually active setting member. This role is both created and reinforced by the structure and organization of men's homosocial, sexual environments. To be present, and to present oneself as an individual others may define and respond to as a sexually motivated individual, is facilitated by the number of men present in such settings. By being present, emulating the activities (waiting behaviors, eye contact, gestures, silence, and slow circulation throughout the setting), an observer has access to the full range of behaviors men enact in public sex environments. This includes being identified and propositioned for anonymous sexual encounters. Such a role presentation provides first-hand experiences of the processes involved, not merely observation. However, perhaps the primary distinction between the potential participant role and one of a complete member is the limitation the potential participant role imposes: data can be gleaned only on the experiential components up to the point of sexual propositions. To further experience setting activities would invite serious ethical questions. However, because many sexual encounters are truly public in these settings, pure observational data on sexual activities, to some degree, is accessible (see Styles, 1979 and Weinberg and Williams, 1975).

In both adult bookstores and public parks, the majority of men initiate sexual approaches to other men only when no third parties are present. It is in this regard that presenting oneself as potentially interested in sexual activities is critical to data access. If a researcher were to adopt a role suggesting he was merely observing, or accidentally happening by, his presence may in fact impede and inhibit the very behaviors and interactions he is seeking to observe and understand. Furthermore, the accidental passerby is limited in the number of times he can realistically happen by the setting; more than one or two short visits to the research setting are likely to raise suspicions, as some sexually involved men spend lengthy periods, and visit repeatedly, such environments.

Perhaps the greatest advantage offered by the potential participant role is the experiential insight provided to the researcher, while balancing against personal and professional ethical positions. Whereas a complete participant role certainly provides the greatest depth of experiential data, in sexualized environments and with studies of "marginal" sexual populations and activities, stresses will undoubtedly arise. The ways in which a complete participant responds to and manages such stresses can easily make or break a research project, as well as (perhaps) the researcher's career.

How better to understand sexual propositions than to receive them? As a potential participant in adult bookstores and public parks, receiving sexual propositions is a key component to the research. Simply observing cannot and will not provide complete data. One important reason for this is that only the most aggressive (or least cautious) setting participants are likely to proposition others in a researcher's presence. A second reason full data are inaccessible with a strict reliance on observation is that the critical experiential components are not available. Clearly, the "real" activities of the setting would not be uncovered using a traditional observational approach.

Rites of Passage

By looking at perceived setting norms and rites of passage, it is clear that a potential participant role facilitates researchers' integration in sexual environments. Ethnographers access to valid data can be significantly enhanced through covert approaches in which the researcher successfully "passes" as a setting native. Access to settings may require special permission, knowledge, or skills (Lofland and Lofland, 1995). Studying highly stigmatized, secretive settings (such as an adult bookstore or a sexualized public park) may present researchers with initially seeming, anomalous encounters; but, upon closer inspection these events can be seen as heavily veiled rites-of-passage ceremonies. These seemingly minor, or to some perhaps, indistinguishable occurrences are gatekeeping procedures known as such only by knowledgable, true setting participants.

In order to most effectively present oneself as a potential participant, it is necessary to be able to act (and when necessary interact) as one who knows "how the game is played." However, when seeking entrance and acceptance in hidden populations some researchers may find themselves having only rudimentary knowledge (or more often, expectations) about how setting participants "really act." After all, if we knew very much about what goes on, the research might not be necessary.

When entering a hidden, sexual setting it may be necessary to enter and find your way as opportunities present themselves. This trial-and-error approach can be highly stressful, and, if not successfully navigated, it can set the investigator up for embarrassment, ostracization, and, in extreme cases, deal a fatal blow to the research. These situations are not unique to researchers, however. Filters and gatekeeping procedures are established for the explicit purposes of insulating the setting and its participants from unwanted intruders and prying "outsiders." The researcher is an outsider, striving for acceptance and endorsement for his presence. In short, rites-of-passage rituals confront all newcomers to the setting.

The rites of passage encountered in hidden, sexual environments illustrate Arnold van Gennep's (1960) three-stage conceptualization of rites of passage. When entering a new cultural environment, three stages of tests (actually composing one larger, all-encompassing rite of passage) are encountered. These separate rites can be distinguished as stages of separation, transition, and incorporation.

In hidden, sexual environments these stages are operationalized respectively by the entrance behaviors, acknowledgment of others present, and methods of receiving sexual approaches. All three stages present apparently normless situations that differentiate between those who do and those who do not know setting norms. A truly astute and quick-thinking researcher may be able to successfully navigate the separation and transition rites phases, however, only the truly knowledgable will pass the third rite of passage stage.

The researcher who successfully navigates all three rites of passage by maintaining normative behaviors will have access to the environment that true participants enjoy. At this point the researcher is on equal footing with true-setting participants and can present himself as a potential sexual partner.

An obvious hazard in the potential participant role is the risk some may face of going native, and losing objectivity (per the Chicago school) or violating professional ethical standards. It remains of utmost importance to carefully delineate one's role as researcher and observer. The researcher needs to project an image as a potential participant but at all times maintain a focus on the primary mission: observation.

This raises an obvious limitation regarding participant observation research. Regardless of how carefully planned and implemented a research methodology may be, it still falls short (to some degree) of actual participation. Observational researchers must continuously assess their abilities to pass in reference to the available benchmarks (re: rites of passage examinations).

Ethical Considerations

Ethical standards also necessitate a distinction between a researcher who successfully completes rites-of-passage examinations and a researcher who deliberately misrepresents either 1. his/her identity, or 2. his/her purpose for being present in the research setting. Discussing the ethical demands of observational research, Erikson (1967:373) defines two rules regarding misrepresentations:

> *1. It is unethical . . . to deliberately misrepresent his identity for the purpose of entering a private domain to which he is not otherwise eligible.*
>
> *2. It is unethical . . . to deliberately misrepresent the character of the research in which he is engaged.*

Although simple and straightforward, such requirements are somewhat contrary to the inherent demands of any form of covert observation. A potential participant does not violate these standards. Careful definition, design, and execution of the role provides the means for ethical conduct. Hidden, sexual environments acknowledge and, by default, legitimize observations of others. In this way, one's identity is not misrepresented, but, rather, identities and purposes are presented. Second, whereas the research is conducted covertly, no definition of the research need be presented to setting participants. Hence, the adoption of a potential participant role requires neither the researcher's identity nor his purpose to be misrepresented.

A corresponding ethics issue centers on informed consent. When observing and recording the interactions of others, ideally, all should be informed and should consent to being observed. As discussed earlier, the hidden nature of such a setting and behaviors prohibit the utilization of informed consent. In a setting of anonymous individuals engaging in highly stigmatized behavior the likelihood of any setting participants positively responding to invitations for participation is highly unlikely. If consent were sought, knowledge of the research focus would likely spread among the participants, thereby stigmatizing the researcher and impeding any further research efforts. Certainly the degree of privacy that needs to be accorded to setting participants may be debated. Hidden, sexual environments are, by definition, open environments. It is clear, nevertheless, that an attempt to protect observed subjects from any possible negative consequences necessitates absolute confidentiality and anonymity. This is easily maintained by careful attention to the actual definition and implementation of the researcher role.

The point here is that some, if not many, critics may criticize researchers (such as myself) for purportedly being true participants in sexual activity. I have never engaged in sexual encounters in these settings, nor have I made contacts for off-site sexual activity. This, however, is not to say that such activities could not be beneficial to the research effort (see Styles, 1979). However, the violation of ethical standards is obvious. Not only would the researcher directly influence setting activities, but the very nature of engaging in sexual activities with those one studies is a violation of ethical canons.

The consequence of such a personal decision regarding "complete" data collection is that experiential data can be gathered only up to a certain point in the sequence of behavior. The processes involved in these latter stages of interactions, though, do pose numerous questions for subsequent research. Although perhaps controversial, covert research designs can be an effective and ethical method of obtaining valid, in-depth data on interactional processes of hidden, sexual settings.

The completion of such research is possible while remaining within the parameters of ethical standards. Ethical considerations do impose some limitations on data collection. However, with careful and continuous attention to the definition and implementation of the researcher's role, data collection in sexualized settings is possible while also ensuring protection of setting participants' rights.

Although far from an easy task, research in hidden sexual environments is a valuable endeavor and can be conducted in an ethical manner. The key to successful research in such settings appears to be the actual conduct of the researcher. Covert participant-observers in sexualized settings are bound by professional ethics (as well as personal morals) to provide absolute anonymity and confidentiality, minimal influence and intrusion on the setting, and no risk of physical, psychological, or so-cial harm to each and every setting participant. Such settings certainly present ob-stacles for researchers to overcome, but none so great as to deter the committed, professional, social scientist.

References

Adler, P. A. & Adler, P. (1987). *Membership Roles in Field Research.* Newbury Park, CA: Sage Qualitative Research Methods Series, No. 6.

Corzine, J. & Kirby, R. (1977). Cruising the Truckers: Sexual Encounters in a Highway Rest Area. *Urban Life, 6,* 171–192.

Delph, E. (1978). *The Silent Community: Public Homosexual Encounters.* Beverly Hills, CA: Sage.

Donnelly, P. (1981). Running the Gauntlet: The Moral Order of Pornographic Movie Theaters. *Urban Life, 10,* 239–264.

Erikson, K. (1967). Disguised Observation in Sociology. *Social Problems, 1,* (4), 368.

Freilich, M. (1970). *Marginal Natives.* New York: Harper & Row.

Gennep, A. (1960). *The Rites of Passage.* Chicago: University of Chicago Press.

Gold, R. L. (1969). Roles in Sociological Field Observation, in G. J. McCall & J. L. Simmons (eds.) *Issues in Participant Observation.* Reading, MA: Addison-Wesley.

Gray, J. (1988). *The Tearoom Revisited: A Study of Impersonal Homosexual Encounters in Public Settings.* Unpublished PhD dissertation, The Ohio State University, Columbus.

Hammersley, M. & Atkinson, P. (1983). *Ethnography: Principles in Practice.* New York: Tavistock.

Horowitz, I. L. (1967). *The Rise and Fall of Project Camelot.* Cambridge, Mass.: MIT Press.

Humphreys, L. (1970). *Tearoom Trade.* Chicago, IL: Aldine.

Kamel, G. W. L. (1980). Leathersex: Meaningful Aspects of Gay Sadomasochism. *Deviant Behavior, 1,* 171–191.

Lofland, J. & Lofland, L. H. (1995). *Analyzing Social Settings (3rd ed).* Belmont, CA: Wadsworth Publishing.

Miller, J. M. (1995). Covert Participant Observation: Reconsidering the Least Used Method. *Journal of Contemporary Criminal Justice, 11,* (2), 97–105.

Ponte, M (1974). Life in a Parkling Lot: An Ethnography of a Homosexual Drive-In *Deviance: Field Studies and Self-Disclosures,* edited by J. Jacobs. Palo Alto, CA: National Press Books.

Styles, J. (1979). Outsider/Insider: Researching Gay Baths. *Urban Life,* 8:135–152.

Tewksbury, R. (1995). Adventures in the Erotic Oasis: Sex and Danger in Men's Same-Sex, Public Sexual Encounters. *Journal of Men's Studies,* 4, (1):9–24.

Tewksbury, R. (1996). Cruising for Sex In Public Places: The Structure and Language of Men's Hidden, Erotic Worlds. *Deviant Behavior,* 17, (1):1–19.

Covert Participant Observation: Reconsidering The Least Used Method

J. MITCHELL MILLER

"The goal of any science is not willful harm to subjects, but the advancement of knowledge and explanation. Any method that moves us toward that goal is justifiable" (Denzin 1968).

Social scientists have virtually ignored the qualitative technique covert participant observation. This variation of participant observation is either not mentioned or described in less than a page's length in social science research methods texts. The majority of qualitative methods books provide a few illustrative examples, but scarcely more in terms of detailed instruction. Manifested in the selection of alternative field strategies, this disregard has made covert observation the truly least used of all the qualitative methods.

It is unfortunate that covert research is so rarely conducted because a veiled identity can enable the examination of certain remote and closed spheres of social life, particularly criminal and deviant ones, that simply cannot be inspected in an overt fashion. Consequently, covert research is well-suited for much subject material of concern to criminology and the criminal justice sciences. Also applicable in some situations where overt designs appear the appropriate or only option, covert schemes are infrequently considered.

• • •

This brief commentary reintroduces covert participant observation and presents the principal advantages of using the technique. Theoretical, methodological, and pragmatic grounds are offered for exercising covert research. Ethical matters long associated with the stifling of its use are also reconsidered in the context of criminal justice. The ethicality of secret research, relative to other qualitative methods, is upheld for some research problems with certain stipulations.

J. Mitchell Miller. "Covert Participant Observation: Reconsidering the Least Used Method." *Journal of Contemporary Criminal Justice, Vol. 11, No. 2, May 1995.* Copyright 1995. Reprinted by permission of Sage Publications.

Defining Covert Participant Observation

Covert participant observation is a term that has been used rather interchangeably with other labels: "secret observation" (Roth 1962), "investigative social research" (Douglas 1976), "sociological snooping" (Von Hoffman 1970), and most frequently "disguised observation" (Erickson 1967;1968; Denzin 1968). Disguised observation has recently been defined as "research in which the researcher hides his or her presence or purpose for interacting with group" (Hagan 1993:234). The distinguishing feature is that the research occurrence is not made known to subjects within the field setting.

Disguised observation is too inclusive a term often used in reference to those who simply hide in disguise or secret to observe, such as Stein's (1974) observation via a hidden two-way mirror of prostitutes servicing customers. Covert participant observation likewise involves disguise, however, the researcher is always immersed in the field setting. Additional elements—intentional misrepresentation, interpersonal deception, and maintenance of a false identity over usually prolonged periods of time are entailed. "Covert participant observation" is therefore a more technically correct term than "disguised observation" because it better indicates the active nature of the fieldwork essential to the technique (Jorgensen 1989).

Covert participant observation is essentially "opportunistic research" (Ronai and Ellis 1989) conducted by "complete-member researchers" (Adler and Adler 1987) who study phenomena in settings where they participate as full members. Admission to otherwise inaccessible settings is gained by undertaking a natural position and then secretly conducting observational research. Examples of the methods include Steffensmeier and Terry's (1973) study of the relationship between personal appearance and suspicion of shoplifting involving students dressed either conventionally or as hippies, Stewart and Cannon's (1977) masquerade as thieves, Tewksbury's (1990) description of adult bookstore patrons, and most recently Miller and Selva's (1994) assumption of the police informant role to infiltrate drug enforcement operations.

The most pronounced example of covert research, however, is Laud Humphreys' infamous Tearoom Trade (1970). Shrouding his academic interest in sexual deviance, Humphreys pretended to be a "watchqueen" (i.e., a lookout) for others so that he might observe homosexual acts in public bathrooms. He also used this role to record his subjects' license plate numbers to obtain their names and addresses in order to interview them by means of another disguise—survey researcher interested in sexual behaviors and lifestyles.

There are other versions of disguised or covert participant observation wherein certain confederates are made aware of the researcher's true identity, purpose and objectives (Formby and Smykla 1981; Asch 1951). The reasons for working with cooperatives are plain: to facilitate entry and interaction in the research site, to become familiar with nomenclature and standards of conduct, to expedite the happening of that which the researcher hopes to observe, and to avoid or at least minimize potential danger. Such reliance may be counterproductive, though, in that observations and consequent analysis of the social setting may be tainted by confederates' values, perceptions, and positions within the research environment.

If only a few individuals within a research site are aware of the researcher's true identity, it is possible, indeed likely, that interaction will be affected and spread to others within the setting. Hence, data distortion can become a potential validity and reliability problem with the use of confederates. The researcher must be completely undercover to avoid this problem and utilize the covert role so as to optimally exploit a social setting.

The goals of covert participant observation are no different than the standard objectives of overt participant observation: exploration, description, and, occasionally, evaluation (Berg 1989).

• • •

Most aspects of the methodological process, such as defining a problem, observing and gathering information, analyzing notes and records, and communicating results, are nearly identical to conventional participant observation as well. The covert approach may thus be considered a type of participant observation rather than a distinctive method.

There are aspects of the covert participant observation research cycle, however, that are unconventional. One controversial point is gaining entry to a setting through misrepresentation. It is the closed nature of backstage settings and the politics of deviant groups that negates announcement of the researcher's objectives and requires deception via role assumption if certain topics are to be examined.

The character of the participation is also much different and more demanding on the researcher. Covert role assumption means full participation in various group and individual activities, many of which contain risks. The direct study of crime by means of an undercover role can be doubly enigmatic to both the researcher's well-being and the inquiry. Assuming a role either as a criminal or in close proximity to crime for the purpose of research does not absolve the researcher from real or perceived culpability; thus moral decisions and the possibility of arrest and legal sanction must be considered prior to the onset of fieldwork.

The recording of notes from a clandestine position would divulge the researcher's cover and is obviously inadvisable. Extended periods of time in the field often yield rich and rare insight, but, without a chance to withdraw and log events, recollection of temporal/causal sequence can become muddled due to information overload and understandable fatigue. Resolves to this concern have been the use of mnemonics—a process of memorizing through abbreviation and association (Hagan 1993:195), taking photographs when possible, and the use of hidden mini-tape recorders and even body wires (Miller and Selva 1994).

The Ethics of Covert Observation

The ethicality of disguised or covert observational techniques has long been controversial as evidenced by the "deception debate" (Bulmer 1980; Humphreys 1970; Roth 1962; Galliher 1973). Participants in this debate have tended to assume one of two polarized positions: moralistic condemnation or responsive justification. Deception is explicitly equated with immorality and is so unconscionable for some they would have covert observation banned from social science research altogether

(Erikson 1967). The major objection is that deceptive techniques often violate basic ethical principles including informed consent, invasion of privacy, and the obligation to avoid bringing harm to subjects.

Critics further contend that misrepresentation not only causes irreparable damage to subjects, but also to the researcher, and to science by evoking negative public scrutiny and making subject populations wary of future researchers (Polsky 1967). Risk to the researcher, however, is a matter of individual decision.

• • •

The argument of isolating future research populations is seemingly unsound as well. Many settings of interest to criminal justice are essentially restricted and typically occupied with subjects already suspicious of strangers due to the threat of legal penalty associated with disclosure. Because researchers as outsiders will usually be distrusted and excluded from such settings, it is logical to assume that its occupants are already ostracized from researchers. The more substantial points that remain and must be confronted are interrelated: the use of deceit and the harm subjects may encounter as a result of the research process.

The topic of dishonesty in covert research is not as clear as opponents of the method suggest and nebulous in comparison to the frequent disregard for ethical standards demonstrated in other qualitative deviance research. Klockars' award winning "The Professional Fence," for example, describes research conduct far more offensive than the duplicity intrinsic to covert participant observation. This case history of a thirty year career of dealing in stolen goods was enabled by an intentionally misrepresentative letter in which the researcher admittedly lied about: 1. his academic credentials, 2. his familiarity and experience with the subject of fencing, 3. the number of other thieves he had interviewed, and most seriously 4. the possible legal risks associated with participating in the project (Klockars 1974:215). Klockars deception is reasoned in near blind pursuit of his research objective:

> *"I thought the claim would strengthen the impression of my seriousness" and "the description of what I wanted to write about as well as the whole tone of the letter is slanted . . . and did not warn Vincet (the research subject) of his rights" (Ibid).*

Surprisingly, Klockars book and projects have not produced controversy on par with covert strategies. The terms "case history" and "personal interview" simply do not provoke the interest and suspicion generated by the labels "covert" and "disguise." Covert methods can be considered, relative to the exercise of some techniques, forthright in that the level of deception is predetermined and calculated into the research design (Stricker 1967). The decision of whether or not to use deception to gain entry and thus enable a study can be made on the ends versus the means formula described below.

A Basis for Covert Research?

Justifications for the use of covert techniques have been presented on various levels. The most common practical argument is that those engaged in illegal or unconventional behavior, such as drug dealers and users, simply will not submit to or participate in a study by overt methods. Likewise, those in powerful and authoritative positions have been considered secretive and difficult to openly observe (Shils 1975). Police chiefs, white-collar criminals, prison wardens, and drug enforcement agents benefit from the existing power structure which inhibits study of their behavior in these official roles. A covert design is often the only way to conduct qualitative evaluation research of certain enforcement and intervention programs closed to principal participants.

Beyond a "last-resort" rationale, there are other reasons, methodological and theoretical, for employing the covert technique. An evident reason is that of qualitative methodology in general—the desirability of capturing social reality. By concealing identity and objective, researchers can avoid inducing a qualitative Hawthorne effect (i.e., a covert approach can minimize data distortion). Covert participant observation is justified theoretically by dramaturgical and conflict perspectives. If Goffman (1959) is to be taken seriously, then all researchers should be viewed as wearing masks and the appropriateness of any inquiry viewed in its context. Following Goffman, Denzin has also argued that ethical propriety depends upon the situation:

> *"the sociologist has the right to make observations on anyone in any setting to the extent that he does so with scientific intents and purposes in mind" (1968:50).*

Dramaturgy also provides a theoretical framework from which to assess topics of concern to the covert observer. The duplicity of roles already present in criminal settings under analysis (eg., undercover police, fence, snitch, racketeer) are only multiplied when such a role is assumed with the additional post of social scientist.

Consideration of the well known consensus-conflict dialectic also provides logic supportive of covert research. Conventional field methods, such as in-depth interviewing and overt observation, are based on a consensus view of society wherein most people are considered cooperative and willing to share their points of view and experiences with others (Patton 1990). This assumption is highly suspect however, in stratified and culturally diverse societies. To the extent that acute conflicts of interests, values, and actions saturate social life to the advantage of some and not others, covert methods should be regarded proper options in the pursuit of truth.

• • •

Perhaps the most compelling basis for the use of disguise in some research, however, is "the end and the means" position first stated by Roth (1962), then Douglas

(1972) and Homan (1980), and most recently Miller and Selva (1994). Employing this reasoning in defense of covert observation, Douglas (1972:8–9) notes:

"Exceptions to important social rules, such as those concerning privacy and intimacy, must be made only when the research need is clear and the potential contributions of the findings to general human welfare are believed to be great enough to counterbalance the risks."

That the purpose may absolve the process has also been acknowledged by the British Sociological Association, which condones the covert approach "where it is not possible to use other methods to obtain essential data" (1973:3); such is the case in many criminal justice research situations. The benefits of investigating and reporting on expensive, suspicious, and dysfunctional facets of the criminal justice system, then, may outweigh its potential costs. Failure to study how various initiatives and strategies are actually implemented on the street could condemn other citizens to misfortune and abuse should the behavior of the system be inconsistent with stated legitimate objectives.

To rule out study of covert behavior, whether engaged in by the powerful or the powerless, simply because it cannot be studied openly places artificial boundaries on science and prevents study of what potentially may be very important and consequential activities in society. The propriety and importance of research activities must always be judged on a case by case basis. Drug enforcement's use of asset forfeiture, for example, has been questioned by the press and media with such frequency and intensity that scholarly evaluation is warranted. The very nature of the allegations, however, have prompted the police fraternity to close ranks, thus compelling covert analysis. Abandoning such a study because it can not be out overtly would mean that potential misconduct and betrayal of public trust by government officials would remain unexposed.

The means and end rule, of course, requires the subjective interpretation of plausible harm to subjects, what exactly constitutes benefit, and who will be beneficiaries. To assess the balance between these elements it is necessary that they be highly specified, a requirement that is not easily met. The means and end formula is thus ambiguous and the choice to use a covert technique must be carefully deliberated. Certainly, deceptive observation carries ethical baggage less common to other qualitative methods, yet its ethicality is negotiable through detailed purpose and design.

Conclusion

The study of crime invites and sometimes requires the covert method as does examination of the clandestine nature of many facets of the formal social control apparatus. How other than through covert participant observation can topics such as undercover policing and inmate-correctional officer interaction be fully understood and evaluated? Those in the criminal justice system, as well as criminals, have vested interests in maintaining high levels of autonomy which require degrees of secrecy. This is evident in various labels such as "police fraternity", "gang", and "confidential informant."

The very things that make a criminal justice or criminological topic worthy of investigation and suitable for publication in a social science forum can preclude overtly exploring it. Methodologically sustained by the theoretical foundations of qualitative inquiry, covert designs tender opportunities to reach relatively unstudied topics.

• • •

This comment has briefly surveyed the methodological, theoretical, and practical reasons to utilize covert participant observation in criminal justice research. The most difficult facet of using this method will undoubtedly remain ethical factors that must be dealt with on a case by case basis. But these too can be overcome with caution, conviction, and adherence to established scientific guidelines for qualitative research (Glaser and Strauss 1967). The spirit of selecting methods on technical merit and relevance to research objectives rather than ethical pretense is an outlook consistent with the goals of social science. To the extent that this perspective thrives, covert participant observation may well become more commonplace; perhaps to the point of no longer being the least used method.

References

Adler, P. A. and P. Adler. (1987) "The Past and Future of Ethnography." *Journal of Contemporary Ethnography* 16:4–24.

Asch, Solomon E. (1951) "Effects of Group Pressure upon the Modification and Distortion of Judgement." in H. Guetzkow (Ed.) *Groups, Leadership and Men.* Pittsburgh, PA: Carnegie Press.

Berg, Bruce L. (1989) *Qualitative Research Methods for the Social Sciences.* Boston, MA: Allyn and Bacon.

British Sociological Association. (1973) Statement of Ethical Principles and their Application to Sociological Practice.

Bulmer, Martin. (1980) "Comment on the Ethics of Covert Methods." *British Journal of Sociology* 31:59–65.

Denzin, Norman. (1968) "On the Ethics of Disguised Observation." *Social Problems* 115:502–504.

Douglas, Jack D. (1976) *Investigative and Social Research: Individual and Team Field Research.* Beverly Hills, CA: Sage.

Erickson, Kai T. (1967) "Disguised Observation in Sociology." *Social Problems* 14:366–372.

Formby, William A. and John Smykla. (1981) "Citizen awareness in Crime Prevention: Do They Really Get Involved?" *Journal of Police Science and Administration* 9:398–403.

Galliher, John F. (1973) "The Protection of Human Subjects: A Reexamination of the Professional Code of Ethics." *The American Sociologist* 8:93–100.

Glaser, Barney G. and Anselm Strauss. (1967) *The Discovery of Grounded Theory.* Chicago, IL: Aldine.

Goffman, Erving. (1959) *The Presentation of Self in Everyday Life.* New York: Doubleday.

Hagan, Frank E. (I 993) *Research Methods in Criminal Justice and Criminology.* 3rd ed. New York: Macmillian Publishing Co.

Homan, Roger. (1980) "The ethics of covert methods." *British Journal of Sociology* 31:46–59.

Humphreys, Laud. (1970) *Tearoom Trade: Impersonal Sex in Public Places.* New York: Aldine Publishing Co.

Jorgensen, Danny L. (1989) *Participant Observation: A Methodology for Human Studies.* Newburry Park, CA: Sage.

Klockars, Carl B. (1974) *The Professional Fence.* New York: The Free Press.

Miller, J. Mitchell and Lance Selva. (1994) "Drug Enforcement's Double-Edged Sword: An Assessment of Asset Forfeiture Programs." *Justice Quarterly* 11:313–335.

Patton, M. Q. (1990) *Qualitative Evaluation and Research Methods.* 2nd ed. Newbury Park, CA: Sage.

Polsky, Ned. (1967) *Hustlers, Beats, and Others.* New York: Anchor Books.

Ronai, C. R. and C. Ellis. (1989) "Turn-ons for money: Interactional strategies of the table dancer." *Journal of Contemporary Ethnography* 18:271–298.

Roth, Julius A. (1962) "Comments on Secret Observation." *Social Problems* 9:283–284.

Shils, Edward A. (1975) "Privacy and Power" in *Center and Periphery: Essays in Macrosociology.* Chicago, IL: University of Chicago Press.

Stein, Martha L. (1974) *Lovers, Friends, Slaves . . . : The Nine Male Sexual Types.* Berkeley, CA: Berkeley Publishing Corp.

Stewart, John E. and Daniel Cannon. (1977) "Effects of Perpetrator Status and Bystander Commitment on Response to a Simulated Crime." *Journal of Police Science and Administration* 5:318–323.

Stricker, L. J. (1967) "The True Deceiver." *Psychological Bulletin* 68:13–20.

Tewksbury, Richard. (1990) "Patrons of Porn: Research Notes on the Clientele of Adult Bookstores." *Deviant Behavior* 11:259–271.

Von Hoffman, N. (1970) *"Sociological Snoopers."* Washington Post (Jan. 30).

Covert Participant Observation

On Its Nature and Practice

RICHARD A. HILBERT

The aim of this article is to address a number of issues pertinent to covert participant observation not ordinarily discussed in other work. The article is concerned neither with the advantages and disadvantages of covert research nor with ethical questions related to relative secrecy. My concern lies mainly with the nature of covert participant observation per se, that is, what it is that covert analysts are actually doing when they engage in covert activity. I shall argue that analysts' practical concerns with protecting their identities closely coincide with other methodological strategies of ethnographic investigation.

I should add, however, that much of what follows is of direct relevance to traditional concerns, and I shall indicate some of these relevancies toward the conclusion of this discussion. In anticipation of these relevancies, I might state that the distinction between secret and nonsecret observation may challenge the assumption that analysts explicitly and consciously "choose" to be covert, overt, or somewhere in between. As a consequence, the question of ethics, though of considerable importance as an issue, will have to be settled according to standards other than "how covert" somebody's research is. Finally, the question of the advantages and disadvantages of covert research becomes moot, as such matters are situational, being essentially decided within the terms of research settings themselves.

JOURNAL NOTE: Doing covert research remains a problem for researchers trying to resolve the ethical and practical dilemmas inherent in "secret" observation. Richard Hilbert suggests that not all covert participant observation research is necessarily unethical, although such research does invariably create its own particular problems. Among these are the need to maintain a credible identity and the problems of gathering data in an unobtrusive, yet accurate manner. Drawing from his own experiences in covert research, Hilbert describes selected strategies, often coinciding with the observed activities which he himself found useful in his own research.

Urban Life & Culture, Vol. 9 No. 1, April 1980; 51–78. © 1980 Sage Publications, Inc. Reprinted by permission of Sage Publications, Inc.

Covert Participant Observation as an Unstudied Phenomenon

Traditional concerns with methodological advantages of covert participant observation and the ethical problems of secrecy have failed to address the nature of the research activity itself and the general strategies located within it. This is the topic I am undertaking here. The ideas developed below were inspired by a one-year ethnographic investigation, related to the completion of my doctoral dissertation, of an elementary teaching credentials program. My chosen strategy was enrollment in the program with a decided preference for not revealing my research interests. Though I successfully completed the program (securing certification), these research interests were paramount. Until quite late in the academic year, my research interests were not known by most of the program personnel, staff, students, or teachers with whom I worked in the public schools. My intended public identity, for the most part, was that of student, student teacher, and prospective schoolteacher.

In this article, I intend not to report findings relevant to teacher education or to other theoretical issues to which my study was directed. Rather what concerns me is the nature of the research itself, particularly the congruence of secrecy-guarding with practical, methodological strategies. The claim will be made that my experience was not accidental or idiosyncratic but was a consequence of the essential nature of the research activity itself. As such, it is of interest both theoretically as a sociological phenomenon and practically as an explication of methodological strategies for analysts about to embark on similar research ventures.

The sort of research I wish to generalize about involves full participation in a social gathering, group, or organization. I am further discussing research in which it is the analyst's task to come to terms with what it takes to sustain competent membership covertly in the group in question. Thus I am not concerned with simple spying or deception for purposes of access to secret files of "facts and figures," or of gaining the confidence of key officials who subsequently "tell all." The research I am discussing focuses on the mundane realities of day-to-day social existence and the problem of how the perceived stabilities of such realities are produced and managed. Conventional solutions to this problem recommend discovering the "subjective realities" or internalized rules governing proper conduct within social settings. Such solutions have no doubt led to traditional discussions of validity when it comes to the use of "informants." Informants can ostensibly "tell" researchers about these subjective realities, and it is therefore incumbent upon researchers to ensure that their informants are being truthful, represent the judgments of "typical" group members, and so forth. It will be argued here, however, that covert participant observation is participation par excellence and as such is itself "typical"—if the term is at all meaningful—of whatever it is that actors do to sustain competent membership.

The Secret in Covert Participant Observation

Insofar as analysts have determined that full disclosure would be injurious to their research interests, an abiding concern must be for maintaining a secret. We might initially think of the analyst's research role as the "reality" behind a manufactured or projected social identity. In short, we have the sociologist trying to pass himself or herself off as "something else."

In a classic investigation into the life of an intersexed person, Garfinkel (1967: 116–185) characterizes this sort of activity as "passing," i.e., behavior directed toward achieving a social identity other than what one might achieve without this behavior. What is instructive in this article is that the subject of the study, known only as Agnes, artfully secured her social right to be natural, normal member of a female population within a wider population consisting only of men and women whose ascribed sexual status, as Agnes knew, was beyond their control, just as hers was for her. However, throughout her passing performance, Agnes protected a secret which if revealed would have brought certain ruin. Her secret consisted of (a) her past upbringing as a boy until the age of seventeen, (b) her plans to secure surgically the anatomy that "nature intended," and (c) her present male genitals. While these three items were equally important to her secret, it was the last of them that proved most problematic to Agnes in her day-to-day encounters.

If Agnes's secret can be trichotomized, so can that of the covert analyst. The covert researcher guarding the secret must generally attend to aspects of his or her past, present, and future, which if revealed could lead to the breakdown of the projected identity. (a) The fact that he or she has been trained as a sociologist, has written literature reviews relevant to the setting, and possibly has written a research proposal are all potentially tricky areas to manage should they become public, as any research-motivated method of access to the setting might be. (b) Similarly, the fact that the analyst plans to write about the setting generally has to be withheld from other participants. (c) Most problematic, however, are certain aspects of analysts' present, day-to-day professional lives. A number of things could be involved, such as routine discussions with colleagues about the progress of the study, but the most likely, and probably most basic thing concerns the fact that analysts take extensive field notes and spend a great amount of time away from the field (possibly while other members are sleeping or watching television) poring over the notes, typing them, filing them, keeping records of conversations which to members are trivial and forgotten, and so forth. One might wonder, while typing these conversations alone at night, what it would be like for participants to these conversations to walk in unexpectedly or otherwise see the notes.

Some might say that despite the strategic necessity of guarding the secret, guarding the secret is after all secondary to the actual purposes of the research. Guarding the secret, so the argument might go; is a methodological device making it possible to conduct the research itself, namely discovering shared attitudes and norms through observation and interaction. Such characterizations overlook the sense in which guarding the secret *is* the research, *is* the method through which analysts discover whatever it is about group membership that is "typical." This is so, at least insofar as the secret is managed and successful passing is accomplished.

Sociologists electing to use covert field methods are aware that full disclosure will alter their participant status and will as a consequence affect their abilities to participate "typically." By the same token, the way in which they guard the secret must be consistent with their membership activity. That is, they must make use of their knowledge of "what typical members do" in order to protect the secret; they must protect the secret by doing those things. Not to do so risks disclosure. At the same time, if this is successfully managed, analysts succeed in finding out "what typical members do," i.e., what they, the analysts, themselves were actually doing vis-à-vis a relevant social community. Their dual interests—that of managing the secret and that of doing search—fundamentally coincide. They are inseparable.

• • •

Covert participant observers share in Agnes's problem. In order to learn what constitutes membership in a social setting, they have to assure themselves that what they are witnessing, what they are doing, is not colored by the mere *fact* that they are, in addition to participating in group processes, doing research. Simultaneously they seek to notice features of group membership that for other members may go unnoticed or unthematized. These are not contradictory objectives; but as indicated above they are synonymous. Successfully managing the secret *requires* attention to areas which to other members may be nonproblematic. Successfully managing the secret is also what we mean when we say successfully maintaining competent, "typical" membership.

Some General Features of Social Settings Which Covert Participant Observers Can Depend On

To restate: Covert research oriented toward discovering features of interaction which constitute typical membership does not depend upon guarding the secret simply for purposes of establishing a perspective otherwise inaccessible. Rather, guarding the secret is the process through which typical membership is realized. Simultaneously, the analyst uses his or her already established, albeit incomplete, knowledge concerning what typical membership consists of in order to manage the secret successfully. Thus, managing the secret and sustaining typical group membership are mutually elaborating activities which together constitute covert participant observation research activity.

What follows is a list of features general enough to apply to nearly any social setting. Items in the list are neither exhaustive nor mutually exclusive. They represent setting features that covert analysts can initially depend upon in their research activity. When I say analysts can depend on them, I am not indicating their literal or nonproblematic status, nor am I proclaiming them to be "true" in any precise sense. Rather, I am saying that they can be useful to analysts in managing the secret and sustaining group membership; they represent idealized resources whose specific sense awaits discovery from setting to setting and from occasion to occasion. I have also included examples from my own experience to fill in some of the shadowy detail.

1. First and most useful is the tendency for people to view others as what they claim to be (see Goffman, 1959)—in cases relevant to this discussion, as fellow members. People are not therefore inclined to see anyone as doing sociological research. This may hardly need mentioning, but to sociologists entering a setting for covert research purposes, the likelihood of exposure may be drastically overestimated. In my own case, the setting itself included an academic department in which the art of ethnography is taught to graduate students. To an astonishing degree, the possibility that I was simultaneously doing research while getting a teaching credential was not entertained, even though program personnel knew of my identity as a sociology graduate student. This was so, despite the fact that numerous unannounced research projects were conducted throughout the year using us, students in the program, as unsuspecting subjects. Thus, even within a setting where both ethnography and "secret research" were available to staff and personnel as day-to-day concepts, the possibility that the setting itself was simultaneously being systematically noticed for research purposes was apparently so remote as to escape any consideration whatsoever. I eventually came to feel that I had been overprotective of the secret, almost as though no one would have believed it if invited to do so. This was extremely helpful and is relevant to the paragraphs below.

2. All participants to the setting have past biographies and future intentions which conform to patterns only "more or less." Their pasts and futures are "typical," but this is an occasioned typicality accomplished through talk. It is possible, then, for the analyst to engage in such talk without pretext. Talk which for members is essentially equivocal is, for the analyst, purposefully vague. On many occasions, I had the opportunity to discuss past "experiences in academia," doubts that I would ever be a schoolteacher, and "alternative career lines" (including sociology) in ways that conformed to other students' talk about disquiet and doubt concerning their present purposes in the credentials program.

3. Similarly, membership itself is "typical" by virtue of membership activity. In this regard, most social settings allow for eccentricity (see Lofland, 1971: 100–101). The degree to which this is so depends upon unspecifiable, situationally specific features of the setting which can only be revealed in the course of the research. The *fact* that this is so, however, makes it possible for analysts to probe areas that others may find ludicrous without surrendering their status as "typical" members. The extent to which it is advantageous for a sociologist to accept and cash in on the social label "a little bit odd" is something that has to be decided by individual analysts. The point is that it can be done and it can be useful.

4. In keeping with the above, there often will be other participants in the setting who are labeled eccentric (see Vidich, 1955: 357). There will also be those judged marginally competent or incompetent altogether. These people should be watched. They take risks the analysts may be unwilling to take. Sometimes their activity will be of the sort the analyst would indeed like to engage in, and with similar results. One of my colleagues, upon reading an early draft of my study, thought I was referring to myself sometimes in the first person and sometimes as "a student" and recommended that I standardize my writing style. What other students did, asked, and said often so closely resembled the sort of thing I would do for research purposes that my reader initially thought that I had been doing all of it. *This* was the point that needed clarification in subsequent drafts.

5. Nothing counts as "the action that was taken" independent of talk about action. What is typical behavior within a social setting is typical by virtue of its linguistically accomplished typicality. Thus within indeterminate limitations, the analyst can engage in research activity without direct attention to covering it up. There is nothing about that activity that is self-evidently research activity. In fact, insofar as members attend to that activity at all, they will not "see" research activity; they will see some sort of membership activity instead. This is to say that they will tend to see it as somehow in conformity with notions of normal membership activity. It is therefore in the analyst's interest at times like these to allow members to inform him or her of what he or she is actually doing or has done vis-à-vis the setting. That is, vis-à-vis the setting, the activity is not research activity. By noting members' compliments, observations, complaints, and so on, the analyst can turn necessary practicalities of research activity into opportunities to generate data—allowing members to provide accounts of how that activity conforms to notions of typical membership.

6. Talk is irremediably vague (see Garfinkel, 1967: 1–11). This enables the analyst to talk about issues, ask questions, and so forth; to members, such talk appears less monumental than it does to the analyst; i.e., small talk to members can be significant talk for the researcher. Many times I asked questions of instructors, supervising teachers, and other program personnel regarding specific course requirements, practical questions for getting the assignments done. On occasion, these questions masqueraded my intent to explore sociological themes interesting to me at the moment; more often these questions simultaneously served mundane and research ends. In still other cases, I asked questions for purely pragmatic purposes and the sociological import of the exchange did not strike me until months later when I was reviewing my notes.

7. The equivocal nature of language also allows analysts to enter, more or less freely, into talk about past training, future plans, and present sociological interests. When directly asked about matters that might affect the integrity of the secret, analysts can follow Agnes's lead and select characterizations that are likely answers to questions typically asked of members of the setting. They can, furthermore, state their responses in such a way that despite essential ambiguities will not require further information or invite further inquiry. While no clear recipe for doing this will be forthcoming, analysts can never the less depend upon their abilities to improvise answers and any further clarification with the certain knowledge that routine interaction will not require them to disclose more than what remains under their control. This knowledge rests on a fundamental feature of talk in any setting: Absolute clarification, where all is known and brought to light, is an essential impossibility (see Garfinkel, 1967). Put differently, nothing counts as "telling all," and members both know that and count on it. To quote Wittgenstein (1953: 1) "Explanations come to an end."

Several occasions arose in which my background as a sociologist became thematized. Students knew me from TA sections, had friends I "should know," or had heard through various channels that I had a master's degree. It was relatively effortless for me to allow students to reveal their practical concerns with these matters: Could I "do" anything with an M.A.? (No.) Didn't I "just hate sociology?" (At times.) Did I think labeling theory was just another form of Marxism? (I hadn't thought of that.) Often students' interests revolved around the issue of my M.A. either with respect to my starting salary or my very employability as a schoolteacher. Sometimes I concertedly turned conversations in these directions, talking about whether I would ever "go back" to sociology, get a Ph.D. and the rest of it. In fact, by emphasizing the disadvantages of a Ph.D. in the school-teaching job market, I was able to speculate quite freely on the possibility of using my experiences in the credentials program to write a dissertation. I might add, parenthetically, that several students encouraged me to do just that, saying that "somebody should get *something* out of all this!"

8. When new information arises, members have at their disposal procedures for viewing that information not as information withheld but as what-could-have-been-said-earlier-but-never-came-up. Thus as parts of the secret are disclosed, or perhaps as the secret itself is being revealed (as indeed it often must be), analysts can trade on members' inclination not to view themselves as having been "fooled." That is, this inclination is an invaluable resource for the analyst in managing either inadvertent slip-ups or the ultimate debriefing of setting participants. If successfully managed, debriefing can itself become an occasion for analysts to display typical membership and to learn how members normalize such revelations as insufficient to warrant doubting analysts' "after all" status as members.

I began formal debriefing of key personnel during the last eight weeks of the academic year. Insofar as I had been established as a competent student and student teacher, I found full disclosure to be an unrealizable ideal; i.e., my student role, in each case, assimilated my revelation. The secret was received in most cases with mild lack of interest. Students appeared not to believe me or thought I was fantasizing because of the poor job market. One former supervising teacher said: "So why are you telling *me* this? It seems you'd have to get somebody in sociology to help you on that." The supervising teacher I was working with at the time was quite interested and even wanted to know some of the specifics; however, after a lengthy discussion of my dissertation and my upcoming advancement to candidacy (for which I would need time off), she shifted the topic to "practical" matters—my need to write "plans of some sort" for an all-class takeover I was about to conduct. The fact that she did not want to see these written plans herself, her acknowledgement that I "might not really *need* them," and her assertion that writing them anyway would be "good practice" for the types of things I would be doing in the future ("Sometimes a principal may walk in and want to see them . . . you just never know . . .") all contributed to a hunch that my revelations were somehow assimilated by my "after all" status as student teacher. This hunch subsequently proved correct.

Two Examples

In this section we take up two general research strategies which depend upon setting features enumerated above. The congruence of managing the secret and membership activity will be illustrated by emphasizing first how normal membership activity can be turned to research advantage (secret interview) and subsequently how necessary research procedures (secret note-taking) can be construed within social settings to be normal membership activity. To some degree, the specifics of what follows are consequences of my own research setting; however, their central import should not be lost on those generally interested in participant observation.

Participation-as-research: the secret interview. Analysts concerned with normal membership can learn from other members' knowledge concerning this activity. Thus it is proper to ask questions (see Vidich, 1955: 354–360). In so doing, covert analysts are using their knowledge that requesting and providing information are features of almost any social setting; analysts can begin there. Asking for information accomplishes at least three things:

a. It provides responses which to the analyst serve as examples, models, and indicators of proper talk within the setting under study. These reponses are data in the same way that any observed talk is data. Here, however, the analyst controls the topic, intervenes as it were, and solicits talk about areas particular to his or her research interests—talk which otherwise would not take place.

b. Simultaneously, the analyst, in asking questions, is practicing the art of talk within the setting. Certain sorts of questions are not taken seriously. They may, for example, appear to go beyond the bounds of "what everybody knows"—and instead of responses may only draw bewildered looks (see Stoddart, 1974). Thus the analyst can be an apprentice in members' talk in the very process of attempting to solicit it.

c. Combining these facts, it becomes possible to identify certain parameters of members' talk, that is, boundaries which competent members do not ordinarily cross. Such boundaries have been referred to as "idealizations" in the ethnomethodological literature—unstated premises, assumptions, presuppositions, and background expectancies which provide for the perceived reasonableness of all members' talk while at the same time being elaborated and documented as "after all correct" whenever such talk takes place.

Whenever analysts talk within the setting, they could be conducting secret interviews. A concerted interview, however, aimed at the objectives outlined in the last paragraph, will generally require some degree of risk. The analyst may want to approach the boundaries of perceived reasonableness or cross them temporarily for purposes of satisfying himself or herself as to "where" those boundaries are; the line of demarcation is routinely avoided by members, and it may be possible to identify it only by crossing it—with caution. Such practices, if engaged in continuously, will be costly in terms of role credibility. Much can be gained, though, from using these devices strategically and sparingly. "How much" to use them can only be determined in the context of doing the research itself; such determinations simultaneously become research data.

In my own research, a tremendous resource resided in the fact that students in the program were *expected* to ask questions. We were supposed to be learning how to teach. In framing questions as directed toward the presumed objective, I was able to generate data concerning how to be a student within the credentials program learning how to teach. Both in the responses provided and in the way questions were taken, I learned something about schooling that is so taken for granted that it should only seldom be brought up for review, and even then only in theory or in jest. I learned the sorts of questions students can ask. Sometimes I was told in college classes that such-and-such was a "good" question and that it deserved an answer, but that I should ask it somewhere else. Students sometimes groaned when I began flirting with such issues as how bureaucratically mandated "behavioral objectives" can tell teachers what is going on inside a child's mind or by what justification a child not "conforming to school expectations" or working up to "grade level" can be called a problem child. At one point late in the first term, a staff member called me into her office to relay some complaints made by students and instructors about some of my questions. She was unable to tell me what kinds of questions I should ask, but she suggested I keep to questions like: "When is it due?" or "how many pages should it be?"

As already suggested, analysts cannot overly engage in such risk-taking if they are to maintain typical membership. This is not to say that the secret would be revealed, but significant tendencies on the part of members to see analysts as incompetent or otherwise obstructionist will probably not be beneficial to ongoing research concerns. It should be noted in this regard, however, that several of the teachers in one of my student teaching assignments commented on my questioning, saying that it was my "strongest point" and that it indicated I was a "really conscientious student."

Research-as-participation: taking field notes. Field notes are possibly the most universal ingredient of participant observation and of ethnography in general. Most textbooks on field methods provide suggestions for taking and processing notes (see Forcese and Richer, 1973: 149–151; Lofland, 1971: 101–113, 117–133). What is not addressed, possibly because little has been said about covert field methods, is the sense in which note-taking for research purposes can be systematically concealed and made to conform with membership activity. Analysts can use whatever it is about the setting that transforms "paper and ink" into tools of membership in order to accomplish their practical ends of note-taking while simultaneously discovering further aspects of what they are doing vis-à-vis the same setting.

The credentials program was particularly amenable to this sort of practice, since students were expected to take notes and even to keep a "journal" of day-to-day activities and observations. An observation guide was provided listing 38 areas with which students were to become familiar. Many of these areas closely approximated my own research interests. A program coordinator elaborated on the list, suggesting that we avoid being overly conspicuous in our note-taking in the public schools. We might, she said, want to "remember" things and write them down later.

All told, I collected 450 pages of typed, single-spaced notes by the end of the year. By far the easiest to manage notes were those that doubled as "class notes." In college classes I wrote nonstop as instructor lectures and student-instructor dialogue took place. My seemingly fanatical notetaking served, within the setting, to document my "seriousness" with respect to my student role. It also served to document my eccentricity. Upon occasions in which students broke into small groups for various purposes and were to choose "recorders" to take notes and report back to the class, I was chosen as the "recorder" on the grounds that "he takes notes on everything anyway." I made it a point in all of my note-taking to reveal my illegible handwriting in order to discourage people from attempting to read my notes.

Taking notes was not as easy or straightforward in other settings within the program, such as "professional seminars" in which students shared mutual problems and successes encountered while student teaching, special topics seminars, informal get-togethers, potluck dinners, and so forth. In these settings, I was able to vary the degree to which my note-taking was in the open by monitoring other students' note-taking activity. Even where little notetaking was taking place, paper and notebooks were usually highly visible. In such cases, I was able to participate in group processes while periodically turning to a piece of paper to jot down some bit of information to be interpreted later in the evening. I also engaged in such practices as writing while looking elsewhere, for example at a book or blackboard, giving the impression that I was copying something down and was not paying attention to the discussion which was the object of my attention.

Note-taking was most difficult to manage in student teaching assignments, which lasted most of the year. It was here that my participant role was all-consuming. I had practical concerns, bureaucratic responsibilities, and problems to resolve. The most useful resource in this setting was the recommendation by program personnel that we take notes, because supervising teachers expected us to take notes. I initially asked one of these supervising teachers if such note-taking made her nervous. Her response was: "Are you kidding? After how used to being observed I am?" She said she was glad to see that I was a "conscientious student" and that she herself had taken "notes like that" as a student teacher. She also said that it made her feel important to see me taking notes; "Like it makes me think I'm doing something worth writing down."

Occasionally, however, problems arose. For example, during one student teaching assignment, my note-taking became potentially troublesome when the supervising teacher wanted to read my notes. "I probably ought to look at them to see what I'm doing that I might not even know about." I was not sure how to handle this, and I stalled for a few days. Later, when she was taking notes on my student teaching performance, she remarked that she did not want me to read her notes "for the same reason you don't want me to read yours." In the course of this conversation, I learned that it was routine for evaluators to take notes on teachers, notes which if read by the teachers being evaluated, might be misinterpreted as overly negative. Thus teachers routinely withhold their written observations, and vis-à-vis the setting, this is what I appeared to be doing.

The point I wish to emphasize here is that taking notes need not be seen simply as the recording of events and occurrences within the setting in which the analyst is also a participant. Rather the note-taking ought properly to be viewed as a constituent feature of that very setting. Thus the analyst's technical research work is part of his or her very role as a participant. Members view it that way; that they view it that way is part of competent membership, and as such it is a topic for analysis. Analysts can then use this acquired information as resources for further managing the problem of discreet note-taking. Throughout the year I was able to take notes while waiting to see what I was doing. Taking notes in the teachers' lunchroom was drawing up "lesson plans"; taking notes on teachers' talk concerning "control devices" of the classroom was the accumulation of such devices for future use as a schoolteacher. The point here is that what was an unfortunately necessary component of field work was simultaneously competent student-teacher activity. Thus my analyst activity and my membership activity were congruent.

As suggested above, the specifics of my research setting may provide for some exaggerated claims regarding the possibility of open and unabashed note-taking. Nevertheless, it is always in the analyst's interest to discover the taken for granted corpus of knowledge operating within a setting regarding the normal, routine use of paper and ink, or whatever facilities are available for taking notes. This corpus of knowledge can be simultaneously discovered in the actual course of taking notes and used to manage notetaking, allowing the analyst both to discover and to display typical membership activity in and through necessary research procedure.

Some Objections

The central point I have been making is that for covert participant observers, managing the secret is not incidental to the research itself, nor is it incidental to the display of typical membership. It is not as though managing the secret is hiding one's "real" identity for purposes of gaining access to a setting or a participant's "perspective" from which it then becomes possible to do research. Managing the secret *is* the research, *is* the display of typical membership. These activities are not independent of one another, nor can they be analytically segregated. They coincide, they are congruent, they are inseparable.

Objections can be raised to these arguments, and I will attempt to deal with some of them in this section. I have been discussing these matters as though everything analysts do in their capacities as researchers consists of managing the secret, as though that were all they do. One might ask whether analysts need constantly be on guard in this way. Certainly during most of the time spent in a setting, the secret is in no immediate danger; there simply is no foreseeable thematic opening for the topic to arise. At times like these, however, it is the analyst, and only the analyst, who has made the determination to relax his or her guard. And even within these contexts, the analyst cannot know precisely when and how guarding the secret might reemerge as relevant. It is in this sense, then, that the analyst must continually monitor and manage the secret, pay close attention, be ever vigilant.

I also might be misunderstood on the following point: I do not mean to suggest that all of the material gathered in the process of managing the secret will be relevant to the analyst's immediate theoretical concerns. When I say that managing the secret is simultaneously membership activity and research activity, I mean that it is through such practices that analysts can assure themselves of typical membership. Such assurances are crucial for analysts in determining the validity of their data. That is, without these assurances, their possibly flaws participant status may undercut the credibility of their research activity, whatever their immediate theoretical research interests might be.

A more serious objection might be that the secret is, after all, a secret, and the analyst could be discredited; this in and of itself renders the analyst atypical of group members. Such an objection presupposes several things about social life, most notably that all "typical" members are "up-front," have "nothing to hide," or in some objective way fit a "mold" of typicality. Such a "mold" is conventionally characterized as conformity to a set of internalized group norms, such conformity "causing" the observed typicality. The arguments presented here, however, are informed by a perspective which regards "typicality" as an accomplishment of occasioned, ongoing membership activity which includes the presentation of self through an array of practices of selecting relevancies, glossing incidentals, ignoring or often concealing idiosyncratic biographical specifics which otherwise might call competent membership into question, and disregarding an unlimited number of alternative ways of constituting what "really is going on" or "what I'm really doing, what my interests really are" (see Garfinkel, 1967).

A related objection might be raised: Is it not the case that researchers engaged in such analyses are depending for their data upon case studies of one, namely themselves? Worse, are they not overly dependent upon their own subjective impressions regarding "what it takes" to sustain membership where other members' impressions might significantly differ? Answers to these questions revolve around an emphasis upon what it is that analysts interested in what it takes to sustain membership are concerned with: *doing*. They are not concerned with subjective formulations, attitudes, or opinions. What it takes to sustain membership is not inside anyone's head but consists of socially accountable activity. Furthermore, analysts, in engaging in such activity, are not doing so in isolation. Indeed, successful passing on their part is not possible without the active cooperation of other members of the setting; other members facilitate analysts' performance. Thus successful passing does not mean coming to view things from a "typical perspective," but rather depends upon full participation in the setting with other members who also participate and whose participation renders analysts' participation typical. In the final analysis, then, it can be stated: The analyst *is* a typical member by virtue of successful passing.

• • •

Concluding Remarks

The ideas presented in this article were inspired by a covert participant observation study within an elementary school teaching credentials program. These experiences suggest that the characterization "covert research" can often be misleading. While my research required the preservation of secrecy and warranted the label covert, it indicated the congruence between the *covert* and *public* natures of any research role. Thus this discussion can be extended to participant observation in general.

A participant observation is irremediably covert to some degree, because of the essential glossing practices any member engages in to produce typicality. But for participant observers, these practices normally have a special significance. Not only is it seldom desirable for research motivated behavior to emerge as dominant in the eyes of fellow participants, it is probably difficult for analysts to reveal the entire character of their research interests and goals, even if this were their research policy; indeed it is doubtful they could articulate it fully even to themselves (see Forcese and Richer, 1973: 146). Yet it is through guarding the integrity of such concerns that analysts both achieve acceptance within a social community and accomplish their research ends, assuring that whatever their research interests might be, they are after all participating typically within the setting. In short, all participant observers must, in some sense and to some degree, pass.

References

Becker, H. et al. (1961) Boys in White: Student Culture in Medical School. Chicago, IL: University of Chicago Press.

Bogdan, R., and S. J. Taylor (1975) Introduction to Qualitative Research Methods. New York: John Wiley.

Bruyn, S. T. (1966) The Human Perspective in Sociology: The Methodology of Participant Observation. Englewood Cliffs, NJ: Prentice-Hall.

Davis, F. (1960–1961) "Comment on 'Initial interaction of newcomers in Alcoholics Anonymous.' " Social Problems: 364–365.

Denzin, N. K. (1970) The Research Act: A Theoretical Introduction to Sociological Methods. Chicago, IL: Aldine.

Erikson, K. T. (1967) "A comment on disguised observation in sociology." Social Problems 14: 366–373.

Fichter, J. H. and W. L. Kolb (1953) "Ethical limitations on sociological reporting." Amer. Soc. Rev. 18: 544–550.

Forcese, D. P. and S. Richer (1973) Social Research Methods. Englewood Cliffs, NJ: Prentice-Hall.

Garfinkel, H. (1967) Studies in Ethnomethodology. Englewood Cliffs, NJ: Prentice-Hall.

Goffman, E. (1959) The Presentation of Self in Everyday Life. Garden City, NY: Doubleday.

Gold, R. L. (1958) "Rules in sociological field observations." Social Forces 36:217–223.

Helmstadter, G. C. (1970) Research Concepts in Human Behavior: Education, Psychology. Sociology. Englewood Cliffs, NJ: Prentice-Hail.

Hilbert, R. A. (I 977) "Approaching reason's edge: 'nonsense' as the final solution to the problem of meaning." Soc. Inquiry 47:25–31.

Junker, B. H. (1960) Field Work: An Introduction to the Social Sciences. Chicago, IL: University of Chicago Press.

Lofland, J. (1971) Analyzing Social Settings: A Guide to Qualitative Observation and Analysis. Belmont, CA: Wadsworth.

———. (1960–1961) "Reply to Davis." Social Problems 8:365–367.

———. and R. A. Lejeune (1960) "Initial interaction of newcomers in Alcoholics Anonymous: A field experiment in class symbols and socialization." Social Problems 8:102–111.

Riesman, D. and J. Watson (1964) "The sociability project: a chronicle of frustration and achievement," in P. E. Hammond (ed.) Sociologists At Work. New York: Basic.

Roth, J. (1962) "Comments on 'secret observation'." Social Problems 9:283–284.

Schatzman, L. and A. Strauss (1973) Field Research: Strategies for a Natural Sociology. Englewood Cliffs, NJ: Prentice-Hall.

Shils, E. A. (1959) "Social inquiry and the autonomy of the individual," pp. 114–157 in D. Lerner (ed.) The Human Meaning of the Social Sciences. New York: Meridian.

Stoddart, K. (1974) "Pinched: notes on the ethnographer's location of argot," pp. 173–179 in R. Turner (ed.) Ethnomethodology. New York: Viking.

Vidich, A. J. (1955) "Participant observation and the collection and interpretation data." Amer. J. of Sociology 60:354–360.

Wieder, D. L. (1974a) Language and Social Reality: The Case of Telling the Convict Code. The Hague: Mouton.

———. (1974b) "Telling the Code,' " pp. 21–26 in R. Turner (ed.) Ethnomethodology. New York: Viking.

———. (1970) "On meaning by rule," pp. 107–135 in J. D. Douglas (ed.) Understanding Everyday Life, Chicago, IL: Aldine.

Wilson, T. P. (1970) "Normative and interpretive paradigms in sociology," pp. 57–79 in J. D. Douglas (ed.) Understanding Everyday Life. Chicago, IL: Aldine.

Wittgenstein, L. (1953) Philosophical Investigations. New York: Macmillan.

Zimmerman, D. H. (1970) "The practicalities of rule use," pp. 221–238 in J. D. Douglas (ed.) Understanding Everyday Life. Chicago, IL: Aldine.

———. and D. L. Wieder (1970) "Ethnomethodology and the problem of order: comment on Denzin," pp. 285–295 in J. D. Douglas (ed.) Understanding Everyday Life, Chicago, IL: Aldine.

Doing Research in Prison: The Strengths and Weaknesses of Full Participation as a Guard

JAMES W. MARQUART

Prison research has traditionally been conducted by outsiders, or researchers in non-participant roles. This paper, however, demonstrates that involvement in the prison as a prison guard, an insider, is a viable and needed form of participant observation. As an insider, the author was able to collect data on behaviors often concealed from other fieldworkers. However, participation as a member was not problem-free and this paper addresses the strengths, weaknesses, and ethical dilemmas of full participation as a research role. The paper also addresses whether full participation hinders or hampers data collection when the researcher returns to the same setting but in the traditional or outside role.

The dominant mode of prison guard research is survey methodology, and in the past decade guards have been polled on such numerous topics as role stress (Poole and Regoli 1980), turnover (Jacobs and Grear 1977), role conflict (Hepburn and Albonetti 1980), occupational socialization (Crouch and Alpert 1982), and race relations and the guard culture (Jacobs and Kraft 1978). These inquiries have contributed greatly to the literature on guards and their role within prison organizations. Questionnaire data, however, are collected from a "distance" and fail to penetrate the inner or backstage prison behavioral settings. On the other hand, some investigators (e.g., Sykes 1958; Carroll 1974; Jacobs and Retsky 1975) have collected qualitative data on guards, but they entered the setting in the typical observer role as nonparticipants or "outside-as-researchers." These prison methodologies offer only a restricted or limited view of guards and their organizational role. Specifically prison researchers, unlike those who have become police officers to study police work (see Van Maanen 1973), have avoided full participation as a means to study guards and prisons.

J.W. Marquart. *Justice Quarterly,* Vol. 3 No. 1, March 1986 © 1986 Academy of Criminal Justice Sciences.

In the spring of 1981, I became a prison guard to examine the official and unofficial methods of prisoner control and discipline in a large maximum security penitentiary within the Texas prison system. I worked as a researcher-guard for nineteen months (June 1981 through January 1983) and collected ethnographic materials while working, participating, and observing in a variety of locations and activities (e.g., cell blocks, dormitories, visitation areas, recreation periods, dining halls, shower rooms, solitary confinement, disciplinary hearings, and hospital). I eventually obtained unlimited access to the unwritten and more sensitive aspects of guard work, prisoner control, and the guard culture.

The activities of entering the prison, negotiating a research role, establishing field relations, studying social control and order, and exiting the field were not the clear and orderly processes so often described in ethnographic reports. Instead, immersion in the prison scene placed some unusual demands on me as an observer (and person) not generally experienced by other more "traditional" qualitative researchers (see also Styles 1979; Van Maanen 1982). Complete participation is a viable research role, yet there are some pitfalls. This paper addresses the strengths, weaknesses, and ethical implications of the researcher-guard role and full participation as a prison methodology.

Becoming an Outside-Insider

My first experience with Texas prisons was in the summer of 1979 when I participated in a project evaluating guard training, supervision, and turnover throughout the Texas prison system. During the research, I met a warden who in turn made arrangements for me to visit the Eastham Unit*—a maximum security facility housing 3200 prisoners over the age of twenty-five who had been incarcerated more than three times. My first visit was spent touring the institution with the warden, meeting various ranking guards, observing disciplinary court, and driving around the prison's 14,000-acre agricultural operation. The warden informed me at the end of the tour that I was welcome to visit Eastham.

For the next year and a half I went to Eastham almost every other month, with each trip lasting five to eight hours. I had complete freedom to walk unescorted throughout the compound and converse with guards at work and with inmates while they ate, worked, spent recreation time in the gym or lounged in their cells. I often followed an officer for several hours to observe his work routine. During these trips, I met several "old time" convicts who described in detail the rich folklore surrounding Texas prisons. Moreover, each time I visited Eastham, my guard and inmate contacts pressed me to work as a guard to see the "real" penitentiary. I avoided their suggestions, explaining that I wanted to remain impartial, free to roam the prison. Actually, my real reason was outright fear of the prisoners. Yet I knew they were correct and after assessing my research goals, I real-

*All names in this paper are pseudonyms.

ized full participation would foster the necessary inside perspective to examine prisoner control. In April 1981, the warden arranged for me to begin work in June 1981.

I entered Eastham without a clearly-defined role (c.f., Jacobs 1977). Although the warden, a few guards, and several inmates knew I was a graduate student in sociology, they did not know the exact details of my research plans. The Texas prison system was at this time embroiled in the bitterly contested prison reform case of *Ruiz v. Estelle* (1980). This suit alleged, among other things, that guard brutality was rampant and that the building tender system (using dominant/aggressive inmates to control other inmates) was abusive. Eastham was a target unit in the case. One of my research goals was to observe and analyze the building tender system (see Marquart and Crouch 1984). I felt, however, that if I revealed my aims to the security staff they would not allow me to work as a guard or even conduct research. Therefore, I kept the specifics of the project vague and told the warden of my interest in guards, guard work, and the ways in which various court orders have affected the staff's ability to maintain control and order. Moreover, my presence as a researcher-guard was not officially announced to the prison community. I had no official letter from the director of the prison system or the warden identifying me as a researcher. I was to be treated as any other employee, which was reflected in my first shift assignment—the third shift (9:45 p.m.–5:45 a.m.).

I never at any time misrepresented my identity. I "passed" as a sociology doctoral student who was tired of the books and sought real prison experience. If asked about my personal or educational background, I gave true information in order to prevent suspicion and rumor. But this strategy was not enough of an explanation and precipitated several rumors. The prison grapevine had it that I was an F.B.I. agent or an official from the Department of Justice "placed" at Eastham to investigate and report on prison operations. Some inmates thought I was a writer and followed me for hours detailing their life of crime and violence, hoping I would write their life histories. I was also tagged as Mr. Estelle's (then, the director of the prison system) son, a rumor that lasted throughout the research. I also foolishly contributed to these rumors when I was seen photographing the prison compound. Like most prison field observers (Giallombardo 1966; Carroll 1974; Jacobs 1974), I had to prove constantly that I was not a spy or government agent.

I relied on two contacts, both of whom eventually became trusted informants and friends, to facilitate my acceptance and quell rumors. One was PP, a high ranking guard and Ph.d. student at a nearby university. We had met during an earlier visit and shared our research interests. He was well-respected by the guards and prisoners and introduced me to the two most politically powerful inmates at Eastham. I told them of my background and interest in Texas prisons. They agreed to be interviewed only because they said "PP told us to." In addition, I met MM, an older politically powerful prisoner who introduced me to other important prisoners. These latter contacts in turn introduced me to others and soon I developed (through snowball sampling) an extensive network of inmate informants. As for the guards, I befriended several workmates who became allies and informants. PP's and MM's assistance enhanced my status tremendously; however, their endorsement did not ensure immediate acceptance or totally eliminate doubt about "what I was really up to." Many guards and inmates respected my willingness to work as a guard, but they did not regard me as reputable. In their eyes, I was an untested novice who had to earn their favor before being accepted, respected, and able to collect data.

Character Development and Data Collection

Maximum security prisons are rife with fear, conflict, paranoia, racial animosities, and intense factionalism. Building rapport and establishing trust in the context of a research role is difficult and time-consuming. Prison researchers are on center stage and their behavior is constantly scrutinized by officers and inmates who look for clues (or cues) that reveal the observer's character and intentions. I followed a careful strategy in establishing field relations.

First, I kept a low profile and concentrated on working hard to establish a reputation as a reliable employee. In this institution, following orders without hesitation was an important value within the guard subculture. I accepted without complaint difficult and boring work assignments, broke up inmate fights, and wrote disciplinary reports on several inmates. My eagerness so impressed my supervisors that I was promoted to Hall "Boss" (inmates referred to the guards as "boss" or "bossman"). Hall bosses were regarded by the guards and prisoners alike as the cream of the non-ranking officers. Obtaining one of these positions was also viewed as a promotion by the officers, his peers, supervisors, and prisoners. Moreover, all line staff sought to become one of these officers because they were free from cell block duty and worked closely with ranking guards which aided in rank-obtaining promotions. Among the three shifts, there were around 25 hall officers, the majority of whom were white. With this advancement, I became quickly and deeply involved in the guard world and I was an ally of the building tenders, who taught me the official and unofficial means of prisoner control.

Second, I began weightlifting and boxing in the prison gym with several prisoners. One inmate, WW, was my "teacher" and we worked out daily, played basketball, jogged, as well as trained on the "heavy bag." . . . I soon won their trust because I listened and never questioned their knowledge, but instead let them tell me what to do—a reversal of their normally subordinate status. By deferring to them, I demonstrated my acceptance of their expertise and this fostered a bond that established a high degree of rapport. While we exercised, they described how the guards recruited snitches, used unofficial force to punish and control inmates, and told me which officers were respected and why. Moreover, weightlifting and boxing (especially in prison) were prized masculine activities and my eagerness to learn enhanced my status among the prisoners. In fact, many prisoners based their respect for other inmates and officers on their ability to exhibit superior strength (mental and physical) or compulsive masculinity (see Toby 1966).

The third and most important factor which established my credibility, and earned the guards' and prisoners' respect was an occurrence on December 15, 1981. This event and my subsequent behavior solidified my reputation as a "good" officer (i.e., not afraid of the inmates, firm but fair) and a "true" insider. At approximately 11:25 p.m., another hall officer and I went to 1-block (a solitary confinement area) to help several other hall officers search inmate Friar's property which was in a large canvas sack. He had been placed in solitary confinement earlier that day for assaulting an officer. Friar, who weighed nearly 300 pounds, stood in the Hall (central corridor in the prison) waiting for us to inventory his property. I ordered him to take his property out of the sack. He remained motionless. I then said, "unsack it." He lifted the bag and spilled the contents on the floor, threw the sack in the air, and then punched me in the forehead nearly knocking me unconscious. I was forced to defend myself. With the help of two other hall officers, Friar was finally subdued and quartered in solitary confinement. I required medical attention for a large knot on my forehead.

Early the next morning, I was standing near the Commissary (prison store) when Supervisor L approached me and said:

L: "Hey, there's the raging bull. Tell us what happened. What happened?"

I then retold the story to his delight., The following morning another ranking guard pointed at me and yelled "Hey, there's Bruiser." Then he came over and started shadow boxing with me. That evening two second shift hall officers, who had previously avoided me, also asked me about the incident. After finishing the story, these officers stated they would help me with anything they could.

The fact that I had been assaulted and had defended myself in front of several officers and building tenders raised my esteem and established my reputation. The willingness to fight inmates was an important trait rewarded by the ranking guards (see Marquart and Roebuck 1984). Due to this "fortunate" event, I earned the necessary credibility to establish rapport with the prison participants and allay their previous suspicions of me. I passed the ultimate test—fighting an inmate even though in self-defense—and was now a trustworthy member of the guard subculture. I had character, or the "balls" or "nuts," to stand up for and defend myself.

• • •

I entered Eastham as a guard to discover "how things really operated," but this was not a ticket to obtaining good data. As an outsider-insider, I had to prove myself through hard work and by standing up to the inmates. More important, I had to share and actually experience the traumas, risks, violence, and dangers of the prison environment. My presence and acceptance depended on how well I negotiated these daily realities. Although the Friar incident ultimately secured my acceptance, I continually had to demonstrate loyalty to the guards and building tenders. Few research roles are ever finalized (complete acceptance) and this situation heightens the fieldworker's awareness of the necessity to constantly guard against overconfidence in matters of acceptance (Lofland 1971). . . .

Insider Status and Data Collection

Hard work, often involving "dirty work," and the willingness to use official force enabled me to recruit informants among the guards and inmates, particularly the building tenders. I quickly made friends with several officers, told them my research interests, and they willingly agreed to work as surrogate observers, describing events or incidents on the other shifts (see Scott 1965). I also interviewed officers in their homes, in bars, or on the job. From these interviews and countless conversations, data was obtained on, for example, morale, the staff's recruitment of snitches, and when and where the guards used unofficial force (beatings) to subdue, control, and terrorize "unruly" inmates. These home interviews were tape-recorded while those on the job were written down and reconstructed later.

From my inmate informants, I collected data on how the guards officially recruited and coopted the most dominant and aggressive inmates to become building tenders. Because of my guard role, I closely associated with these inmate elites and nearly a dozen were key informants. They showed me how they made liquor or "pruno," stole food from the prison kitchen, made knives, and sold tattoo patterns and machines. These latter activities were clearly illegal but I kept their trafficking confidential; this too demonstrated my trustworthiness. The ability to "keep one's mouth shut" was a highly prized asset and I quickly internalized this important value. I also made sure that all interviewees were told that their conversations were confidential and off the record. The gathering of information, however, was not one-sided and I reciprocated when and wherever possible (see Wax 1971). I often helped inmates obtain job or cell changes, new uniforms or shoes, or hospital appointments. I also periodically bought my key inmate informants sodas, cigars, candy, or coffee. After exiting the field, I wrote letters of recommendation to the parole board for five prisoners, all of whom are now free citizens.

Building rapport and earning trust in the prison community was initially difficult but my actions eventually secured my acceptance. Like Jacobs (1974), once I was regarded as an insider, I had little trouble making the necessary contacts to obtain information. However, with my ability to establish trust came the problem of deep involvement in the guard subculture. I tried to balance my roles, to be both a sociologist studying prisoner control and a legitimate member of the prisoner control apparatus. The participative or outside-inside role is emotionally and physically taxing because the researcher, in any scene or setting, must in essence wear "two hats." One persistent problem, to be discussed below, was that the guard role often superseded my sociological interests.

Problems of the Participative Research Role

. . . The participative research role was not problem-free and three major difficulties were encountered throughout the fieldwork.

Occupational Pressures

One of the most pervasive problems, stemming from my work role, was remaining a uniformed sociologist (or outsider). I spent my first three months working cell blocks and this assignment severely restricted my ability to make contacts or ask questions. In the fourth month, I was promoted to hall "boss," which afforded the needed mobility to traverse the prison compound. Yet at certain times of the day my work duties (e.g., counting, searching cells, monitoring inmate traffic to and from meals, showers, and work) tied me down for several hours. Prison is a structured world and the work role demanded that I do the same things each day at the same time. To manage this role conflict, I scheduled my "free" time to interview, gather records, and review ideas or data with informants. This does not mean that I did not collect data while actually working. On the contrary, I observed, interviewed, listened to, and conversed with inmates and guards wherever and whenever I could. But as a guard, it was necessary to be security conscious first and a researcher second—a problem inherent in the participative prison research role. This strain would also pose problems for investigators who become police officers or hospital orderlies—the official work role in these cases must supercede, when the situation arises, research interests.

I also collected data off-duty while exercising with several inmates in the prison gym. Once rapport was established, they eventually became key informants and I used these recreation periods to interview, reformulate ideas, or simply discuss our personal lives. I was extremely close to these inmates, who provided a rich data source. As for the officers, we sometimes spent after-hours playing football, swimming, target shooting, drinking beer and shooting pool, eating pizza, and relaxing. I listened to and participated in their conversations about guard work, fights they had with inmates (or other officers), their supervisors, other guards, troublesome inmates, or the Texas prison system. I made mental notes of their comments and reconstructed these conversations later. I even had several key officer informants tape record their thoughts about work, prisoner control, careers, or other prison-related subjects. Not only did these off-duty sessions provide data, but they enabled me to form lasting and meaningful friendships.

Clearly, the most difficult problem in being an outside-insider was role conflict. During the first few months on the "job," I had little difficulty remaining a uniformed sociologist. However, I slowly adopted the guard perspective due to my participation and deep involvement in the guard world. I laughed while guards teased and taunted inmate homosexuals, nodded approvingly when others described how they ripped apart an inmate's cell during a search, and kept a straight face when supervisors threatened to kill inmates. I also remained silent when observing guards and building tenders beat and physically injure inmates. Where and when possible, I defended the system and guards to naive outsiders. I explained to them that guards were the "good guys" and that prisons were necessary to isolate social predators. In many respects I was an apologist for the guards (see Manning 1972).

I was a guard forced to confront the enormous pressures of occupational socialization; this is the major drawback of full participation. I was expected to think, act, and talk like a guard. It was a personal battle to refrain from "going native," especially after the promotion to sergeant in November, 1982. Three factors helped me to adjust and maintain some role stability and distance. First, I left the prison on my designated days off. I worked seven days and then was off three days, which were spent debriefing in my dissertation advisor's office, with friends, and with other faculty members. Maintaining non-guard associations were critical in remaining objective. Second, I never insulted or fought inmates for fun. Many new guards displayed bravado ("John Wayne syndrome"), acting and talking tough to the inmates.

I completely avoided this fronting behavior because I knew prison was too dangerous a place to act tough. Some guards paid the price both physically and mentally when an inmate called their bluff. Finally, I made extensive field notes about this role conflict and kept myself aware of how "deeply" I was moving into the guard subculture. In short, I was extremely sensitive to this problem and forced myself not to lose all objectivity.

Reactivity

The concept of reactivity specifies the proclivity of the research subjects to alter their behavior as a consequence of the researcher's presence (Vidich 1970). Because of his or her presence, a researcher does not observe the subjects' true behavior—a problem endemic to participant observation. Did the guards and prisoners alter their behavior in my presence? I entered Eastham with the full knowledge and approval of several high ranking prison officials. Even though I was known to some of the subjects beforehand, the majority had no idea who I was and treated me as another guard. However, some of the prison participants regarded me as a possible undercover agent investigating Eastham for the Department of Justice. Rumors were also spread about my "intentions" and several guards avoided me.

To negate these suspicions, I embarked on a strategy of earning the guards' trust to combat their false impressions of me and to minimize reactivity. I made it a point to work hard and share the emotional highs and lows of institutional life. In addition, it took nearly eight months of careful interaction, laying low, and "passing" various character tests to prove I was trustworthy. Most fieldworkers do not have this amount of time to invest in character development. After eight months, I was considered to be a "good" officer and this reputation facilitated data collection.

I also observed a great deal of backstage behavior. For example, I witnessed fifty incidents in which guards beat inmates (some were severely injured)—and all of these guards were well aware of my identity as a researcher. Had ranking staff members been afraid or leery of my presence, they would have assigned me to isolated duty posts. Instead, they viewed me as a loyal member of the subculture. To them, I was an employee and they did not have time to alter their behavior in my presence when breaking up brawls, fighting inmates in cells, disciplining inmates, searching cells or inmates, rushing attempted suicides or self-mutilators to the prison hospital, or stopping knife fights among inmates. These behaviors were spontaneous and occurred in similar fashion with or without my presence. Other researchers have noted that once respondents have accepted you (in whatever role) they tend to act as if you were one of them or as if you were not on the scene (see Skolnick 1966).

The vast majority of the inmates considered me to be "just another guard." Some initially told me that they, like some guards, were hesitant to talk with me. The support of third parties allayed some of their apprehensions but my reputation as a fair officer won their confidence, enabling me to secure key informants. Most of my inmate allies were building tenders who occupied positions of power and status within the prisoner society. They candidly answered questions and trusted me because I expressed a true interest in their welfare. Most importantly, I kept everything they said strictly confidential.

Although I cultivated the friendship of a number of inmate elites, I had great difficulty interviewing the "run of the mill" inmates. My uniform was a barrier that limited access to these prisoners and I never completely resolved this problem. I was able to get close to only ten "ordinary" inmate informants who described, from their perspective, snitching, homosexuality, staff use of force, rules and regulations, and verbal threats from the guards. To obtain this information, I often interviewed them in their cells, shower rooms, or on their way to and from meals. The insider role "slotted" me in the prison social structure and almost completely curtailed any contact with Hispanic inmates (c.f., Davidson 1974). For cultural reasons and because of their minority status, these inmates generally stayed away from other inmates and avoided almost all contact (e.g., saying hello, talking about sports, asking questions about various rules) with the staff. For many Hispanic inmates, voluntary interaction with guards was viewed as "ratting" and something to be avoided. Therefore, my contacts with these and most other ordinary inmates were primarily official.

Coping with Violence

Maximum security prisons are conflict-ridden societies where violence or the threat of it is a daily reality. As an outside-insider, I saw, took part in, and was personally affected by the inescapable presence of violence. Full participation brought me face-to-face with actual fear and terror, emotions most field observers never encounter (c.f., Van Maanen 1982). It is difficult for me to describe how I felt when I saw officers punch, kick, and knock inmates senseless with riot clubs as they screamed and begged for mercy. On several occasions I assisted guards in restraining inmates while medics sutured their wounds without any anesthetic. These incidents were shocking experiences. I also observed building tenders throw inmates head first into the bars and "blackjack" others who failed to report for work, remained too long in the dining hall, or cheered for the Houston Oilers instead of the Dallas Cowboys. One brawl involving four building tenders and one inmate so unnerved me that I almost quit. This event was so disturbing that I could not even write about it until several weeks later.

I knew prisons were violent, but only through the writings and experiences of other people. I learned to cope with the everpresent violence and tension by accepting it as an element of this milieu. Violence in prison is banal and everyone must learn to cope with it or else retreat from the situation. For officers, retreat often resulted in quitting and for inmates, in isolation. My particular coping strategy was indifference, the route of most prison participants. If people got hurt, especially inmates, I maintained a cold detachment. However, inwardly I was hurt because human suffering appalled me. In the end, I coped and survived as well as I could (see Jacobs 1974).

Moral and Ethical Dilemmas of Full Participation

All fieldworkers run the risk, due to their presence, of obtaining "guilty knowledge" (see Van Maanen 1982). Because of my insider status, I was privy and party to discrediting information about the nature of guard work and prisoner control. I was firmly entrenched in the prison world—and this may raise some complaints from other researchers. There are ethical dilemmas surrounding this methodology which stem primarily from the observation of numerous violations, not only civil but legal as well.

• • •

. . . Like Van Maanen (1982) in his police fieldwork, I witnessed many illegalities at Johnson but "did not see them." To block or neutralize the moral predicament of seeing "too much," I kept quiet and simply observed. In fact, I could not "tell all" because this would have violated the implicit research bargain assumed by the officials when I entered the situation—an agreement not to use information to injure the subjects. I could not stop the violence and perhaps no one ever will. During the project, the Texas prison system came under a sweeping court order (*Ruiz v. Estelle*) to end guard and building tender brutality. I was contacted by an attorney in the Special Master's Office, who knew of my background, to testify against the Texas Department of Corrections. I told the lawyer that I had nothing to say. I believed my materials were confidential and even envisioned going to jail for contempt of court. Fortunately, this never happened.

I rationalized the violence as being a part of prison life and as something a full participant would in all likelihood have to face. Complete involvement or immersion means just that, and like it or not the insider must sometimes come to grips with various difficult and trying situations (see Styles 1979). Direct observation is unpredictable and the researcher has little control over the strange and unusual events in the setting. There are no formal standards for doing this research and therein lies the problem of full participation. In some cases, getting too close to the data might force the observer to compromise his or her values and morals in order to remain a trusted member. In the end, ethics are purely situational and no research method is completely safe for the researcher and the subjects (Humphreys 1970).

Conclusions

The research process is filled with our own biases and preconceptions which influence the groups or settings that we study and how we study them (Styles 1979). The question "to participate or not?" presents the investigator with a profound moral decision. Indeed, there are strengths and weaknesses associated with both the outside and inside research roles. I am not arguing that one way is superior to another, this is a value judgment that depends on what one wants to study (Becker 1978). Both are important methodologies that should be carefully evaluated before entering the field. I chose to study the prison setting in the participative role. By studying prisoner control as a guard, I collected some unique data but observed much wrong-doing. Yet this is the necessary risk in full participative field research; I took this risk when I made the decision to become a guard. In a positive light, involvement enabled me to experience face-to-face the totality of prison life. In addition, the insider role promotes a firsthand view of the institution and whether or not policies are being complied with or circumvented. Prison reform and prisoner control have historically been intense political and social issues. For this reason, an insider's knowledge can be extremely useful to officials or administrators.

When a researcher decides to participate as a prison guard, several issues must be weighed beforehand. First, the participative role restricts access to some events and can lead to biased sampling. That is, the participant-researcher cannot continuously be on the scene. Further, the fact that he or she is "slotted" in an official role hinders the researcher's ability to make contacts with some prisoner groups. Second, full participation is extremely time-consuming due to the special problems of building rapport and earning respect. I "had" to suffer a physical attack before I was regarded as "alright." Third, this methodology can create complex ethical issues for the researcher. The problem of personal commitments versus social issues can become overwhelming and affect the research process. Finally, full participation breeds questions about reactivity. The direct observer must document how and in what ways, if any, his or her presence affects the scene and validity of the data.

As in any form of research, there are a variety of costs and benefits. By studying prisons from the inside, we can learn how desperately we need new theories and techniques to understand these institutions adequately. If we can obtain this information, then we can provide informed input into new policies and procedures, thus making a genuine contribution to reform.

References

Abbot, J. H. (1981), *In the Belly of the Beast.* New York: Random House.

Becker, H. S. (1978), "Practitioners of Vice and Crime." In N. K. Denzin (editor) *Sociological Methods: A Sourcebook.* New York: McGraw-Hill.

Bettelheim, B. (1943), "Individuals and Mass Behavior in Extreme Situations." *Journal of Abnormal and Social Psychology* 38:417–452.

Bulmer, M. (1982), "When is Disguise Justified? Alternatives to Covert Participant Observation." *Qualitative Sociology* 4:251–264.

Carroll, L. (1974), *Hacks, Blacks and Cons: Race Relations in a Maximum Security Prison.* Lexington, MA: Lexington Books.

Charriere, H. (1970), *Papillion.* New York: Basic Books.

Clemmer, D. C. (1940), *The Prison Community.* New York: Holt, Rinehart and Winston.

Crouch, B. M. and G. Alpert (1982), "Sex and Occupational Socialization Among Prison Guards: A Longitudinal Study." *Criminal Justice & Behavior* 9(2):159–176.

Davidson, R. T. (1974), *Chicano Prisoners: Key to San Quentin.* New York: Holt, Rinehart, and Winston.

Giallombardo, R. (1966), *Society of Women: A Study of Women's Prison.* New York: John Wiley.

Hepburn, J. R. and C. Albonetti (1980), "Role Conflict in Correctional Institutions." *Criminology* 17 (4):445–459.

Humphreys, L. (1970), *Tearoom Trade.* Chicago, IL: Aldine.

Irwin, J. (1970), *The Felon.* Englewood Cliffs, NJ: Prentice-Hall.

Jacobs, J. (1974), "Participant Observation in Prison." *Urban Life and Culture* 3(2):221–240.

——— (1977), *Stateville: The Penitentiary in Mass Society.* Chicago, IL: University of Chicago Press.

Jacobs, J. and M. Grear (1977), "Drop-outs and Rejects: An Analysis of the Prison Guard's Revolving Door." *Criminal Justice* 2(2):57–70.

Jacobs, J. and L. Kraft (1978), "Race Relations and the Guard Subculture." *Social Problems* 25(3):304–318.

Jacobs, J. and H. Retsky (1975), "Prison Guard." *Urban Life* 4(l):5–29.

Lofland, J. A (1971), *Analyzing Social Settings.* Belmont, CA. Wadsworth.

Manning, P. K. (1972), "Observing the Police: Deviants, Respectables, and the Law." In J. Douglas (editor) *Research on Deviance.* New York: Random House.

Marquart, J. W. and B. M. Crouch (1983), "Coopting the Kept: Using Inmates for Social Control in a Southern Prison." Paper presented at the American Society of Criminologists annual meetings, Toronto.

Marquart, J. W. and J. B. Roebuck (1994), "The Use of Physical Force by Prison Guards: Individuals, Situations, and Organizations." Paper to be presented at American Sociological Assoc. Meetings in San Antonio (August).

Poole, E. and R. Regoli (1980), "Role Stress, Custody Orientation and Disciplinary Actions." *Criminology* 18:215–227.

Roebuck, J. (1965), *Criminal Typology.* Springfield, IL: Charles C. Thomas.

Ruiz v. Estelle, 503 F. Supp. 1265 (S.D. Texas) 1980.

Scott, W. R. (1965), "Field Methods in the Study of Organizations." In J. G. March (editor) *Handbook of Organizations.* Chicago, IL: Rand McNally Co.

Schutz, A. (1944), "The Stranger: An Essay in Social Psychology," *American Journal of Sociology* 49:499–507.

Simmel, G. (1908), *Sociology.* Leipzig: Dunker and Humblot.

Skolnick, J. H. (1966), *Justice Without Trial: Law Enforcement in Democratic Society.*

Solzhenitsyn, A. I. (1973), *The Gulag Archipelago.* New York: Harper and Row.

——— (1975), *The Gulag Archipelago II,* New York: Harper and Row.

Styles, J. (1979), "Outsider/Insider: Researching Gay Baths." *Urban Life* 8:135–152.

Sykes, G. (1958), *The Society of Captives.* Princeton, NJ.: Princeton University Press.

Thomas, J. (1979), "Some Aspects of Negotiated Order, Coupling and Mesostructure in Maximum Security Prisons." *Symbolic Interaction* 4:213–231.

Toby, J. (1966), "Violence and the Masculine Ideal: Some Qualitative Data." *ANNALS* 364 (March):19–27.

Van Maanen, J. (1973), "Observations on the Making of Policemen." *Human Organization* 32:407–418.

——— (1982), "Fieldwork on the Beat." In J. Van Maanen et al. (editors) *Varieties of Qualitative Research.* Beverly Hills, CA: Sage Publications.

Vidich, A. (1970), "Participation Observation and the Collection and Interpretation of Data." In W. J. Filstead (editor) *Qulitative Methodology: Firsthand Involvement With the Social World.* Chicago, IL: Markham.

Wax, R. H. (1971), *Doing Fieldwork: Warnings and Advice.* Chicago, IL: University of Chicago Press.

Webb and Morris (1978), *Prison Guards: The Culture and Perspective of an Occupational Group.* Coker Books.

Comparison of Self-Reported Recycling Attitudes and Behaviors with Actual Behavior

KATHLEEN BARKER, LYNDA FONG, SAMARA GROSSMAN, COLIN QUIN, and RACHEL REID

Summary.—This study was designed to investigate the congruence of 102 college students' self-reported paper-recycling behaviors and attitudes with actual behavior. The hypothesis that college students would report positive attitudes toward paper recycling and associated behaviors in a survey was supported. Unobtrusive observation, however, indicated that self-reports did not predict actual paper recycling for most respondents. Only 14 students who had previously reported prorecycling attitudes and behaviors were observed to recycle. The implications of the results for research on college students' recycling and conservation behavior are discussed.

Since 1975, a substantial amount of research on recycling has been conducted by social scientists (Burn, 1991). Studies of recycling attitudes and behaviors have depended on self-report data via questionnaires or interviews (Arbuthnot & Lingg, 1975; Baldassare & Katz, 1992; Oskamp, Harrington, Edwards, Sherwood, Okuda, & Swanson, 1991; Schahn & Holzer, 1990; Shama & Wisenblit, 1984; Vining & Ebreo, 1990). However, in at least four papers, authors have expressed concern about the validity of self-report data in predicting actual recycling or conservation behavior (McGuinness, Jones, & Cole, 1977; McGuire, 1984; Oskamp, 1983; Oskamp, et al., 1991). While one researcher has noted the cost-efficiency of self-report data over observational data (Humphrey, Bord, Hammond, & Mann, 1977), others have remarked that questions remain when measures of actual behavior are not pursued as vigorously as self-reported attitudes (Schahn & Holzer, 1990).

We were able to locate seven studies in which actual behaviors were compared with attitudinal data. The results were mixed across these studies. In some studies, re-

Adapted and reproduced with permission of authors and publisher from: Barker, K., Fong, L., Grossman, S., Quin, C., and Reid, R. Comparison of self-reported recycling attitudes and behaviors with actual behavior. *Psychological Reports*, 1994, 75, 571–577. © Psychological Reports 1994.

cycling or conservation behavior was predicted by attitudes (Humphrey, *et al.,* 1977; Lansana, 1992; McGuinness, *et al.,* 1977), attitudes and education (Webster, 1975), and knowledge regarding the consequences of recycling (Hopper & Nielsen, 1991). In other studies, there was no or only, a minimal relationship between household recycling attitudes and behavior (McGuire, 1984: Steininger & Voegtlin). Studies of actual recycling behavior among college students have focused on behavior modification and the effectiveness of interventions (e.g., Hamad, Cooper, & Semib, 1977; Wang & Katsev, 1990; Witmer & Geller, 1976).

Why should researchers be so concerned about the reliance of the recycling literature on self-reported behavior? We know that the research process may interfere with the outcomes of research (Stern, 1979). Social desirability (Paulhus, 1991), apprehension about evaluation (Rosenberg, 1965, 1969), and becoming attuned to "demand characteristics" (Orne, 1962) may distort the research process and the outcomes when based on self-report measures. Especially when people are asked about socially proscribed behaviors such as recycling, social desirability may tilt self-perceptions about attitudes and behaviors in an inaccurate direction.

Therefore, we sought to examine the relationship between self-reported attitudes and behaviors obtained via a survey with actual behavior measured by trace accretion. Because recycling is a behavior which is positively valued in the USA, especially among younger people (e.g., Hamilton, 1985), it was predicted that the majority of college students would report positive attitudes toward recycling and that they themselves do recycle. However, given the problems associated with self-reports, we predicted that few students with self-reported prorecycling attitudes and behaviors would actually recycle. Finally, we also sought to explore the issue of personal responsibility and efficacy. Schwartz (1977) reported a positive relationship between progressive environmental attitudes and acceptance of personal responsibility for the environment. Therefore, we sought to explore this issue but, given the context of the research, we also sought to explore participants' reactions to the effectiveness of the institution in recycling.

Method

Sampling and Participants

Sampling.—Participants were undergraduates at a four-year liberal arts college. Half of the student population was sampled by mailing a questionnaire via campus mail to every other student for a total of 507 students. Fourteen questionnaires were returned by postal staff because they were placed in unused mailboxes. The target sample size was 493.

Participants.—Of the 493 mailed questionnaires, 152 were returned for a response rate of 31%. Of the 152 participants, 59.2% ($n = 90$) were women and 40.8% ($n = 62$) were men. Participants were 20 years of age on the average, with an age range of 17 to 26 years.

Materials

Questionnaire.—Each questionnaire was labeled with the number of the box in which it was deposited. Instructions for completing the survey instrument also included the statement, "By filling out this questionnaire, you are agreeing to participate in our study of the attitudes and behavior of (college name) students concerning recycling." The questionnaire was comprised of demographic questions plus 10 questions concerning the student's own behaviors and attitudes toward paper recycling and recycling in general. Answering on a 4-point scale in Likert response format (strongly agree, agree, disagree, strongly disagree), questions probed general and specific recycling attitudes, for example, "Recycling is my responsibility" and behavior, for example, "I use _____'s paper recycling bins." An additional item probed responses regarding institutional effectiveness.

Bogus notice.—Four days after distribution of the questionnaire, a bogus notice was sent to the original sample of 493 students via their campus mailboxes. The notice was printed with information on both sides to render it useless for other purposes. The information contained in the notice concerned a college deadline that had already passed and about which students had already been apprised in an earlier college mailing. A separate identification number was paired with each mailbox number. Each notice was then imprinted with the identification number and delivered to the appropriate mailbox. This permitted matching each original questionnaire with a discarded bogus notice.

• • •

Setting.— The study took place in the college's campus mail room over a seven-day period. The mail room is a U.S. Post Office and campus mail facility for students and faculty and has clearly designated paper-recycling bins and garbage bins.

For the next three days the researchers took shifts recovering the bogus notice from the general area of the mail room. At regular intervals (every 15 minutes), a researcher on duty would go to the mail room and adjoining rooms to search for discarded bogus notices. This involved searching trash receptacles, recycling bins, counters, and floors, and recording on the back of each notice from where it had been recovered, e.g., garbage bin, recycle bin, or "other."

Results

After seven days, at the end of the collection period, 308 of the bogus notices had been recovered and, of these, 102 matched a returned questionnaire. Therefore, the final sample of participants numbered 102 college students, 63 women and 39 men.

The two hypotheses predicted that college students would report positive attitudes and behaviors but that, given the social desirability of recycling, self-reported attitudes and behaviors would be independent of actual recycling behavior. All survey items were coded such that a higher score indicated a prorecycling response. The percent endorsing a prorecycling position was calculated by a response of "strongly agree" or "agree" on a 4-point scale for each item.

Table 1   Agreement With Recycling Survey Items By Type of Item and Percentage of Respondents Who Actually Recycled For Sample of *N* = 102

Survey Item Statement	% Endorsing a Prorecycling Position	% Endorsing a Prorecycling Position and Who Actually Recycled
Although recycling is a good idea, I don't recycle.	90.2[a]	14.1
Unrecycled waste paper poses a threat to the environment.	96.1	14.3
Recycling is futile.	95.1[a]	14.4
It is not worth my extra time to recycle.	92.2[a]	14.9
I use the school's paper-recycling bins.	89.2	14.3
Recycling is a passing fad.	88.9[a]	15.9
I make an effort to find and use recycling bins.	88.2	14.4
I recycle paper when I'm not at school.	69.0	17.4
Recycling is my responsibility.	69.0	17.4
My recycling makes a difference.	67.4	15.6

[a]Reversed-scored item.

The first hypothesis was confirmed. The percentages in Column 2 of Table 1 indicate that students overwhelmingly reported high recycling behavior and positive attitudes toward recycling. When students were asked about their own responsibility and importance to the recycling effort, percentages of prorecycling endorsement dropped.

The second hypothesis concerned the subset of the sample who endorsed a prorecycling position. Column 3 of Table 1 displays the actual percentage of participants who both endorsed a prorecycling stance on an item and recycled. Approximately one-sixth of the sample of individuals who reported prorecycling attitudes and behavior actually engaged in the recycling behavior under study. A total of 14 individuals in the sample (12 of whom were female) actually recycled the bogus notice.

• • •

Discussion

These results provide weak evidence that self-report measures regarding positive attitudes toward recycling and prorecycling behaviors predict actual paper-recycling behavior. Except for a minority of students who were consistent between self-reported attitude and actual behavior, the accuracy of individuals in estimating their attitude-behavior consistency was disappointing. Even when the behavior measures

("I use [college name] paper recycling bins") were specific to the location—a specific college and paper recycling itself—such measures did not predict actual behavior.

• • •

A clear outcome of this study is that general attitudes and self-reported recycling behaviors are primarily positive. However, given the positive attitudes expressed in this study and the convenient recycling bins, results departed from those reported by Lansana (1992) who found that recycling was predicted by over-all convenience. Similar to Lansana, recycling was significantly correlated with a positive environmental attitude that recycling is a good idea. Less dramatic but not less meaningful was the finding that the minority who expressed negative attitudes and recycling behavior were consistent in their actual behavior.

• • •

The issue of self-report and actual behavior has a long history in methodological discussions (e.g., Eagly & Chaiken, 1992; Schuman & Kalton, 1985; Wicker, 1969). One argument is that a single criterion measure is not substantial enough to measure actual behavior adequately (Fishbein & Azjen, 1974). Others have argued that in applied settings there are circumstances in which there is only a single instance of behavior that is of psychological or practical importance, for example, using a condom, voting, etc. (McGuinness, *et al.,* 1977). Recycling in a public venue such as at a college mail room may constitute another such "single" instance of behavior: students vote on recycling each time they visit the mail room. In this case, students may not have realized that "notices" constitute opportunities to recycle.

Researchers should consider the feasibility of capturing repeated observations to increase the reliability of behavioral measures. Strengths of the study included systematic and persistent unobtrusive observation which, although costly and typically difficult to conduct, enabled a glimpse at the potential mismatch between professed attitudes, self-reported behaviors, and actual behaviors. However, even though all attempts were made to ensure that the bogus notice was not worth "holding onto" and research teams were thorough and systematic in recovering all traces, some students may have recycled their materials away from the mail room, thus contributing to the observed low congruence between attitudes and behaviors on most items.

The data of this study suggest that the classification of individuals as "non-recyclers" on the basis of self-reports may be more valid than the classification of "recyclers." The use of self-report data in studies of recycling or conservation merits further discussion and empirical consideration.

References

Arbuthnot, J., & Lingg, S. (1975) A comparison of French and American environmental behaviors, knowledge, and attitudes. *International Journal of Psychology,* 4, 275–281.

Baldassare, M., & Katz, C. (1992) The personal threat of environment problems as predictor of environmental practices. *Environment and Behavior,* 24, 602–616.

Burn, S. M. (1991) Social psychology and the stimulation of recycling behaviors: the block leader approach. *Journal of Applied Psychology,* 21, 611–629.

Eagly, A. H., & Chaiken, S. (1992) *The psychology of attitudes.* New York: Harcourt Brace Jovanovich.

Fishbein, M., & Azjen, I. (1974) Attitudes toward objects as predictors of single and multiple behavioral criteria. *Psychological Review*, 81, 59–74.

Hamad, C. D., Cooper, D., & SEMB, G. (1977) Resource recovery: use of a contingency to increase paper recycling in an elementary school. *Journal of Applied Psychology*, 62, 768–772.

Hamilton, L. C. (1985) Concern about toxic wastes: three demographic predictors. *Sociological Perspectives*, 28, 463–486.

Hopper, J. R., & Nielsen J. M. (1991) Recycling as altruistic behavior: normative and behavioral strategies to expand participation in a community recycling program. *Environment and Behavior*, 23, 195–220.

Humphrey, C. R., Bord, R. J., Hammond, M. M., & Mann, S. H. (1977) Attitudes and conditions for cooperation in a paper recycling program. *Environment and Behavior*, 9, 107–124.

Lansana, F. M. (1992) Distinguishing potential recyclers from nonrecyclers: a basis for developing recycling strategies. *Journal of Environmental Education*, 23, 16–23.

McGuinness, J., Jones, A. P., & Cole, S. G. (1977) Attitudinal correlates of recycling behavior. *Journal of Applied Psychology*, 62, 376–384.

McGuire, R. H. (1984) Recycling. *American Behavioral Scientist*, 28, 93–114,

Orne, M. T. (1962) On the social psychology of the psychological experiment: with particular reference to demand characteristics and their implications. *American Psychologist*, 17, 776–783.

Oskamp, S. (1983) Psychology's role in conserving society. *Population and Environment: Behavioral and Social Issues*, 6, 255–293.

Oskamp, S., Harrington, M. J., Edwards, T. C., Sherwood, D. L., Okuda, S. M., & Swanson, D. C. (1991) Factors influencing household recycling behavior. *Environment and Behavior*, 23, 494–519.

Paulhus, D. L. (1991) Measurement and control of response bias. In J. P Robinson, P. R. Shaver, & L. S. Wrightsman (Eds.), *Measures of personality and social psychological attitudes.* New York: Academic Press. Pp. 17–59.

Rosenberg, M. J. (1965) When dissonance fails: on eliminating evaluation apprehension from attitude measurement. *Journal of Personality and Social Psychology*, 1, 28–42.

Rosenberg, M. J. (1969) The conditions and consequences of evaluation apprehension. In R. Rosenthal & R. L. Rosnow (Eds.), *Artifact in behavioral research.* New York: Academic Press. Pp. 279–349.

Schahn, J., & Holzer, E. (1990) Studies of individual environmental concern: the role of knowledge, gender, and background variables. *Environment and Behavior*, 22, 767–786.

Schuman, H., & Kalton, G. (1985) Survey methods. In G. Lindzey & E. Aronson (Eds.), *Handbook of social psychology.* Vol. 1. (3rd ed.) New York: Random House. Pp. 635–697.

Schwartz, S. H. (1977) Normative influence in altruism. In L. Berkowitz (Ed.), *Advances in experimental social psychology.* Vol. 8. San Diego, CA: Academic Press. Pp. 174–188.

Shama, A., & Wisenblit, J. (1984) Values of voluntary simplicity: lifestyle and motivation. *Psychological Reports*, 55, 231–240.

Steininger M., & Voegtlin, K. (1976) Attitudinal bases of recycling. *Journal of Social Psychology*, 100, 155–156.

Stern, P. C. (1979) *Evaluating social science research.* New York: Oxford Univer. Press.

Vining, J., & Ebreo, A. (1990) What makes a recycler? A comparison of recyclers and nonrecyclers. *Environment and Behavior*, 22, 55–73.

Wang, T. H., & Katsev, R. D. (1990) Group commitment and resource conservation: two field experiments on promoting recycling. *Journal of Applied Social Psychology,* 20, 265–275.

Webster, F. E. (1975) Determining the characteristics of the socially conscious consumer. *Journal of Consumer Research,* 2, 188–196.

Wicker, A. W. (1969) Attitudes vs. actions: the relationship of verbal and overt behavioral responses to attitude objects. *Journal of Social Issues,* 25, 41–78.

Wittmer, T. E, & Geller, E. S. (1976) Facilitating paper recycling: effects of prompts, raffles, and contests. *Journal of Applied Behavior Analysis,* 9, 315–322.

Conclusion

The articles in this section introduced methodological approaches not usually addressed in conventional methods texts, however they are important research options to be considered, especially when the topic of analysis involves deviance or crime. These approaches (potential participation, covert participation, and full participation) all enable researchers to study remote, esoteric, and often dangerous facets of our society. These settings are removed from social scientific examination if the choice of research design is limited to typical traditional options. Moreover, the people within deviant and criminal contexts usually have strong, personal, vested interests in maintaining secrecy and keeping a degree of distance from outsiders.

These methods, then, are important because they enable the examination of otherwise closed and inaccessible settings and groups. Clearly, there are numerous considerations, both methodological and ethical, that accompany the choice of these comparatively extreme methods. Consider carefully the following questions concerning the first five selections. When you are able to answer them, you will have acquired a basis for better understanding the remaining sections.

Questions for Discussion

1. In what ways do covert and full participation research strategies differ from more traditional research designs?

2. Why are these methods considered extreme and controversial?

3. Can you identify the risks, benefits, and costs of employing an extreme method?

4. Do you think that failure to disclose the conduct of research is unethical?

5. What do you think about intentional misrepresentation by the researcher?

6. Do the goals (ends) of research justify the strategies (means) used?

Section 2
Establishing Entrée and Rapport

One of the neccessary keys for researchers to successfully address research questions through extreme methods is gaining access (entrée) to research subjects and, when actually working *with* those being studied, to gain the trust and acceptance of these individuals. Becoming trusted and seen as someone with whom research participants are comfortable spending time, talking, and sharing their lives is called "establishing rapport." In order for a researcher to truly understand the world from the perspectives of those being studied and to see how persons being studied think about their world it is critically important for rapport to be established.

The articles in Section 2 all address ways that researchers can approach their projects, subjects, participants, and activities so as to maximize their likelihood of having rapport with the people they are studying. Although all qualitative researchers who interview or "hang out with" the people they study need to have a rapport with their research participants, rapport is even more important for researchers who study extreme groups or who use extreme methods. When persons are engaged in highly deviant activities, or believe that they are stigmatized by society, or suspect that they may be arrested, harassed, fired, or shunned for their activities or lifestyles, they tend to be suspicious of "researchers." This means that extreme methods researchers face a double-edged problem. First, establishing rapport is even more important than it is for researchers using traditional approaches (or studying mainstream activities and communities), and, second, gaining access to people and gaining their trust and comfort may be more difficult than for traditional researchers.

The four articles in this section all look at ways that researchers who use extreme methods and study "extreme groups" can overcome the obstacles of establishing the relationships that are vital to effective research. The first two articles examine general approaches and offer advice to researchers for identifying, approaching and establishing relationships with participants in extreme contexts. The last two articles discuss specific ways that researchers have put such suggestions into practice.

The first article is a classic discussion by Berk and Adams of ways that researchers can work to develop rapport with deviant groups. Although the discussion in this article applies to all types of deviance researchers, the points it raises are especially relevant for extreme methods researchers. What is stressed in this article is that researchers need to carefully consider whom they are studying, anticipate how these individuals/groups might perceive the researcher, and then plan for ways to overcome the obstacles that might be present in these perceptions. What is key, then, is planning and anticipating.

This same theme is present in the Tewksbury and Gagné article. In this piece, the authors focus on ways in which researchers are perceived by participants in research projects and in the communities in which researchers work. The central issues in this discussion are how researchers can manage their behaviors and appearances, so as to increase the likelihood that they will be positively perceived, and ultimately accepted by those whom they are trying to research. By drawing on their own experiences, with a variety of hidden and stigmatized groups, the arguments in this article suggest that researchers using extreme methods, and/or studying extreme groups, need to devote a significant amount of attention and energy to managing how they are perceived by the communities in which they work.

In the next two articles, the discussion focuses on how the methods of gaining access to and developing rapport with research subjects can be carried out in specific types of settings. The first of these, by Wright, Decker, Redfern and Smith, looks at how a group of researchers studied burglars who were actively engaged in breaking into and stealing from homes. The research reported in this article comes from intensive interviews and fieldtrips that were conducted by the research team with persons who were actively working as burglars. In this research, both the persons being studied and the ways that the research was conducted is an example of extreme methods. Working with active criminals and doing so in ways that include not only explicit discussions of how, where, when, and why their crimes were committed but also traveling through the community to see the locations where crimes were committed involves a great deal of danger for researchers. Also, the creativity that goes into finding and developing trust with such persons is an excellent example of extreme approaches to research.

The final article by Hamm combines the practical-advice approaches of the first two articles with the direct applications approach advocated by Wright et al. In this piece, the author discusses existing research on gangs and outlines how the different approaches that have been taken by researchers have both advantages and disadvantages. What we see in this article is that the way that a researcher approaches her/his topic and the actual method of collecting data have a great influence on what the researchers actually discover. The importance of this article, then, is that it shows us that extreme methods can provide insights and understandings that more traditional approaches cannot.

In their entirety, then, the four articles show us that, although extreme research methods can be important for understanding difficult-to-access groups, communities, and individuals, these approaches to research can also be difficult to carry out. The important step of the research process that is outlined here is the means of gaining access to those who are being studied, and the ways that researchers can (and must) work with such persons to gain their trust and full cooperation. Gaining entrée, and establishing rapport, are critical if an extreme methods researcher wishes to be able to tap into the perspectives and activities of research participants in ways that allow them to see the world through the eyes of those being studied.

Questions to Consider

1. What does a researcher need to do to effectively gain access to closed groups?

2. Why do extreme researchers believe it is important to study deviants and criminals in their own settings?

3. How can a researcher manage his/her own presentation of self so as to increase the chances of being accepted by deviants and criminals?

Establishing Rapport with Deviant Groups

RICHARD A. BERK
The Johns Hopkins University
and JOSEPH M. ADAMS
University of Maryland

Under the best of conditions, participant observation poses problems in which complex human and methodological considerations are inextricably entwined. Among the most problematic of these considerations are the necessary processes by which the investigator establishes and maintains rapport with his subjects. If there exists a large gap in social background between the investigator and his subjects and if the subjects are unusually hostile and suspicious, gaining ongoing rapport often becomes an especially formidable task. This paper draws on the field experiences of the authors as long-term participant-observers of juvenile delinquents and drug addicts, in order to present what we feel to be useful suggestions for handling some of the problems that typically arise in the attempts to establish rapport with distrustful groups that also differ considerably in life style, presumably, from the typical social scientist.

Introduction

Under the best of conditions, participant observation poses problems in which complex human and methodological considerations are inextricably entwined. Among the most problematic of these considerations are the necessary processes by which the investigator establishes and maintains rapport with his subjects. Even when the researcher intends to gather the most non-threatening kinds of information in situations where he has a great amount of experience, he may never get to the point where he can start collecting data. Such failures are not infrequent. And under certain conditions to be discussed shortly, the probability of failure drastically increases. The following description from Gans (1962:341) is a good example of what can go wrong in a somewhat difficult research situation.

> I finally chanced on one [tavern] which served as a hangout for a group of young Italian adults of the type that Whyte called "corner boys." From then on, I visited there only. But as much as I tried to participate in the conversation, I could not do so. The bar, though open to the general public, was actually almost a private club. The same dozen or so men came there every night, and—since some of them were unemployed or not working during daylight hours—during the day as well. Moreover, I suspect that some of them were engaged in shady enterprises. In any case they were extremely loath to talk to strangers, especially one like myself who came unintroduced, alone and then only irregularly about once a week. Also, much as I tried, I could not really talk about the subject they covered or use the same abundance of four-letter profanity. After several unsuccessful attempts, I gave up trying to intrude and sat by, from then on, as an observer.

Whyte (1955:289) provides a similar narrative of his first efforts to gain entry into the "district." Baffled by the many false starts, Whyte decided to take the advice of a colleague who suggested he visit a drinking place.

> I looked around me again and now noticed a threesome: one man and two women. It occurred to me that here was a maldistribution of females which I might be able to rectify. I approached the group and opened with something like this: "Pardon me. Would you mind if I joined you?" There was it moment of silence while the man stared at me. He then offered to throw me downstairs. I assured him that this would not be necessary and demonstrated as much by walking right out of there without any assistance.

The failures by Whyte and Gans to establish the necessary rapport in the situations presented above are open to a number of explanations. However, there are at least two crucial disabilities that apparently plagued both investigators. First, both researchers appeared on the scene with very limited information of what to expect. They had not been well "briefed" by an informant from the neighborhood, and it is unlikely that either had had a great amount of experience with similar situations. Second, in both cases there are good reasons to believe that the investigators were attempting to gain entry into groups that were naturally suspicious of outsiders. Gaining rapport is always problematic; but when the groups involved can be characterized as unusually distrustful, the participant observer is faced with special difficulties.

It does not seem unreasonable to generalize from the experiences of Gans and Whyte as follows. First, the greater the social distance between the participant observer and the subjects, the greater the difficulty in establishing and maintaining rapport. The rationale here is that when the investigator comes from a background considerably different from the people he is attempting to study, he has less information about the kinds of behavior that are acceptable to the group and less practice in acting appropriately. His own personal experiences probably have little to say about how to behave; and even if he knew what was "proper," such behavior would probably not come naturally. Thus, he is much more likely to commit a *faux pas* that could leave him vulnerable to negative evaluation. An investigator who is ridiculed or distrusted because he behaves improperly is less likely to be able to establish ongoing rapport. Second, insofar as the group to be studied is naturally suspicious, the participant observer will have a more difficult time in gaining ongoing rapport. There are a number of reasons why certain groups might be unusually suspicious. Some are listed below.

1. Often participant observers become interested in groups that are involved in illegal activities and self-preservation would dictate that these groups be distrustful of strangers. . . .
2. Suspicion can be based on the expectation that many actions of the group, though not illegal, would be considered improper (or at least "deviant") by the larger society. . . . Thus, certain groups might avoid strangers simply to keep from being ridiculed, lectured, or patronized. . . .
3. Another basis for distrust would be past experience in certain groups with people who were trying to "score" or take advantage of people and situations. . . .
4. Most people experience anxiety when they anticipate having to face situations with which they are unfamiliar. Many groups studied by participant observers have lived in such relatively isolated environments (a ghetto, for example) that they have little knowledge of the world outside their immediate community. People from that outside world will thus trigger a certain amount of anxiety simply because the group in question knows little about that person or his life style.

For many of those groups that society labels as most "deviant," there is a unifying theme underneath these four specific explanations why certain groups might be unusually suspicious. The members of many of the groups most marginal to the larger society have had long experience in environments that take on a number of characteristics of a Hobbesian war of all against all. . . . And this kind of life experience will make the participants extremely suspicious of anyone, let alone outsiders. There is a pervasive cynicism that implies that everyone is out for himself. Everyone has an angle, and the game is zero sum. In short, the members of such groups expect the worst in almost any kind of human interaction, and the burden is on the person who wants to interact honestly to demonstrate the sincerity of his intent.

The essential point is that establishing and maintaining rapport are crucial and somewhat difficult in almost any situation; but when the participant observer is placed among people very different from himself, and when the groups in question are unusually suspicious, the necessary task of gaining ongoing rapport may be an extremely troublesome obstacle. . . .

The rest of this paper outlines a number of suggestions for establishing and maintaining rapport for researchers interested in doing participant-observation. A few of the suggestions will seem obvious and trivial. Nevertheless, it is often the most obvious considerations that are forgotten simply because they seem to be common knowledge. The unfortunate consequences of such oversights have convinced the authors of the utility of the inclusion of "trite" recommendations. Also, the suggestions have a specific slant, because they are based on the experiences of the two authors, who have been doing participant observation with deviant groups in Baltimore's inner city. One has been studying heroin addicts for four years, the other, juvenile delinquents for three and a half years. The groups of addicts and delinquents who are subjects in the authors' work represent people not just extremely different in life styles from that of the authors, but also extremely deviant in terms of ordinary social standards; that is, they embody not only social class differences, but also various kinds of psychological maladjustments, so that they differ considerably even from people in their own immediate neighborhoods and environments. Thus, the suggestions are based on extensive experience with situations that represent about as wide a gap in background as may be possible, and, therefore, an extreme case of a participant observer not having personal experience that will help him in knowing how to behave. Also, both groups being studied are extremely hostile toward outsiders for most of the reasons mentioned earlier.

Given the nature of the groups, it is not at all clear if our suggestions are equally applicable in situations where smaller social gaps exist or where the groups are more trustful. However, the necessity of establishing ongoing rapport is present in all participant observation; and if the specific strategies outlined in this paper are not easily generalized, at least the need for such techniques, regardless of the situation, is underlined.

Technique for Establishing and Maintaining Trust

No one likes to be threatened or exploited. And this sensitivity to being victimized is often extremely acute among groups from some of the more disadvantaged segments of society. If the participant observer intends to gather data from these kinds of groups, he must be aware of the unusual amount of distrust with which he will often be greeted. One way of helping to overcome this is to demonstrate consistent commitment to the goals of the investigation. If it becomes clear to the subjects that the observer is sincerely involved in gathering his data, the observer's trustworthiness increases. Commitment by the observer first acts to decrease the credibility of other, more threatening, explanations of his presence. Second, it tends to demonstrate that the observer is a responsible individual and not motivated by morbid curiosity. The following suggestions, then, can be regarded as ways to help convince the subjects that the researcher is sincere in his intent to gather data and that the researcher is the kind of person one can trust.

1. *Always* be honest with the subjects. Besides the ethical considerations which make such a position necessary, there are few observers who can be consistently clever enough to avoid "blowing a cover." A good participant observer will be with his subjects in many kinds of situations, and often in situations requiring complete concentration on a number of difficult problems. (For example, being frisked by a suspicious policeman.) The observer will thus have a great deal to think about, and this added to the burden of trying to maintain a front will often tax the observer to the point of his making a mistake serious enough to expose him. The complete honesty suggested should include all topics and not just his reasons for being in the neighborhood. As rapport develops, questions about the observer's personal life will be asked. These should be answered with complete candor as long as information of that kind and that degree of intimacy is considered appropriate for persons in that group.

2. Another useful technique for convincing subjects that the investigator is indeed serious and committed is for the investigator to appear in the subject's neighborhood to do his participant-observing when it is obviously inconvenient for the investigator to be there. Working weekends is one example of this. Furthermore, this approach helps to avoid the "social worker aura," since addicts and delinquents are accustomed to seeing social workers in the area on a nine to five basis and never on weekends, holidays or "after hours.". . .

3. When the investigator says he will do something, he *must* follow through. Many of the groups that need to be understood better through participant observation are just those groups who will be especially distrustful. Constant effort by the investigator to live up to promises and statements go a long way toward minimizing this distrust. As trivial as it may sound, the investigator should appear promptly for all appointments even if it is extremely inconvenient. And when it sometimes becomes necessary to cancel appointments, the investigator should try to let the subjects know well in advance. A few unexplained absences or several tardy appearances can ruin months of hard work trying to gain rapport. Further, lack of punctuality or unexplained absences on the part of the participant observer will tend to reinforce similar behavior already present in many deviant individuals. Therefore, if the observer desires that his subjects appear for appointments and on schedule, he must set the proper example.

4. It is extremely important that the participant observer present the reasons for his investigation in as flattering terms as possible. And this is often very difficult to do honestly. One of the reasons why it is often so difficult is that many researchers have gotten into the business of studying certain groups because these groups are defined as "social problems." Further, many of the members of such groups are very aware of their label. For example, teenage gang members who are subjects in the study by one of the authors know that society thinks of them in rather hostile and/or insulting ways (all they have to do is read a newspaper or watch television), and even go so far as to use the perjorative labels which society has provided for them as excuses for their own behavior. "Sure, many apartments get sacked around here, man. What do you expect? This is a slum." Or, "How else do you expect me to act? I was brought up in this neighborhood."

The point is that though many are aware of what society thinks of them and on the surface seem to have gotten used to the idea, the typical bravado so common in discussions of such labels suggests underlying feelings of resentment and self doubt. "I'm a punk and a danger to society." And insofar as the rationale for the presence of the researcher is phrased in terms of social problems or deviant behavior, establishing ongoing rapport will be extremely difficult.

The author working with the delinquent gangs has used two approaches in explaining the goals of his research. In the first approach, he presented his rationale as simple, direct curiosity based on the fact that he was brought up in a community very different from the one he wanted to study. "I'm just trying to find out what it is like to live around here. I don't know anything about this neighborhood, and I thought that maybe you guys could help me to find out." The second approach was based on the white teenagers' perception that the black community was getting all the publicity and thus getting the most positive response from the city government. The author stated that he wanted to get their side of the story. Note that both approaches emphasize not the deviance of the community or its members, but rather the fact that the gang members have certain knowledge and skills that the researcher does not have. Perjorative labels are avoided. In short, many groups are increasingly extremely sensitive to the reasons why they are being studied; and unless the researcher can justify in non-demeaning and non-threatening terms why he wants to do the research, rapport will be difficult to achieve.

Techniques for Establishing and Maintaining Respect and Acceptance

Thus far we have been discussing some suggestions for gaining and maintaining trust when doing participant observation with groups who are likely to be especially distrustful and suspicious. What follows will be a series of suggestions that focus on how to gain acceptance. (However, the suggestions also have relevance for the section above on trust.) Being trusted is a prerequisite for any participant observation work . . . .

For successful participant observation to be accomplished, the investigator must demonstrate traits that gain respect and liking from his subjects. Being trustworthy is not only crucial in permitting the subjects to reveal themselves . . . but also promotes liking and respect for the investigator. Other characteristics mentioned below also help in this establishment of rapport. . . . In general, one could say that "likeable" persons will be likeable in most situations, and those traits that make an investigator likeable among his colleagues will make him likeable among his subjects. Thus, when it comes to listing those traits that are apt to make a person accepted by his subjects, we offer little other than saying that some people relate well with other people, and these people will make better participant observation investigators than those people who do not relate well. Nevertheless, we do have some specific suggestions on ways to maximize the gaining of rapport assuming this basic quality is present.

1. It is usually unwise to speak in the slang style of the subjects unless this is a natural thing for the investigator to do. If the slang style is noticeably forced, the researcher runs the risk of "coming on too strong" and engendering suspicion or, through ineptitude, making a fool of himself. . . .

Examples of researchers trying to be "together" and embarrassing themselves through ineptitude are common. Thus Whyte (1955:304) addressed himself to this issue:

> *At first, I concentrated upon fitting into Cornerville, but a little later I had to face a question of how far I was to immerse myself in the life of the district. I bumped into that problem one evening as I was walking down the street with the Nortons. Trying to enter the spirit of small talk, I cut loose with a string of obscenities and profanity. The walk came to a momentary halt as they all stopped to look at me in surprise. Doc shook his head and said: "Bill, you're not supposed to talk like that. That doesn't sound like you."*

. . . The investigator must present himself as he really is. If he is the kind of person who naturally has a manner that will be totally unacceptable to the group, he should not engage in participant observation with that group. To put on an act will usually result in the investigator making a fool out of himself and will prevent gathering relevant data.

Fortunately, it is usually not necessary for a potential investigator to be "hip" to be accepted as a participant observer. Often the subjects will be flattered that the investigator shows interest, and the fact that he has a different life style will increase the credibility of his expressed desire to gather information about the subject. As long as the investigator can be trusted, and as long as the investigator is liked and respected . . ., rapport can be established. "Hipness" is not the only standard by which the investigator will be evaluated by his subjects; and if he has other traits that are valued, he will be accepted. Some of these traits are, for example, a sense of humor, warmth, knowledge about things of interest to the group, poise in the face of danger, and a confident manner with women. For example, one of the authors (who is married) was approached by a woman and propositioned in the following way: "Do you sport?" (She recognized that he was married.) His reply was, "Yeah, if it is free." She laughed and said, "You don't do much sporting, do ya?"

2. The investigator must not appear shaken by what he sees. Often the physical conditions of the neighborhoods in which the subjects live will be truly shocking, especially to the inexperienced investigator. There will often be stomach-turning smells, rats, and disease. It is often useful to experience things like this with subjects, but the investigator must not lose his composure while doing so. To lose composure will label the investigator as someone not worthy of respect and in some cases will encourage the subjects to make fun of him. Generally, deviant groups highly value the ability with which a person "carries himself." This means that poise and coolness under stress are important characteristics for the investigator to possess.

The suggested poise discussed above applies not only to the physical condi‾tions of the neighborhood but the behavior of the individuals in it. If an investigator cannot remain composed in the face of various kinds of deviant and sometimes dangerous activities, he should not attempt participant observation with particularly deviant groups. . . .

3. Closely related to the attribute of "poise" is being keenly aware that the investigator is not the only one who is observing. The investigator will be constantly watched and tested by the very people he is studying. This is especially true in such groups as delinquents who are likely especially to value poise in the face of danger. Both authors have experienced a number of occasions when they were threatened with physical violence. For the most part, these were bluffs. For example, one of the authors has a frequent problem with youths in their middle teens who are constantly trying to demonstrate to older youths that they are "bad" enough to be accepted. Often they will try to challenge the author in a sort of playful way to a shoving match. Obviously, for the author to pick up the gauntlet would create a dangerous confrontation. On the other hand, to be pushed around would mean loss of face. The best response to the situation on the part of the author has been something as follows. "Ease off, man. Why're you leaning on me? If you really think you're bad, go pluck Beaver." (Beaver is the reigning brawler in the neighborhood.)

No matter whether it is a bluff or not, it is best to remain cool. If for example, someone threatens to "cut" you, you have several choices. One is to run. This is entirely reasonable. However, if he was bluffing, you may not be able to return to the neighborhood. The alternative of trying to disarm him, on the other hand, is a dangerous one; even if you succeed, you will have caused someone to lose face and thus created an enemy for yourself in the neighborhood. Probably the best general strategy is to remain cool and try to talk your way out. The best tack to take here might involve your minimizing the threat (treating it as though you don't really believe he's serious) and making sure that neither of you loses face. Other times, the best strategy is to come on very tough yourself ("You motherfucker, put that away, who do you think you're messin' with?"), assuming you can play this role with some credibility. Obviously, any strategy one tries has a certain probability of failure (and in many cases that probability is high), but we feel that usually your best solution is to stay around and try to talk your way out of it. However, this decision on strategy in the face of a threat must be made in light of all the information you have. For example, if the subject is on amphetamines, the risk of failure goes up. . . .

4. This brings us to the next point. *Anticipate* what kinds of things are likely to happen. This cannot be stressed enough. There are a number of situations like those discussed above where once the confrontation has taken place, getting out can be very sticky. Yet many times these kinds situations can be avoided. The point can be generalized as follows.

Insofar as the investigator is interested in studying potentially dangerous kinds of behavior, he should understand the risks. This is often difficult to do in advance because the investigator is often very uninformed about the life styles of his subjects. Therefore, he should approach the situations cautiously, not placing himself immediately in obviously risky situations. For example, with delinquent gangs and addicts it is best to begin establishing relationships in the early evening. Do not stay too late at night and avoid Friday nights altogether. As situations come up where the investigator may want to gather data, he should try to anticipate what could happen and then decide if it is worth the risks. Studying riots in process may be very interesting; but it is obviously not worth the risk of getting arrested, injured, or killed. This crucial skill of anticipating and weighing risks is important not only in deciding when to go to a certain area, but in deciding when to leave. A quiet, peaceful chat on a corner can quickly escalate into a violent argument. The investigator should try to anticipate such changes and then decide if he wants to take the risks involved in staying around. And if he anticipates well enough in advance, and decides to leave, he can leave under most any pretext, thus avoiding the possible acccusations of being a "sissy." If caught in a dangerous situation, deserting may be the only reasonable response, even at the risk of losing some face, but this can generally be avoided by thinking ahead. (Less face will be lost if one avoids establishing an unsupportably masculine image to begin with.)

5. It is important to try to remain neutral in arguments among group members. Once the subjects gain some liking and respect for you, they will often try to bring you into an argument to back up their side. Even if this backup is intended to be only verbal, it must be avoided. Obviously, if the investigator backs one party and is on the losing side, he has been "put down." And if he backs the winning party, he will be resented by the loser. Fortunately, there are usually a number of tactful ways to avoid taking sides. Two tactics which have proven successful for the authors are appealing to another local party to serve as mediator, or reminding the group members of some valued norm (such as group solidarity) which will tend to break up the argument. Sometimes it is best simply to state that you like both parties and do not want to take sides. . . .

6. Generally, it is not a good idea to lend money to the subjects. This will be a constant problem in participant observation, since the investigator will usually want to gain acceptance as soon as possible, and the subjects are all too happy to "borrow." It has been our experience that except in obvious emergencies (like cab fare to a hospital) it is bad policy to lend money. You are quite likely, especially early in the establishment of a relationship, to be taken. In fact, the subjects are often testing you to see if you can be "suckered." By freely lending money, which the subjects have no intention of paying back, you have defined yourself as an "easy mark." And even if they intend to pay you back, they often cannot. Then the debtor winds up resenting the investigator. As will be discussed later, most deviant groups have a set of general norms governing the exchange of money and other kinds of favors. When the investigator learns these regulating factors (it often takes many months) and can relate with the subjects within these norms of exchange, it may then be permissible to lend *small amounts* of money. But even after the investigator feels accepted in the system of exchange, he must always be cautious, for the testing process never really ceases and "borrowing" money is one quick test to see if a person is a "mark."

Another problem of a similar nature which constantly plagues one of the authors is that his subjects constantly attempt to "con" him into performing taxi services. This service should be performed only in emergencies. For example, the author took an addict and her daughter to the hospital for emergency treatment (for the daughter). It is important to note that this act was almost as useful as a month in the field and points out that consciously *careful* dispensing of favors not only prevents one from being "taken," but can be used by the perceptive investigator to further establish good relationships.

7. Wagering among the members of groups presents another set of problems. Fortunately, these can be handled in ways which parallel the methods suggested for leading money. It is perfectly reasonable (and often an excellent means for maintaining rapport) to participate in betting games as long as the researcher can do so in ways consistent with the norms of the group. The norms that apply to the group members should also apply to the researcher. It should be clear, however, that it takes time for an outsider to be accepted by the group, especially if he is a middle-class social scientist. To try to enter into betting games soon will probably result in the newcomer being "suckered.". . .

Fortunately, it is relatively easy to stay out of wagers; or pick those that might be useful in maintaining rapport, while avoiding those that would be counterproductive. All that the participant observer has to do if he wants to stay of out a wager is not take a strong position in the discussion preceding the wager. It is generally not a good idea for the researchers to take an argumentative stance on anything; and so if a reasonable, flexible style is maintained, the decision whether or not to take a strong position rarely comes up. If the researcher does get into an argument (almost always a mistake) it is extremely difficult to back out without some loss of face. In such cases, however, the loss of face is probably better than an actual bet which in effect formalizes and underlines the disagreement. It is crucial to remember that wagering is competitive, and the participant observer must never become a threat to any of his subjects.

If the researcher wants to be part of a wager, all he has to do is ask to be "in on the action." When this takes place in a friendly atmosphere in which the competitive elements are minimal, such participation can greatly aid the maintaining of rapport.

8. It is best to dress in a manner that is comfortable for you and that reflects the way you normally dress, providing that style does not call too much attention to the investigator. As mentioned earlier about speech, do not try to be something you are not. You will only make a fool of yourself. Certainly it is wise to dress appropriately for the activities planned, but dress as you would always dress for such an activity.

9. When trying to establish rapport, it is often a good idea to try to be accepted first by the leaders of the group (insofar as the group has leaders). This serves two important functions. First, it is an efficient way of getting cooperation. Once you win over leaders, the rest will follow quite easily. Second, by trying to relate to the leader first you are not undermining the present pecking order. You are not threatening the leader. If you make special efforts at gaining the approval of some of the followers and ignore the leader, you will soon have him as a very dangerous enemy.

Techniques Useful While Gathering Data

The discussion so far has suggested a number of ways of establishing and maintaining trust, respect, and acceptance. Below are some suggestions for the actual gathering of data, after trust, respect, and liking have been established. In practice, the investigator must not plunge into the taking of notes or the giving of instruments without careful consideration of many of the issues that have been raised in the discussion above.

1. It is generally a good idea not to become overly intent on gathering data until acceptance by the group is clear. Too many researchers, either overambitious or limited by time, money, and patience, try to gather data before rapport is established. (It may take a year to gain the necessary rapport.) Although sometimes data gathered before rapport is established can be useful, it is rarely as reliable as information gathered after. This is especially true of participant observation with groups that are likely to be especially distrustful and who have a lot of illegitimate activities to hide. . . . Thus, it is better to go very slowly in starting to gather data. You lose only time if you wait too long, but you will lose your subjects if you begin too soon. Also, by waiting you demonstrate commitment and sincerity.

Thus, it is useful for the participant observer to be acutely aware of those signs that signal acceptance in the group he is observing. As discussed earlier, in working with delinquent gangs the observer should only rarely lend money, but when a series of exchanges can take place with the youths offering cigarettes, soft drinks or beer to the investigator, with the investigator sometimes reciprocating, it is usually a sign that the subjects feel comfortable with the investigator. The investigator must be especially cautious of being taken for a "mark," but as long as he is sure that the exchanges he makes with subjects are roughly comparable to those they make among themselves, it is likely that the exchanges reflect acceptance rather than exploitation.

Another indicator of trust is when the investigator is asked to witness or even participate in activities that, if reported to the police, would mean great costs to the subjects involved.

2. Insofar as the investigator is interested in intimate or illegal behavior in groups which feel they have a lot to hide, the investigator should gather data as casually as possible. When the observer part of his role must be exercised, he should do his best not to "go in like gang busters." We know of a number of instances where participant observers have spent a great deal of time gaining the trust of a group and then spoiled it by tactlessly dropping the participant role and (almost literally) slipping on a white coat. It should be clear to the subjects that the investigator will be gathering data. Once this is communicated to the subjects, and the investigator is sure that he has their approval to observe (this approval may change from situation to situation and the investigator must be aware of these changes), he should go about his business of observing in as subtle a manner as possible. This is very simple to state in print, and it seems perfectly obvious; but in fact, this type of mistake is easily committed. Even subjects who appear completely to understand that the investigator will be gathering data, will sometimes be startled when the investigator permits the observer part of his role to become more salient.

3. Earlier we noted the need for the investigator to be completely honest about his role and to answer with complete candor any questions, even personal ones, that come up. We qualified this by saying that the candor should be tempered with what may be a reasonable amount of intimacy for the kind of groups and kind of role in which the investigator is involved. This position can be elaborated in two ways.

First, to be too intimate and warm, especially at first, will often be seen as being soft. This label is not usually attached as a compliment. Thus, honesty and candor in response to questions must be tempered with what the group feels is an appropriate amount of intimacy. If the male role is seen as somewhat aloof, it may be a good idea for the investigator to be a little less intimate than he had originally planned. Also, the degree of intimacy will vary from person to person in the group and from situation to situation. Where the norms of the group may highly value warmth and camraderie at a party, they may value aloofness on a street corner.

Second, revealing intimate facts about himself can be a useful tool for the clever investigator. By releasing intimate information when it is appropriate, he increases the probability that he will be accepted by the group (as long as the intimacies do not reveal the observer as someone who cannot be trusted). He is, in fact, acting to increase the saliency of a *participant* part of his dual role. By remaining aloof from discussions about intimate subjects, he is stressing the *observer* part of his dual role. The investigator can thus manipulate the balance of these two facets through the degree to which he shares intimate information. However, we feel it is usually never in the investigator's best interests to *volunteer* intimate information. He should only respond to questions. (There may be rare exceptions, late in his relationship with group members, but these will be recognized only by the really experienced worker.) This is one convenient way to maintain the "go slow" approach to participant observation stressed in this paper.

Special Problems

1. Thus far we have presented some suggestions for carrying out participant observation with deviant groups. In one sense, the study of any group's behavior viewed exclusively from the perspective of that group could be considered distorted because other perspectives from people associated, however indirectly, with the group would have been ignored. We feel this criticism is unwarranted. As Becker (1963:174) states, "what we are presenting is not a distorted view of reality but the reality which engages the people we have studied, the reality they create by their interpretation of their experience in terms of which they act. If we fail to present this reality, we will not have achieved full sociological understanding of the phenomenon we seek to explain."

2. The intimate involvement of an investigator with deviant (and often illegal) activity has been seriously questioned by researchers such as Yablonsky (1965:56). He has suggested that the investigator has an obligation as a citizen and moral being to report illegal behavior to the proper authorities. It seems to us that this position presents the following problem. How can the investigator expect to gain the trust necessary to gather information about deviant activities if his subjects know (and Yablonsky rightly says they must be told) that such activity may be reported to the police? Obviously then, one cannot study deviant behavior that is also illegal if one feels the need to act as a citizen agent of the authorities. As Polsky (1969:134) says, and we fully agree, "If one is effectively to study adult [or juvenile] criminals in their natural settings he must make the moral decision that in some way he will break the law himself. He need not be a 'participant' observer and commit the criminal acts under study, yet he has to witness such acts or be taken into confidence about them and not blow the whistle. That is, the investigator has to decide that when necessary he will 'obstruct justice' or have 'guilty knowledge' or be an 'accessory' before or after the fact, in the full legal sense of those terms. He will not be enabled to discern some vital aspects of criminal life styles and subcultures unless he (1) makes such a moral decision, (2) makes the criminals believe him, and (3) convinces them of his ability to act in accord with his decision. That third point can sometimes be neglected with juvenile delinquents, for they know that a professional studying them is almost exempt from police pressure to inform, but adult criminals have no such assurance, and hence are concerned to assess not merely the investigator's intentions but his ability to remain a 'stand-up guy' under police questioning."

Conclusions

We began this paper with the premise that the establishment of ongoing rapport was a necessary and often difficult prerequisite for any participant observation research. We then noted that under certain conditions establishing and maintaining rapport was especially difficult. First, insofar as there is great social distance between the investigator and the subjects, the researcher is more likely to make errors in behavior, based on lack of experience, that leave him vulnerable to negative evaluations. Second, groups that are especially distrustful tend to assume that the participant observer has the worst intentions until he proves otherwise. This latter problem is a tremendous obstacle because the pervasive cynicism makes almost any action on the part of the investigator susceptible to a threatening interpretation. Though the two conditions were presented conceptually as somewhat separate problems, our discussion strongly implied that they often interact.

A number of suggestions on the establishing and maintaining of rapport with deviant groups, though based on experiences with juvenile delinquents and addicts, offer the potential for wider applicability. The techniques recommended focus on overcoming the problems of social distance and mistrust. And if there was one theme that ran through all of the recommendations for doing participant observation, it was that participant observation, at least with these extremely deviant groups, takes a great deal of time. The nature of the subjects and the material to be gathered make quick "hit and run" interviews next to worthless. Many months are necessarily spent developing rapport before data are collected, and the natural suspicion of groups such as those studied by the authors makes the maintenance of trust a constant problem. In short, this is not something one could execute during a free summer. As for our specific recommendations, even if they prove sound, they are not substitutes for sensitivity, common sense, and especially experience. All that we hope is that they may provide some preparation for meeting novel situations that often demand an immediate response from the investigator, where the progress of the research depends upon the appropriateness of his reaction.

References

Becker, Howard S. 1963. *Outsiders.* New York: Free Press.

Dean, John P. 1954. "Participant observation and interviewing." Pp. 229–239 in John T. Doby (ed.), *Introduction to Social Research.* Harrisburg, PA: The Stackpole.

Donovan, John C. 1967. *The Politics of Poverty.* New York: Pegasus.

Gans, Herbert J. 1962. *The Urban Villagers.* New York: Free Press.

Gordon, Robert. 1967. "Social level, social disability, and gang interaction." *American Journal of Sociology 73*(July).

Kluckhohn, Florence R. 1940. "The participant observation technique in small communities." *American Journal of Sociology 46* (November): 331–343.

Marris, Peter and Rein, Martin. 1967. *Dilemmas of Social Reform.* New York: Doubleday.

Polsky, Ned. 1969. *Hustlers Beats and Others.* New York: Doubleday.

Schorr, Alvin L. 1968. *Exploration in Social Policy.* New York: Basic Books.

Whyte, William F. 1955. *Street Corner Society.* Chicago, IL: University of Chicago Press.

Yablonsky, Lewis. 1965. "Experiences with the criminal community." Pp. 55–73 in Alvin W. Gouldner and S. M. Miller (eds.), *Applied Sociology.* New York: Free Press.

Assumed and Presumed Identities: Problems of Self-Presentation in Field Research

RICHARD TEWKSBURY
University of Louisville
and PATRICIA GAGNÉ
University of Louisville

Understanding how qualitative researchers utilize and manage identities in the conduct of field research is a critical, yet underdeveloped, field of inquiry. This article explores the ways that qualitative researchers can facilitate their work through management of their presented identities. Central issues of establishing rapport and gaining trust, especially with stigmatized social groups, are examined in light of the authors' experiences. Drawing upon a diverse range of fieldwork experiences, this article addresses confronting erroneous assumptions about researchers' identities, managing multiple identities, the difficulties of competing field and professional identities, and the stresses that may arise from managing the politics of stigmas. Drawn together, these issues are presented as problematic, yet manageable and constructive influences on the conduct of field research.

Qualitative research often seeks to specify and elaborate on the varieties of identity and identity components that characterize social actors. Qualitative investigations are not explorations of concrete, intact frontiers; rather, they are movements through social spaces that are designed and redesigned as we move through them. The research process is fueled by the raw materials of the physical and social settings and the unique set of personalities, perspectives, and aspirations of those investigating and inhabiting the fluid landscape being explored.

Feminist and postmodern thought has well established that variances in researcher identities yield differing outcomes of the research process. However, it is not only the outcome—the data themselves—that are differentially constructed, but also the tone, direction, composition, and social placement of the research process itself (see Clough 1992). Understanding the ways the process and outcomes of the qualitative endeavor are shaped is not so much a science as an art. It is not a simple calculation of how the predetermined parts mix and congeal, but rather an art of finding, examining, and placing in context the perceptions of those involved in the interactions that inspire the attributes of the interactional process.

Rapport is critical between researchers and those researched. The importance of a strong, positive rapport is intensified when the research endeavor involves a sensitive topic or a stigmatized population (see Lee 1993; Renzetti and Lee 1993). Among those of discredited character, body, or tribe (Goffman 1963), there commonly exists a trepidation concerning the approach of outsiders; however, trust may be facilitated when researchers accept stigma by association (but see also Anderson and Calhoun 1992).

The key to successful research with stigmatized groups is their willingness to "embark on a risky course of action" (Lee 1993, p. 123). This decision is based on trust and the rapport that precedes it. If and when the stigmatized feel accepted and respected and perceive some degree of similarity with their explorers, a relationship can proceed, and the qualitative researcher can pursue investigation of inhabitants' identities, identity components, and experiences (Bergen 1993).

The foundation for any relationship between researcher and researched is the set of perceptions and interpretations that both hold of one another. The social world operates on the basis of attributions, interpretations, and individual self-presentation (Goffman 1959; Berger and Luckman 1966; McCall and Simmons 1978). Self-presentation, however, is not something that field researchers can necessarily always guide to a desired outcome. Even for the most experienced and skilled, it may not be possible to select and completely construct how we are perceived. "We frequently discover that we are being linked with images and backgrounds we cannot hope to maintain. . . . The impressions we project—indeed, sometimes market—are only partially under our own management" (Miller et al. 1993, p. v). Thus, although we may try to present ourselves as accessible, trustworthy, and worthy visitors to the communities we study, we can never be certain of how members of such communities perceive us.

The task, then, becomes to identify how entrée can be gained, rapport established, and trust built, and how one's self-presentation can be managed to optimize the degree and likelihood of these crucial elements of research being completed. On some issues, management is relatively simple: The selection of interviewers should focus on personal and visible physical or social traits that complement those of the population under study (Warren and Rasmussen 1977; Reinharz 1992; Bergen 1993; Coxon et al. 1993). However, more important than simply manipulating the status of the field researcher, and perhaps more costly (in terms of physical, psychic, and scholarly energies), qualitative researchers' presentation of self must be attuned to issues of masking and unmasking actual social identities and constructing and presenting virtual social identities (Goffman 1963).

Within the research terrain, identity management and interpretations encompass both focused and unfocused interactional realms (Goffman 1963). *Focused interactions* are the range of structured contexts where actors reciprocally acknowledge one another and strive to sustain a solitary point of attention. *Unfocused interactions* encompass a broader range of time and space circumstances in which actors may or may not acknowledge one another, yet are nonetheless provided with opportunities to assess one another. Unfocused interactions operate on the basis of interpretation of appearances, artifacts, and presented behaviors. In these circumstances, the actor who is not closely attuned to the management of his or her identity presentation can and often does appear in ways that destroy or weaken the establishment of rapport.

It is important to maintain a focus on the fact that identity management is a process at work among those being researched as well as among researchers (Douglas 1972; Daniels 1983; El-Or 1992; J. Miller 1995). Furthermore, the interpretation of the researcher by the subjects works to shape and determine the management strategies used by investigators. Interactions rely not only on appearances, but on the meshing of multiple sets of perceptions and interpretations that are complementary (see Goffman 1963).

In a research setting, therefore, it is the researcher's responsibility to seek to construct the research—including gaining entrée, establishing rapport, earning trust, and gathering data—in a way that will result in the collection of valid and complete data. This construction requires a positive relationship, which is the product of the researched arriving at and maintaining particular perceptions of the researcher. Although specifically about ethnographers, Van Maanen's (1982, p. 112) observations are valuable advice in general: "A good part of fieldwork is simply being attentative to the impressions one's presence and activities cast off." Our discussion focuses on the role of the qualitative, interview-based researcher in structuring and managing the research process through the presentation of self. It has been our experience, paradoxically and despite careful management of self in the field and among our colleagues, that erroneous assumptions have been made about our identities and the motivations behind our work. Drawing upon experiences where our identities have been presumed, we seek in this article to identify the ways stigmatized, marginalized groups' perceptions of qualitative researchers influence the possibility of gaining entrée to the community, the establishment of rapport, the earning of trust; and to identify how these three crucial elements of qualitative research in turn affect the ability to gather and report valid and complete data. Our secondary goal is to discuss the strategies we have found to be successful and unsuccessful in facilitating our research on marginalized or highly stigmatized groups.

Background Studies

During the winter and spring of 1986–1987, Gagné conducted ethnographic research to examine the lives of Appalachian women, with a specific focus on their experiences with domestic violence and patriarchal control. The research consisted of part-time residence with a family in the region, participant observation in the community, and semistructured, in-depth interviews with resident women (see Gagné 1992). In a separate project, from 1992 to 1994, Gagné conducted in-depth interviews with battered women who had been convicted of killing or assaulting abusive mates or stepfathers and who, while incarcerated, had been granted clemency for their crimes. In this project, a snowball sampling method was used, with the initial list of contacts provided by Ohio's former First Lady, Dagmar Celeste. Through contacts made while in the field, Gagné ultimately was introduced to and interviewed 12 of the 26 women who had received clemency (see Gagné 1996).

Since 1991, Tewksbury has worked conducting in-depth interviews with more than 70 individuals living with HIV disease. Throughout this work interviewees have been recruited through social service agencies, advertisements, and personal referrals. Following the completion of interviews, averaging 3 to 5 hr in length, interviewees have commonly reported the experience as highly positive and personally beneficial. For Tewksbury the process has been highly productive and very stressful. Not only have there been the numerous usual stresses of recruiting, scheduling, completing, coding, analyzing, and writing up the research, but there have also been the stresses of attending participants' funerals and listening to deathbed discussions of frustrations and dissatisfactions with family, friends, medical providers, social service agencies, and society in general. Whereas many interviewees reported the research experience to be empowering, the exact opposite has been the case for the researcher (see Tewksbury 1994a, 1995a, 1995b).

Tewksbury's previous work has included participant observation in adult bookstore video peepshows and participant observation with traveling troupes of male strippers. In the first project Tewksbury spent afternoons, evenings, and late nights attending and "potentially participating" in the activities of men slowly circulating through the hallways of peepshows, reviewing the posted advertisements for sexually explicit videos playing in individual booths, and cruising for sexual partners (see Tewksbury 1990, 1993a). In the study of male strippers, Tewksbury spent more than 2 years, first interviewing dancers and later traveling and working with one troupe of male dancers (see Tewksbury 1993b, 1994b).

Since 1994, both authors have conducted research on transgendered people, specifically transsexuals, cross-dressers, and gender radicals. The research has consisted primarily of semistructured in-depth interviews ranging from 2 to 4 hr, with participant observation of support groups during times when we were recruiting volunteers for our work. All but one of the people we have interviewed were born male and have adopted temporary or permanent identities as women. We have solicited respondents through actual and virtual (e-mail) support groups, with the assistance of highly visible members of the community. While recruiting volunteers through actual support groups, it has been necessary for one of us to attend meetings and interact with the group. In these settings, we have presented ourselves as outsiders who are interested in and empathetic with the group. Most fieldwork and interviews have been conducted by Gagné, who had limited exposure to the transgender community prior to this research project. Initially, she found the research to be very stressful, in part because of questions about self-presentation and the way she was perceived by others. After beginning to learn the norms of the subculture, she became somewhat relaxed and was able to adopt a persona as a somewhat knowledgeable, empathetic outsider, eager to learn as much as members of the community were willing to teach her about their experiences and lives.

Insider-Outsider Issues

In the work of the present authors, the need for careful management of presented identities—or what Van Maanen (1982) has called "character display"—has been clearly established. In the study of rural Appalachian women living with domestic violence, Gagné (1992) found it necessary to establish herself as a member of the community, attached to and under the control of men who were known and trusted in the region. Tewksbury's (1990) work in adult bookstore video peepshows necessitated the presentation of an appearance suggesting subcultural knowledge and interactional willingness. Without such presented virtual social identities, access, trust, and interactions would not have transpired and the research could not have been accomplished. Examples abound in the literature to show the necessity of managing how qualitative researchers are perceived by inhabitants of the territory of interest. Brief perusal of the debate regarding the ethics of covert participant observation (Roth 1962; Humphreys 1970; Galliher 1973; Bulmer 1980; J.M. Miller 1995) or closed, highly suspicious organizations (Lofland 1966; Berk and Adams 1970; Robbins et al. 1973; Van Maanen 1982; Rochford 1985; Ayella 1993) make the centrality of this issue all too clear.

In pursuing a qualitative research agenda with stigmatized populations, several strategies involving the management of self-presentation may be used to gain access to valid and reliable data. It is well established that trust and rapport may be diminished and bias introduced when interviewer and interviewee are of significantly different social statuses (Berk and Adams, 1970; Landis et al. 1973; Freeman and Butler 1976; El-Or 1992; Johnson and Moore 1993). However, it would be naive to suggest that status congruence or complementarity alone can enhance trust and rapport, leading to a more productive and valid interview. Rather, as Wise (1987) has argued, it is the complex combination of status-based relationships and researcher skills that interact to produce interviews in which the respondents feel comfortable in the act of self-revelation. Or, as Riessman (1987) has suggested, researchers and interviewees can understand one another when they share "cultural patterns." Shared status (such as gender) is not enough. Nonetheless, when researchers share similar or marginally similar experiences with those being investigated, the research process may be enhanced by communicating similarities where they exist. Where researchers and respondents differ in obvious or subtle ways, investigators may establish rapport by communicating empathy for the group based on similar philosophies or world views. In some cases, such communication may simply be impossible for researchers, for example among extremists who advocate or practice violence (Scully 1990; however, see also Mitchell 1993); they must then work harder to establish trust and rapport in other ways, by communicating a commitment to unbiased research, assurances of confidentiality, and reflexive listening. However a researcher ultimately decides to manage a project, the first obstacle to be overcome in any research endeavor is to gain entrée to the group under investigation.

Gaining Entrée

Efforts to overcome the potential or, in some observers' view, likely obstacles to an effective and efficient research process can take any of several forms. Interestingly, however, very little literature exists addressing the problems that accompany efforts to gain entrée and the consequences of the fact that some persons will grant researchers access to settings and others will not (Lee 1993; however, see Herman 1995). Even when researchers clearly are not members of the communities they study, there can be roles constructed or discovered that facilitate research entrée (see Adler and Adler's 1996 discussion of the parent as researcher). Common assumptions (often implicit) in the literature suggest that entrée can be a very difficult task with stigmatized or criminal populations. This, we believe, is a largely faulty assumption. Our research, like Hagedorn's (1988) work with gangs and Wright et al.'s (1992) research with burglars, suggests that although gaining entrée may be a long, sometimes frustrating process, entrée certainly is achievable.

The lack of attention to how entrée is gained, in the eyes of at least one observer, may be for the best: "Nor are researchers necessarily wise while in the field to look too closely at why access has been granted. In so doing they might raise further and unwelcome questions in the minds of gatekeepers about whether the decision to permit the researcher entry was correct in the first place" (Lee 1993, pp. 119–120). We disagree with this view. In the study of stigmatized populations, one must first ask how entrée may be gained and then consider the potential benefits and consequences of any point of entry that is adopted.

In the realm of criminal justice (especially corrections) research, there is a growing movement to incorporate a team research approach in which a community insider and an outsider cooperatively pursue research (Schmid and Jones 1991, 1993; Jones 1995; Taylor and Tewksbury 1995). A second approach centers on presenting oneself as a potential community member, indicating a generally sympathetic view of the group and individuals that are the focus of the study (Lofland, 1966; Robbins et al. 1973; Rochford 1985). Alternatively, one can gain status and present oneself as a marginal member of the community or group, playing on membership in the community but ignorance of the finer points of community membership and life (Stack 1974; Hafley and Tewksbury 1996). Alternatively, it is possible to present oneself as a knowledgeable insider (Styles 1979; Levi Kamel 1980; Ronai and Ellis 1989) or as a semiknowledgeable, empathetic outsider (Smith and Batiuk 1989; Myers 1992; Leinen 1993; J. Miller 1995). Finally, in some instances, especially when negotiating access with a highly closed community or group, it can be beneficial to have a visible and respected individual who holds a position of authority, high respect, or leadership introduce one to the group (Whyte 1955; Boles and Garbin 1974; Foltz 1979; Van Maanen 1982; Herman and Miall 1990; Hopper and Moore 1990; Calhoun 1992; Jacobs 1992; Leinen 1993) or to provide direct referrals (Wright et al. 1992). When such a person takes an active role in facilitating access, he or she is likely to do so in one of three manners: as a bridge to link into a new social world, as a guide who points out what occurs and how culturally different actions are locally meaningful, or as a patron who helps to secure the trust of community members (Lee 1993).

The presentations of self the present authors have used to gain entrée and establish effective status-based relationships are (a) knowledgeable insider, (b) potential participant, (c) marginal member, (d) empathetic outsider, and (e) knowledgeable outsider working with a knowledgeable insider. In conjunction with these strategies, particularly in our investigations of highly closed groups, we have used a visible and respected community member to help us gain entrée, establish rapport, earn trust, and understand locally meaningful events. In Gagné's research on Appalachian women, entrée to the community was gained through a family friend, a member of the community who was known and respected by most in the region. As a marginal member of the community—one who spent weekends in Appalachia and weekdays at graduate school—she needed to gain the trust of men in the community, who served as gatekeepers to their own and other men's wives, daughters, and girlfriends. To persuade her host to sponsor her in the community, she needed to convince him that she was empathetic to the men's world view, that her research report would be unbiased toward men, and that helping her would be a favor to his housemate, her husband. To gain his trust, she presented herself in a manner very foreign to her actual identity, by behaving according to feminine gender norms within the community. Her actions included washing the dishes, cleaning the house, asking permission to leave the house, and deferring to men's decisions about daily activities. In short, she emulated women in the community through presentation of self. (Also, see Warren 1988 for a discussion of how gender may need to be managed for women to gain access to some research settings.) Over time, she gained his trust, and he began to serve as both a guide, explaining the cultural significance of local events and relationships, and as a patron, securing the trust of men in the community. Once contact with women outside the household was established, she needed to gain their trust so interviews could be scheduled and establish enough rapport so that respondents would talk freely about their experiences. To do so, she presented herself as the wife of a new man in the area and a marginal member of the geographic and cultural community, as well as the community of women who had experienced abusive relationships.

Similarly, in a separate project on battered women who received clemency, Gagné was initially dependent on the sponsorship of the former first lady of Ohio,

Dagmar Celeste. In an initial exploratory interview, Celeste served as a guide who explained the history of the battered women's movement and how it related to the clemency decisions. By providing permission to "drop" her name, Dagmar Celeste served as a bridge into the world of activism and state decision making. To gain entrée with activists in the battered women's movement, Gagné needed to assure them she was sympathetic to their actions and ideologies. The use of the first lady's name was enough to do so in most cases, although a few feminists required further assurance that Gagné was sympathetic to their activism. To gain entrée with authorities, she needed to convince them either that she was unbiased or that she favored the decision and to imply that she would not write about it unfavorably. To gain entrée with the women granted clemency, she needed an introduction from a trusted insider, and to further establish rapport and engender trust, she needed to convince them she was empathetic to their experiences and the decisions they had made.

Tewksbury's identification and access to persons with HIV disease was enhanced by referrals and initial contacts made by a major, well-known social service agency. In this project, dependence on his role as a highly visible HIV educator in the community allowed him to approach interviewees with a request to have them assist in formalizing "what we all know already." This approach, coupled with his highly visible role, may have led to some selection bias on the part of interviewees; however, whatever costs were encountered are believed to have been offset by his wide acceptance in the HIV community. The employment of the role of "expert" often facilitates entrée. When researching politicized, stigmatized communities, the presentation of self as an empathetic expert (and truly being one) may be the only way to gain full entrée.

In our cooperative work with the transgender community, we gained entrée through our acquaintance with a highly visible and respected community leader who served as a patron, securing trust and providing introductions. Within the transgender community, there is a great deal of overlap in support groups' membership. Once we had gained entrée and established rapport and trust in one group, members who also belonged to or served in leadership positions in other groups served as patrons in the new groups. In essence, we relied on a "snowball patron" approach for facilitating our entrée to new groups. Within each group, our sponsors alerted us to potential social or political factions, making it easier for us to manage the recruitment and interview processes, except when our patrons were part or the cause of such rifts. In such cases, some people were more cautious than others during initial phases of interviews, until they became assured that the patron was simply an acquaintance, not a good friend. To reduce perceptions that we were too closely allied with a particular individual or faction, we publicly reduced our contacts with our patrons once the initial introductions were made. At public meetings, we were always careful to speak to our patron, but then to pursue other contacts quickly. When discussions of other individuals arose, we kept silent, and, if asked for an opinion, simply reminded the group that we needed to maintain our professional neutrality. In private interactions with patrons, we sought information about events and individuals but avoided commenting about them.

In our interactions with transgendered individuals, both in the field and during interviews, we have presented ourselves as empathetic outsiders (although we have been occasionally mistaken for actual or potential group members). When we have been mistaken for insiders or potential insiders, we have used humor when possible, conveyed our empathy with the group, and drawn upon our theoretical belief that gender is a social construction.

Despite the obvious benefits of having a high profile insider facilitate access and introductions, there are less obvious pitfalls. In all of these projects, some community members voiced hesitancy to consent to interviews or to disclose experiences and feelings fully because of the initial referral or contact from a visible—and sometimes disliked—community member. As Stack (1974) has argued, gaining entrée through authorities provides a biased view of the community under study. Clearly, some communities (especially stigmatized communities) may be distrustful of authorities and "professionals"; therefore, as many feminist researchers advocate, it may be advantageous to minimize one's professional status in interactions (Reinharz 1992). Although we acknowledge such concerns, we believe that all points of entrée produce potentially different phenomenological realities and, therefore, result in bias. In our own research, the authoritative introduction was facilitative, but in a minority of instances political maneuverings internal to the community under study introduced additional obstacles to be overcome. To engender trust and establish rapport with less trustful group members, we carefully selected and managed our self-presentations. This management resulted in a broader sample than would otherwise have been possible, leading to a broader phenomenological reality being revealed.

Community Perceptions of Researchers

When seeking entrée to work with stigmatized others, we found that it was not un-common for community members to assume, or ask if, we shared the statuses that stigmatized members. Assumed identities are common; they are frequently deduced through one's interests, associates, or appearance. The fact that researchers possess virtual social identities is unavoidable, and needs to be recognized as such. "The mis-taken belief that the researcher's role is unmitigated by those whom he or she studies remains the positivist's unachievable hope" (Mitchell 1993, p. 13). The ways that re-searchers present themselves to communities of study can shape and direct the expec-tations others have of the researchers. Similarly, the information not shared can also influence others' constructed identities for researchers (Mitchell 1993). Assumptions regarding researchers' identities can also be made in the absence of active identity management efforts on the part of researchers. In unfocused interactions, when re-searchers are attentive to instrumental task completion, community members may very well be attentive to the reasons researchers give for pursuing their line of research, whom the researchers know in the community, and details of physical appearance and interactional styles. From such cues, whether given intentionally or unintentionally, assumptions are made and expectations formed. In short, "any aspect of a researcher's identity can impede or enhance the research process (Reinharz 1992, p. 26).

Letters of introduction and telephone calls requesting interviews are frequently the earliest impressions researchers make on potential respondents. Although most of us are careful to write a well-crafted letter or to explain ourselves clearly on the telephone, it is essential to remain aware that the names of associates one drops to engender trust or establish rapport become central cues in the presentation of self. This technique may create the dilemma of requiring the researcher to know about group factions and the affiliations of members while she or he is in the process of learning about the political landscape under investigation. In her research on the clemency decisions, Gagné gained permission to mention the names of those people who identified further potential respondents. She naively assumed that anyone who would grant permission for his or her name to be used would probably be on good terms with those to whom she was referred. Therefore, in all initial contacts, she mentioned the name of the person who had suggested she contact the respondent. In all but two instances, the contact person was one with whom the respondent was friendly or in philosophical agreement. In those two cases, however, authorities who thought the clemencies were politically inexpedient for the governor declined to be interviewed when the name of the person who suggested they be included was mentioned. In much the same way, Tewksbury's work with persons with AIDS, in which most introductions included mention of his professional affiliation with the social service agency, occasionally resulted in refusals to participate and active avoidance. Tewksbury quickly realized that it was necessary to investigate individuals' roles in the community so as to anticipate how best to make introductions and structure initial contacts.

When soliciting interviewees during the course of fieldwork involving face-to-face interaction, the cues one gives are often inadvertent—or "given off" (Goffman 1959)—unless one is extremely conscious in impression management and knowledgeable about the group under study. Almost without exception, when Tewksbury first encountered new members of the HIV community he would be offered food, a glass of water, or a hug. Although initially the participants seemed simply to be a very gracious and warm set of individuals, it soon became apparent that by such acts of kindness they were actually testing his comfort and knowledge of HIV. Somewhat differently, upon entrance to transgender support groups for the first time, we found that members were extremely attentive to the actions and reactions of the researcher(s) present. During interviews, group members explained that they watch all women closely to learn their mannerisms and other aspects of social presentation. However, it was Gagné's perception that during initial, and particularly public, interactions, members were scrutinizing and assessing her to see if she was, in fact, comfortable with the group and sympathetic to their experiences. For example, upon walking into a group meeting for the first time, one member approached and introduced herself, saying, "Hi, I'm 'Jane.' Are you here for the freak show?" At another meeting, held in a restaurant, Gagné arrived early with her patron, a cross-dresser. As members arrived, everyone looked closely at Gagné's face when approaching and attended closely to her clothing, voice, and mannerisms. After being introduced, several asked her hostess, "So, is she one of us?" Later that evening, the group adjourned to a bar, where they were joined by other transgenderists. Gagné went around the bar introducing herself, explaining our research, and asking for volunteers to be interviewed. During the process, she was approached several times by people asking, "So, are you a guy, or what?" In these interactions, it was imperative that Gagné (a genetic female) use humor to defuse awkward situations, admit when she did not know or understand part of the subculture, and convey empathy with the experiences and worldviews of the group. By presenting herself as a somewhat naive but empathetic outsider she was able to establish rapport with the group as one they would educate so that she could, in turn, educate others. Nonetheless, it is not enough for one to be able to fall back on naiveté. Although it is imperative to admit ignorance, rather than feign knowledge, the researcher must carefully manage the impression being made and base the presentation of self on as complete information as is available.

A diversity of interviewees in any project can make the management of self-presentations a tricky and stressful activity. This problem was made abundantly clear in Tewksbury's interviews with persons with AIDS when, one day after completing an interview with a self-defined punk performance artist, Tewksbury was "jokingly" told that he probably could not understand much of what the multiple-pierced man with barbed wire tattooed across his body had said, because Tewksbury was "such a conservative, middle-class type." Immediately following this exchange he drove to a second interview, where the 27-year-old medical student greeted him and commented, "You're a lot more liberal-seeming than I expected." Even managed identities can be interpreted very differently, and no matter how careful researchers may be about self-presentations, we can never be in total control of the impressions we make on others.

Ethical Dilemmas of Presumed Identity

When researchers know, or strongly suspect, that research subjects have attributed identities to them that are in fact different from their actual social identities, the question of whether to self-disclose information that would "correct" these assumptions is raised. This question rests on the more general issue of whether researchers should engage in any form of significant self-disclosure with interviewees. As is common with such issues, the answer is that it depends on the situation.

Daniels (1983) has argued that self-disclosures can be beneficial to the process and has suggested that it establishes a relationship based on exchanges of information. More adamantly, Hosie (1986, p. 206) has argued, "it is conversely unfair to expect a person to bare his/her soul without reciprocity." Such a position suggests that researchers hold a moral obligation to self-disclose. However, in some situations, the exchange of information may, in fact, act to dissuade subjects from open discussion (See Bombyk et al. 1985, cited in Reinharz 1992). In his work with persons with HIV disease, when interviewees assumed that Tewksbury was HIV-positive, they would often discuss at length their positive and negative experiences with a variety of health care providers. In reality, Tewksbury was HIV-negative at the time of the interviews, and many of the doctors, nurses, and therapists being discussed were his associates. When respondents entered interviews knowing of his organizational affiliations, only brief, superficial, and almost always positive comments were offered regarding health care providers. Obviously, disclosure quieted some subjects; it did not establish a relationship based on mutual exchange.

When the researched believe they have something to gain from the researcher, including simple knowledge, the offer of such disclosures after the completion of the formal interview can facilitate the research process. However, while respondents may be willing to trade information or favors, such offers of information may put researchers in the awkward situation of having to tell the truth. For example, at the end of our interviews with transgendered individuals, we always ask whether respondents have any questions they would like to ask us. Typically, we are asked how we became interested in the topic, when the research will be published, and how respondents may obtain a copy of our work. Occasionally we have been challenged with comments indicating that interviewees "know" we must be cross-dressers. Such challenges must be handled carefully, because the misinterpretation must be corrected without appearing to distance ourselves from the stigma. On occasion we have been asked to comment on the "convincingness" of interviewees' self-presentations as women. Particularly with those new to transgenderism, this situation can be very awkward. However, we have learned that constructive criticism is appreciated.

In summary, the dynamics of the situation need to be assessed, as well as the expectations and needs interviewees show for interactions, in determining whether researchers should engage in self-disclosure. In considerations of the special circumstances where self-disclosure would serve to alter assumptions held about researchers' identities, these issues become yet more complex. Not only must subjects' expectations and needs be assessed in general, but they must also be examined in terms of stigma politics. In our interviews with transgenderists, we have been unable to draw upon any status similarities between ourselves and our subjects. During interviews and other interactions when our research motives have been questioned or respondents have become defensive or reticent, we have been able to reestablish empathy by explaining that we believe gender is socially constructed and exists along a continuum. In all of our collaborative and individual research projects, when we have disagreed with the moral or ethical nature of our respondents' actions, we have reminded ourselves that we are not there to argue or judge, only to listen or observe. In short, we temporarily suspended judgement while in the field. It has been our strategy to play up similarities of status and worldview and downplay differences. When respondents' interpretations have clearly been based on untruths, we have corrected the mistake by explaining the degree of similarity, not difference, with the group under investigation.

Stated slightly differently, it is not necessarily the presentation of a virtual social identity in accord with one's actual social identity that is critical to the efficient and productive interview; rather, it is the presentation of commitment that matters.

Although perhaps presenting ethical concerns in some instances, one does not always have to present oneself wholly and exclusively "accurately." A managed, and generally accurate, presentation of self that emphasizes similarities with interviewees and that displays empathy is more likely to be fruitful. Researchers can benefit from presenting themselves as having a strong commitment to the goals of their research (Berk and Adams 1970; Shaffir et al. 1980) and to the interviewee. As put forth by Daniels (1983, p. 199), in the interview situation, "Reciprocity, generosity, sympathy, and responsibility to informants are rewarded." It appears to be more important to present oneself as a caring, concerned person, and as a researcher who is dedicated to the research issue, than to concoct false status similarities to convince the stigmatized individual to trust one.

The Pragmatism of Presumed Identity

From our experiences, it appears that when a researcher seeks and gains entrée to stigmatized populations, members often assume or believe that the researcher is actually or potentially a member of the community. It is not uncommon for questions, both direct and indirect, to be posed to determine if the reading the community members have of the researcher's virtual social identity is accurate (Bergen 1993). This assumption may well be because of the strength of the stigmas felt by community members. Because they themselves are discredited in society, it is not surprising that such individuals may believe that only similarly stigmatized persons would be interested in them and their experiences.

It may well also be that their readings of appearances—physical, reputational, status-based, and managed—lead to community members' presumptions. When entering new and perhaps threatening interactions, interviewees bring with them interaction needs. One way to perceive the interview setting and process with less apprehension is to believe that the setting is "safe." For stigmatized individuals, the safest environments are those in which co-presenting others are similarly situated.

However, not only interviewees bring interactional needs to the interview setting; so do researchers. By way of identity management—manipulation of identity cues—researchers can and actively do construct virtual social identities (see Daniels 1983). Although researcher management of identity presentations may facilitate gaining entrée, some may question whether it is ethical for researchers actively to manipulate such aspects of self. On one hand, there is a degree of deception that is practiced in such instances. However, identities and appearances are always socially constructed, and the process of interpretation and reaction to appearances occurs, anyway. Because the investigator is necessarily going to be interpreted, it behooves the research process for the investigator to consider carefully his or her self-presentation and maximize its potential to garner entrée and facilitate rapport and trust. However, although one may "stretch" a marginal or potential identity, the researcher must carefully avoid fabricated virtual identities that simply do not exist. Interviewees can and do actively respond to what they perceive as researcher identities, based on presentations of self.

As social knowledge, the "truthful" answer to the question of whether a researcher is a community member may not be as simple as expected on first glance. Recognizing that membership in a stigmatized community comes in varying degrees and that statuses are interpretations of "facts," it may well be that, even if researchers do not actively define themselves as members of the communities under study, members may perceive the facts of researchers' biographies as indicating some degree of group membership. In some instances, both identity definitions may, in fact, be accurate. For example, Tewksbury was and is an activist in the HIV community although at the time of his fieldwork not HIV-positive. Similarly, while observing in bookstores, he was, in a sense, cruising: Although not following through on received sexual propositions, he was carefully watching others, just as the sexually interested patrons were doing. Because Gagné had never been seriously beaten, had never killed anyone, and had never been incarcerated, her self-revelations to some in the community that she had in fact been in an abusive relationship became very awkward when it became apparent that respondents had overinterpreted them. The dilemma of this overinterpreted identity was never more evident than when she was introduced to a support group for women who had killed or attempted to kill their abusers as, "This is Dr. Gagné. She's one of us."

What, then, if anything, should be done in response when researchers recognize that they are being perceived as a member of the community to which they are seeking research access or continued access? As we see it, there are four basic responses that may be used. First, researchers can let the incorrect assumption stand and use it to their benefit. Second, the attribution can be corrected, either directly with those with whom the researcher interacts or by informing members of the community's communication network and allowing the information to filter back to previous interviewees at a later date. Third, the assumption can be allowed to stand until the time that (more) interviews are conducted and corrections can be among the initial conversation topics at that time. Or, fourth, researchers can approach the dilemma as a nonissue, letting the assumption stand and not attending to whether corrections are made. Decisions on how to handle this dilemma can be based on whether the perceptions are true, the researchers' comfort with the "gray areas" of their similarities with group members, and the degree to which such misperceptions are overtly expressed. Particularly among highly stigmatized or marginal groups, it is imperative that corrections be made in such a way that respondents do not perceive that researchers are distancing themselves, either from the group or from the stigma. Even after interviews are completed, community members may talk to other potential respondents, conveying their perceptions of researchers' discomfort or efforts to distance themselves from stigma. Maintaining entrée, rapport, and trust within a community, even when interviews are completed, is an essential part of the process of managing a qualitative project. Even as they leave one geographic area for another, researchers must be ever mindful that there may be considerable overlap of membership among groups, and the impressions they make with a single respondent may make it easier or more difficult to gain access to the next group.

The Dilemma of Field Identities and Professional Persona

Qualitative researchers have devoted relatively little attention to the explicit stresses of their work, and especially to their need to manage identities in conducting field-work while simultaneously maintaining (or attaining) professional status (however, see Zigarmi and Zigarmi 1980; Warren 1988; Ronai 1992). In all qualitative research, decisions about the presentation of self are an inherent part of managing the project. In some cases, researchers may find it necessary to present different identities to varying audiences in one field of investigation while simultaneously wondering if those being presented are the "right" or "best" ones. At the same time, researchers must continue to manage their professional identities. Such worries as how public knowledge may affect one's private life and how courtesy stigmas may affect professional attainment or standing are an additional source of strain. For example, in her efforts to gain entrée to women in a small Appalachian community, Gagné had to convince men who could provide introductions in the area that she was no threat to them and that it was safe for their wives to be interviewed. She did so by always introducing herself as the wife of one of the men who lived in the region, and if his name was not recognized, she mentioned that they stayed with "John," a long-time, trusted community member. The key to acceptance was convincing people that, were it not for her college career—which was probably a waste of time—she would be living there with her husband. This method brought up the obvious dilemma of presenting herself as someone she could have become, had she chosen not to pursue an advanced degree. During this period, she was also seeking to attain the status of sociologist by presenting herself at the university as a (potentially) knowledgeable professional. In the field, particularly around men, she had to be careful not to talk or know too much and always to defer to men's judgment. In interview settings, when she was alone with women, she needed to convince them that she was, in fact, knowledgeable about life in Appalachia, women's issues, and wife abuse, and she had to consider how much of her own abusive history to reveal. At the university, when discussing her research, she obscured her personal ties to the community in an effort to downplay her membership in a stigmatized group and to emphasize her professional standing. Being a chameleon in a diverse landscape is one skill an investigator must acquire; learning to discern the proper presentation of self based on knowledge of the landscapes and cues provided by research subjects and professional colleagues is another.

Identity construction and management can push researchers to question and reformulate their "true" identities. Those who conduct research in communities where they already have a significant degree of familiarity and involvement are most likely to encounter identity-based dilemmas. Adler and Adler (1996) have reported that the parent-as-researcher role can be very complex and presents numerous potential ethical questions. Whittier (1991) reported that by listening to the stories of lesbian feminist activists she came to recognize that her research and other activities qualified her as an activist. Similarly, in the midst of interviewing persons with AIDS, Tewksbury was approached by a researcher requesting an interview about his "HIV activism." It was not until this time that he realized he was an activist, and apparently so defined by others. To recognize that one is perceived differently than assumed is usually at least somewhat disturbing. Whereas feminist methodology accepts the breakdown of the "subject/object" dichotomy (Cook and Fonow 1990), positivism demands objectivity and the separation of researcher and respondent. Even among those who are trained in feminist methodologies, researchers frequently recognize, and at some level internalize, the higher status afforded positivist research methods. As an academic striving to be, and be seen as, an objective scientist, indisputable evidence of others' perceptions of one as a politicized actor can be disheartening. Recognition of his or her own activism can lead the neophyte researcher to question his or her legitimacy as a scientist—which is exactly what Tewksbury did.

Managing multiple identities may be a primary source of stress for field researchers. While touring with male strippers, Tewksbury was also a doctoral student and adjunct faculty member at several colleges and universities. Numerous awkward situations arose when students saw their sociology teacher arrive and work with the dancers. Similarly, even well-seasoned fieldworkers may add to the stresses of those managing multiple identities. Such was the case when a feminist qualitative methodologist in Tewksbury's department insisted that he "must be dancing" and reacted angrily when he "wouldn't invite her to one of his shows." Succeeding in both worlds can sometimes be interpreted as being a member of both.

On top of these stresses are the ethical dilemmas of the ethnographic "white lie," implied when one acts differently among varying groups and the stress involved in getting it right each time. Unless one is experienced in the field under investigation, we advise against the management of multiple identities.

Identity and Project Politics

Our experience in the field suggests that when researchers emphasize similarities of status or worldview to gain entrée to a community, members hold a tacit, or frequently overt, assumption that research reports will depict them in a favorable and uncritical fashion. Similarly, Mitchell (1993, p. 14) has suggested that "whatever fieldworkers intend their roles to be they are most often perceived initially as naive sympathizers." Such assumptions have the potential to create a moral dilemma for researchers.

The dilemma of respecting the trust of group members may be resolved in two ways. The first is to use the research report as praxis (see Lather 1986). Based on assumptions and goals of critical and feminist theory, research-based praxis seeks to decenter privileged groups and assumptions, holds a deep respect for the intellectual and political capacities of the dispossessed, and works toward social change and the empowerment of marginal or stigmatized groups (Lather 1986). For example, in her work with Appalachian women, Gagné conceptualized a continuum of methods used by men to control women and discussed women's efforts to assert autonomy in a patriarchal social setting. Similarly, rather than examining the lives of AIDS "victims,"

Tewksbury analyzed the sexual adaptations of persons *living with* HIV and their efforts to resist externally imposed stigmatizing labels by reclaiming the language used to construct their identities.

The second means of balancing the expectations of community members with researchers' needs is based in interpretive theory's goal for social research, which is simply to enhance understanding of a community. Weber's ([1913] 1981) concept of *verstehen* is particularly useful here. Although researchers may personally condemn or approve of the behaviors, lifestyles, and worldviews of communities under investigation, interpretive theory demands that descriptions of the group be written from the perspectives of community members. Analyses that help readers understand the community and the unusual behaviors or worldviews of its members are likely to be accepted by the community under study. For example, respondents in our research on transgenderism have frequently expressed the belief that we will write research reports advocating transgenderism. In the field, we have corrected such misperceptions by explaining that we believe gender is socially constructed and exists along a continuum and that our goal is to understand the transition process from the perspectives of those who have lived it. We have also explained that once we have described the transformation processes, we will also analyze the sociological factors that encourage or impede the transition from one gender category to another (see Gagné and Tewksbury 1996).

Researchers need not agree with or depict in a favorable light all aspects of group beliefs or behaviors, but it is imperative that they make an effort to include the perspectives of those under investigation. By providing a critical examination of the social context of the community under investigation, researchers may advance understandings about the social factors that lead to group members' behaviors. Respondents may or may not agree with researchers' analyses of their situations, but if the perspective of the group is depicted accurately and completely, analyses are likely to be respected, if not held in agreement. In short, whereas researchers may emphasize similarities in status or worldview to gain entrée to a community, they must demonstrate commitment to the research project without violating the trust of the community in reporting their findings.

Conclusion

In any qualitative examination of stigmatized groups, gaining entrée, establishing rapport, and building trust are essential to the success of the research project. Among stigmatized groups, rapport and trust are most likely to be engendered when researchers emphasize their similarities with the group members. However, managing what the researched perceive about the researchers is not always easy, efficient, or even possible. It is not uncommon for those being studied to presume identities of researchers, often erroneously. This problem may very possibly result in ethical dilemmas and practical difficulties for those seeking to pursue a research agenda efficiently.

When trying to manage the research setting and their own identity presentations, researchers may encounter uncertainties regarding how individual members of researched communities will, in fact, construct virtual social identities for them. Although this goal is perhaps not entirely possible, it is critical that all qualitative field researchers carefully attend to the cues—both obvious and subtle—that the researched give off (Goffman 1959). Both direct and indirect interactional markers need to be observed, especially in unfocused interactions, where the attributions and identity definitions held by the researched concerning researchers may best be discerned. Both verbal and nonverbal communications can be instructive for identifying how one is being constructed in the eyes of others.

What we find in the end is an affirmation of the belief that qualitative fieldwork is more of an art than a science (if we apply traditional definitions). To know *how* to do fieldwork, one must experience fieldwork. To understand if, when, where, and with whom approaches are efficient and effective may require experimentation. To know when a piece of fieldwork is "good" requires the observer to know what it is like to be in the field. Knowing about fieldwork means knowing about what it is like to be in the field.

We hope this discussion has accomplished two tasks. First, it has been our intention to make clear that identity management is something that simply must be done, something of which researchers must be aware at all times in pursuing qualitative fieldwork. Identities are constructed, and continually reconstructed, throughout the fieldwork process. Knowing that how they wish to be perceived may not be how they really are perceived can attune researchers to both practical and ethical dilemmas in their work.

Second, we hope that this discussion will reinvigorate a dialogue about the pragmatic issues involved in conducting qualitative fieldwork. By sharing our experiences, and discussing them in the above outlined conceptual framework, we hope we have shed some light on issues of identity management of which other (both novice and experienced) qualitative researchers may be unaware. To discuss the theoretical, philosophical, and political underpinnings of qualitative methods can be fruitful; but so can frank, honest discussions of what works, and what does not work, in the field.

At the core of the fieldwork experience, we believe, is the identity management process. Here is the art, not the science, of qualitative work. Despite the difficulties of constantly attending to identity management, with the researchers required to make rapid "gut-level" judgements on the courses of action to take, successful management of assumed and presumed identities will continue to yield important sociological data that would be impossible to gather under more rigidly imposed positivist rules.

References

Adler, P., and P. Adler. 1996. "Parent-as-Researcher: The Politics of Researching in the Personal Life." *Qualitative Sociology* 19(1):35–58.

Anderson, Leon, and Thomas C. Calhoun. 1992. "Facilitative Aspects of Field Research with Deviant Street Populations." *Sociological Inquiry* 62:490–498.

Ayelia, M. 1993. " 'They Must Be Crazy': Some of the Difficulties in Researching 'Cults'."
Pp.108–124 in *Researching Sensitive Topics,* edited by C. M. Renzetti and R. M. Lee.
Newbury Park, CA: Sage.

Berg, B. 1995. *Qualitative Research Methods for the Social Sciences,* 2nd ed. Boston, MA:
Allyn & Bacon.

Bergen, R. K. 1993. "Interviewing Survivors of Marital Rape: Doing Feminist Research on
Sensitive Topics." Pp. 197–211 in *Researching Sensitive Topics,* edited by C. M. Renzetti
and R. M. Lee. Newbury Park, CA: Sage.

Berger, P. L., and T. L. Luckman. 1966. *The Social Construction of Reality.* New York: Doubleday.

Berk, R. A., and J. A. Adams. 1970. "Establishing Rapport with Deviant Groups." *Social Problems* 18:102–117.

Boles, J., and A. P. Garbin. 1974. "The Strip Club and Stripper: Customer Patterns of Interaction." *Sociology and Social Research* 58:136–144.

Bombyk, M., M. Bricker-Jenkins, and M. Wedenoja. 1985. "Reclaiming our Profession
Through Feminist Research: Some Methodological Issues in the Feminist Practice
Project." Paper presented at the annual meeting of the Council on Social Work Education.

Bulmer, M. 1980. "Comment on the Ethics of Covert Methods." *British Journal of Sociology*
31:59–65.

Calhoun, T. C. 1992. "Male Street Hustling: Introduction Processes and Stigma Containment."
Sociological Spectrum 12:35–52.

Clough, P. 1992. *The End(s) of Ethnography.* Newbury Park, CA: Sage.

Cook, J., and M. M. Fonow. 1990. "Knowledge and Women's Interests: Issues of Epistemol-
ogy and Methodology in Feminist Sociological Research." Pp. 69–93 in *Feminist Research Methods: Exemplary Readings in the Social Sciences,* edited by J. M. Nielsen.
Boulder, CO: Westview Press.

Coxon, T., P. M. Davies, A. J. Hunt, T. J. McManus, C. M. Rees, and P. Weatherburn. 1993.
"Research Note: Strategies in Eliciting Sensitive Sexual Information: The Case of Gay
Men." *The Sociological Review* 41: 537–555.

Daniels, A. K. 1983. "Self-Deception and Self-Discovery in Fieldwork." *Qualitative Sociology*
6:195–214.

Douglas, D. 1972. "Managing Fronts in Observing Deviance." Pp. 93–115 in *Research on Deviance,* edited by J. D. Douglas. New York: Random House.

El-Or, T. 1992. "Do You Really Know How They Make Love? The Limits on Intimacy with
Ethnographic Informants." *Qualitative Sociology* 15:53–72.

Foltz, T. 1979. "Escort Services: An Emerging Middle Class Sex-for-Money Scene." *California Sociologist* 2:105–133.

Freeman, J., and E. W. Butler. 1976. "Some Sources of Interviewer Variance in Surveys." *Public Opinion Quarterly* 40:79–92.

Gagné, P. 1992. "Appalachian Women: Violence and Social Control." *Journal of Contemporary Ethnography* 20:387–415.

Gagné, P. 1996. "Identity, Strategy, and Feminist Politics: Clemency for Battered Women Who
Kill." *Social Problems* 43:77–93.

Gagné, P., and R. Tewksbury. 1996, August. "Hiding in Plain Sight: Conformity Pressures in
the Transgender Community." Paper presented at the annual meetings of the Society for
the Study of Social Problems, New York.

Galliher, J. F. 1973. "The Protection of Human Subjects: A Reexamination of the Professional Code of Ethics." *The American Sociologist* 8:93–100.

Goffman, E. 1959. *The Presentation of Self in Everyday Life.* Garden City, NY: Doubleday Anchor Books.

Goffman, E. 1963. *Stigma: Notes on the Management of Spoiled Identity.* Englewood Cliffs, NJ: Prentice-Hall.

Hafley, S. R., and R. Tewksbury. 1995. "The Rural Kentucky Marijuana Industry: Organization and Community Involvement." *Deviant Behavior* 16:201–221.

Hafley, S. R., and R. Tewksbury. 1996. "Reefer Madness in Bluegrass County: Community Structure and Roles in the Rural Kentucky Marijuana Industry." *Journal of Crime and Justice* 19(1):75–94.

Hagedorn, J. M. 1988. *People and Folks: Gangs, Crime and the Underclass in a Rustbelt City.* Chicago, IL: Lake View Press.

Herman, N. J. 1995. "Accessing the Stigmatized: Gatekeeper Problems, Obstacles, and Impediments to Social Research." Pp. 132–145 in *Deviance: A Symbolic Interactionist Approach,* edited by N. J. Herman. Dix Hills, NY: General Hall.

Herman, N. J., and C. Miall. 1990. "The Positive Consequences of Stigma: Two Case Studies in Mental and Physical Disability." *Qualitative Sociology* 13: 251–269.

Hopper, C., and J. Moore. 1990. "Women in Outlaw Motorcycle Gangs." *Journal of Contemporary Ethnography* 18:363–387.

Hosie, P. 1986. "Some Theoretical and Methodological Issues To Consider When Using Interviews for Naturalistic Research." *Australian Journal of Education* 30:200–211.

Humphreys, L. 1970. *Tearoom Trade: Impersonal Sex in Public Places.* New York: Aldine.

Jacobs, B. 1992. "Undercover Drug Evasion Tactics: Excuses and Neutralization." *Symbolic Interaction* 15:435–453.

Johnson, T. P., and R. W. Moore. 1993. "Gender Interactions Between Interviewer and Survey Respondents: Issues of Pornography, and Community Standards." *Sex Roles* 28:243–261.

Jones, R. 1995. "Prison as a Hidden Social World." *Journal of Contemporary Criminal Justice* 11:106–118.

Landis, J. R., D. Sullivan, and J. Sheley. 1973. "Feminist Attitudes as Related to Sex of the Interviewer." *Pacific Sociological Review* 16:305–314.

Lather, P. 1986. "Research as Praxis." *Harvard Educational Review* 56:257–277.

Lee, R. 1993. *Doing Research on Sensitive Topics.* Newbury Park, CA: Sage.

Leinen, S. 1993. *Gay Cops.* New Brunswick, NJ: Rutgers University Press.

Levi Kamel, G. W. 1980. "Leathersex: Meaningful Aspects of Gay Sadomasochism." *Deviant Behavior* 1:171–191.

Lofland, J. 1966. *Doomsday Cult.* Englewood Cliffs, NJ: Prentice-Hall.

McCall, G. J., and J. L. Simmons. 1978. *Identities and Interactions: An Examination of Human Associations in Everyday Life,* Rev. ed. New York: Free Press.

Miller, J. 1995. "Gender and Power on the Streets: Street Prostitution in the Era of Crack Cocaine." *Journal of Contemporary Ethnography* 23:427–452.

Miller, J. M. 1995. "Covert Participant Observation: Reconsidering the Least Used Method." *Journal of Contemporary Criminal Justice* 11:97–105.

Miller, M. L., P. K. Manning, and J. Van Maanen. 1993. "Editors' Introduction." Pp. v–vi in *Secrecy and Fieldwork* (Qualitative Research Methods Series, Vol. 29), edited by R. G. Mitchell. Newbury Park, CA: Sage.

Mitchell, R. G. (Ed.) 1993. *Secrecy and Fieldwork* (Qualitative Research Methods Series, Vol. 29), Newbury Park, CA: Sage.

Myers, J. 1992. "Nonmainstream Body Modification: Genital Piercing, Branding, Burning, and Cutting." *Journal of Contemporary Ethnography* 21:267–306.

Reinharz, S. 1992. *Feminist Methods in Social Research.* New York: Oxford University Press.

Renzetti, C. M., and R. M. Lee (Eds.). 1993. *Researching Sensitive Topics.* Newbury Park, CA: Sage.

Riessman, C. 1987. "When Gender is Not Enough: Women Interviewing Women." *Gender & Society* 2(l):172–207.

Robbins, T., D. Anthony, and T. Curtis. 1973. "The Limits of Symbolic Realism: Problems of Empathetic Field Observation in a Secretive Context." *Journal for the Scientific Study of Religion* 12:259–272.

Rochford, E. B. 1985. *Hare Krishna in America.* New Brunswick, NJ: Rutgers University Press.

Ronai, C. R. 1992. "The Reflexive Self Through Narrative: A Night in the Life of an Erotic Dancer/Researcher." Pp. 102–124 in *Investigating Subjectivity: Research on Lived Experience,* edited by C. Ellis and M. G. Flaherty. Newbury Park, CA: Sage.

Ronai, C. R., and C. Ellis. 1989. "Turn-Ons for Money: Interactional Strategies of the Table Dancer." *Journal of Contemporary Ethnography* 18:271–298.

Roth, J. A. 1962. "Comments on Secret Observation." *Social Problems* 9:283–284.

Schmid, T. J., and R. S. Jones. 1991. "Suspended Identity: Identity Transformation in a Maximum Security Prison." *Symbolic Interaction* 14:415–432.

Schmid, T. J., and R. S. Jones. 1993. "Ambivalent Actions: Prison Adaptation Strategies of First-Time, Short-Term Inmates." *Journal of Contemporary Ethnography* 21:439–463.

Scully, D. 1990. *Understanding Sexual Violence.* Boston, MA: Unwin Hyman.

Shaffir, W., V. Marshall, and J. Haas. 1980. "Competing Commitments: Unanticipated Problems of Field Research." *Qualitative Sociology* 2(3):56–71.

Smith, N. E., and M. E. Batiuk. 1989. "Sexual Victimization and Inmate Social Interaction." *The Prison Journal* 69(2):29–38.

Stack, C. 1974. *All Our Kin: Strategies for Survival in a Black Community.* New York: Harper and Row.

Styles, J. 1979. "Outsider/Insider: Researching Gay Baths." *Urban Life* 8:135–152.

Taylor, J. M., and R. Tewksbury. 1995. "From the Inside Out and Outside In: Team Research in the Correctional Setting." *Journal of Contemporary Criminal Justice* 11:119–136.

Tewksbury, R. 1990. "Patrons of Porn: Research Notes on the Clientele of Adult Bookstores." *Deviant Behavior* 11:259–271.

Tewksbury, R. 1993a. "Peepshows and 'Perverts': Men and Masculinity in an Adult Bookstore." *The Journal of Men's Studies* 2:53–67.

Tewksbury, R. 1993b. "Male Strippers: Men Objectifying Men." Pp. 168–181 in *Doing "Women's Work": Men in Nontraditional Occupations,* edited by C. Williams. Newbury Park, CA: Sage.

Tewksbury, R. 1994a; " 'Speaking of Someone with AIDS': Identity Constructions of Persons with HIV Disease." *Deviant Behavior* 15:337–355.

Tewksbury, R. 1994b. "A Dramaturgical Analysis of Male Strippers." *The Journal of Men's Studies* 2:325–342.

Tewksbury, R. 1995a. "Sexuality of Men with HIV Disease." *The Journal of Men's Studies* 3:205–228.

Tewksbury, R. 1995b. "Sexual Adaptations among Gay Men with HIV Disease." Pp. 222–245 in *Men's Health & Illness: Gender, Power and the Body,* edited by D. Sabo and D. Gordon. Newbury Park, CA: Sage.

Van Maanen, J. 1982. "Fieldwork on the Beat." In *Varieties of Qualitative Research,* edited by J. Van Maanen, J. M. Dobbs, Jr., and R. R. Faulkner. Beverly Hills, CA: Sage.

Warren, C. 1988. *Gender Issues in Field Research* (Qualitative Research Methods Series Vol. 9). Newbury Park, CA: Sage.

Warren, C., and Rasmussen, P. 1977. "Sex and Gender in Field Research." *Urban Life* 6:349–369.

Weber, M. [1913] 1981. "Some Categories of Interpretive Sociology." *The Sociological Quarterly* 22:151–180.

Whittier, N. 1991. *Identity Construction in Interviewing: Feminist Postmodem Methodological Dilemmas in Research in Lesbian Feminist Communities.* Paper presented at the annual meetings of the North Central Sociological Association, April, Dearborn, MI.

Whyte, W. F. 1955. *Street Corner Society.* Chicago: University of Chicago Press.

Wise, S. 1987. "A Framework for Discussing Ethical Issues in Feminist Research: A Review of the Literature." *Studies in Sexual Politics* 19:47–88.

Wright, R., S. H. Decker, A. K. Redfern, and D. L. Smith. 1992. "A Snowball's Chance in Hell: Doing Fieldwork with Active Residential Burglars." *Journal of Research in Crime and Delinquency* 29:148–161.

Zigarmi, D., and P. Zigarmi. 1980. "The Psychological Stresses of Ethnographic Research." *Education and Urban Society* 12:291–322.

A Snowball's Chance in Hell: Doing Fieldwork with Active Residential Burglars

RICHARD WRIGHT, SCOTT H. DECKER,
ALLISON K. REDFERN, and DIETRICH L. SMITH

Criminologists long have recognized the importance of field studies of active offenders. Nevertheless, the vast majority of them have shied away from researching criminals "in the wild" in the belief that doing so is impractical. This article, based on the authors' fieldwork with one-hundred five currently active residential burglars, challenges that assumption. Specifically, it describes how the authors went about finding these offenders and obtaining their cooperation. Further, it considers the difficulties involved in maintaining an on-going field relationship with those who lead chaotic lives. And lastly, the article outlines the characteristics of the sample, noting important ways in which it differs from one collected through criminal justice channels.

Criminologists long have recognized the importance of field studies of active offenders. More than 2 decades ago, for example, Polsky (1969, p. 116) observed that "we can no longer afford the convenient fiction that in studying criminals in their natural habitat, we would discover nothing really important that could not be discovered from criminals behind bars." Similarly, Sutherland and Cressey (1970) noted that:

> Those who have had intimate contacts with criminals "in the open" know that criminals are not "natural" in police stations, courts, and prisons, and that they must be studied in their everyday life outside of institutions if they are to be understood. By this is meant that the investigator must associate with them as one of them, seeing their lives

Richard Wright et al. in *Journal of Research in Crime and Delinquency*, Vol. 29 No. 2, May 1992 148–161
© 1992 Sage Publications, Inc. Reprinted by permission by Sage Publications, Inc.

and conditions as the criminals themselves see them. In this way, he can make observations which can hardly be made in any other way. Also, his observations are of unapprehended criminals, not the criminals selected by the processes of arrest and imprisonment. (p. 68)

And McCall (1978, p. 27) also cautioned that studies of incarcerated offenders are vulnerable to the charge that they are based on "unsuccessful criminals, on the supposition that successful criminals are not apprehended or at least are able to avoid incarceration." This charge, he asserts, is "the most central bogeyman in the criminologist's demonology" (also see Cromwell, Olson, and Avery 1991; Hagedorn 1990; Watters and Biernacki 1989).

Although generally granting the validity of such critiques, most criminologists have shied away from studying criminals, so to speak, in the wild. Although their reluctance to do so undoubtedly is attributable to a variety of factors (e.g., Wright and Bennett 1990), probably the most important of these is a belief that this type of research is impractical. In particular, how is one to locate active criminals and obtain their cooperation?

The entrenched notion that field-based studies of active offenders are unworkable has been challenged by Chambliss (1975) who asserts that:

The data on organized crime and professional theft as well as other presumably difficult-to-study events are much more available than we usually think. All we really have to do is to get out of our offices and onto the street. The data are there; the problem is that too often [researchers] are not. (p. 39)

Those who have carried out field research with active criminals would no doubt regard this assertion as overly simplistic, but they probably would concur with Chambliss that it is easier to find and gain the confidence of such offenders than commonly is imagined. . . .

We recently completed the fieldwork for a study of residential burglars, exploring, specifically, the factors they take into account when contemplating the commission of an offense. The study is being done on the streets of St. Louis, Missouri, a declining "rust belt" city. As part of this study, we located and interviewed 105 active offenders. We also took 70 of these offenders to the site of a recent burglary and asked them to reconstruct the crime in considerable detail. In the following pages, we will discuss how we found these offenders and obtained their cooperation. Further, we will consider the difficulties involved in maintaining an on-going field relationship with these offenders, many of whom lead chaotic lives. Lastly, we will outline the characteristics of our sample, suggesting ways in which it differs from one collected through criminal justice channels.

Locating the Subjects

In order to locate the active offenders for our study, we employed a "snowball" or "chain referral" sampling strategy. As described in the literature (e.g., Sudman 1976; Watters and Biernacki 1989), such a strategy begins with the recruitment of an initial subject who then is asked to recommend further participants. This process continues until a suitable sample has been "built."

The most difficult aspect of using a snowball sampling technique is locating an initial contact or two. Various ways of doing so have been suggested. . . . In attempting to find active offenders for our study, we avoided seeking referrals from criminal justice officials for both practical and methodological reasons. From a practical standpoint, we elected not to use contacts provided by police or probation officers, fearing that this would arouse the suspicions of offenders that the research was the cover for a "sting" operation. One of the offenders we interviewed, for example, explained that he had not agreed to participate earlier because he was worried about being set up for an arrest: "I thought about it at first because I've seen on T.V. telling how [the police] have sent letters out to people telling 'em they've won new sneakers and then arrested 'em." We also did not use referrals from law enforcement or corrections personnel to locate our subjects owing to a methodological concern that a sample obtained in this way may be highly unrepresentative of the total population of active offenders. It is likely, for instance, that such a sample would include a disproportionate number of unsuccessful criminals, that is, those who have been caught in the past (e.g., Hagedorn 1990). Further, this sample might exclude a number of successful offenders who avoid associating with colleagues known to the police. Rengert and Wasilchick (1989, p. 6) used a probationer to contact active burglars, observing that the offenders so located "were often very much like the individual who led us to them."

A commonly suggested means of making initial contact with active offenders other than through criminal justice sources involves frequenting locales favored by criminals (see Chambliss 1975; Polsky 1969; West 1980). This strategy, however, requires an extraordinary investment of time as the researcher establishes a street reputation as an "all right square" (Irwin 1972, p. 123) who can be trusted. Fortunately, we were able to short-cut that process by hiring an ex-offender (who, despite committing hundreds of serious crimes, had few arrests and no felony convictions) with high status among several groups of Black street criminals in St. Louis. This person retired from crime after being shot and paralyzed in a gangland-style execution attempt. He then attended a university and earned a bachelor's degree, but continued to live in his old neighborhood, remaining friendly, albeit superficially, with local criminals. We initially met him when he attended a colloquium in our department and disputed the speaker's characterization of street criminals.

Working through an ex-offender with continuing ties to the underworld as a means of locating active criminals has been used successfully by other criminologists (see e.g., Taylor 1985). This approach offers the advantage that such a person already has contacts and trust in the criminal subculture and can vouch for the legitimacy of the research. In order to exploit this advantage fully, however, the ex-offender selected must be someone with a solid street reputation for integrity and must have a strong commitment to accomplishing the goals of the study.

The ex-offender hired to locate subjects for our project began by approaching former criminal associates. Some of these contacts were still "hustling," that is, actively involved in various types of crimes, whereas others either had retired or remained involved only peripherally through, for example, occasional buying and selling of stolen goods. Shortly thereafter, the ex-offender contacted several street-wise law-abiding friends, including a youth worker. He explained the research to the contacts, stressing that it was confidential and that the police were not involved. He also informed them that those who took part would be paid a small sum (typically $25.00). He then asked the contacts to put him in touch with active residential burglars.

• • •

Throughout the process of locating subjects, we encountered numerous difficulties and challenges. Contacts that initially appeared to be promising, for example, sometimes proved to be unproductive and had to be dropped. And, of course, even productive contact chains had a tendency to "dry up" eventually. One of the most challenging tasks we confronted involved what Biernacki and Waldorf (1981, p. 150) have termed the "verification of eligibility," that is, determining whether potential subjects actually met the criteria for inclusion in our research. In order to take part, offenders had to be both "residential burglars" and "currently active." In practice, this meant that they had to have committed a residential burglary within the past 2 weeks. This seems straightforward, but it often was difficult to apply the criteria in the field because offenders were evasive about their activities. In such cases, we frequently had to rely on other members of the sample to verify the eligibility of potential subjects.

We did not pay the contacts for helping us to find subjects and, initially, motivating them to do so proved difficult. Small favors, things like giving them a ride or buying them a pack of cigarettes, produced some cooperation, but yielded only a few introductions. Moreover, the active burglars that we did manage to find often were lackadaisical about referring associates because no financial incentive was offered. Eventually, one of the informants hit on the idea of "pimping" colleagues, that is, arranging an introduction on their behalf in exchange for a cut of the participation fee (also see Cromwell et al. 1991). This idea was adopted rapidly by other informants and the number of referrals rose accordingly. In effect, these informants became "locators" (Biernacki and Waldorf 1981), helping us to expand referral chains as well as vouching for the legitimacy of the research, and validating potential participants as active residential burglars.

The practice of pimping is consistent with the low level, underworld economy of street culture, where people are always looking for a way to get in on someone else's deal. One of our contacts put it this way: "If there's money to make out of something, I gotta figure out a way to get me some of it." Over the course of the research, numerous disputes arose between offenders and informants over the payment of referral fees. We resisted becoming involved in these disputes, reckoning that such involvement could only result in the alienation of one or both parties (e.g., Miller 1952). Instead, we made it clear that our funds were intended as interview payments and thus would be given only to interviewees.

Field Relations

The success of our research, of course, hinged on an ability to convince potential subjects to participate. Given that many of the active burglars, especially those located early in the project, were deeply suspicious of our motives, it is reasonable to ask why the offenders were willing to take part in the research. Certainly the fact that we paid them a small sum for their time was an enticement for many, but this is not an adequate explanation. After all, criminal opportunities abound and even the inept "nickel and dime" offenders in the sample could have earned more had they spent the time engaged in illegal activity. Moreover, some of the subjects clearly were not short of cash when they agreed to participate; at the close of one interview, an offender pulled out his wallet to show us that it was stuffed with thousand dollar bills, saying:

> I just wanted to prove that I didn't do this for the money. I don't need the money. I did it to help out [the ex-offender employed on our project]. We know some of the same people and he said you were cool.

Without doubt, many in our sample agreed to participate only because the ex-offender assured them that we were trustworthy. But other factors were at work as well. Letkemann (1973, p. 44), among others, has observed that the secrecy inherent in criminal work means that offenders have few opportunities to discuss their activities with anyone besides associates—which many of them find frustrating, As one of his informants put it: "What's the point of scoring if nobody knows about it." Under the right conditions, therefore, some offenders may enjoy talking about their work with researchers.

We adopted several additional strategies to maximize the cooperation of the offenders. First, following the recommendations of experienced field researchers (e.g., Irwin 1972; McCall 1978; Walker and Lidz 1977; Wright and Bennett 1990), we made an effort to "fit in" by learning the distinctive terminology and phrasing used by the offenders. Here again, the assistance of the ex-offender proved invaluable. Prior to entering the field, he suggested ways in which questions might be asked so that the subjects would better understand them, and provided us with a working knowledge of popular street terms (e.g., "boy" for heroin, "girl" for cocaine) and pronunciations (e.g., "hair ron" for heroin). What is more, he sat in on the early interviews and critiqued them afterwards, noting areas of difficulty or contention and offering possible solutions.

A second strategy to gain the cooperation of the offenders required us to give as well as take. We expected the subjects to answer our questions frankly and, therefore, often had to reciprocate. Almost all of them had questions about how the information would be used, who would have access to it, and so on. We answered these questions honestly, lest the offenders conclude that we were being evasive. Further, we honored requests from a number of subjects for various forms of assistance. Provided that the help requested was legal and fell within the general set "of norms governing the exchange of money and other kinds of favors" (Berk and Adams 1970, p. 112) on the street, we offered it. For example, we took subjects to job interviews or work, helped some to enroll in school, and gave others advice on legal matters. We even assisted a juvenile offender who was injured while running away from the police, to arrange for emergency surgery when his parents, fearing that they would be charged for the operation, refused to give their consent.

One other way we sought to obtain and keep the offenders' confidence involved demonstrating our trustworthiness by "remaining close-mouthed in regard to potentially harmful information" (Irwin 1972, p. 125). A number of the offenders tested us by asking what a criminal associate said about a particular matter. We declined to discuss such issues, explaining that the promise of confidentiality extended to all those participating in our research.

Much has been written about the necessity for researchers to be able to withstand official coercion (see Irwin 1972; McCall 1978; Polsky 1969) and we recognized from the start the threat that intrusions from criminal justice officials could pose to our research. The threat of being confronted by police patrols seemed especially great given that we planned to visit the sites of recent successful burglaries with offenders. Therefore, prior to beginning our fieldwork, we negotiated an agreement with police authorities not to interfere in the conduct of the research, and we were not subjected to official coercion.

Although the strategies described above helped to mitigate the dangers inherent in working with active criminals (see e.g., Dunlap et al. 1990), we encountered many potentially dangerous situations over the course of the research. For example, offenders turned up for interviews carrying firearms including, on one occasion, a machine gun; we were challenged on the street by subjects who feared that they were being set up for arrest; we were caught in the middle of a fight over the payment of a $1 debt. Probably the most dangerous situation, however, arose while driving with an offender to the site of his most recent burglary. As we passed a pedestrian, the offender became agitated and demanded that we stop the car: "You want to see me kill someone? Stop the car! I'm gonna kill that motherfucker. Stop the fuckin' car!" We refused to stop and actually sped up to prevent him jumping out of the vehicle; this clearly displeased him, although he eventually calmed down. The development of such situations was largely unpredictable and thus avoiding them was difficult. Often we deferred to the ex-offender's judgment about the safety of a given set of circumstances. The most notable precaution that we took involved money; we made sure that the offenders knew that we carried little more than was necessary to pay them.

Characteristics of the Sample

Unless a sample of active offenders differs significantly from one obtained through criminal justice channels, the difficulties and risks associated with the street-based recruitment of research subjects could not easily be justified. Accordingly, it seems important that we establish whether such a difference exists. In doing so, we will begin by outlining the demographic characteristics of our sample. In terms of race, it nearly parallels the distribution of burglary arrests for the City of St. Louis in 1988, the most recent year for which data are available. The St. Louis Metropolitan Police Department's Annual Report (1989) reveals that 64% of burglary arrestees in that year were Black, and 36% were White. Our sample was 69% Black and 31% White. There is divergence for the gender variable, however; only 7% of all arrestees in the city were female, while 17% of our sample fell into this category. This is not surprising. The characteristics of a sample of active criminals, after all, would not be expected to mirror those of one obtained in a criminal justice setting.

Given that our research involved only currently active offenders, it is interesting to note that 21 of the subjects were on probation, parole, or serving a suspended sentence, and that a substantial number of juveniles—27 or 26% of the total—were located for the study. The inclusion of such offenders strengthens the research considerably because approximately one third of arrested burglars are under 18 years of age (Sessions 1989). Juveniles, therefore, need to be taken into account in any comprehensive study of burglars. These offenders, however, seldom are included in studies of burglars located through criminal justice channels because access to them is legally restricted and they often are processed differently than adult criminals and detained in separate facilities.

Prior contact with the criminal justice system is a crucial variable for this research. . . .

More than one-quarter of the offenders (28%) claimed never to have been arrested. (We excluded arrests for traffic offenses, "failure to appear" and similar minor transgressions, because such offenses do not adequately distinguish serious criminals from others.) Obviously, these offenders would have been excluded had we based our study on a jail or prison population. Perhaps a more relevant measure in the context of our study, however, is the experience of the offenders with the criminal justice system for the offense of burglary, because most previous studies of burglars not only have been based on incarcerated offenders, but also have used the charge of burglary as a screen to select subjects (e.g., Bennett and Wright 1984; Rengert and Wasilchick 1985). Of the 105 individuals in our sample, 44 (42%) had no arrests for burglary, and another 35 (33%) had one or more arrests, but no convictions for the offense. Thus 75% of our sample would not be included in a study of incarcerated burglars.

• • •

Conclusion

By its nature, research involving active criminals is always demanding, often difficult and occasionally dangerous. However, it is possible . . . [that] some of the offenders included in such research may differ substantially from those found through criminal justice channels. It is interesting, for example, that those in our sample who had never been arrested for anything, on average, offended *more* frequently and had committed *more* lifetime burglaries than their arrested counterparts. These "successful" offenders, obviously, would not have shown up in a study of arrestees, prisoners, or probationers—a fact that calls into question the extent to which a sample obtained through official sources is representative of the total population of criminals.

Beyond this, researching active offenders is important because it provides an opportunity to observe and talk with them outside the institutional context. As Cromwell et al. (1991) have noted, it is difficult to assess the validity of accounts offered by institutionalized criminals. Simply put, a full understanding of criminal behavior requires that criminologists incorporate field studies of active offenders into their research agendas. Without such studies, both the representativeness and the validity of research based on offenders located through criminal justice channels will remain problematic.

References

Bennett, Trevor and Richard Wright. 1984. *Burglars on Burglary: Prevention and the Offender.* Aldershot, England: Gower.

Berk, Richard and Joseph Adams. 1970. "Establishing Rapport with Deviant Groups." *Social Problems* 18:102–17.

Biernacki, Patrick and Dan Waldorf. 1981. "Snowball Sampling: Problems and Techniques of Chain Referral Sampling," *Sociological Method & Research* 10:141–63.

Blumstein, Alfred and Jacqueline Cohen. 1979. "Estimation of Individual Crime Rates from Arrest Records." *Journal of Criminal Law and Criminology* 70:561–85.

Chambliss, William. 1975. "On the Paucity of Research on Organized Crime: A Reply to Galliher and Cain." *American Sociologist* 10:36–39.

Cromwell, Paul, James Olson, and D'Aunn Avary. 1991. *Breaking and Entering: An Ethnographic Analysis of Burglary.* Newbury Park, CA: Sage.

Dunlap, Eloise, Bruce Johnson, Harry Sanabria, Elbert Holliday, Vicki Lipsey, Maurice Barnett, William Hopkins, Ira Sobel, Doris Randolph, and Ko-Lin Chin. 1990. "Studying Crack Users and Their Criminal Careers: The Scientific and Artistic Aspects of Locating Hard-to-Reach Subjects and Interviewing Them about Sensitive Topics" *Contemporary Drug Problems* 17:121–44.

Greenwood, Peter. 1982. *Selective Incapacitation.* Santa Monica, CA: RAND.

Hagedorn, John. 1990. "Back in the Field Again: Gang Research in the Nineties." Pp. 240–59 in *Gangs in America,* edited by C. Ronald Huff. Newbury Park, CA: Sage.

Irwin, John. 1972. "Participant Observation of Criminals." Pp. 117–37 in *Research on Deviance,* edited by Jack Douglas. New York: Random House.

Letkemann, Peter. 1973. *Crime as Work.* Englewood Cliffs, NJ: Prentice-Hall.

McCall, George. 1978. *Observing the Law.* New York: Free Press.

Miller, S. M. 1952. "The Participant Observer and Over-Rapport." *American Sociological Review* 17:97–99.

Petersilia, Joan, Peter Greenwood, and Marvin Lavin. 1977. *Criminal Careers of Habitual Felons.* Santa Monica, CA: RAND.

Polsky, Ned. 1969. *Hustlers, Beats, and Others*. Garden City, NJ: Anchor.

Rengert, George and John Wasilchick. 1985. *Suburban Burglary: A Time and a Place for Everything*. Springfield, IL: Thomas.

————. 1989. *Space, Time and Crime: Ethnographic Insights into Residential Burglary*. Final report submitted to the National Institute of Justice, Office of Justice Programs, U.S. Department of Justice.

Sessions, William. 1989. *Crime in the United States—1988*. Washington, DC: U.S. Government Printing Office.

St. Louis Metropolitan Police Department. 1989. *Annual Report—1988/89*. St. Louis, MO: St. Louis Metropolitan Police Department.

Sudman, Seymour. 1976. *Applied Sampling*. New York: Academic Press.

Sutherland, Edwin and Donald Cressey. 1970. *Criminology—8th Edition*. Philadelphia, PA: Lippincott.

Taylor, Laurie. 1985. *In the Underworld*. London: Unwin.

Walker, Andrew and Charles Lidz. 1977. "Methodological Notes on the Employment of Indigenous Observers." Pp. 103–23 in *Street Ethnography*, edited by Robert Weppner. Beverly Hills, CA: Sage.

Watters, John and Patrick Biernacki. 1989. "Targeted Sampling: Options for the Study of Hidden Populations." *Social Problems* 36:416–30.

West, W. Gordon. 1980. "Access to Adolescent Deviants and Deviance." Pp. 31–44 in *Fieldwork Experience. Qualitative Approaches to Social Research*, edited by William Shaffir, Robert Stebbins, and Allan Turowitz. New York: St. Martin's.

Wright, Richard and Trevor Bennett. 1990. "Exploring the Offender's Perspective: Observing and Interviewing Criminals." Pp. 138–51 in *Measurement Issues in Criminology*, edited by Kimberly Kempf. New York: Springer-Verlag.

Doing Gang Research in the 1990s: Pedagogical Implications of the Literature

MARK S. HAMM

Indiana State University

Social images of gangs abound in our world today. From the "white heat" of movies and television to the emotional volatility of militant rap music, urban gangs are portrayed as more violent now than ever before in the American experience. Ambitious politicians from all points on the political spectrum have decried the upsurge in gang violence; and in the wake of the Los Angeles riots of 1992; some politicians have predicted that gangs have the potential to become the major social problem facing urban America in the next century.

Not surprisingly, university courses exploring gang violence seem to attract more students of criminology and criminal justice than almost any other subject. This chapter explores—in desperate brevity—the pedagogical implications of American gang literature. The product is intended to serve as a primer that may be used by educators to introduce their students to the complexities of doing gang research in the 1990s.

Gaining Access

The most important step in conducting gang research is the development of a pool of subjects. This demands that researchers overcome two major obstacles: paranoia and violence.

By its very nature, social science research creates conditions that can put gang members at risk for both arrest by police, and retaliation from other members of the gang. Thus, researchers—whose goal is to expose the individual and organizational features of gangs—are potentially seen as threats to the gang in general, and to its members in specific. Because the researcher is an intruder into the gang, members are likely to be paranoid about participating in any study. In turn, this paranoia can lead to

Hamm, Mark S. (1996). "Doing Gang Research in the 1990s: Pedagogical Implications of the Literature." In J. M. Miller and Jeffery P. Rush (eds.). *Gangs: A Criminal Justice Approach.* Cincinnati, Ohio: Anderson Publishing Co.

violence against the researcher. Over the years, criminologists have relied on four primary strategies for entering the inner circle of American street gangs. Each has attempted, with varying degrees of success, to avoid the problems of paranoia and violence. I begin with the most traditional method.

Participant Observation

Historically, scholars have entered gangs through the method of participant observation.... This technique has been preferred because of its ability to bring the researcher face to face with their subjects. Through this face-to-face interaction, researchers are afforded sensitizing and inductive methods for understanding the individual and organizational features of gangs.

. . . [P]articipant observation is exemplified in the research of Martin Sanchez Jankowski (1991)—a work heralded by veteran gang researcher Ruth Horowitz in the liner notes to Jankowski's *Islands in the Street,* as "important and elegant . . . this will be the book on gangs for the next ten years, if not longer."

Jankowski offers a rare comparative study of 37 gangs from Los Angeles (n = 13 gangs), New York City (n = 20), and Boston (n = 4), conducted over a 10-year period of intensive participant observation (1978–1988). The author successfully entered Irish gangs and African-American gangs; Puerto Rican gangs and gangs of Chicanos, Dominicans, Jamaicans, and Central Americans. Jankowski conducted interviews with more than 1,000 gang members, and observed more than 5,000 acts of violence committed by them. He also provides extensive eyewitness accounts of gang beatings, stabbings, and drive-by shootings. To gain access to these gangs, Jankowski was required—first and foremost—to undergo a test of courage. He writes that:

> *[In] all of the gangs . . . [t]his test had to do with determining how tough I was. While there were variations in exactly how the test was administered, it involved a number of members starting a fight with me. This was done to see how good a fighter I was and to see if I had "heart" (courage) . . . . The fact that I had training in karate did not eliminate the anxiety that such situations create, but it did help to reduce it. Although the tests often left bruises, I was never seriously hurt. Quite remarkably, in the more than ten years during which I conducted this research, I was only seriously injured twice (1991:12).*

In sum, Jankowski entered the inner circle of 37 violent gangs and received a physical beating each time he did. Once he endured this brutal rite of passage, Jankowski went on to commit gang violence himself—which resulted in two serious injuries.

> *I participated in nearly all the things they did. I ate where they ate, I slept where they slept, I stayed with their families, I traveled where they went, and in certain situations where I could not remain neutral, I fought with them (Jankowski, 1991:13).*

This study carries two overarching pedagogical implications for those of us who teach the criminology of gang research in the 1990s. First, in addition to teaching theory and research methods, we must begin to educate and train our students in the martial arts. The skill of self defense, it seems, is now a prerequisite for entering violent youth collectives. Second, because researchers themselves are often required to commit gang violence, students must be educated in the morality of vengeance—which makes interpersonal aggression justifiable in those situations where researchers cannot remain neutral. . . .

The Purists

Jankowski's experiences are highly unique to the tradition of participant observation research. In fact, never before in the entire corpus of American gang literature has a researcher documented so many personal experiences with violence. This can be explained by the researcher's introduction to the various gangs. In each of the 37 gangs studied, Jankowski relied on the assistance of community leaders, social workers, and/or clergy to make his initial contact with gang members—any gang member.

First impressions, according to a vast body of social psychology, are profoundly important. The first impressions made by Jankowski—specially among the hundreds of gang underlings he met—marked him as being associated with a system of gang control (see Klein, 1971 for a concise discussion of this problem). This wavering from the purity of participant observation research led to Jankowski's tests of courage—which resulted in his 37 beatings and two serious injuries. Jankowski's rationale for using social control agents was that they were instrumental in gaining access. "[H]aving decided what gangs to study," he argues, "one does not simply show up on their streetcorners and say, 'I am a professor and I want to study you.' This would be naive and quite dangerous" (1991:9)

Yet, this was precisely the method used for gaining access to gangs in such participant observation classics as William J. Chambliss' (1973) *The Saints and the Roughnecks,* R. Lincoln Keiser's (1969) *The Vice Lords,* Walter Miller's (1958) *Lower Class Culture as a Generating Milieu of Gang Delinquency,* Irving Spergel's (1964) *Racketville, Slumtown, Haulburg,* and William Foote Whyte's (1943) *Street Corner Society.* . . . It was also the method used in more recent criminological studies of collective violence such as Adler's (1985) analysis of cocaine smugglers in Northern California, Campbell's (1987) study of Puerto Rican gangs in New York City's South Bronx, Hamm's (1993) analysis of violence among American neo-Nazi skinhead youth, Horowitz's (1983) exposé on a Chicano gang in Chicago, Mieczkowski's (1986, 1988) studies of African-American heroin and crack cocaine dealers (drug crews) in Detroit, and Vigil's (1988) research on the barrio gangs of East Los Angeles.

In these studies, researchers have entered the field as criminology natives unaffiliated with agents of social control. They presented themselves alone; as impartial social scientists with a purely academic interest in the lives and behaviors of individual gang members. Often, these researchers have focused on gang leaders, assuming that leaders will display the highest rates and severity of violence. Based on face-to-face interaction and interpersonal trust, researchers have convinced gang leaders that they had nothing to fear. In this way, the purists removed the dual threats of paranoia and violence. And through their honesty, they displayed courage.

For example, Chambliss (1973) simply approached the leaders of the Saints and the Roughnecks outside a Seattle pizza parlor. Working independent of community agencies, social workers, or the clergy, Chambliss established trust with his subjects and went on to observe numerous acts of violence perpetrated by the Saints over a two-year period. Because of the trust established with his subjects (by working alone and first introducing himself to gang leaders), Chambliss never once had to defend himself. And, to be sure, Chambliss never engaged in gang violence.

Perhaps more instructive is Horowitz's (1983) research on a Chicano gang called the Lions. "Readers may wonder," she asks in the Introduction to *Honor and the American Dream*, "how a woman could possibly have joined gang members as they loitered on street corners and around park benches and developed relationships that allowed her to gather sufficient and reliable data" (1983:6). After all, she laments, "I am Jewish, educated, small, fairly dark, a woman, dressed slightly sloppily but not too sloppily, and only a few years older than most of those I observed" (1983:6). Horowitz solved this research dilemma by entering the gang "without local sponsorship" (1983:7). She simply walked into a poverty-stricken area of South Chicago, by herself, and took a seat on a bench in a park where Chicano gangs were known to congregate. Horowitz sat on this park bench—alone, from noon until midnight, for three days straight. Then,

> On the third afternoon of sitting on the bench, as I dropped a softball that had rolled toward me, a young man came over and said, "You can't catch" (which I acknowledged) and "You're not from the hood (neighborhood), are you?" This was a statement, not a question. He was Gilberto, the Lions' president. When I told him I wanted to write a book on Chicano youth, he said I should meet the other young men and took me over to shake hands with eight members of the Lions (1983:7).

So began Horowitz's three-year study of the Lions, during which time she observed numerous fights involving clubs, baseball bats, chains, bricks, and guns. Horowitz describes the precipitating phases of a gang war and the build up of a veritable arsenal of shotguns and pistols. She observed it all from her park bench. Horowitz was never injured by the Lions or any rival gang member. Indeed, she was often protected by the Lions who, over the course of the study, came to see her as a friend. Her favorable first impression had allowed Horowitz to enter the Lions peacefully. This allowed her to follow the gang and make observations. . . .

The pedagogical implications of the purist approach are these: Students—especially women—must be taught how to walk into depressed and dilapidated urban areas alone, demonstrating no fear whatsoever, where they must hunt down and introduce themselves to gang leaders and negotiate interviews with leaders and their gang underlings. This implication is important and must be stated as clearly as possible: Always go to gang leaders first, and never go to a gang underling first. In short, students must be taught courage. Not courage through karate as suggested by Jankowski, but courage through honesty which has proven to be effective in controlling paranoia and violence by Chambliss,

Horowitz and a legion of gang scholars dating back to the Chicago School of the 1920s. Courage overcomes fear, and fear is the wellspring of all violence. . . .

Community Agency Field Studies

Other researchers have collaborated with gang members, former gang members, and/or university graduate students to enter gangs under the auspices of community agencies. Through this collaborative effort, researchers have protected themselves from paranoia and violence by handing these pressures over to those gang members, former members, and/or students who were in their employ. However, these arrangements have always had a significant affect on the research process itself. As a result, studies conducted in the community agency field study tradition have never documented the extreme levels of gang violence found in participant observation research (e.g., Hamm, 1993; Jankowski, 1991; Vigil, 1988).

The community agency field study approach began with the work of Lewis Yablonsky (1962/1983). During the late 1950s, Yablonsky was appointed by a government-funded community agency to develop and direct a New York City gang prevention program on the upper West Side of Manhattan called "Morningside Heights, Inc:" Yablonsky lived and worked in the area and gang members would "often hang out" at his office and occasionally visit his home (1983:xi).

Yablonsky's contribution to gang research was built on 51 gang members' responses to 16 open-ended questions related to the structure and behavior of one Morningside Heights, Inc. gang called the Balkans. The Balkans were a group of Puerto Rican youths responsible for an unspecified number of homicides, assaults, robberies, burglaries, and drug addictions. Yablonsky called them The Violent Gang.

Yet unlike those gang researchers working in the participant-observation tradition, Yablonsky did not conduct his interviews in a face-to-face fashion. Instead, he used his influence as the director of Morningside Heights, Inc. and offered two Balkan leaders—named Duke and Pedro—$10 apiece for each completed questionnaire they administered to their gang underlings. This was an unprecedented strategy for entering a gang. Gang leaders were now themselves employees of the research project, and their behaviors were viewed as legitimate (see Bookin-Weiner & Horowitz, 1983 for a splendid account of this important shift in American gang research).

Duke and Pedro's method of administering the questionnaire was also unprecedented. Unlike the purists who invoked honesty and interpersonal trust in their collection of interview data, Yablonsky trained Duke and Pedro to use coercion and intimidation to administer his survey. "Their approach," recalled Yablonsky, "seemed to vary between a polite request for information at one extreme and a threatening 'You fill it out 'cause I say so' interview at the other" (1983:103). In essence, Yablonsky recognized Duke and Pedro's coercive authority within the Balkans, and he began to train them in methods of data collection through the threat of violence. . . .

Yablonsky found that "Duke's interview technique was 'forceful,' he had a talent for getting information" (1983:104). Indeed he did. Within three weeks, Duke and Pedro conducted a total of 51 interviews for Yablonsky, and they were rewarded $510 for their efforts. . . . Thus, Yablonsky remained safe from the threats of paranoia and violence by handing these pressures over to Duke and Pedro for a handsome price. Yet Duke and Pedro would ultimately pay for their participation in gang research.

> *The gang-boy respondents had mixed reactions to Duke and Pedro as researchers. Some . . . felt they were stoolies working for the cops, and some non-Balkans reacted with overt hostility. On one occasion, Duke arrived at my office, displaying some . . . fresh lacerations on his face, and claimed he had been beaten and robbed of 10 filled-out questionnaires by six unidentified Negroes in central Harlem (Yablonsky, 1983:103).*

The Managers

Despite the ethical ramifications of bringing harm to the subjects of social science research (Babbie, 1992), Yablonsky's techniques have been duplicated by others. Most notable is the often-cited work of Joan Moore (1978) who founded a community-based research project that utilized a combination of former East Los Angeles gang members (known as pintos, or ex-convicts) and graduate students. Like the research of Yablonsky, Moore's collaboration was funded by outside sources (the National Science Foundation and the National Institute of Drug Abuse). And also like Yablonsky, her collaboration produced a litany of problems. In the Introduction to *Homeboys,* Moore regrets that her research staff "shared collective traumas and most of us went through individual crises in connection with the work" (1978:x).

These problems all arose from paranoia. But not paranoia between the researcher and the gang member, (indeed, there is no evidence that Moore actually met an active gang member herself)—but between the pintos and the academic students who comprised the research team. According to Moore, the pintos feared negative stereotyping from students, and students feared that pintos could not "identify with contributing to knowledge as a goal" (1978:184). The pintos feared manipulation on the part of students, and vice-versa. Pintos mistrusted students and students were fearful and contemptuous of the pintos' capacity to engage in illegal behavior (eg., shooting heroin). Both groups distrusted the long-range goals of the research. And, most important, Moore's research organization was brought to its knees by the problem of gossip.

> *Rumors about criminal activity are a great and obvious hazard to a pinto project. . . . In an atmosphere of mixed conceptions of normality, gossip is dangerous. The academic people suffered from rumors among fellow academics about neurotic motivations. . . . The pinto staff was accused of selling out to the establishment for personal profit. The charges were always accompanied by negative implications. [The] gossip implied that both the pinto and the academic staff were using each other for unspeakable reasons (Moore, 1978:185–186).*

The cumulative effect of this was a total transformation of the research project. The experiment was stressful," Moore concluded, "—so much so that one major element, most of the graduate student assistants, became alienated and withdrew" (1978:187).

This resulted in a major modification of the research goals. Originally designed as a survey-driven study of the individual and organizational characteristics of modern barrio gangs, Moore's research now turned toward an oral history and conceptualizing approach emphasizing the socialization of Chicano males. Accordingly, no new data were generated on the proclivity of urban gangs to engage in violence. The scholastic energy to understand such complex phenomena had been consumed by an inept bureaucracy.

During the mid-1980s, Moore and John M. Hagedorn—a Milwaukee gang prevention specialist and community activist—became co-principal investigators of the "Milwaukee Gang Research Project" funded by a small grant from a private organization called the Milwaukee Foundation. This collaboration led to the publication of Hagedorn's (1988) *People and Folks*. . . . Hagedorn made four important modifications to the community agency field study approach.

Hagedorn's Contribution. First, Hagedorn adopted a stripped-down version of the "collaborative model" that proved to be so troublesome in East Los Angeles. Gone were the numerous graduate students and ex-convicts. Instead, Hagedorn chose to work with only one former gang leader and ex-prisoner, named Perry Macon. Second, Hagedorn focused specifically on 47 founding street gang members. "Those interviewed were the 'top dogs' of Milwaukee's gangs," he wrote, ". . . [and] We paid twenty dollars for each interview" (1988:32). Third, Hagedorn conducted most of the 47 interviews himself. He conducted these interviews in his home or at his office at the University of Milwaukee research center which housed his project. Macon's job was to recruit former top dogs off the streets and deliver them to Hagedorn for interviewing. Finally, rather than asking gang members to fill out questionnaires on their attitudes and behaviors, Hagedorn's subjects spoke into a tape recorder.

Hagedorn's methods contributed significantly to the community agency field study tradition because they brought the researcher back to his historical roots where he was provided inductive and sensitizing methods for understanding gangs. By eliminating bureaucracy, Hagedorn came face to face with his subjects and developed rich insights into the social dynamics that lead young people to join urban gangs in the first place. But unlike the participant-observation researchers, Hagedorn discovered that violence played only a small role in Milwaukee gangs. He concluded that:

> *All gangs we studied in Milwaukee were "fighting gangs," but the fighting period was generally when the gang members were "juniors" or in their early teens. As the gang matured, their interests turned to fundamental problems of survival (Hagedorn, 1988:100).*

Now, there may be four interrelated reasons why Hagedorn discovered low levels of violence among Milwaukee gangs.

1. The majority of Hagedorn's subjects were gang founders who had subsequently left their gangs. Hence, Hagedorn's subjects may have held negative attitudes about gangs. If so, they may have underreported what they could remember about violence back in the days when they were the top dogs.

2. The role of the intermediary (Macon) may have influenced the selection of subjects brought before Hagedorn for interviewing.
3. Hagedorn's use of an electronic recording device may have affected subjects' responses.
4. Hagedorn may not have asked the right questions. Of the 124 questions used in the interviews, only three related to violence. Hagedorn made no attempt to study the effects of social processes (e.g., gun ownership, alcohol and drug use, ideology, religion, and contemporary music) on the incidence of gang violence.

Thus, the pedagogical implications of the community agency field study approach are complicated. Yablonsky's (1983) research suggests that we begin to train our students in the art of persuasion, so that students may one day train gang leaders to coerce and intimidate gang underlyings into filling out questionnaires. Moore's (1978) research suggests that the managerial complications of community agency field study approach are so overwhelming that they deform the very process of social science itself. Therefore, students should be taught a healthy skepticism of the community agency field study tradition. Yet Hagedorn (1988) shows that a community researcher can effectively overcome the obstacles of paranoia and violence by working with a single former gang member, and by studying only former gang leaders in a face-to-face exchange. And if students follow his procedures, Hagedorn's work indicates that students will almost never witness an act of gang violence.

Detached Caseworker Studies

Levine (1972:132) argues that "deductive reasoning can prove nothing." By this, Levine implies that at least something may be learned from inductive reasoning. The most reliable source of information on gang violence is the observed behavior of, and testimony of, gang members themselves. This observed behavior and testimony served as the intellectual grist for gang scholars working in the participant-observation tradition. From specific instances of violence, the participant-observation researchers looked "outward" in search of general theoretical principles to explain their observational and interview data. This is the essence of inductive reasoning. Other researchers have worked from a deductive model: They began with a general theory of gang violence, and then went in search of specific gangs to confirm their theoretical expectations. However, consistent with the community agency field study approach (e.g., Hagedorn, 1988; Moore, 1978), these researchers have provided little meaningful knowledge on gang violence.

The Corporate Executives

Another community-oriented technique for entering gangs has been survey research conducted in conjunction with social workers. This technique began with the research of James F. Short and Fred L. Strodtbeck (1965). . . .

In their pathbreaking study, *Group Process and Gang Delinquency,* Short and Strodtbeck examined 38 Chicago street gangs through what they called "detached caseworkers" affiliated with the City's YMCA. The detached caseworkers spent most of their time with gang members; gaining their trust, steering them away from delinquency, and encouraging participation in more conventional activities—such as playing basketball. Relying on a five-year grant from the National Institute of Mental Health (1959–1962), Short and Strodtbeck were the employers of these detached caseworkers. The researchers directed their employees to fill out an extensive questionnaire on each gang members' norms, values, and self-reported acts of delinquency and violence.

Essentially, they found nothing. But this is not the message transmitted in textbooks. Orcott, for instance, describes Short and Strodtbeck's gang theory as being capable of "explaining consistent and revealing patterns of social interaction leading to violence" (1983:171). Yet after two years of interviewing (1959–1961), Short and Strodtbeck's detached caseworkers produced a total of 598 completed questionnaires that failed to identify a single delinquent gang member in the entire City of Chicago. This happened despite the fact that the Chicago street gangs accounted for 25 percent of all teenage homicides during the late 1950s (see Spergel, 1990). The authors fully acknowledge this severe limitation of their research with the following caveat.

> *The failure to locate a full-blown criminal group, or more than one drug-using group, despite our highly motivated effort to do so, is a "finding" of some importance, for it casts doubt on the generality of these phenomena, if not on their existence (Short & Strodtbeck, 1965:13).*

In other words, the subjects in Short and Strodtbeck's historic research were not violent at all. Hence, there can be no "consistent and revealing patterns of social interaction that leads to violence" among youths who have never engaged in violence to begin with. At bottom, Short and Strodtbeck were left with exhaustive survey data on nearly 600 youngsters who were guilty of nothing more than horseplay. "We were led in the end" they write, "to seek groups not primarily oriented around fighting, but with extensive involvement in the pursuit of 'kicks' " (1965:13).

The pedagogical implications of Short and Strodtbeck's research are these. First, students must be taught skills in grant writing and management. They must aspire to become corporate executives of large-scale research projects dedicated to understanding the pursuit of kicks. Because the detached caseworker approach consistently fails to discover delinquency and violence—and because the researcher never actually comes into contact with gang members—lessons in courage are irrelevant. Second, skills in corporate executive management are of utmost importance in today's marketplace of ideas on doing gang research. Currently, nearly every federal agency concerned with research on gangs assumes the efficacy of the detached caseworker approach and consequently limits research outside this tradition on the grounds that alternative methods are less likely to produce results of policy significance (see U.S. Department of Justice, 1992).

The Mathematical Olympian. This trend is exemplified by the federally funded research of Jeffrey Fagan (1989, 1990; see also Wilson, 1990). Like the YMCA research of Short and Strodtbeck, Fagan recruited his subjects through gang prevention programs sponsored by social service agencies, neighborhood advocacy groups, and community centers in Los Angeles, San Diego, and Chicago. Fagan called this group of gang prevention specialists "intermediaries." The intermediaries, who lived and worked in the field, persuaded active gang members to come to neighborhood community centers, where gang members were asked to fill out questionnaires by yet another group of "proctors" (community center employees) who were also part of the research team. On completion of their questionnaires, gang members were rewarded T-shirts, baseball caps, and music cassettes. Across three cities, this entire operation (i.e., prices paid to intermediaries, proctors, and gang members) was funded by Fagan's grant from the National Institute of Justice.

This research enterprise led to 151 usable questionnaires on gang organization and behavior. Fagan's sample, therefore, provided enough statistical power to establish grounds for quantitative criminology. Through an unprecedented display of complex statistical proofs, Fagan made two discoveries about the nature of violent gangs in America today: (1) the organizational structures of gangs facilitates violence, and (2) gang violence is usually presaged by drug use and/or drug dealing.

Fagan's study was successful because it was safe. While gang members were encouraged and rewarded for participating in the study, Fagan did not come in contact with his subjects. Thus he was spared the threats of paranoia and violence. Ultimately, however, Fagan's research was also affected by the detached caseworker approach. While Fagan discovered a uniform prevalence of violence among his subjects, he also found variance in the incidence of violence. . . .

The pedagogical implications of Fagan's research are as follows. To do gang research in the 1990s, it is first of all necessary to be the proprietor of a large government grant. This grant will provide resources to overcome paranoia and violence by removing the researcher from his or her subjects, and by rewarding research staffs and gang members for participating in the study. Second, students must be taught to manage large and complex statistical files on high-speed . . . computers. And third, students must be taught this: The detached caseworker approach will automatically introduce error variance into statistical predictions of gang violence whenever it is computed.

Prison Field Studies

Perhaps the most untapped sources of information about gangs are the *post hoc* recollections of former gang members who are now incarcerated in prison. In the prison field study approach, the researcher conducts interviews with incarcerated former gang members who have been identified by correctional officials. Therefore, the researcher has a steady pool of subjects and the safety of a nearby prison guard who is trained to eliminate paranoia and violence. This arrangement places the researcher face-to-face with subjects, and it places subjects in less danger than if they were being interviewed in the community while at large for a violent crime (see Polsky, 1967).

This emerging strain of gang research is represented in the work of Skolnick (1988) who drew a purposive sample of 39 incarcerated former gang members who were heavily involved in the California crack trade. And by the research of Winfree,

Vigil, and Mays (1991) who posit a stochastic model of gang violence based on the results of questionnaire data drawn from a purposive sample of former gang members incarcerated in New Mexico prisons.

The pedagogical implications of the prison field study method are that students must be taught how to construct reliable and valid survey questionnaires based on extant gang research and theory Then, they must convince correctional administrators that their research is worthwhile. Students can do this without a grant. All they need to do is contact the warden of a nearby prison, and explain—with impeccable clarity—the goals of their research; and then, follow the warden's advice for implementing a research project to meet these goals. In strictly criminological terms, the overarching goal of all gang research is to explain the propensity for violence (Thrasher, 1927, Chapter IX).

Conclusions

Klein (1992) offers a helpful comment on conducting gang research in the 1990s. In his critical review of *Islands in the Street,* Klein argues that "It is difficult to sep[a]rate the [researcher's] attempts to take new ground from his procedures—both research and presentation" (1992:81). Consistent with this, I have attempted to show that as researchers move farther and farther away from inductive reasoning—and therefore, farther away from explanations concerning the way gang members view their own world—researchers tend to rely more and more on their own value-laden assumptions (derived from deductive reasoning) about human nature and the way society should and does operate. Along the way, these researchers tell us almost nothing about the problem of gang violence. If the goal of gang research is to understand violence, then the end result of the community agency and detached caseworker methods is scientific ossification.

Reified scientific beliefs confirm prevailing opinions among law enforcement officers, community activists, legislators, correctional administrators, citizens, rap artists, and students of criminology and criminal justice. These mainstream opinions—shaped by the social and political contentions of the times—support and sustain the views of social control agents, rather than the empirical realities of the criminal phenomena researchers are interested in to begin with.

I have suggested that this academic and public policy stagnation can be corrected through university courses that encourage students to return to a more traditional approach to doing gang research. Following Mills (1959), I have attempted to show that government grants and advanced technology have been responsible for transforming gang researchers into bureaucrats and technicians. Mills explained that a "quality of mind" was necessary to "achieve lucid summations of what is going on in the world". In distinguishing the social scientist from the bureaucrat/technician, Mills described the former as having a capacity to shift from one intellectual perspective to another, a playfulness of mind that integrates ideas in novel ways, and a "fierce drive to make sense of the world" (1959:211).

With respect to gang violence, such "playfulness of mind" can be achieved only by seeing gang violence first-hand, and/or by directly interviewing gang members who have committed violence. This criminological lesson is not learned in the cloistered hallways of a university; nor is it learned at a computer keyboard. It is never learned in an office of grants and contracts. It is learned only on the streets—through courage.

References

Babbie, E. (1992). *The Practice of Social Research.* Belmont, CA: Wadsworth Publishing Co.

Bookin-Weiner, H. & R. Horowitz. (1983). "The End of the Youth Gang: Fad or Fact?" *Criminology* 21:585–602.

Chamblis, W. J. (1973). "The Saints and the Roughnecks." *Society* 11:24–31.

Fagan, J. (1989). "The Social Organization of Drug Use and Drug Dealing Among Urban Gangs." *Criminology* 27:649–652.

Gotfredson, M. R. & T. Hirschi. (1990). *A General Theory of Crime.* Stanford, CA: Stanford University Press.

Hagerdon, J. M. (1988). *People and Folks.* Chicago, IL: Lake View Press.

Hamm, M. S. (1993). *American Skinheads: The Criminology and Control of Hate Crime.* Westport, CT: Praeger.

Horowitz, R. (1983). *Honor and the American Dream: Culture and Identity in a Chicano Community.* New Brunswick, NJ: Rutgers University Press.

Jankowski, M. S. (1991). *Islands in the Street: Gangs and American Urban Society.* Berkeley, CA: University of California Press.

Keiser, R. L. (1969). *The Vice Lords: Warriors of the Streets.* New York: Holt.

Klein, M. W. (1971). *Street Gangs and Street Workers.* Englewood Cliffs, NJ: Prentice-Hall.

Levine, R. A. (1972). *Public Planning: Failure and Redirection.* New York: Basic Books, Inc.

Mieczkowski, T. (1986). "Geeking Up and Throwing Down: Heroin Street Life in Detroit." *Criminology* 24:645–666.

———. (1988). "Crack Distribution in Detroit." Presented at the annual meeting of the American Society of Criminology. Chicago, IL.

Miller, W. B. (1958). "Lower-Class Culture as Generating Milieu of Gang Delinquency." *Journal of Social Issues,* 12:5–19.

Mills, C. W. (1959). *The Sociological Imagination.* New York: Oxford University Press.

Moore, J. (1978). *Homeboys: Gangs, Drugs, and Prisons in the Barrios of Los Angeles.* Philadelphia, PA: Temple University Press.

Orcutt, J. D. (1983). *Analyzing Deviance.* Chicago, IL: The Dorsey Press.

Short, J. F. & J. J. Stodtbeck. (1965). *Group Process and Gang Delinquency.* Chicago, IL: University of Chicago Press.

Siegel, L. J. & J. J. Senna. (1981). *Juvenile Delinquency: Theory, Practice & Law.* St. Paul, MN: West Publishing Co.

Spergel, I. & G. D. Curry. (1990). "Strategies and Perceived Agency Effectiveness in Dealing With the Youth Gang Problem." In C. R. Huff (ed.). *Gangs in America,* pp. 288–309. Newbury Park, CA: Sage.

Thrasher, F. M. (1927). *The Gang: A Study of 1,313 Gangs in Chicago.* Chicago, IL: The University of Chicago Press.

U.S. Department of Justice. (1993). *Crime in the United States 1992: Uniform Crime Reports.* Washington, DC: U.S. Department of Justice.

Vigil, J. D. (1988). (1988). *Barrio Gangs: Street Life and Identity in Southern California.* Austin, TX: University of Texas Press.

Whyte, W. F. (1943). *Street Corner Society: The Social Structure of an Italian Slum.* Chicago, IL: The University of Chicago Press.

Wilson, J. Q. (1990). "Drugs and Crime." In M. Tonry & J. Q. Wilson (eds.) *Drugs and Crime.* Chicago, IL: University of Chicago Press.

Winfree, L. T., T. Vigil & G. L. Mays. (1994). "Social Learning Theory and Youth Gangs: A New Twist on a General Theory of Crime and Delinquency." *Youth and Society* 26:147–177.

Yablonsky, L. (1962). *The Violent Gang.* New York: Macmillan.

Conclusion

This section has addressed the dynamics of human interaction inherent in observational- and participation-based qualitative methods. The human dimension is less an issue with traditional, variable-analysis-based research designs (e.g., telephone survey), but the qualitative researcher understands that the success or failure of a certain project often rests on the ability to gain entree and to establish and maintain rapport. When the subjects are deviants and criminals (as we have just seen, sometimes active criminals) the fundamental problems are compounded by the elements of paranoia and violence.

That times have changed regarding these research issues is evident by comparing the classical article by Berk and Adams with the Hamm selection. Although there has clearly been a steady movement in the direction of extremes (in terms of the extent of field immersion and exposure to danger), there remains a continuity regarding the significance of researcher-subject interaction. The questions below invite discussion of how the practical, ethical, and even legal issues that come into conflict in the course of research may be resolved.

Questions for Discussion

1. What are the primary obstacles to gaining access to deviant and criminal subject groups?

2. What strategies are advocated by Berk and Adams to facilitate rapport? By Hamm?

3. What are the advantages to studying active criminals?

4. Given that a case can be made for studying criminals in their active state, why do so many researchers shy away from doing so?

5. To what extent does the researcher's self-presentation become a factor in fieldwork?

Section 3

Get a Little Dirt on Your Hands: Illustrations of Extreme Fieldwork

The research produced by extreme methods is often the type of research that is considered marginal, weird, dangerous, or simply *extreme*. Such labels are given to research of this variety because the topics are often outside of the mainstream of things that "normal" (i.e., traditional, respectable, or rigid) researchers would study. However, when criminologists and sociologists study people and communities on the edges of society, they are, in many ways, also studying the people and communities in the mainstream. It is only by understanding what is on the edges that one can understand what makes something mainstream. The articles in this section all highlight the ways that extreme methods can be used to better understand both marginal social groups and activities and mainstream social life.

In the first article, Miller and Selva report on a research endeavor that included a researcher's working undercover in the narcotics market. The research is based on data gathered by way of covert participant observation and highlights latent functions of the war on drugs. The activities of both drug industry participants and law enforcement agencies were observed and compared with publicly stated and endorsed government objectives. The research took an extreme methodological position in this work in several ways. First, the topic of the research (undercover narcotics operations) is a dangerous and difficult social world to access. However, the fact that the research was conducted without the knowledge of those being studied and the fact that both sides of the oppositional communities were accessed presents a set of issues that accent the creativity and degree of carefulness that was necessary to examine this otherwise esoteric phenomenon.

The second article takes a slightly different approach, looking at only one community, but focusing attention on a usually neglected segment of the community. Hopper and Moore look at the role of women in outlaw motorcycle gangs. Outlaw motorcycle gangs, because of both their actual activities and the way in which they have historically been treated by law enforcement and other "official" agencies, are difficult groups to infiltrate. However, drawing on one researcher's contacts inside the outlaw motorcycle world, these authors know how some of the more secretive aspects of biker life transpire. As reported in this article, some of the situations in which the research was conducted included extreme forms of behavior. If those being studied had known that they were being studied and that their actions were going to be reported to outsiders, it is likely that they would have barred the researcher(s) from observing secret, hedonistic, criminal acts. Clearly, as suggested by the experiences of these researchers, simply having some points of contact with a community do not guarantee that the community will welcome researchers.

Lozano and Foltz, in the third article, report on their work with a religious group considered only marginally acceptable to most of society. By entering and partially participating in a coven of witches, this team of researchers shows how a community is structured and how their values are expressed in their activities. What makes this research extreme is the fact that the community being studied is closed to outside observers, and the researchers found that the only way they could be granted access to observe the group's activities was that they would be expected to participate. Although not necessarily a form of spirituality that they initially valued, these researchers did agree to participate in some (but not all) activities of the coven, in exchange for being accepted at most community activities.

In the fourth article, the theme of getting one's hands "dirty" is perhaps most clearly seen. So too is the idea of participation in the community being studied carried to an extreme. Whereas the first two articles report on researchers who went undercover to study others, Ronai reports (with Ellis) on how her work as an erotic dancer (i.e., stripper) allowed her to study both the world of strip clubs and the experience of erotic dancing. Where this research differs from the other research reported on in this section is that Ronai employs an extreme method of research known as *reflexive*. Rather than simply studying all the aspects of the research, reflexive methodologies also include the personal perceptions and "feelings" (i.e., experiences) of the actual researcher. By employing a methodology that exploits the researcher's own experiences and reactions to those experiences, this project provides readers with an intimate view of the world of the erotic dancer.

The idea of carrying through on participating in a community under study is again seen in Myer's article on genital piercing, branding, burning, and cutting. In most Americans' minds, activities such as the piercing of genitals and branding is "extreme." However, the fact that this is the type of activity being studied in Myers' work is only one (and not the most important) reason that this article is an example of extreme research. Myers, like Ronai, fully participates in the topic he studies and draws on his own experiences to help readers understand. Whereas Ronai's study of erotic dancers emphasizes the reflexive aspect of the researcher's experiences, Myers' research includes his own experiences as only one of several forms of data. However, by immersing himself in a community of persons who "modify" their bodies by branding, burning, or cutting themselves, or who pierce their genitals, Myers goes beyond the traditional boundaries of social science research by showing how a "real participant" can not only establish rapport more easily with those being studied, but such a researcher can also better understand that which he sees and hears from participants. The full involvement of the researcher is not so much a data collection technique as it is a means of preparation for better understanding the data that is collected. For the majority of social scientists, such an approach (whether in a world such as body modifiers or not) is definitely going above and beyond the call of duty.

What these articles clearly show is that, when a researcher is willing to get his/her hands dirty by becoming involved in the worlds they are studying, they are much better able to understand what they are studying. Sometimes the involvement with those being studied is for the purposes of gaining insights and information. Sometimes it is for the purpose of being able to understand the information that is gathered in other ways. And, sometimes becoming involved in "different" worlds allows researchers to both gain information they would not otherwise be able to get, as well as to be better able to understand what they are seeing, hearing, feeling, and experiencing. Studying something using extreme research methods often involves some rather unsavory, if not downright frightening and bothersome, things that we would not otherwise do. However, sometimes such things are necessary, in the name of research.

Questions to Consider

1. How can researchers separate their personal experiences and feelings from their role as scientists? Is it important to keep these two roles separate?

2. How much of themselves should researchers be expected to invest in a research project?

3. What are the advantages for researchers to completely immerse themselves in the settings they study?

Drug Enforcement's Double-Edged Sword: An Assessment of Asset Forfeiture Programs

J. MITCHELL MILLER
University of Tennessee
and LANCE H. SELVA
Middle Tennessee State University

• • •

The 1988 Anti-Drug Abuse Bill created new legal tools to handle the special enforcement problems presented by crack cocaine, gang-related violence, and domestic marijuana production, all of which appeared to be increasing steadily (Weisheit 1991). The bill provided for additional allocation of resources for equipment and manpower, as well as stiffer legal penalties for drug law offenders. It also created an Asset Forfeiture Fund. This fund is modeled after the Racketeer-Influenced and Corrupt Organizations (RICO) and the Continuing Criminal Enterprise statutes as well as the Federal Criminal Forfeiture Act of 1984, which legalized seizing the fruits of criminal activities (Moore 1988).

The Asset Forfeiture Fund is much more than a depository for income generated by liquidating seized assets, whether cash, automobiles, jewelry, art, or real estate. It is the central component in a reciprocal relationship between law enforcement agencies and federal and state treasury departments, from which the attorney general may authorize

> *payment of any expenses necessary to seize, detail/inventory, safe-guard, maintain, advertise or sell property under seizure or detention pursuant to any law enforced.... Payments from the fund can be used for awards for information or assistance related to violation of criminal drug laws.... Deposits to the fund will be from the*

J. Mitchell Miller and Lance H. Selva. *Justice Quarterly*, Vol. 11 No. 2, June 1994. © 1994 Academy of Criminal Justice Sciences.

forfeiture of property under any law enforced or administered (Lawrence 1988:2).

The Asset Forfeiture Fund was created with the intention of helping law enforcement agencies to combat drug lords whose wealth gave them refuge from traditional enforcement tactics. Proponents were optimistic that seizing assets would limit the amount of working capital available to drug dealers, thereby reducing their ability to facilitate criminal activity (Drug Policy Foundation 1992; Fried 1988).

The fund calls on federal agencies to form special units for conducting operations to make seizures. Most state law enforcement agencies and several metropolitan police departments soon noted the monetary benefits of the fund and copied the federal approach, making asset seizure and forfeiture a sweeping narcotics policing strategy (United States Department of Justice 1988). Like any legal innovation, however, it had the potential for unintended consequences.

Critics contend that seizing assets and money has become a concern of vice divisions in smaller enforcement agencies, primary to the exclusion of traditional enforcement goals of deterrence and punishment (Stuart 1990; Trebach 1987). The routinization of seizure and forfeiture, others allege, has prompted enforcement agencies to develop new strategies of narcotics policing that are directed more toward asset hunting than toward reducing illegal drug use (Miller 1991; Trebach and Zeese 1990). Furthermore, this new policing strategy appears to be increasingly intrusive. A number of journalistic accounts describe civil liberties violations related directly to asset forfeiture enforcement (Jacobs 1992; Morganthau and Katel 1990). A series published by the Pittsburgh Press, titled *Presumed Guilty: The Law's Victims in the War on Drugs* (Schneider and Flaherty 1991), portrays the frequent, severe victimization of ordinary citizens through forfeiture. These excellent reports, based on reviews of 25,000 DEA seizures and 510 court cases, reveal that "enormous collateral damage to the innocent" is the effect of a new standard of presumed guilt. Other information on asset forfeiture comes from legal critiques dissecting the language of the 1988 Anti-Drug Abuse Act and surveying its feasibility as an effective drug enforcement initiative (Goldstein and Kalant 1990; Krauss and Laezear 1991). No grounded studies have been conducted, however, to examine asset forfeiture in the field and to assess whether it is fair practice or foul play.

This study is an empirical examination of asset forfeiture as a tool of drug enforcement policy. It differs from previous work in this area in that it examines the implementation of the laws from within forfeiture programs, explaining experimentally rather than speculatively why and how one aspect of the drug war has gone astray. We begin with a survey of the literature, focusing on the legal basis of forfeiture policy and describing the extent of its use. This section also highlights major criticisms regarding problematic aspects of asset forfeiture programs. This discussion is followed by an explanation of the study. Next, we present observations. We conclude with an assessment of asset forfeiture.

Background

An initial assessment of the 1988 Anti-Drug Abuse Bill might suggest that it is little more than an intensification of preexisting laws and enforcement programs. Most of the provisions are either replicas or renovations of previous initiatives, but closer examination of the component establishing the Asset Forfeiture Fund reveals new developments. A brief survey of the use of forfeiture in the United States provides a framework for examining these recent changes.

The seizing of assets, both as an enforcement tactic and as a sanction, was practiced long before the creation of the 1988 Anti-Drug Abuse Bill. Historically, a felony was defined as a crime for which a person could be required to forfeit all property (Reid 1991). The power of forfeiture was recognized and approved by the American colonies and was used by the First Congress of the United States to confiscate smuggling, pirate, and slave ships (Greek 1992; Myers and Brzostowski 1982). Hundreds of forfeiture laws have been created and are now enforced by both state and federal governments.

The strategy of asset forfeiture was first used against drug dealers in 1970, when persons operating a trafficking organization were required to forfeit illegally acquired profits and assets according to the Comprehensive Drug Abuse Prevention and Control Act of 1970 *(United States Code* V.21). Subsequently Congress authorized federal attorneys to file *in rem* actions, civil lawsuits staking the government's claim to property and money related to the illicit drug industry. This step potentially enabled the government to obtain legal possession of property and currency even despite dismissal of criminal charges based on a legal technicality such as a faulty search warrant or a *Miranda* rights violation. In addition, prosecutors enjoyed the reduced burden of proof required under civil law; a simple preponderance of the evidence, as opposed to the "beyond a reasonable doubt" standard recognized in criminal courts.

The consequences were considerable. During 1979, the first full year of implementation, the DEA seized close to $10 million in assets; this figure reached $54.4 million in 1981 (Myers and Brzostowski 1982). In 1983 more than $100 million in cash and property was forfeited to the government (Stellwagen 1985); an astronomical $460 million was forfeited in 1990 (Bureau of Justice Statistics 1991). Despite these impressive statistics, advocates of asset forfeiture considered the power to be seriously underutilized.

In the early 1980s all states were seizing illicit substances during routine narcotics operations, but few were following the federal example of seizing drug profits. In 1982, to encourage states that had yet to pass laws attacking the profits of drug trafficking, the DEA developed a Model Forfeiture of Drug Profits Act and published a training manual titled "Drug Agents" Guide to Forfeiture of Assets (Myers and Brzostowski 1982). The federal agency suggested that states adopting the Act, or a similar provision, allocate revenue generated through seizure and forfeiture to drug enforcement. By 1985, 47 states had passed legislation resembling the 1982 DEA Act (Stellwagen 1985). Federal policy recommendations, formulated in a 1985 U.S.

Department of Justice study of 50 prosecutors, including extending statutes to condemn additional types of property and hiring staff for financial investigations and asset management (U.S. Department of Justice 1988). The practice of returning seized money to drug enforcers was incorporated in the 1988 Anti-Drug Abuse Bill and is the heart of the controversy surrounding asset forfeiture and its offspring, a seizure-based style of narcotics policing.

The importance of the Asset Forfeiture Fund, and the element that makes it more than a mere intensification of previous seizure laws, centers on the redirection of the income produced by asset forfeiture (Osborne 1991). Before provision was made for an Asset Forfeiture Fund, income raised by liquidating assets was generally channeled into treasury departments for redistribution into the national or state budgets. Under the present provision, however, a percentage of the funds generated by asset seizures is returned Government treasury departments to law enforcement agencies to supplement their budgets. In 1988, in fact, the United States Justice Department shared $24.4 million with state and local law enforcement agencies that participated in investigations and arrests producing forfeitures (Burden 1988:29). A cycle was created, which allowed narcotics operations to make seizures that could be used to finance other operations in which yet more assets might be seized.

Proponents of asset seizure claim that it is necessary for enforcing the law and could turn the tide in the war on drugs. Substantial cash seizures, they argue, cripple large drug trafficking operations. The Los Angeles County Sheriff s Department, for example, seized more than $26 million in drug money in 1987 and another $33 million in 1988 (Stuart 1990). Forfeitures have included a Chevrolet dealership, a recording studio, a thousand-acre plantation, and numerous luxury homes, cars, boats, and planes (Wrobleski and Hess 1990:429). The distribution of the proceeds varies among federal agencies and from state to state. Under Louisiana's Drug Racketeering and Related Organizations law, all property associated with illegal drug activity is subject to forfeiture. Division of the spoils in Louisiana are 50 percent to the state, 25 percent to the district attorney's office; and 25 percent to the narcotics division of the seizing law enforcement agency. The Illinois Narcotics Profit Forfeiture Act allocates 50 percent for local drug policing, 25 percent for narcotics prosecution, and 25 percent to the State Drug Traffic Prevention Fund (U.S. Department of Justice 1988).

Problems

Success in drug work traditionally has been measured by the protection it provides society through ferreting out drugs and drug dealers, eradicating the substances, and apprehending offenders (Carter 1990; Moore 1977). The goal has been to diminish drug use and trafficking. Despite a problematic history, narcotics policing has employed strategies and tactics that at least appeared to be consistent with policy objectives (Carter and Stephens 1988; Mockars 1983; Manning and Redlinger 1977;

Wilson 1961). Many of the traditional problems of drug control, such as exposure to pressures and invitations to corruption (Carter 1990; Chambliss 1988; Wilson 1978), still must be addressed, but new problems have developed since the implementation of asset forfeiture programs.

Journalistic accounts suggest that seizing assets has become a high-priority objective in drug enforcement (Dortch 1992; Shaw 1990; Willson 1990). According to Dan Garner, an undercover narcotics agent in southern California, drug enforcement success is measured by the amount of money seized:

> You see that there's big money out there, you want to seize the big money for your department. For our unit, the sign of whether you were doing good or poorly was how much money you seized, and the kind of cases you did. And my supervisor made it extremely clear that big money cases were a lot more favorable for your overall evaluation than big dope cases (Stuart 1990).

Garner and some of his fellow agents were accused of stealing drug profits during seizure operations. Their story has called attention to a growing problem, as have other highly publicized drug related police scandals such as the Miami River murders of drug dealers by officers who stole their profits, and the arrest of more than half of the Sea Girt, New Jersey Police Department by the DEA on drug trafficking charges (Dombrink 1988).

Asset forfeiture was designed to be used against major dealers involved heavily in criminal activity. In practice, however, suspects not associated significantly with criminal activity often become the targets of operations because they have valuable assets. Under forfeiture laws, the potential value of assets strongly affects the priority of cases, thus determining who the suspects will be. The goal of raising revenue encourages selection of cases according to the suspect's resources. Targets of police surveillance thus are chosen for their resources rather than for their criminal activity, giving credence to frequent insinuations that the police facilitate crime (Block 1993; Braithwaite, Fisse, and Geis 1987; Marx 1988).

Observers argue that when narcotics officers become revenue producers, the system itself becomes corrupt (Carter 1990; McAlary 1987; Trebach 1987). As one critic points out,

> Once you focus on cash as the goal for the officers, they accept that and they forget about the ultimate goal of eliminating dope dealers. Seizure operations are simply revenue raising devices for departments, and divert officers' attention from the real goal, stopping dope (Stuart 1990).

According to one study, police in both Los Angeles and Miami routinely took assets from dealers but did not arrest them. Officers seized money from individuals and asked them to sign a disclaimer form before release. The disclaimer form stated that the suspect was not the owner of the seized money, had no knowledge of where it came from, and would not attempt to claim it. Such forms were used in investigations where money was seized but no drugs were found. The purpose, according to agency memos, "was to assist the department in gaining legal possession of the money" (Stuart 1990).

Examination of the forfeiture process from seizure to revenue highlights the steps involved in liquidating assets. Seized currency moves through the system more rapidly than do assets such as automobiles and real estate, which must be warehoused (when appropriate), advertised, and auctioned. By seizing cash, law enforcement agencies obtain their percentage of the revenue produced much sooner than by seizing property. For this reason, narcotics operations employ strategies designed to generate cash.

The "reverse sting" (Miller 1991) has emerged as the predominant choice of narcotics divisions. This type of operation features undercover agents as the sellers of drugs, rather than as buyers who seek out illicit substances. This controversial method involves negotiation, frequently through confidential informants, aimed at arranging a time and place at which undercover agents posing as drug dealers will provide felonious resale quantities of an illicit substance for a predetermined price. After the transaction has been completed, a "take-down" team of agents arrests the suspect and seizes any assets than can be associated with the deal (frequently an automobile) as well as any cash involved. The reverse sting is the preferred approach because agents can control and calculate the amount of money a deal will involve before they commit time and resources.

Traditional tactics, such as executing search warrants, often may produce arrests and confiscation of illegal substances, but no certain cash seizure. Narcotics enforcement is becoming a business, in which officers and equipment are allocated so as to maximize profits rather than to control or eradicate drugs. Efficiency is measured by the amount of money seized rather than by the impact on drug trafficking. In achieving efficiency, however, law enforcement has so misused the power of seizure that the Supreme Court recently has limited the scope of forfeiture laws.

In *Austin v. United States* (1993) the high court examined whether the Excessive Fines Clause of the Eighth Amendment applies to forfeitures of property. Although the court declined an invitation to establish a multifactor test for determining whether a forfeiture is excessive, it held that the principle of proportionality serves as a basis by which lower courts may decide individual cases. Thus the court determined that the government exacted too high a penalty (forfeiture of a home, $4,500, and an auto body shop) for the offense (sale of two grams of cocaine). Also, in *U.S. v. A Parcel of Land* (1993), some protection was provided to innocent owners of property related to the drug industry. Although these cases may slow the momentum of future asset-gathering operations, they address only a few of the real and potential dangers presented by forfeiture laws. Observations of undercover reverse sting operations point out these dangers and evidence the contradictions of such an approach.

The Study: A Year Under Cover

The data for this study come from the observations and experiences of one of the authors, who assumed the role of confidential informant in undercover narcotics operations in a southern state. This position provided a rare opportunity to examine, through covert participant observation, the clandestine work of narcotics operations units and to observe undercover narcotics agents, typically an inaccessible subject group.

While the researcher was a graduate student in a criminal justice program, he became friendly with fellow students who were drug enforcement agents. They invited him to participate in narcotics cases as a confidential informant. Although these fellow graduate students enabled his initial entry, the researcher then interacted with drug agents who did not know him and who had no knowledge of his research objectives. The label *confidential informant* should not be misconstrued; the position typically involves undercover work more often than the revealing of privileged knowledge to narcotics agents. The primary functions of a confidential informant are negotiating with and manipulating suspects so as to involve them in reverse sting operations.

The sense of police fraternity (Wilson 1961) is intensified in narcotics units, making them neither open nor receptive to research. As a confidential informant, the researcher was not accepted fully in the group. Nevertheless, his position allowed him to penetrate the hidden activities of narcotics operations and provided an excellent vantage point for conducting a study of drug enforcement. Informants interact with agent and criminal alike, often serving as a communication link between the two. This position allows proximity to the thoughts, feelings, motives, and strategies of both agents and suspects, thus permitting an investigation of asset forfeiture as implemented at the street level.

The researcher remained in this position for one year; he participated in 28 narcotics cases with agents and officers from very small city police departments, larger county sheriffs departments, urban and metropolitan forces, and two state law enforcement agencies. Here a case is defined operationally as a series of events that culminated in arrest, seizure of assets, or both. Cases often overlapped because they ranged in duration from a few days to several months. The events of each case were recorded upon leaving the various field settings, maintained in separate files, and updated as each case progressed.

As a "complete-member-researcher" (Adler and Adler 1987), the author conducted "opportunistic research" (Ronai and Ellis 1989) by studying phenomena in a setting in which he participated as a full member. This method also has been called "disguised observation" (Erikson 1967). Its distinguishing feature is that the research objectives are not made known to others in the field setting. The use of disguised or covert observational techniques often has been regarded as ethically controversial, as evidenced by the "deception debate" (Bulmer 1980; Galliher 1973; Humphreys 1970; Roth 1962). Participants in the debate tend to assume one of two polarized positions: moralistic condemnation or responsive justification. Opponents of this method hold that covert strategies should be banned from social science research (Erikson 1967). Their major objection is that these techniques often violate basic ethical principles such as informed consent, invasion of privacy, and the obligation to avoid causing harm to subjects. Specifically, the critics allege that misrepresentation can cause irreparable damage to subjects, to the researcher, and to science by evoking negative public scrutiny and by making subject populations wary of future researchers (Galliher 1973; Polsky 1967).

Justifications for the use of covert techniques have been presented on both practical and philosophical levels. One practical argument is that persons engaged in illegal or unconventional behavior, such as drug dealers and users, simply will not submit to or participate in study by overt methods. Similarly, those in powerful and authoritative positions, such as drug enforcement agents, have been considered secretive and difficult to observe openly (Shils 1975). From a philosophic perspective, Denzin (1968) argues, following Goffman (1959), that all researchers wear masks and ethical propriety thus depends on the context. Denzin suggests that

the sociologist has the right to make observations on anyone in any setting to the extent that he does so with scientific intents and purposes in mind (1968:50).

The basis for this disguise in this study, however, is "the end and the means" position stated first by Roth (1962) and later by Homan (1980). That the end may justify the means also is acknowledged by the British Sociological Association, which allows the covert approach "where it is not possible to use other methods to obtain essential data" (1973:3); such is the case in the present situation. We believe that the benefits of investigating and reporting on this expensive and dysfunctional drug enforcement strategy outweigh its potential costs. Failure to study how this strategy is implemented on the street would condemn other citizens to the misfortunes and abuses we describe below. In addition, scarce resources in the war on drugs would continue to be misused.

Drug enforcers' use of asset forfeiture has been questioned by the press and media so frequently and with such intensity that scholarly examination is warranted. The very nature of the allegations, however, has prompted the police fraternity to close ranks, thus making disguised entry a necessity. To rule out study of covert behavior, whether by the powerful or by the powerless, simply because it cannot be studied openly imposes artificial limits on science and prevents study of what may be important and consequential activities in society. The propriety and the importance of research activities always must be judged case by case. In this particular case, abandoning the study because it could not be conducted with overt techniques would cause the potential misconduct and betrayal of public trust by government officials to remain unexposed. We hope others will agree not only that the end justifies the means in the context of this research, but that it takes ethical precedence.

Observations: Some Typical Cases

The following examples of cases involve acts and decisions by narcotics agents that illustrate several troubling aspects of asset forfeiture. These concern the impact of forfeiture on both the type of cases selected for undercover operations and the function of covert policing in society.

The researcher first came to understand how cases were assigned priority while he was working with the police department of a medium-sized city in 1989. Still unaware of the profit-seeking nature of narcotics divisions, he began undercover work by "feeling out" possible deals and meeting with an undercover agent to discuss potential cases. The researcher mistakenly believed that a large quantity of drugs or a "known" dealer made a case desirable, and accordingly proposed two possible deals. The first deal involved 2½ pounds of marijuana that a dealer was willing to sell to the researcher's buyer (the agent). The second involved a factory worker who was shopping for a half-pound of marijuana to resell to friends and co-workers. The agent asked the researcher to note the license plate numbers of the suspects' vehicles. The researcher believed the plate numbers were to be used for gathering information such as the suspects' ages, addresses, and arrest records. The primary purpose, however, was to learn whether the suspect owned the vehicle or whether a lien holder was involved. This information enabled the agent to determine the amount of equity in a suspect's vehicle.

The equity in a vehicle represented potential profit that officers could expect to receive if the vehicle was seized. If a person whose car had been seized had a clear title, he or she was likely to lose the car. It would be sold later at auction, and the seizing agency would receive a percentage of the money. If a person was still making payments, the situation was more complex. Normally the defendant was given the option of making a "contribution" to the arresting department's drug fund, equal to the level of equity, in exchange for the seized vehicle.

The agent in charge of this case compared the two proposed deals in order to assess which one would generate more income. The first case involved five times as much marijuana as the second. Also, by working the first deal, officers would take 2 ½ pounds of marijuana out of circulation because the dealer would be selling. The seller was a full-time drug dealer with two prior drug-related convictions, and was on probation at the time of this case. The suspect in the second deal had no arrest record and appeared to be a relatively small-time user who hoped to make a modest profit by selling quarter-ounce bags of marijuana. Although the first deal seemed more serious, the second would guarantee seizure of at least $700 when the suspect purchased drugs from the agent. In addition, the latter suspect owned a truck, whereas the professional dealer had only a little equity in a late-model sports car. The officer explained that the first deal simply was not profitable and would not be pursued.

The researcher was instructed to arrange for the latter suspect to meet the "seller." When he expressed concern that the officer was encouraging the suspect to commit a crime, the officer justified the operation by contending that the suspect would secure marijuana elsewhere and eventually would become a major dealer. In this way, according to the officer, the problem would be "nipped in the bud" because the suspect would be deterred from future criminal activity. The purchase was consummated with the agent, the suspect was arrested, and his cash and vehicle were seized.

This case provided the agent's department with a small profit. The buyer may or may not have been deterred from future criminal behavior. On the other hand, no drugs were taken out of circulation, and the buyer might never have acted on his intentions to purchase a felonious quantity of drugs if the researcher and the agent had not presented him with such an opportunity.

The strategy involved in this case was termed a "reverse" sting because the visual undercover function of buying narcotics was the opposite of this arrangement: here, officers became sellers. This strategy was preferred by every agency and department with which the researcher was associated because it allowed agents to gauge potential profit before investing a great deal of time and effort. Reverses occurred so regularly that the term *reverse* became synonymous with the word *deal*.

This case was not an isolated incident; it was one of many such cases in which the operational goal was profit rather than the incapacitation of drug dealers. The pursuit of profit clearly influenced policies on case selection.

The researcher was told that only exchanges involving a certain amount of money or narcotics would be acceptable. It was apparent that these guidelines came from supervisors who did not want squads to work comparatively small cases or those of low monetary value, when more profitable options existed. These standards proved to be contrary to the notion of taking distributors off the street.

The drug trade, an illicit market, is similar to licit markets in several ways. One likeness is natural price regulation through the mechanics of supply and demand (Manning and Redlinger 1977). Upon seeing a large bust, supervisors tended mistakenly to believe that the drug markets in their jurisdictions were flooded with a particular substance. Consequently they imposed limits for agents and informants. Ironically, the arrest that prompted the decision was often an isolated incident that did not accurately reflect local drug trading activity.

These limits were a constant source of annoyance for both the researcher and the officers with whom he worked. One case, in which the researcher and an agent had spent a week preparing a suspect for a deal, provides a revealing example.

The researcher had established a relationship with the suspect, having bought marijuana from him on one occasion and cocaine on another. The suspect was informed that he could discuss business with the researcher's connection, who could supply quantities of marijuana at a low price. Having gained the suspect's confidence and whetted his appetite for a substantial bargain, the researcher arranged a conference between his supplier (an undercover agent) and the suspect. A deal was struck whereby the agent would sell two pounds of marijuana to the suspect for $2,500. The deal was canceled before the transaction, however, because the agent's supervisor decided that only reverses of five pounds or more would be worked. The researcher was told to give the suspect a reason why the deal could not take place.

After two unproductive weeks, the supervisor realized that he had been unrealistic in setting a five-pound limit. He lowered the limit to the previous level of one pound and then ordered the agent to try to recover the deal he had canceled two weeks earlier. The deal could not be saved, however, because the suspect no longer trusted the researcher. The undercover work and the money spent on compensating the researcher had been wasted. In addition, the suspect, a recidivist with criminal intent, remained free to solicit illicit substances.

Another case that was lost because of imposed limits involved a well-known suspect whom an agent had kept under surveillance for more than a year. The suspect, a college student, dealt primarily in "ECSTASY", a hallucinogenic drug in tablet form. The agent told the researcher that previously he had served a search warrant at the suspect's apartment, but had found nothing to warrant an arrest. The student had abused the agent verbally and threatened to sue his department for harassment. Later the researcher learned when and where this suspect was to deliver a quantity of ECTASY and marijuana. Although the agent wanted to arrest this suspect, largely for revenge, his supervisor was reluctant to pursue the case because it was not regarded as profitable.

Episodes such as these not only involved nonenforcement of narcotics' laws, but also promoted cynicism among officers, a troublesome aspect of police work (Carter 1990; Manning 1980). The ever-changing limits on deals magnified this problem as some officers began to question the nature and the true purpose of their occupation.

Other drug agents, however, demonstrated acceptance of asset forfeiture operations. When asked why a search warrant would not be served on a suspect known to have resale quantities of marijuana in his apartment, one officer replied: "Because that would just give us a bunch of dope and the hassle of having to book him (the suspect). We've got all the dope we need in the property room. Just stick to rounding up cases with big money and stay away from warrants."

Selecting cases on the basis of potential gain creates another problem, one that not only causes neglect of obligatory police functions but also tampers with civil rights. To raise revenue, asset gathering operations must focus on suspects with money and other resources. Large-scale dealers could not have achieved their status without connections and suppliers. Their ties and their discretion make them largely inaccessible to seizure operations because they are not easily "reversible." Many of these dealers value safety more, than profit, and work by selling drugs on credit in an operation known as "fronting." They recognize the legal advantage of keeping cash separate from illegal drugs. The big dealers do not make natural suspects for seizure strategies, nor are they easy prey. Consequently agents take the suspects they can get, namely lower-level dealers and ordinary users who fall victim to enterprising informants.

Another incident involved a 19-year-old male college sophomore, who came under surveillance while making routine deliveries of various drugs in a certain county jurisdiction. To obtain information, the researcher arranged and made an authorized purchase of two ounces of marijuana from the suspect. This individual turned out to be a "mule," a person who transports drugs but usually does not make buys or negotiate deals. The regular procedure in situations such as this was to arrest the suspect and then coerce him into cooperating with law enforcement by setting up the bigger dealer with whom he was working.

The researcher was surprised when the agent requested that a meeting be arranged with the suspect. A few days later, the researcher brought the suspect to a bar where the agent was waiting. The agent, having gained the suspect's confidence through conversation and by paying for drinks, persuaded him to secure a personal loan from a bank by using his vehicle as collateral so that he might purchase five pounds of marijuana. The ploy was successful and the suspect was arrested a few days later. This student was not searching for a large quantity of drugs, nor did he view himself as a dealer until the agent showed him how to become one. Thus, at times, undercover policing actually may promote crime by manipulating individuals who are naive, suggestible, or corruptible. Such activity not only victimizes ordinary people but also affects the conduct of police and their function in society.

The Impact of Forfeiture on Police Conduct

The following example demonstrates how the seizure motive can undermine police interest of service to the community. The suspect, one of the larger "players" whom the researcher encountered, dealt in marijuana, barbiturates, cocaine, and stolen property. The researcher had conducted two "buy-walks" with the suspect in order to establish a relationship. A buy-walk occurs when officers or their assistants purchase illegal substances, but officers do not make an arrest so that they may observe a situation and determine whether it will lead them higher in a drug ring's hierarchy.

The state agent wanted to reverse the suspect, but realized that a reverse strategy was impractical for this situation. The alternative was to serve a search warrant that ideally would occur when the suspect possessed a large amount of cash that could be seized. As a result, the researcher was required to stay in close contact with the suspect for two days; during that time the dealer received a quarter-kilogram of cocaine, a large shipment. This shipment was worth about $7,000 in bulk and as much as $13,000 on the street. The researcher relayed this information to the agent in charge of the operation.

In this case the researcher felt that the only decision to be made was when the warrant should be served. He believed that the narcotics division of the involved state agency would wish to intervene before the drugs could be resold. Proper police procedure does not mandate that agents act immediately on information which makes an arrest possible. If that were so, valuable periods of surveillance could not be conducted. The researcher, however, was surprised when he was instructed to observe the suspect's transactions to determine the rate at which the cocaine was being resold. Less drugs meant more cash, and the agent's objective was to seize currency rather than cocaine. The case was successful as to proceeds, but perhaps not in view of the quantity of cocaine that officers knowingly permitted to reach consumers. This incident illustrates that a focus on revenue requires police to compromise law enforcement in a manner that may harm rather than protect society.

The pressure created by a demand for productivity created competition among agents from nearby jurisdictions. This was magnified in rural county agencies that also had a city or town police force. Agents consequently became "turf conscious," regarding negatively the arrests of mutual suspects by agents from other agencies because those agents had taken away potential profit and had nullified the time and effort invested in surveillance. Thus operations often disintegrated because of a general lack of interagency cooperation, and numerous suspects were left at large.

One large case collapsed for this reason. A well-known drug dealer, who traded crack and cocaine in a small rural town, had been frequenting a neighboring jurisdiction to visit a woman with whom the researcher became acquainted. The suspect had been delivering drugs on weekly visits and was said to always have a large supply on his person. A city narcotics agent arranged for the researcher and a second undercover informant, a female posing as the researcher's date, to meet with the suspect for a small party at a residence approximately two miles from the city limit, the agent's jurisdictional boundary. The researcher notified the agent when the suspect was coming and described the route he would take.

The researcher and his associate noticed that the suspect possessed a kilogram of cocaine and had an unknown amount of cash in a gallon-sized plastic freezer bag. They attempted to manipulate the dealer into entering the city police department's jurisdiction by suggesting various bars that the group might patronize. The suspect refused to go, and the deal stalled.

Other agents learned what was happening by monitoring surveillance equipment, hidden wires fixed to each informant, but they were powerless to act because of the jurisdictional dilemma. Nothing prevented them, however, from contacting the county sheriff's department or notifying the state agency, who might have conducted a vehicle stop. Even so, the agents took no action, and the suspect slipped away with his bag of money and cocaine.

Even in cases involving children's welfare, officers sometimes failed to notify other agencies. In one such case, officers of a state agency monitored the daily activities of a marijuana and cocaine dealer for a long period because he was a vital link in an interstate drug ring. On one occasion, while the researcher was waiting with the suspect late at night for a phone call regarding a shipment of cocaine, he saw the suspect overdose; he had been injecting cocaine repeatedly for two hours. The man came staggering from a bathroom and muttered something unintelligible as he walked toward a patio. He forgot to open a sliding glass door and rammed his body through the glass, cutting his face and arms badly. His wife called for an ambulance and then revealed that he had overdosed twice before.

Less than a week later, the researcher was invited to a party to celebrate the suspect's release from the hospital. The party was disrupted when a friend of the suspect brought warning of a possible raid, thus prompting the suspect to retreat to a motel room with his wife and her 12-year-old son from a previous marriage. Suffering from intense paranoia, they remained there for eight days where the researcher visited them twice.

The boy in this family had failed three grades in school and was permitted to smoke pot and drink beer. The case was unfolding in late September, when he should have been attending school. This issue was raised by the suspect's wife, who had received warnings of legal action due to the boy's excessive absences. Furthermore, during this period, the suspect traveled with his wife to a bordering state to secure drugs, leaving the youth alone in the motel room for two days.

The researcher relayed the details of this situation to the agents working the case, who listened with indifference. The researcher recommended that the agents contact the Department of Human Services (DHS), but was told that such action would only disrupt the case; DHS would be notified after an arrest was made.

This case dragged on for another month before the suspect was arrested in a marijuana field in another county. When the researcher inquired about the boy, two agents explained that the time required to contact a social worker and complete the paperwork associated with that step could be better spent in making another case.

During the summer of 1990, the researcher spent several weeks concentrating on locating marijuana patches. This task was difficult because of the secretive nature of marijuana farming and the suspicion among farmers who previously had lost crops to thieves. To induce growers to reveal the location of their crops, the researcher joined suspects in planting other patches, thus becoming a "partner." This act fostered a common bond, which often produced the information that agents desired. The researcher observed that marijuana growers took a great deal of pride in their work and often bragged about their botanical abilities. When he expressed doubt about the truthfulness of growers' claims, occasionally they showed him a patch as proof of their cultivation skills.

One eradication case demonstrated how the objective of raising revenue undermined the police functions of apprehending criminals and enforcing narcotics laws. The researcher traveled with a suspect to a rural county, while six state agents in three vehicles tailed the suspect's truck to the site where the researcher had visited twice. Another group of state agents, the "take-down" team, waited in the woods at the edge of a marijuana field. This was the researchers's largest case in terms of the number of agents involved, the amount of marijuana (approximately 50 pounds), and the potential value of the plants. The marijuana grew in three loosely connected rectangular patches, each containing approximately 30 plants 12 to 16 feet high.

The researcher and the suspect arrived at the location and hiked two miles to reach the patches. This period was very suspenseful because armed, camouflaged agents were filming every move. The suspect was armed with a semi-automatic shotgun and a nine-millimeter pistol; the researcher carried a rifle. The possibility of gunfire and the size of the deal created a great deal of anxiety.

The suspect had come to the patches on this occasion to fertilize the plants with a liquid nitrogen solution. After he and the researcher had tended to about half of the plants, agents emerged from the brush, pointing automatic weapons. Both the suspect and the researcher were ordered to lie on the ground, and were handcuffed. To protect the researcher's identity, the agents subjected him to everything that was done to the suspect, such as frisking and interrogating. The agents cut down the plants, seized the suspect's firearms, took approximately $300 in cash, which was in his wallet, and another $200 from the glove box in his truck. A quick records check on the truck showed that the grower did not own it; thus seizure of this vehicle was an unattractive option.

After taking everything of value, the agents ordered the grower to enter his truck and leave, without formally arresting him for cultivating marijuana. In effect they appeared to rob the suspect. When the researcher inquired about this questionable use of discretion, an agent replied that the grower was subject to being indicted at a later date. The suspect had not been charged formally when this study was concluded.

In several cases that the researcher observed, members of the law enforcement community compromised legitimate police functions to secure profits. This last case is significant because the pursuit of higher goals was completely abandoned. Usually the objectives of seizure operations were disguised and mixed with traditional activities, including arrests, but in this case the taking of assets was displayed boldly as the foremost concern.

An Assessment of Asset Forfeiture

Before asset forfeiture policies were established, narcotics cases were assigned priority by the amount of drugs involved and the level of threat to society posed by suspects. The observations made here, however, show that asset seizure has become the primary objective of drug enforcement. The problematic nature of asset forfeiture policy became apparent when the development of specific narcotics cases was observed. Before the procedural stage of the observed cases, the fundamental function of narcotics divisions was made clear to officers and agents through supervisors' decisions as to which cases would be pursued.

Selection of cases on the basis of seizure policy creates two basic problems. First, the process of raising revenue through asset forfeiture often requires police to concentrate on cases that offer little or no direct social benefit. Second, the suspects involved in these cases often are not engaged in serious criminal activity. Their personal profiles differ greatly from those of the drug lords, for whom asset forfeiture strategies were designed.

Equally disturbing is the effect of asset-hunting operations on police conduct; they elevate both the image and the reality of the private soldier over those of the public servant. Too often the tactics required to generate regular seizures conflict with the ideals of protecting and serving the public. A situation has developed, which allows narcotics supervisors to choose justifiably between strategies that produce revenue and those which acknowledge the demands of justice.

The recent Supreme Court decisions have done little to alter the present approach of forfeiture programs. Both *Austin v. United States* (1993) and *U.S. v. A Parcel of Land* (1993) set limits on forfeiture, thus protecting citizens' civil liberties. These restrictions, however, will not necessarily limit the scope of victimization and intrusion; they may even worsen the present condition. The principle of proportionality, for example, confines law enforcement to less property per seizure, but may invite more frequent application of the tactic so as to maintain revenue levels already fixed in agency budgets.

In certain cases, asset forfeiture has proved to be a valuable enforcement tool. This potential benefit, however, must be weighed against unfavorable consequences. This study addresses what recently has been considered a primary question concerning forfeiture laws: "What impact will asset forfeiture have on police operations and management?" (Holden 1993:1). It is apparent that asset forfeiture is already being institutionalized within law enforcement; this process is influencing its disposition. Although the narcotics units observed in this study were confined to one general locale, the mid-south, neither empirical studies nor journalistic accounts suggest that seizure-based policing tactics differ elsewhere. Certainly, further examinations of asset forfeiture programs should be pursued. Interrelated topics to be addressed include comparative analysis of the levels of assets seized by federal and state agencies, by regions of the country; the relationship of forfeiture to the fiscal autonomy of the police (Miller and Bryant Forthcoming); the soundness of conceptualizing forfeiture as legitimized police deviance; and selective targeting by race and class.

The redirection of narcotics enforcement is manifested theoretically in broader implications for the entire interaction of law enforcement with society at large. The inherent contradictions of asset seizure practices have surfaced as highly controversial civil liberties violations which increasingly have eroded our sense of fairness and have caused drug enforcers to subordinate justice to profit. This insidious redirection is rooted in and propelled by American values of success, specifically profit. Societal and governmental opposition rarely succeeds in deterring means of income generation. The enforcers' inability to combat the pervasive illicit drug market does not justify legal mechanisms whereby law enforcement agencies share the wealth of drug trafficking under the guise of "service" to society.

Asset forfeiture has given drug enforcers a powerful incentive to maintain and manage economic mechanisms that allow the illegal drug market to continue. In this market, the drug enforcers and the drug traffickers become symbiotic beneficiaries of the "War on Drugs." Ironically, in its failure to reduce the marketing of illegal drugs, drug enforcement has succeeded in profiteering. Unfortunately, continued "success" in this area portends further and more widespread subversion of our ideals of fairness and justice.

References

Adler, P. A. and P. Adler (1987) "The Past and Future of Ethnography." *Journal of Contemporary Ethnography* 16:4–24.

Block, A. (1993) "Issues and Theories on Covert Policing." *Crime, Law and Social Change: An International Journal* (special issue) 18:35–60.

Braithwaite, J. B. Fisse, and G. Geis (1987) "Covert Facilitation and Crime: Restoring Balance to the Entrapment Debate." *Journal of Social Issues* 43:5–42.

British Sociological Association (1973) *Statement of Ethical Principles and Their Application to Sociological Practice.*

Bugliosi, V. T. (1991) *Drugs in America: The Case for Victory.* New York: Knightsbridge.

Bulmer, M. (1980) "Comment on the Ethics of Covert Methods." *British Journal of Sociology* 31:59–65.

Burden, O. P. (1988) "Finding Light at the End of the Drug War Tunnel." *Law Enforcement News,* December 15, pp. 8.

Bureau of Justice Statistics (1991) *Sourcebook of Criminal Justice Statistics.* Washington, DC: National Institute of Justice.

Carter, D. L. (1990) "Drug Related Corruption of Police Officers: A Contemporary Typology." *Journal of Criminal Justice* 18:85–98.

Carter, D. L. and D. W. Stephens (1988) *Drug Abuse by Police Officers: An Analysis of Policy Issues.* Springfield, IL: Thomas.

Chambliss, W. (1988) *On the Take: From Petty Crooks to Presidents.* Bloomington, IN: Indiana University Press.

Currie, E. (1993) *Reckoning: Drugs, the Cities, and the American Future.* New York: Hill and Wang.

Denzin, N. (1968) "On the Ethics of Disguised Observation." *Social Problems* 115:502–504.

Dombrink, J. (1988) "The Touchables: Vice and Police Corruption in the 1980's." *Law and Contemporary Problems* 51:201–32.

Dortch, S. (1992) "356 Marijuana Plants, House, Weapons Seized." *Knoxville News-Sentinel,* August 29, pp. 1.

Drug Enforcement Administration (1992) *Illegal Drug/Price Purity Report.* Washington, DC: Drug Enforcement Administration.

Drug Policy Foundation (1992) "Asset Forfeiture: Fair Practice or Foul Play?" (Film) *Drug Forum,* Date Not Available.

Elsasser, G. (1990) "A Just Cause: Washington Group Wages War on the War on Drugs." *Chicago Tribune,* May 24, pp. 13.

Erikson, K. T. (1967) "Disguised Observation in Sociology." *Social Problems* 14:366–72.

Fried, D. J. (1988) "Rationalizing Criminal Forfeiture." *Journal of Criminal Law and Criminology* 79:328–36.

Galliher, J. F. (1973) "The Protection of Human Subjects: A Reexamination of the Professional Code of Ethics." *The American Sociologist* 8:93–100.

Goffman, E. (1959) *The Presentation of Self in Everyday Life.* New York: Doubleday.

Goldstein, A. and H. Kalant (1990) "Drug Policy: Striking the Right Balance." *Science,* September 28, pp. 9–13.

Greek, C. (1992) "Drug Control and Asset Seizures: A Review of the History of Forfeiture in England and Colonial America." In Thomas Mieczkowski (eds.), *Drugs, Crime, and Social Policy,* pp. 4–32 Boston, MA: Allyn & Bacon.

Holden, R. N. (1993) "Police and the Profit-Motive: A New Look at Asset Forfeiture." *ACJS Today* 12:2.

Homan, R. (1980) "The Ethics of Covert Methods." *British Journal of Sociology* 3146–59.

Humphreys, L. (1970) *Tearoom Trade: Impersonal Sex in Public Places.* New York: Aldine.

Inciardi, J. A. (1991) *The Drug Legalization Debate.* 2nd ed. Newbury Park, CA: Sage.

Jacobs, D. (1992) "Police Take $700 from Man, Calling It Drug Money." *Knoxville News-Sentinel,* February 23, pp. 1.

Kleiman, M.A.R. (1989) *Marijuana: Costs of Abuse, Costs of Control.* New York: Greenwood.

———. (1992) *Against Excess: Drug Policy for Results.* New York: Basic Books.

Klockars, C. (1983) *Thinking About Police.* New York: McGraw-Hill.

Krauss, M. B. and E. P. Laezear, eds. (1991) *Searching for Alternatives: Drug-Control Policy in the United States.* Stanford, CA: Hoover Institution Press.

Lawrence, C. C. (1988) "Congress Clears Anti-Drug Bills." *Congressional Quarterly Weekly Report,* October 29, pp. 3145.

Manning, P. K. (1980) *The Narc's Game: Organizational and Informational Limits on Drug Enforcement.* Cambridge, MA: MIT Press.

Manning, P. K. and L. J. Redlinger (1977) "Invitational Edges of Corruption: Some Consequences of Narcotic Law Enforcement." In P. Rock (ed.), *Drugs and Politics,* pp. 279–310. Rutgers, NJ: Transaction Books.

Marx, G. (1988) *Undercover: Police Surveillance in America.* Los Angeles: Twentieth Century Fund Books.

McAlary, M. (1987) *Buddy Boys: When Cops Turn Bad.* New York: Putnam's.

Miller, J. M. (1991) "Inside Narcotics Policing Operations." Master's thesis, Middle Tennessee State University.

Miller, J. M. and K. Bryant (Forthcoming) Predicting Police Behavior: Ecology, Class, and Autonomy." *American Journal of Criminal Justice.*

Moore, M. (1977) *Buy and Bust: The Effective Regulation of an Illicit Market in Heroin.* Lexington, MA: Lexington Books.

———. (1988) "Drug Trafficking." In *Crime File,* pp. 1–4. Washington National Institute of Justice.

Morganthau, T. and P. Katel (1990) "Uncivil Liberties? Debating Whether Drug-War Tactics Are Eroding Constitutional Rights." *Newsweek,* April 29, pp. 18–21.

Myers, H. L. and J. Brzotowski (1982) "Dealers, Dollars, and Drugs: Drug Law Enforcement's Promising New Program." *Drug Enforcement* (Summer): 7–10.

Osborne, J. (1991) *The Spectre of Forfeiture.* Frazier Park, CA: Access Unlimited.

Polsky, N. (1967) *Hustlers, Beats, and Others.* New York: Anchor.

Reid, S. T. (1991) *Crime and Criminology.* San Francisco, CA: Holt, Rinehart, and Winston.

Reuter, P. and M. A. R. Kleiman (1986) "Risks and Prices." In M. Tonry and N. Morris (eds.), *Crime and Justice: An Annual Review of Research,* pp. 289–340. Chicago, IL: University of Chicago Press.

Ronai, C. R. and C. Ellis (1989) "Turn-Ons for Money: Interactional Strategies of the Table Dancer." *Journal of Contemporary Ethnography* 18:271–98.

Roth, J. A. (1962) "Comments on Secret Observation." *Social Problems* 9:283–84.

Schneider, A. and M. P. Flaherty (1991) "Presumed Guilty. The Law's Victims in the War on Drugs." *Pittsburgh Press,* August 11–16.

Shaw, B. (1990) "Fifth Amendment Failures and RICO Forfeitures." *American Business Law Journal* 28:169–200.

Shils, E. A. (1975) In *Center and Periphery: Essays in Macrosociology,* Chicago, IL: University of Chicago Press.

Stellwagen, L. D. (1985) "Use of Forfeiture Sanctions in Drug Cases." *Research in Brief* (July).

Stuart, C. (1990) "When Cops Go Bad." (Film) *Frontline,* July 18.

Trebach, A. S. (1987) *The Great Drug War.* Washington, DC: Drug Policy Foundation.

Trebach, A. S. and K. B. Zeese (1990) *Drug Prohibition and the Conscience of Nations.* Washington, DC: Drug Policy Foundation.

United States Department of Justice (1988) *Research Brief.* Washington, DC: National Institute of Justice.

Walker, W. O. (1992) *Drug Control Policy: Essays in Historical and Comparative Perspective.* University Park, PA: Pennsylvania State University Press.

Weisheit, R. A. (1991) "Drug Use Among Domestic Marijuana Growers." *Contemporary Drug Problems* 17:191–217.

Willson, E. (1990) "Did a Drug Dealer Own Your Home? (Criminal assets may be seized)." *Florida Trend,* February, pp. 6–9.

Wilson, J. Q. (1961) *Varieties of Police Behavior.* Cambridge, MA: Harvard University Press.

———. (1978) *The Investigators: Managing the F.B.I. and the Drug Enforcement Administration.* New York: Basic Books.

Wistosky, S. (1990) *Beyond the War on Drugs: Overcoming a Failed Public Policy.* Buffalo, NY: Prometheus Books.

Wrobleski, H. M. and K. M. Hess (1990) *Introduction to Law Enforcement and Criminal Justice.* St. Paul, MN: West.

Zimring, F. E. and G. Hawkins (1992) *The Search for Rational Drug Control.* New York: Cambridge University Press.

Cases Cited

Austin v. *United States* 113 S. Ct. 2801 (1993)

U.S. v. *A Parcel of Land* 113 S. Ct. 1126 (1993)

Women in Outlaw
Motorcycle Gangs

COLUMBUS B. HOPPER
and JOHNNY MOORE

This article is about the place of women in gangs in general and in outlaw motorcycle gangs in particular. Street gangs have been observed in New York dating back as early as 1825 (Asbury, 1928). The earliest gangs originated in the Five Points district of lower Manhattan and were composed mostly of Irishmen. Even then, there is evidence that girls or young women participated in the organizations as arms and ammunition bearers during gang fights.

The first gangs were of two types: those motivated primarily as fighters and those seeking financial gain. Women were represented in both types and they shared a remarkably similar reputation with street gang women more than 100 years later (Hanson, 1964). They were considered "sex objects" and they were blamed for instigating gang wars through manipulating gang boys. The girls in the first gangs were also seen as undependable, not as loyal to the gang, and they played inferior roles compared to the boys.

The first thorough investigation of youth gangs in the United States was carried out by Thrasher (1927) in Chicago. Thrasher devoted very little attention to gang girls but he stated that there were about half a dozen female gangs out of 1,313 groups he surveyed. He also said that participation by young women in male gangs was limited to auxiliary units for social and sexual activities.

Short (1968) rarely mentioned female gang members in his studies, which were also carried out in Chicago, but he suggested that young women became gang associates because they were less attractive and less socially adequate compared to girls who did not affiliate with gangs.

According to Rice (1963), girls were limited to lower status in New York street gangs because there was no avenue for them to achieve power or prestige in the

Columbus B. Hopper and J. Moore. *Journal of Contemporary Ethnography,* Vol. 18 No. 4, January 1990 383–387 © 1990 Sage Publications, Inc. Reprinted by permission of Sage Publications, Inc.

groups. If they fought, the boys thought them unfeminine; if they opted for a passive role, they were used only for sexual purposes.

Ackley and Fliegel (1960) studied gangs in Boston in which girls played both tough roles and feminine roles. They concluded that preadolescent girls were more likely to engage in fighting and other typically masculine gang actions, while older girls in the gangs played more traditionally feminine roles.

Miller (1973, 1975) found that half of the male gangs in New York had female auxiliaries but he concluded that the participation of young women in the gangs did not differ from that which existed in the past. Miller also pointed out that girls who formed gangs or who were associates of male gangs were lower-class girls who had never been exposed to the women's movement. After studying black gangs in Los Angeles, Klein (1971) believed that, rather than being instigators of gang violence, gang girls were more likely to inhibit fighting.

The most intensive studies of female gang members thus far were done by Campbell (1984, 1986, 1987) on Hispanic gangs in New York City. Although one of the three gangs she studied considered itself a motorcycle gang, it had only one working motorcycle in the total group. Therefore, all of the gangs she discussed should be thought of as belonging to the street gang tradition.

Campbell's description of the gang girls was poignant. The girls were very poor but not anomic; rather, they were true believers in American capitalism, aspiring to success as recent immigrants always have. They were torn between maintaining and rejecting Puerto Rican values while trying to develop a "cool" streetwise image.

As Campbell reported, girl gang members shared typical teenage concerns about proper makeup and wearing the right brands of designer jeans and other clothing. Contrary to popular opinion, they were also concerned about being thought of as whores or bad mothers, and they tried to reject the Latin ideal that women should be totally subordinate to men. The basic picture that came out of Campbell's work was that gang girls had identity problems arising from conflicting values. They wanted to be aggressive and tough, and yet they wished to be thought of as virtuous, respectable mothers.

Horowitz (1983, 1986, 1987) found girls in Chicano gangs to be similar in basic respects to those that Campbell described. The gang members, both male and female, tried to reconcile Latin cultural values of honor and violence with patterns of behavior acceptable to their families and to the communities in which they existed.

The foregoing and other studies showed that girls have participated in street gangs as auxiliaries, as independent groups, and as members in mixed-gender organizations. While gangs have varied in age and ethnicity, girls have had little success in gaining status in the gang world. As reported by Bowker (1978, Bowker and Klein, 1983), however, female street gang activities were increasing in most respects; he thought that independent gangs and mixed groups were increasing more than were female auxiliary units.

Unlike street gangs that go back for many years, motorcycle gangs are relatively new. They first came to public attention in 1947 when the Booze Fighters, Galloping

Gooses, and other groups raided Hollister, California (Morgan, 1978). This incident, often mistakenly attributed to the Hell's Angels, made headlines across the country and established the motorcycle gangs' image. It also inspired *The Wild Ones,* the first of the biker movies released in 1953, starring Marlon Brando and Lee Marvin.

Everything written on outlaw motorcycle gangs has focused on the men in the groups. Many of the major accounts (Eisen, 1970; Harris, 1985; Montegomery, 1976; Reynolds, 1967; Saxon, 1972; Thompson, 1967; Watson, 1980; Wilde, 1977; Willis, 1978; Wolfe, 1968) included a few tantalizing tidbits of information about women in biker culture but in none were there more than a few paragraphs, which underscored the masculine style of motorcycle gangs and their chauvinistic attitudes toward women.

Although the published works on outlaw cyclists revealed the fact that gang members enjoyed active sex lives and had wild parties with women, the women have been faceless; they have not been given specific attention as functional participants in outlaw culture. Indeed, the studies have been so onesided that it has been difficult to think of biker organizations in anything other than a masculine light. We have learned that the men were accompanied by women, but we have not been told anything about the women's backgrounds, their motivations for getting into the groups, or their interpretations of their experiences as biker women.

From the standpoint of the extant literature, biker women have simply existed; they have not had personalities or voices. They have been described only in the contemptuous terms of male bikers as "cunts," "sluts," "whores," and "bitches." Readers have been given the impression that women were necessary nuisances for outlaw motorcyclists. A biker Watson (1980:118) quoted, for example, summed up his attitude toward women as follows: "Hell," he said, "if I could find a man with a pussy, I wouldn't fuck with women. I don't like 'em. They're nothing but trouble."

In this article, we do four things. First, we provide more details on the place of women in arcane biker subculture, we describe the rituals they engage in, and we illustrate their roles as money-makers. Second, we give examples of the motivations and backgrounds of women affiliated with outlaws. Third, we compare the gang participation of motorcycle women to that of street gang girls. Fourth, we show how the place of biker women has changed over the years of our study, and we suggest a reason for the change. We conclude by noting the impact of sex role socialization on biker women.

Methods

The data we present were gathered through participant observation and interviews with outlaw bikers and their female associates over the course of 17 years. Although most of the research was done in Mississippi, Tennessee, Louisiana, and Arkansas, we have occasionally interviewed bikers throughout the nation, including Hawaii. The trends and patterns we present, however, came from our study in the four states listed.

During the course of our research, we have attended biker parties, weddings, funerals, and other functions in which outlaw clubs were involved. In addition, we have visited in gang clubhouses, gone on "runs," and enjoyed cookouts with several outlaw organizations.

It is difficult to enumerate the total amount of time or the number of respondents we have studied because of the necessity of informal research procedures. Bikers would not fill out questionnaires or allow ordinary research methods such as tape recorders or note taking. The total number of outlaw motorcyclists we studied over the years was certainly several hundred. In addition to motorcycle gangs in open society, we also interviewed and corresponded with male and female bikers in state and federal prisons.

The main reason we were able to make contacts with bikers was the background of Johnny Moore, who was once a biker himself. During the 1960s, "Big John" was president of Satan's Dead, an outlaw club on the Mississippi Gulf Coast. He participated in the rituals we describe, and his own experiences and observations provided the details of initiation ceremonies that we relate. As a former club president, Moore was able to get permission for us to visit biker clubhouses, a rare privilege for outsiders.

Most of our research was done on weekends because of our work schedules and because the gangs were more active at this time. The bikers usually had a large party one weekend a month, or more often when the weather was nice, and we were invited to many of these.

At some parties, such as the "Big Blowout" each spring in Gulfport, there were a variety of nonmembers present to observe the motorcycle shows and "old lady" contests as well as to enjoy the party atmosphere. These occasions were especially helpful in our study because bikers were "loose" and easier to approach while partying. We spent more time with three particular "clubs," as outlaw gangs refer to themselves, because of their proximity.

In addition to studying outlaw bikers themselves, we obtained police reports, copies of Congressional hearings that deal with motorcycle gangs, and indictments that were brought against prominent outlaw cyclists. Our attempt was to study biker women and men in as many ways as possible. We were honest in explaining the purpose of our research to our respondents. They were told that our goal was only to learn more about outlaw motorcycle clubs as social organizations.

Dilemmas of Biker Research

Studying bikers was a conflicted experience for us. It was almost impossible to keep from admiring their commitment, freedom, boldness, and fearlessness; at the same time, we saw things that caused us discomfort and consternation because bikers' actions were sometimes bizarre. We saw bikers do things completely foreign to our personal values. Although we did not condone these activities, we did not express our objections for two reasons. First, we would not have been able to continue our study. Second, it was too dangerous to take issue with outlaws on their own turf.

Studying bikers was a risky undertaking for us, even without criticizing them. At times when we were not expecting any problems, conditions became hazardous. In Jackson, Tennessee, for example, one morning in 1985 we walked into an area where bikers had camped out all night. Half asleep and hung over, several of them jumped up and pulled guns on us because they thought we might be members of a rival gang that had killed five of their "brothers" several years earlier. If Grubby, a biker who recognized us from previous encounters, had not interceded in our behalf, we could have been killed or seriously injured.

Bikers would not humor many questions, and they did not condone uninvited comments. Even seemingly insignificant remarks sometimes caused a problem. In Biloxi on one occasion, we had an appointment to visit a biker clubhouse late on a Saturday afternoon in 1986. When we were admitted into the main room of the building, two women picked up four pistols that had been on a coffee table and scurried into a bedroom. Several men remained in front of a television set, watching a wrestling match.

Because we looked upon professional wrestling as a humorous sham, one of us made a light reference to it. Immediately the bikers became tense and angry; it was clear that another sarcastic comment would have resulted in our being literally thrown out of the clubhouse. In this way, we accidentally learned that some bikers take television wrestling seriously. It would have been a bad mistake to have questioned them about their reasons for liking the dubious sport. There was a human skull on a pole in front of their clubhouse but we thought it better to ignore it!

For practical purposes, both male and female bikers worship the Harley David-son motorcycle. One Mississippi group that we studied extensively had an old flat-head "Hog" mounted on a high tree stump at the entrance to their clubhouse. When going in or out, members bowed to the old Harley or saluted it as an icon of the highest order. They took it very seriously. Had we not shown respect for their obeisance, our relationship would have been terminated, probably in a violent manner.

It was hard to fathom the chasm between bikers and the rest of us. Outlaw cyclists have no constraints except those their club mandates. When a biker spoke of something being "legal," he was referring to the bylaws of his club rather than to the laws of a state or nation. A biker's "legal" name was his club name that was usually inscribed on his jacket or "colors." Club names were typically one word, and this was how other members and female associates referred to a biker. Such descriptive names as Trench Mouth, Grimy, Animal, Spooky, and Red sufficed for most bikers we studied. As we knew them, bikers lived virtually a tribal life-style with few restraints. The freedom they enjoyed was not simply being "in the wind"; it was also emotional. Whereas conventional people fear going to prison, the bikers were confident that they had many brothers who would look out for them inside the walls. Consequently, the threat of confinement had little influence on a biker's behavior, as far as we could tell.

Perhaps because society gave them so little respect, the bikers we studied insisted on being treated with deference. They gave few invitations to nonmembers or "citizens," and they were affronted when something they offered was refused. Our respondents loved to party, and they did not understand anyone who did not. Once we were invited to a club party by a man named Cottonmouth. The party was to begin at 9:00 p.m. on a Sunday night. When we told Cottonmouth that we had to leave at seven in the evening to get back home, we lost his good will and respect entirely. He could not comprehend how we could let anything take precedence over a "righteous" club party.

Bikers were suspicious of all conversations with us and with other citizens; they were not given to much discussion even among themselves. They followed a slogan we saw posted in several clubhouses: "One good fist is worth a thousand words." Studying outlaw cyclists became more difficult rather than easier over the course of our study. They grew increasingly concerned about being investigated by undercover agents. . . . At times, over the last years of our study, respondents whom we had known for months would suddenly accuse us of being undercover "pigs" when we seemed overly curious about their activities.

Our study required much commitment to research goals. We believed it was important to study biker women and we did so in the only way open to us—on the terms of the bikers themselves. We were field observers rather than critics or reformers, even when witnessing things that caused us anguish.

Problems in Studying Biker Women

Although it was difficult to do research on outlaw motorcycle gangs generally, it was even harder to study the women in them. In many gangs, the women were reluctant to speak to outsiders when the men were present. We did not hear male bikers tell the women to refrain from talking to us. Rather, we often had a man point to a woman and say, "Ask her," when we posed a question that concerned female associates. Usually, the woman's answer was, "I don't know." Consequently, it took longer to establish rapport with female bikers than it did with the men.

Surprisingly, male bikers did not object to our being alone with the women. Occasionally, we talked to a female biker by ourselves and this is when we were able to get most of our information and quotations from them. In one interview with a biker and his woman in their home, the woman would not express an opinion about anything. When her man left to help a fellow biker whose motorcycle had broken down on the road, the woman turned into an articulate and intelligent individual. Upon the return of the man, however, she resumed the role of a person without opinions.

The Place of Women in Outlaw Motorcycle Gangs

Although national outlaw motorcycle clubs of the 1980s had restricted their membership to adult males (Quinn, 1983), women were important in the outlaw life-style we observed. We rarely saw a gang without female associates sporting colors similar to those the men wore.

To the casual observer, all motorcycle gang women might have appeared the same. There were, however, two important categories of women in the biker world: "mamas" and "old ladies." A mama belonged to the entire gang. She had to be available for sex with any member and she was subject to the authority of any brother. Mamas wore jackets that showed they were the "property" of the club as a whole.

An old lady belonged to an individual man; the jacket she wore indicated whose woman she was. Her colors said, for example, "Property of Frog." Such a woman was commonly referred to as a "patched old lady." In general terms, old ladies were regarded as wives. Some were in fact married to the members whose patches they wore. In most instances, a male biker and his old lady were married only in the eyes of the club. Consequently, a man could terminate his relationship with an old lady at any time he chose, and some men had more than one old lady.

A man could require his old lady to prostitute herself for him. He could also order her to have sex with anyone he designated. Under no circumstances, however, could an old lady have sex with anyone else unless she had her old man's permission.

If he wished to, a biker could sell his old lady to the highest bidder, and we saw this happen. When a woman was auctioned off, it was usually because a biker needed money in a hurry, such as when he wanted a part for his motorcycle or because his old lady had disappointed him. The buyer in such transactions was usually another outlaw.

Rituals Involving Women

Outlaw motorcycle gangs, as we perceived them, formed a subculture that involved rituals and symbols. Although each group varied in its specific ceremonies, all of the clubs we studied had several. There were rites among bikers that had nothing to do with women and sex but a surprising number involved both.

The first ritual many outlaws were exposed to, and one they understandably never forgot, was the initiation into a club. Along with other requirements, in some gangs, the initiate had to bring a "sheep" when he was presented for membership. A sheep was a woman who had sex with each member of the gang during an initiation. In effect, the sheep was the new man's gift to the old members.

Group sex, known as "pulling a train," also occurred at other times. Although some mamas or other biker groupies (sometimes called "sweetbutts") occasionally volunteered to pull a train, most instances of train pulling were punitive in nature. Typically, women were being penalized for some breach of biker conduct when they pulled a train.

An old lady could be forced to pull a train if she did not do something her old man told her to do, or if she embarrassed him by talking back to him in front of another member. We never observed anyone pulling a train but we were shown clubhouse rooms that were designated "train rooms," and two women told us they had been punished in this manner.

One of the old ladies who admitted having pulled a train said her offense was failing to keep her man's motorcycle clean. The other had not noticed that her biker was holding an empty bottle at a party. (A good old lady watched her man as he drank beer and got him another one when he needed it without having to be told to do so.) We learned that trains were pulled in vaginal, oral, or anal sex. The last was considered to be the harshest punishment.

Another biker ritual involving women was the earning of "wings," a patch similar to the emblem a pilot wears. There were different types of wings that showed that the wearer had performed oral sex on a woman in front of his club. Although the practice did not exist widely, several members of some groups we studied wore wings.

A biker's wings demonstrated unlimited commitment to his club. One man told us he earned his wings by having oral sex with a woman immediately after she had pulled a train; he indicated that the brothers were impressed with his abandon and indifference to hygiene. Bikers honored a member who laughed at danger by doing shocking things

The sex rituals were important in many biker groups because they served at least one function other than status striving among members. The acts ensured that it was difficult for law enforcement officials, male or female, to infiltrate a gang.

Biker Women as Money-Makers

Among most of the groups we studied, biker women were expected to be engaged in economic pursuits for their individual men and sometimes for the entire club. Many of the old ladies and mamas were employed in nightclubs as topless and nude dancers. Although we were not able to get exact figures on the proportion of "table dancers" who were biker women, in two or three cities almost all of them were working for outlaw clubs.

A lot of the dancers were proud of their bodies and their dancing abilities. We saw them perform their routines in bars and at parties. At the "Big Blowout" in Gulfport, which is held in an open field outside of the city, in 1987 and 1988 there was a stage with a sound system set up for the dancers. The great majority of the 2,000 people in attendance were bikers from around the country so the performances were free.

Motorcycle women who danced in the nightclubs we observed remained under the close scrutiny of the biker men. The men watched over them for two reasons. First, they wanted to make sure that the women were not keeping money on the side; second, the cyclists did not want their women to be exploited by the bar owners. Some bikers in one gang we knew beat up a nightclub owner because they thought he was "ripping off" the dancers. The man was beaten so severely with axe handles that he had to be hospitalized for several months.

While some of the biker women limited their nightclub activities to dancing, a number of them also let the customers whose tables they danced on know they were available for "personal" sessions in a private place. As long as they were making good money regularly, the bikers let the old ladies choose their own level of nightclub participation. Thus some women danced nude only on stage; others performed on stage and did table dances as well. A smaller number did both types of dances and also served as prostitutes.

Not all of the money-making biker women we encountered were employed in such "sleazy" occupations. A few had "square" jobs as secretaries, factory workers, and sales persons. One biker woman had a job in a bank. A friend and fellow biker lady described her as follows: "Karen is a chameleon. When she goes to work, she is a fashion plate; when she is at home, she looks like a whore. She is every man's dream!" Like the others employed in less prestigious labor, however, Karen turned her salary over to her old man on payday.

A few individuals toiled only intermittently when their bikers wanted a new motorcycle or something else that required more money than they usually needed. The majority of motorcycle women we studied, however, were regularly engaged in work of some sort.

Motivations and Backgrounds of Biker Women

In view of the ill treatment the women received from outlaws, it was surprising that so many women wanted to be with them. Bikers told us there was never a shortage of women who wanted to join them, and we observed this to be true. Although it was unwise for men to draw conclusions about the reasons mamas and old ladies chose their life-styles, we surmised three interrelated factors from conversations with them.

First, some women, like the male bikers, truly loved and were excited by motorcycles. Cathy was an old lady who exhibited this trait. "Motorcycles have always turned me on," she said. "There's nothing like feeling the wind on your titties. Nothing's as exciting as riding a motorcycle. You feel as free as the wind."

Cathy did not love motorcycles indiscriminately, however. She was imbued with the outlaw's love for the Harley Davidson. "If you don't ride a Hog," she stated, "you don't ride nothing. I wouldn't be seen dead on a rice burner" (Japanese model). Actually, she loved only a customized bike or "chopper." Anything else she called a "garbage wagon."

When we asked her why she wanted to be part of a gang if she simply loved motorcycles, Cathy answered:

There's always someone there. You don't agree with society so you find someone you like who agrees with you. The true meaning for me is to express my individuality as part of a group.

Cathy started "putting" (riding a motorcycle) when she was 15 years old and she dropped out of school shortly thereafter. Even with a limited education, she gave the impression that she was a person who thought seriously. She had a butterfly tattoo that she said was an emblem of the freedom she felt on a bike. When we talked to her, she was 26 and had a daughter. She had ridden with several gangs but she was proud that she had always been an old lady rather than a mama.

The love for motorcycles had not dimmed for Cathy over the years. She still found excitement in riding and even in polishing a chopper. "I don't feel like I'm being used. I'm having fun," she insisted. She told us that she would like to change some things if she had her life to live over, but not biking. "I feel sorry for other people; I'm doing exactly what I want to do," she concluded.

A mama named Pamela said motorcycles thrilled her more than anything else she had encountered in life. Although she had been involved with four biker clubs in different sections of the country, she was originally from Mississippi and she was with a Mississippi gang when we talked to her. Pamela said she graduated from high school only because the teachers wanted to get rid of her. "I tried not to give any trouble, but my mind just wasn't on school."

She was 24 when we saw her. Her family background was a lot like most of the women we knew. "I got beat a lot," she remarked. "My daddy and my mom both drank and ran around on each other. They split up for good my last year in school. I ain't seen either of them for a long time."

Cathy described her feelings about motorcycles as follows:

I can't remember when I first saw one. It seems like I dreamed about them even when I was a kid. It's hard to describe why I like bikes. But I know this for sure. The sound a motorcycle makes is really exciting—it turns me on, no joke. I mean really! I feel great when I'm on one. There's no past, no future, no trouble. I wish I could ride one and never get off.

The second thing we thought drew women to motorcycle gangs was a preference for macho men. "All real men ride Harleys," a mama explained to us. Generally, biker women had contempt for men who wore suits and ties. We believed it was the disarming boldness of bikers that attracted many women.

Barbara, who was a biker woman for several years, was employed as a secretary in a university when we talked to her in 1988. Although Barbara gradually withdrew from biker life because she had a daughter she wanted reared in a more conventional way, she thought the university men she associated with were wimps. She said:

Compared to bikers, the guys around here (her university) have no balls at all. They hem and haw, they whine and complain. They try to impress you with their intelligence and sensitivity. They are game players. Bikers come at you head on. If they want to fuck you, they just say so. They don't care what you think of them. I'm attracted to strong men who know what they want. Bikers are authentic. With them, what you see is what you get.

Barbara was an unusual biker lady who came from an affluent family. She was the daughter of a highly successful man who owned a manufacturing and distributing company. Barbara was 39 when we interviewed her. She had gotten into a motorcycle gang at the age of 23. She described her early years to us:

I was rebellious as long as I can remember. It's not that I hated my folks. Maybe it was the times (1960s) or something. But I just never could be the way I was expected to be. I dated "greasers," I made bad grades; I never applied myself. I've always liked my men rough. I don't mean I like to be beat up, but a real man. Bikers are like cowboys; I classify them together. Freedom and strength I guess are what it takes for me.

Barbara did not have anything bad to say about bikers. She still kept in touch with a few of her friends in her old club. "It was like a family to me," she said. "You could always depend on somebody if anything happened. I still trust bikers more than any other people I know." She also had become somewhat reconciled with her parents, largely because of her daughter. "I don't want anything my parents have personally, but my daughter is another person. I don't want to make her be just like me if she doesn't want to," she concluded.

A third factor that we thought made women associate with biker gangs was low self-esteem. Many we studied believed they deserved to be treated as people of little worth. Their family backgrounds had prepared them for subservience.

Jeanette, an Arkansas biker woman, related her experience as follows:

My mother spanked me frequently. My father beat me. There was no sexual abuse but a lot of violence. My parents were both alcoholics. They really hated me. I never got a kind word from either of them. They told me a thousand times I was nothing but a pain in the ass.

Jeanette began hanging out with bikers when she left home at the age of 15. She was 25 when we talked to her in 1985. Although he was dominating and abusive, her old man represented security and stability for Jeanette. She said he had broken her jaw with a punch. "He straightened me out that time," she said. "I started to talk back to him but I didn't get three words out of my mouth." Her old man's name was tattooed over her heart.

In Jeanette's opinion, she had a duty to obey and honor her man. They had been married by another biker who was a Universal Life minister. "The Bible tells me to be obedient to my husband," she seriously remarked to us. Jeanette also told us she hated lesbians. "I go in lesbian bars and kick ass," she said. She admitted she had performed lesbian acts but she said she did so only when her old man made her do them. The time her man broke her jaw was when she objected to being ordered to sleep with a woman who was dirty. Jeanette believed her biker had really grown to love her. "I can express my opinion once and then he decides what I am going to do," she concluded.

In the opinions of the women we talked to, a strong man kept a woman in line. Most old ladies had the lowly task of cleaning and polishing a motorcycle every day. They did so without thanks and they did not expect or want any praise. To them, consideration for others was a sign of weakness in a man. They wanted a man to let them know who was boss.

Motorcycle Women versus Street Gang Girls

The motorcycle women in our study were similar to the street gang girls described by Campbell and Horowitz because their lives were built around deviant social organizations that were controlled by members of the opposite sex. There were, however, important differences that resulted from the varying natures of the two subcultures.

As our terminology suggests, female associates of motorcycle gangs were women as opposed to the teenage girls typically found in street gangs. The biker women who would tell us their age averaged 26 years, and the great majority appeared to be in their mid-20s. While some biker women told us they began associating with outlaws when they were teenagers, we did not observe any young girls in the clubs other than the children of members.

Male bikers were older than the members of street gangs and it followed that their female companions were older as well. In one of the outlaw clubs we surveyed, the men averaged 34 years old. Biker men also wanted women old enough to be legally able to work in bars and in other jobs.

All of the biker women we studied were white, whereas street gang girls in previous studies were predominantly from minority groups. We were aware of one black motorcycle gang in Memphis but we were unable to make contact with it.

Biker women were not homogeneous in their backgrounds. While street gangs were composed of "home boys" and "home girls" who usually grew up and remained in the areas in which their gangs operated, the outlaw women had often traveled widely. Since bikers were mobile, it was rare for us to find a woman who had not moved around a lot. Most of the biker women we saw were also high school graduates. Two had attended college although neither had earned a degree.

While Campbell found girls in street gangs to be interested in brand name clothes and fashions, we did not notice this among motorcycle women. In fact, it was our impression that biker ladies were hostile toward such interests. Perhaps because so many were dancers, they were proud of their bodies but they did not try to fit into popular feminine dress styles. As teenagers they may have been clothes-conscious, but as adults biker women did not want to follow the lead of society's trend setters.

• • •

As another consequence of the age difference, biker women were not torn between their families and the gang. Almost all of the old ladies and mamas were happy to be rid of their past lives. They had made a clean break and they did not try to live in two worlds. The motorcycle gang was their focal point without rival. Whereas street gang girls often left their children with their mothers or grandparents, biker women did not, but they wanted to be good mothers just the same. The children of biker women were more integrated into the gang. Children went with their mothers on camping trips and on brief motorcycle excursions or "runs." When it was necessary to leave the children at home, two or three old ladies alternately remained behind and looked after all of the children in the gang.

The biker men were also concerned about the children and handled them with tenderness. A biker club considered the offspring of members as belonging to the entire group, and each person felt a duty to protect them. Both male and female bikers also gave special treatment to pregnant women. A veteran biker woman related her experience to us as follows:

> Kids are sacred in a motorcycle club. When I was pregnant, I was treated great. Biker kids are tough but they are obedient and get lots of love. I've never seen a biker's kid who was abused.

As mentioned, the average biker woman was expected to be economically productive, a trait not emphasized for female street gang members or auxiliaries. It appeared to us that the women in motorcycle gangs were more thoroughly under the domination of their male associates than were girls described in street gang studies.

The Changing Role of Biker Women

During the 17 years of our study, we noticed a change in the position of women in motorcycle gangs. In the groups we observed in the 1960s, the female participants were more spontaneous in their sexual encounters and they interacted more completely in club activities of all kinds. To be sure, female associates of outlaw motorcycle gangs have never been on a par with the men. Biker women have worn "property" jackets for a long time, but in the outlaw scene of 1989, the label had almost literally become fact.

Bikers have traditionally been notoriously active sexually with the women in the clubs. When we began hanging out with bikers, however, the men and the women were more nearly equal in their search for gratification. Sex was initiated as much by the women as it was by the men. By the end of our study, the men had taken total control of sexual behavior, as far as we could observe, at parties and outings. As the male bikers gained control of sex, it became more ceremonial.

While the biker men we studied in the late 1980s did not have much understanding of sex rituals, their erotic activities seemed to be a means to an end rather than an end in themselves, as they were in the early years of our study. That is to say, biker sex became more concerned with achieving status and brotherhood than with "fun" and physical gratification. We used to hear biker women telling jokes about sex but even this had stopped.

The shift in the position of biker women was not only due to the increasing ritualism in sex; it was also a consequence of the changes in the organizational goals of motorcycle gangs as evidenced by their evolving activities. As we have noted, many motorcycle gangs developed an interest in money; in doing so, they became complex organizations with both legal and illegal sources of income (McGuire, 1986).

When bikers became more involved in illegal behavior, they followed the principles of sex segregation and sex typing in the underworld generally. The low place of women has been well documented in the studies of criminal organizations (Steffensmeier, 1983). The bikers did not have much choice in the matter. When they got involved in financial dealings with other groups in the rackets, motorcycle gangs had to adopt a code that had prevailed for many years; they had to keep women out of "the business."

Early motorcycle gangs were organized for excitement and adventure; money-making was not important. Their illegal experiences were limited to individual members rather than to the gang as a whole. In the original gangs, most male participants had regular jobs, and the gang was a part-time organization that met about once a week. At the weekly gatherings, the emphasis was on swilling beer, soaking each other in suds, and having sex with the willing female associates who were enthusiastic revelers themselves. The only money the old bikers wanted was just enough to keep the beer flowing. They did not regard biker women as sources of income; they thought of them simply as fellow hedonists.

Most of the gangs we studied in the 1980s required practically all of the members' time. They were led by intelligent presidents who had organizational ability. One gang president had been a military officer for several years. He worked out in a gym regularly and did not smoke or drink excessively. In his presence, we got the impression that he was in control, that he led a disciplined life. In contrast, when we began our study, the bikers, including the leaders, always seemed on the verge of personal disaster.

A few motorcycle gangs we encountered were prosperous. They owned land and businesses that had to be managed. In the biker transition from hedonistic to economic interests, women became defined as money-makers rather than companions. Whereas bikers used to like for their women to be tattooed, many we met in 1988 and 1989 did not want their old ladies to have tattoos because they reduced their market value as nude dancers and prostitutes. We also heard a lot of talk about biker women not being allowed to use drugs for the same reason. Even for the men, some said drug usage was not good because a person hooked on drugs would be loyal to the drug, not to the gang.

When we asked bikers if women had lost status in the clubs over the years, their answers were usually negative. "How can you lose something you never had?" a Florida biker replied when we queried him. The fact is, however, that most bikers in 1989 did not know much about the gangs of 20 years earlier. Furthermore, the change was not so much in treatment as it was in power. It was a sociological change rather than a physical one. In some respects, women were treated better physically after the transition than they were in the old days. The new breed did not want to damage the "merchandise."

An old lady's status in a gang of the 1960s was an individual thing, depending on her relationship with her man. If her old man wanted to, he could share his position to a limited extent with his woman. Thus the place of women within a gang was variable. While all women were considered inferior to all men, individual females often gained access to some power, or at least they knew details of what was happening.

By 1989, the position of women had solidified. A woman's position was no longer influenced by idiosyncratic factors. Women had been formally defined as inferior. In many biker club weddings, for example, the following became part of the ceremony:

You are an inferior woman being married to a superior man. Neither you nor any of your female children can ever hold membership in this club or own any of its property.

Although the bikers would not admit that their attitudes toward women had shifted over the years, we noticed the change. Biker women were completely dominated and controlled as our study moved into the late 1980s. When we were talking to a biker after a club funeral in North Carolina in 1988, he turned to his woman and said, "Bitch, if you don't take my dick out, I'm going to piss in my pants." Without hesitation, the woman unzipped his trousers and helped him relieve himself. To us, this symbolized the lowly place of women in the modern motorcycle gang.

Conclusion

Biker women seemed to represent another version of what Romenesko and Miller (1989) have referred to as a "double jeopardy" among female street hustlers. Like the street prostitutes, most biker women came from backgrounds in which they had limited opportunities in the licit or conventional world, and they faced even more exploitation and subjugation in the illicit or deviant settings they had entered in search of freedom.

It is ironic that biker women considered themselves free while they were under the domination of biker men. They had the illusion of freedom because they lived with men who were bold and unrestrained. Unlike truly liberated women, however, the old ladies and mamas did not compete with men; instead, they emulated and glorified male bikers. Biker women thus illustrated the pervasive power of socialization and the difficulty of changing deeply ingrained views of the relations between the sexes inculcated in their family life. They believed that they should be submissive to men because they were taught that males were dominant. While they adamantly stated that they were living the life they chose, it was evident that their choices were guided by values that they had acquired in childhood.

Although they had rebelled against the strictures of straight society, their orientation in gender roles made them align with outlaw bikers, the epitome of macho men.

References

Ackley, E. and B. Fliegel (1960) "A social work approach to street-corner girls." *Social Problems* 5: 29–31.

Asbury, H. (1928) *The Gangs of New York.* New York: Alfred A. Knopf.

Bowker, L (1978) *Women, Crime, and the Criminal Justice System.* Lexington, MA: D. C. Heath.

Bowker, L. and M. Klein (1983) "The etiology of female juvenile delinquency and gang membership: a test of psychological and social structural explanations." *Adolescence* 8: 731–751.

Campbell, A. (1984) *The Girls in the Gang.* New York: Basil Blackwell.

Campbell, A. (1986) "Self report of fighting by females." *British J. of Criminology* 26: 28–46.

Campbell, A. (1987) "Self-definition by rejection: the case of gang girls." *Social Problems* 34: 451–466.

Eisen, J. (1970) *Altamont.* New York: Avon Books.

Hanson, K. (1964) *Rebels in the Streets.* Englewood Cliffs, NJ: Prentice-Hall.

Harris, M. (1985) *Bikers.* London: Faber & Faber.

Hopper, C. and J. Moore (1983) "Hell on wheels: the outlaw motorcycle gangs." *J. of Amer. Culture* 6: 58–64.

Hopper, C. and J. Moore (1984) "Gang slang." *Harpers* 261: 34.

Horowitz, R. (1983) *Honor and the American Dream.* New Brunswick, NJ: Rutgers Univ. Press.

Horowitz, R. (1986) "Remaining an outsider: membership as a threat to research rapport." *Urban Life* 14: 238–251.

Horowitz, R. (1987) "Community tolerance of gang violence." *Social Problems* 34: 437–450.

Klein, M. (1971) *Street Gangs and Street Workers.* Englewood Cliffs, NJ: Prentice Hall.

Lord, W. (1978) *Day of Infamy.* New York: Bantam.

McGuire, P. (1986) "Outlaw motorcycle gangs: organized crime on wheels." *National Sheriff* 38: 68–75.

Miller, W. (1973) "Race, sex and gangs." *Society* 11: 32–35.

Miller, W. (1975) *Violence by Youth Gangs and Youth Groups as a Crime Problem in Major American Cities.* Washington, DC: Government Printing Office.

Montegomery, R. (1976) "The outlaw motorcycle subculture." *Canadian J. of Criminology and Corrections* 18: 332–342.

Morgan, R. (1978) *The Angels Do Not Forget.* San Diego: Law and Justice.

Quinn, J. (1983) "Outlaw Motorcycle Clubs: A Sociological Analysis." M.A. thesis: University of Miami.

Reynolds, F. (1967) *Freewheeling Frank.* New York: Grove Press.

Rice, R. (1963) "A reporter at large: the Persian queens." *New Yorker* 39: 153.

Romenesko, K. and E. Miller (1989) "The second step in double jeopardy: appropriating the labor of female street hustlers." *Crime and Delinquency* 35: 109–135.

Saxon, K. (1972) *Wheels of Rage.* (privately published)

Short, J. (1968) *Gang Delinquency and Delinquent Subcultures.* Chicago, IL: University of Chicago Press.

Steffensmeier, D. (1983) "Organization properties and sex-segregation in the underworld: building a sociology theory of sex differences in crime." *Social Forces* 61: 1010–1032.

Thompson, H. (1967) *Hell's Angels.* New York: Random House.

Thrasher. F. (1927) *The Gang: A Study of 1,313 Gangs in Chicago.* Chicago, IL: University of Chicago Press.

Watson, J. (1980) "Outlaw motorcyclists as an outgrowth of lower class values." *Deviant Behavior* 4: 31–48.

Wilde. S. (1977) *Barbarians on Wheels.* Secaucus, NJ: Chartwell Books.

Willis, P. (1978) *Profane Culture.* London: Routledge & Kegan Paul.

Wolfe, T. (1968) *The Electric Kool-Aid Acid Test.* New York: Farrer, Straus & Giroux.

Into the Darkness: An Ethnographic Study of Witchcraft and Death

WENDY G. LOZANO
and TANICE G. FOLTZ

This paper explores the religion of radical feminist witches and how it provides both the dying and the living with a meaningful framework for interpreting death. . . . An analysis of a Wiccan funeral demonstrates how the religion gives meaning to life and death, links individuals to the community, helps to reestablish group solidarity, and provides a shared subjective reality for those who acknowledge only a divine female principle called "The Goddess." The data for this paper were collected through participant observation in the coven's rituals and selected social events over a period of one year. In-depth interviews were conducted with all coven members as well.

Introduction

This paper is part of a larger study of a coven of radical feminist witches, a group whose religious or spiritual base derives from what is known as the Old Religion, the Craft, or Wicca and is informed by the second wave of feminism. Contemporary witches believe that the roots of their religion predate Judeo-Christian tradition, drawing from the Goddess-centered cultures believed to have been located in and around Europe, the Mediterranean, and Aegean. They freely admit, however, that they practice the Old Religion in new ways (Starhawk, 1988). They believe these new ways fit societal changes and their own perceived needs. Wicca, in both its radical feminist and more traditional forms, is an example of what Ellwood (1979) calls an "emergent religion" or "alternative spirituality" existing alongside mainline religions, although often suppressed. It possesses a rich system of symbols and a growing community of believers, who are brought together by participating in ritual and magic.

W. Griffin Lozano and T. Foltz. (1990) "Into the Darkness: An Ethnographic Study of Witchcraft and Death." *Qualitative Sociology,* Vol. 13, No. 3, 1990. Copyright © 1990.

Religion and Death

All viable religions allocate an important position in their constitutive symbolism to the experience and event of death, according to functional sociologists Parsons and Lidz. Death has such disorienting effects that a religion

> . . . *must provide a framework for interpreting death that is meaningful and appropriate, in relation to other elements of the culture, for defining attitudes regarding both the deaths of others and the prospect of one's own death (Parsons and Lidz, 1967:135).*

Yinger (1957) also emphasizes that one of the fundamental effects of religion is to rescue individuals and communities from the destructiveness of death.

Integration theories show how religion helps to maintain a state of homeostasis in a community when certain events threaten its stability. Through death and funeral rites, religion provides a potent means of reintegration of the group's "shaken solidarity" and reestablishes its morale (Geertz, 1973; Malinowski, 1948; Vernon, 1970). Funeral behavior thus serves an important social function.

• • •

In stressing the importance of religion to social solidarity, Durkheim observed that religion is ultimately collective, expressing shared meanings and social ideals that unite participants into one moral community (Durkheim, 1915). Collective representations and social rituals are essential to religion precisely because language and symbols depend upon shared meanings. To examine shared meanings reveals a shared reality. By examining the worldview of radical witches, their rituals and their symbols, we can better understand their shared subjective reality.

• • •

Methodology

Data were collected through what Denzin (1970) calls a "triangulation" of qualitative methods. Primary sources of data were fieldnotes written independently by both researchers. Observations covered all ritual activities, planning sessions, and mountain retreats we attended, as well as a wedding and a funeral. After several months in the setting, when we had gained some understanding of appropriate questions, we conducted indepth interviews with all coven members. Our interviews were semistructured, making use of a topical guide (see Gorden, 1969). We employed team research in order to increase perspectives on the setting (see Douglas, 1976). One of us was less experienced in ethnographic methods, but more familiar with feminist theory and some of the group's beliefs about mythology and goddesses. The other was an ethnographer with previous research and publication on a para-religious healing group. We each interviewed witches with whom we felt some affinity. We interviewed the core coven members more than once to cross-validate our data and ask newly formulated questions. Our team fieldwork extended from March 1988 through Summer 1989, when Foltz moved out of the area for job reasons. Lozano continued to attend rituals occasionally and maintain relations with the coven. In addition to fieldwork and interviewing, we sought out literature, artifacts, workshops, and festivals on feminist spirituality, neo-paganism and goddess-worship. We then employed a modified form of "indefinite triangulation" as a validity check (see Circourel, 1964).

Coven Members

The coven we call the Circle of the Redwood Moon was composed of seven core members during the period of our research. The seven included three women defined as Priestesses, one Initiate, and three Apprentices. The women ranged in age from 28 to 48 and came from working class and lower middle class backgrounds. They came to witchcraft at widely different ages—one in her early teens and the latest in her 40s. They came from a variety of Western religions. Yet a common thread was that all but one can be classified as a spiritual "seeker" (see Lofland and Skonovd, 1981) who had actively sought out and explored other religions and spiritual traditions before settling on Wicca. The exception is a core coven member who, at age 11, reported hearing a voice inform her that "she belonged to the Lady." She says she had no idea what that meant at the time, but became a self-avowed pagan by the age of 17 and now has been one for 22 years. Out of respect for her long history and experience with the Craft, she was given the title of Elder Priestess by the coven.

By the time of this study, most of the women had taken some college courses. Two had completed four-year degrees, with one then taking some post-graduate study and the other working on a Master's Degree. Three women held clerical jobs, one was a salesclerk, one a "psych-tech" on a mental ward, and two were unemployed. Five of the seven women were Caucasian, the oldest woman was an African-American, and one woman was a Latina. Only the Elder Priestess, who had been with the coven almost since its start in 1971, was involved in a heterosexual relationship at the time of our research. She and her husband were married by Spiderwoman, Priestess of Ritual and Magic, during the Spring of 1989. All other members were self-identified lesbians, most of whom had held romantic relationships with men in the past. Two of them were previously married, and one has adult children.

The Setting

Most of the ritual activities took place in the home of two of the witches, Aletheia and Spiderwoman. They had been partners for three years by the time we entered the setting. Their condominium was located in a working-class neighborhood on the outskirts of Los Angeles. The decor consisted of soft lighting, a variety of goddess figurines, and numerous "witchy" artifacts, including a pentacle door harp, a frosted glass light in the shape of a crescent moon, and a crystal ball. During rituals, the glasstopped coffee table in the living room was often moved to the side and a small round table was used as an altar in the center of the room. The dining area held bookcases filled with books on philosophy, feminism, lesbianism, witchcraft, and goddess-worship. The large heavy table in the dining area served as a place for the women to gather and plan future rituals and other coven activities. Sometimes this area was used for the ritual, and the large table would be moved outside to a small patio for sharing potluck items afterward. The patio was rimmed by a foot of dirt in which a few abundant rose bushes grew. In the corner was a jacuzzi where the witches sometimes bathed after ceremonies.

Rituals that were open to other women took place at a campsite in a nearby mountain range. The death rituals took place at a funeral home and cemetery described later in this paper.

Gaining Entree

We gained entree to the Circle of the Redwood Moon when an opportunity presented itself near the end of Spring Semester, 1988. One of Lozano's students invited her class to attend a Spring Equinox ritual sponsored by her coven. (We later found that "open ritual" is one way the coven recruits new members, if not to the coven itself, to the religion.) We gained access to the coven by making use of what Reimer (1977) calls an "opportunistic" research strategy. Lozano was informed that everyone attending the ritual was expected to participate actively; no one would be allowed simply to observe. Given the stereotypes of witchcraft and its practitioners, we entered the setting with some trepidation about what we might encounter and what might be expected of us during the ritual. We quickly discovered we had nothing to fear.

The ritual was a spring celebration in which every person was to make a personal commitment to the earth and to the women's community. Members of the coven "raised energy and cast a circle," which is done at the beginning of every ritual as a means of "creating sacred space" (see Starhawk, 1979:55), and various priestesses led visualizations, meditations, dancing and chanting for the next hour or so. The ritual closed with a potluck "feast," women's music, and informal socializing. We left earlier than the others, saturated and exhausted by what we had seen, heard, and felt. Our first experience with Wiccan ritual and our debriefing session on the way home left one of the authors feeling hesitant about pursuing the research, while the other felt the group provided a fascinating setting to explore sociologically. Within a few days, we had both decided to pursue this unique research opportunity.

Lozano contacted the coven to discuss the possibility of our conducting team research. Her student served as "gatekeeper" and lobbied for the project. The other coven members were extremely protective. In a long interview, however, Lozano apparently answered their questions satisfactorily and gained permission on a tentative basis. A bargain was made that the witches would not have editorial control over what we wrote, but could control our access to the ritual settings. We agreed that, while we would not do anything to violate our personal ethics, we would actively participate at some level during the rituals.

Research Roles

In keeping with our epistemological ideal of gaining understanding from a "member's perspective" (Jules-Rosette, 1975), we engaged in participant-observation using a phenomenological approach. Similar to Damrell (1977, 1978), Rochford (1985), and Forrest (1986), we felt it important to experience the subjective meanings that are integral to witchcraft, rather than simply to document what we saw from an "objective" point of view. Since experiencing an altered state of consciousness was deemed critical in grasping the meaning of the coven's worldview, we found it important to immerse ourselves in the ritual experience over time, thereby "becoming the phenomenon" (Mehan and Wood, 1975). This process was limited, however, by the fact that we did not undergo apprenticeship training with the coven.

A central issue in ethnographic research is the role the participant-observer adopts. For example, Gold (1958) located four roles that field researchers adopt on a continuum between the "complete observer" and the "complete participant." Adler and Adler (1987) discussed three "membership roles" that sociologists "carve out" for themselves in fieldwork settings: peripheral-, active-, and complete-member researcher roles. Using the Adlers' terminology, we began our research on the coven in a "peripheral-membership-researcher role." Upon gaining permission to conduct the study, we agreed to participate in rituals to the extent that we were relatively comfortable with them. We were comfortable with being required to express personal commitments to the planet or environment, to the women's community, and to ourselves as part of each ritual, and were not required to take on central roles. Although our agreement to participate was made in order to attend and do research, we did not feel that we had to adopt the witches' worldview, beliefs, and practices as our own in order to conduct the study. We did not "hang out" with the women outside of ritual settings, we debated their beliefs with them, and we asked many questions.

As we attended more rituals, we were greeted more warmly and we felt more comfortable. It became clear to us that, even though we attended coven activities as sociologists, we were viewed as potential converts and friends. Similar to other researchers' experiences in religiously-oriented groups (see Damrell, 1977; Rochford, 1985; Snow, 1980), the witches welcomed us in part because of the possibility of recruiting us to their belief system if not their group. Almost without our recognition, our researcher roles shifted. While attending the Mountain Retreat at the end of the summer of 1988, we were asked to play functional roles in the coven's activities. We had planned to retreat to our tent on occasion to record our fieldnotes and to interview people in our spare time, but it turned out that we had *no* "spare time." As often happens, informants find roles for researchers to take. We were asked to help lead groups, help make food, and be present for and give input into planning and preparation for rituals. Being thrust into these new roles came as a surprise. They were time-consuming and required energy and active participation, limiting our time for observation and fieldnote writing. At the funeral in mid Fall, the author present was introduced as the "coven auxiliary," a term subsequently applied to both authors and used during the rest of our fieldwork, indicating our status as a part of the coven, but not quite real members.

As many scholars have documented, participant-observers' roles are likely to change over time in the setting. . . . Although Gold (1958) has cautioned fieldworkers not to become too involved subjectively and then lose objectivity, other fieldworkers, such as Johnson (1975), Douglas (1976) and Adler and Adler (1987), dispute the notion that the researcher is unable to observe effectively as the participant role increases. Jorgensen (1989:56) submits:

> *Accurate (objective and truthful) findings are* more *rather than less likely as the researcher becomes involved directly, personally, and existentially with people in daily life.*

• • •

As a result of our change in perspective to that of observing participants, we began to understand phenomena in ways that we had not before. We eventually carved out membership roles that were something more than novitiates and yet less than full apprentices. . . . Although we adopted active membership-researcher roles, we did not become complete members. We achieved a "member's perspective" by participating in and experiencing the effects of the rituals as fully as possible, but remained different from members. We made no attempt formally to apprentice ourselves, and our sexual orientation was clearly different from that of most others. Even though we were welcome to do so, we did not regularly attend planning sessions, volunteer to take on central roles during ritual, nor socialize regularly with the witches.

We were, however, enticed by the coven's philosophy and felt a tie with the women who innovated with ritual and brought its meaning to life through their dramatic activities. By the end of our fieldwork, we were participating in rituals far more than we had anticipated. We found them powerfully influencing our outlooks on life, and we both became more reverent in our attitudes and actions toward the earth and environment. . . .

• • •

The Funeral Rites

The importance of symbols as metaphors for a worldview and hence a shared subjective reality becomes . . . clearer when one examines how the symbols are used in times of crisis. During crises, issues concerning the nature of life and death become especially important and religion is called upon to interpret the personal experiences. The sense of community created by shared meanings also becomes particularly valuable.

In the summer of 1988, the father of a member of Redwood Moon was diagnosed as having lung cancer. His daughter Aletheia at first tried solitary magic to effect a cure. The coven, however, decided that the disease had progressed to a point where too much damage had been done. The members believe that dying, like living, can be prolonged. But they decided that the most effective magic would be to send the man energy to help deal with pain. Spiderwoman put it succinctly when she told us, "You can't stop death. You can postpone and prolong it, but you can't stop it."

The death occurred in November. Aletheia's father Sep had remarried years after the death of her mother. He left behind Aletheia and her brother, who rejected his sister because of her sexual orientation. Sep was also survived by his Catholic widow and her adult children from her first marriage. There had been considerable strain between the two families during his lifetime.

. . . After a great deal of argument and difficult negotiation, the family decided that Sep's wife and her children would arrange one service and his adult children by his first marriage another. The outcome was a Catholic mass for the deceased on Friday night, followed by a Wiccan ceremony that the Circle of the Redwood Moon performed in the funeral home on Saturday morning. The coven, family members, and guests then accompanied the body to the Catholic Cemetery, where the coven performed another Dianic ritual over the open grave. Incidentally, this was not the first funeral conducted by the witches, three of whom are empowered by COG and the State of California to "marry and bury."

As the initial arrangements were being made with the undertaker, Aletheia reported experiencing a lack of connection, a lack of meaning. The Christian symbols in the funeral home alienated her. She accordingly asked that a large stained glass window of Jesus in the memorial chapel be covered for the ceremony. She and Spiderwoman were shown row after row of coffins that, according to the latter, were designed to preserve the deceased's remains intact "even in event of nuclear holocaust." At last they came upon a fairly plain oak coffin. Oak is a sacred wood in Wicca, a Celtic symbol of rebirth and regeneration. Aletheia's reaction upon seeing the oak coffin was that, " . . . all of a sudden something had meaning. Dad had to be oak." As a symbol of both mortality and immortality, the oak coffin revitalized for her the framework through which Wicca interprets death and gives it meaning.

The funeral director had serious misgivings about the religious service, especially when informed that the witches were going to "priestess" the ceremony themselves. Aletheia laughed as she remembered:

> He was really worried that we were going to cause some kind of big scene . . . some kind of heretical thing in front of God and everyone at the Holy Cross Cemetery.

When he asked what religion the ceremony represented he was told "neo-pagan." When he balked at that, Spiderwoman told him that it was "nondenominational."

Although he finally agreed, he appeared uncomfortable about the ceremony. He frequently peeked in at the service and later complained about the smell of incense. The arrangements for the interment were made through him, so it is unclear what the officials of the Catholic cemetery were told would occur.

The rites in the funeral home began before any of the guests arrived. One of the coven's apprentices performed a ritual cleansing of the room with a cauldron of burning sage, which is believed to purify everything it touches, and by sprinkling oil, dedicated to Diana, to help create "sacred space." The closed coffin had been aligned with the body's head in the East, the direction which, for Dianics, represents new beginnings and therefore endings, the closing of the circle. The coffin was placed in the front of the memorial chapel under an arch painted with a quote from *John* that promises eternal life through belief in Jesus. The stained glass window had not been covered. The flower arrangements chosen by the coven were seasonal, deep rusts, oranges, and yellows. Each display included oak leaves and shafts of wheat, symbolizing rebirth and regeneration. Wicker baskets filled with evergreen needles and pine cones were on the floor under the casket, repeating the same theme. Later it was disclosed that the needles and cones had been picked that morning from a tree where Sep liked to go when considering issues of life and death. All of the witches, except for Aletheia, wore conservative dark dresses, highlighting the pentacles, moons, and snake jewelry they wore. Aletheia, a large woman who always wears pants, had chosen an expensive man's suit, shirt, and necktie, all black. Around her waist, she had knotted her witch's cord, a red braid. She wore snake and pentacle rings, a pentacle medallion the size of her fist over her necktie, and a silver crescent moon on a copper band around her forehead.

Dianic rituals tends to vary from coven to coven and even within the same coven over time. Rituals of the Circle of the Redwood Moon are usually improvisational, but there was a written agenda for the funeral. Nevertheless, at the last moment, Aletheia decided that she wanted the coven, and its auxiliary, to perform a self-blessing before beginning the service. We stood in a circle in front of the coffin and each of us, in turn, using the same oil that had been sprinkled around the room, anointed the forehead, eyes, nostrils, mouth, breasts, abdomen, genitals, and feet of the woman to our left. Each woman using whatever words came to her while doing this, said in essence as follows:

> *Blessed be thy mind that thou mayst partake of her wisdom, thy eyes that share her vision, thy nostrils that smell her essence, thy mouth to speak her truth, thy breasts to nurture her children, thy womb the source of her creativity, thy yoni the source of her pleasure and energy, and thy feet that they may walk her path. (See Budapest, 1980:96–100)*

The blessing was sealed with a light kiss on the mouth. Several members and friends of Sep's Catholic family walked in during this part of the ceremony. Seeing the anointing and the kiss, they demanded loudly to know just what was going on. An apprentice was sent to reassure them as well as accompany the widow to her pew.

Another apprentice tended a tape recorder playing Sep's favorite music, sea chanties, as the rest of the guests filed in. Spiderwoman took the podium and welcomed everyone. She lit a white tapered candle. One of the apprentices began to burn copal, a resin-based incense she had chosen because it intuitively "felt right." The apprentice discreetly tended the burning incense during the entire ceremony, sprinkling fresh resin on the charcoal block in the small iron cauldron near the coffin and gently fanning the smoke. Nete sounded a small gong and performed a dramatic reading about beginning a new day. She referred to the Goddess as "the Lady" and specifically mentioned "the Lord," her consort. She said later that she had done this with the intention of accommodating "those who believe in a patriarchal religion." Spiderwoman sang "Morning Has Broken" and the coven joined in. She then read the poem that Sep had written to the Goddess, a long ballad-like piece that spoke about Diana's bow and her sacred woods. Individuals were invited to get up and share personal memories about Sep. None of the guests seemed prepared to do this.

The initiate became concerned at the lack of audience participation, which was clearly not what Aletheia had planned. Taking the podium, the initiate said she had met Sep only once, but through Aletheia's talking about him and loving him so much she felt that he had influenced her life through his influence on his daughter. It was a generous, loving thing for Aletheia's "coven sister" to do at a critical point. It pulled the service out of the embarrassed silence it had fallen into. When the initiate finished, she rang the gong and Aletheia took the podium. She shared memories of her father, things he had said, things they had done together. It was difficult for her; sometimes she laughed and sometimes she cried as she spoke. When she was done, she rang the gong and lit a green candle to represent rebirth.

Aletheia then called the coven up to stand in a semi-circle around the coffin. She raised a ceramic chalice that she had used in doing solitary magic for her father and announced that she had placed her wishes for Sep's freedom from pain within the chalice. Then she handed the chalice to the woman on her right. (The insistence on improvisational abilities in the Redwood Moon was important here, since the author present had no idea she was going to be called on to perform in this manner.) The chalice was passed around the circle counterclockwise or "widdershins" to represent dispersal. As each woman accepted the chalice, she announced her wish for the deceased. The wishes ranged from eternal peace to being remembered with joy. The audience was invited to participate in this ritual magic, either silently or out loud. Only Sep's son chose to join the ceremony verbally, announcing tearfully a wish that his father could see and hear the beautiful things that had been said about him.

Then Sep was "cut free of his earthly ties." Spiderwoman, in the West, pulled Aletheia's long broadsword from under the flowers on the coffin and waved it over the lid. As she did so, she called on the powers or goddesses of the West to free Sep. The sword was passed to the priestesses at the South and East, then finally to Aletheia in the North, the direction which represents the body, earth, and darkness. At each point of the compass, the priestesses called in free verse upon Water, Fire, Air, and Earth respectively to set the deceased free. Spiderwoman then began a chant. She sang one line and the coven members repeated it. Phrases involving "deep peace" were chanted over and over, as initiated witches at the four corners placed their hands on the coffin and visualized peace flowing through their bodies and into the body in the coffin.

Aletheia asked us to take our seats and listen to a brief tape of a Celtic autoharp. After a few minutes, Spiderwoman requested that the audience regroup at the cemetery and announced that maps were available in the outer lobby.

Aletheia asked the coven to remain after the rest of the mourners had departed. She raised the coffin lid and tucked the ceramic chalice in the crook of her father's arm. She placed some personal items in his inside coat pocket, including a "charm," a braid made of the hair of some witches who had performed magic for him. She took a small branch from his evergreen tree and laid it on his breast. With Diana oil, she began to bless him. When she came to his genitals, she paused. Dianics are familiar with the word "yoni," but the word "lingham," the male counterpart, was unknown to the separatists in Redwood Moon. After a little shared laughter, Aletheia shrugged and blessed her father's yoni. The funeral director came in and asked us to get a couple of "strong men" for the coffin. Several of the women immediately volunteered to carry it. The rest of us joined the procession to the cemetery.

Near the open grave, everyone lined up behind the coven. We followed the coffin singing a hymn Dianics claim was sung by Italian women who linked arms and walked into the sea to welcome death, rather than be tortured and burned for witchcraft during the witch purges several centuries ago. Nete stood at one end of the coffin and Aletheia at the other, as Nete read from her Book of Shadows about the meaning of the evergreen. She stressed that death precedes life, which always follows death. An apprentice passed through the crowd of family and friends of the deceased, handing out the sprigs of evergreen from the baskets that had been under the coffin during the memorial service. Many people accepted the sprigs, others refused to touch them. Spiderwoman spoke briefly about the debt that was owed to the widow, who had been so loving and caring toward Sep during his illness. Aletheia and her brother laid large pine branches on the coffin and those of us who had taken sprigs followed suit. Spiderwoman blessed the coffin and the grave, then announced that Sep was at rest.

A woman's voice rang out loudly, "And may Jesus Christ have mercy on your soul." One of the widow's daughters had created immediate tension in the small gathering with what appeared to be both a declaration of faith and a challenge to the witches.

An entirely unexpected thing then happened. Aletheia's brother, who had initially been the most angry and argumentative, refusing to attend any religious ceremony, stepped forward to heal the breach. He said that his father had taught him that the true meaning of Jesus Christ was that good lives were led by good people, regardless of their religions. The crowd seemed mollified and slowly dispersed for the reception.

It is important to note that Sep's funeral was not typical. Dianics do not have a typical funeral rite. What is meaningful to individual witches and their families is worked into the service. Symbols of rebirth and regeneration, however, are used consistently, even though reincarnation in a literal sense was not mentioned that day.

Discussion

Attempts at achieving reintegration of the surviving family occurred in the rituals at both the chapel and graveside. The invitations to the mourners to share memories of the deceased and to join in the ritual magic of placing wishes (or spells) in the chalice were obvious attempts to establish a sense of community, as was the passing out of the evergreen sprigs. The attention paid to the widow by the coven, especially the praise and thanks offered to her at the graveside, helped somewhat to reestablish family solidarity. That these efforts were not more successful is only partially due to the deep divisions in the family and its lack of solidarity during Sep's lifetime. Geertz (1973:167) has demonstrated that conflict can occur when a particular funeral rite becomes both "a paean to God" and an affirmation of political belief in spite of their attempt to be inclusive, when they called on the goddess, the radical feminist witches of Redwood Moon were symbolically challenging all social institutions based on patriarchal relationships.

It is significant that Sep's homophobic and sexist son, the most alienated individual present, and the only one without the immediate support of a community, was the one who attempted to heal the breach caused by conflicting religions. Although he professed to be an atheist, the Wiccan funeral and the symbolism it contained held meaning for him. Aletheia reported that the two of them were closer that weekend than they had been in their entire adult lives. She and Sep's widow, who had been estranged from each other during Sep's life, also appeared to renegotiate their relationship, at least on a temporary basis. We were later told that this relationship became strained again over the deceased's financial affairs.

It is also obvious that witchcraft provides a framework for interpreting and giving meaning to death, even in today's society where pain and dying are often prolonged. In so doing, Dianic Wicca also gives greater meaning to life. . . .

Although she claimed not to have a personal belief in literal reincarnation, Aletheia found comfort in using the Dianic symbols of rebirth in dealing with her father's death. This, then, was an affirmation of belief in the life cycle.

Contemporary witchcraft, with its acceptance of death and emphasis on immanence, the interconnectedness of all things, and natural cycles rather than polarities, is a joyous, life-affirming religion, even in death. Spiderwoman epitomized this outlook in a powerful image when she and Aletheia were at the funeral home, wandering among the lead-lined steel coffins with rubber gaskets and special locking devices. As the mortician reminded them that they had to bring underwear to dress the corpse, Spiderwoman turned to him and announced, "When I die, I want to be buried naked, standing up, with a tree planted on my head." Aletheia told us later that she thought this was wonderful.

References

Adler, Margot, 1986. *Drawing Down the Moon.* 2nd ed. 1976; rpt. Boston, MA: Beacon Press.

Adler, Patricia A., and Peter Adler, 1987. *Membership Roles in Field Research.* Beverly Hills, CA: Sage.

Benjamin, Jessica, 1980. "The Bonds of Love: Rational Violence and Erotic Domination." *Feminist Studies.* 6(1), Spring, pp. 144–174.

Budapest, Zsuzsanna, 1986. *The Holy Book of Women's Mysteries, Vol. 1.* 2nd ed. 1979; rpt. Oakland, CA: Susan B. Anthony Coven No. 1.

Budapest, Zsuzsanna, 1980. *The Holy Book of Women's Mysteries, Part II.* Berkeley, CA: Susan B. Anthony Books.

Campbell, Joseph, 1987. *The Power of Myth.* New York. Doubleday.

Circourel, Aaron, 1964. *Method and Measurement in Sociology.* New York: Free Press.

Collins, Sheila D., 1982. "The Personal is Political." in C. Spretnak (ed.) *The Politics of Women's Spirituality.* Garden City, NY: Anchor Press, pp. 362–367.

Damrell, Joseph, 1977. *Seeking Spiritual Meaning.* Beverly Hills, CA: Sage.

Damrell, Joseph, 1978. *Search for Identity.* Beverly Hills, CA: Sage.

Denzin, Norman K, 1970. *The Research Act.* Chicago, IL: Aldine.

Douglas, Jack D., 1970. "The Relevance of Sociology." In J. J. Douglas (ed.) *The Relevance of Sociology.* New York: Appleton-Century-Crofts, pp. 185–233.

Douglas, Jack D., 1976. *Investigative Social Research.* Newbury Park, CA: Sage.

Douglas, J. D., and J. M. Johnson, 1977. *Existential Sociology.* (Editors). New York: Cambridge University Press.

Durkheim, Emile, 1915. *The Elementary Forms of Religious Life.* Translated by J. W. Swain. London: George Allen and Unwin Ltd.

Ellwood, Robert, 1979. *Alternative Altars: Unconventional and Eastern Spirituality in America.* Chicago, IL: University of Chicago Press.

Forrest, Burke, 1986. "Apprentice-participation: Methodology and the study of subjective reality." *Urban Life, 14:* pp. 431–453.

Geertz, Clifford, 1973. *The Interpretation of Cultures.* New York: Basic Books.

Gold, R. L, 1958. "Roles in sociological field observations." *Social Forces 36:* pp. 217–223.

Gorden, Raymond, 1969. *Interviewing: Strategy, Techniques, and Tactics.* Homewood, IL: Dorsey Press.

Hartsock, Nancy, 1985. *Money, Sex, and Power.* Boston, MA: Northeastern University Press.

Jaggar, Alison, 1983. *Feminist Politics and Human Nature.* Totowa, NJ: Rowman & Allanheld.

Johnson, John M., 1975. *Doing Field Research.* New York: Free Press.

Jorgensen, Danny L., 1989. *Participant Observation: A Methodology for Human Studies.* Newbury Park, NY: Sage.

Jules-Rosette, Bennetta, 1975. *African Apostles.* Ithaca, NY: Cornell University Press.

Jules-Rosette, Bennetta, 1976. "The conversion experience: The apostles of John Maranke." *Journal of Religion in Africa 7:* pp. 132–164.

Keller, Evelyn Fox, 1985. *Reflections of Gender and Science.* New Haven, CT: Yale University Press.

Lofland, John, and Norman Skonovd, 1981. "Conversion Motifs." *Journal for the Scientific Study of Religion.* 20(4): pp. 373–385.

Lofland, Lyn, 1978. *The Craft of Dying: The Modern Face of Death.* Beverly Hills: Sage.

Malinowski, Bronislaw, 1948. *Magic, Science, and Religion.* Glencoe, IL: The Free Press.

Mehan, Hugh and H. Wood, 1975. *The Reality of Ethnomethodology.* New York: John Wiley.

Morgan, Robin, 1977. *Going Too Far.* New York: Random House, pp. 306.

Parsons, T. and V. Lidz, 1967. "Death in American Society," pp. 133–170 in E. Shneidman (ed.) *Essays in Self-Destruction.* New York: Science House.

Reimer, Jeffrey, W., 1977. "Varieties of opportunistic research." *Urban Life.* 5(4): pp. 467–477.

Rochford, E. B., Jr., 1985. *Hare Krishna in America.* New Brunswick, NJ.: Rutgers University Press.

Snow, David A., 1980. "The disengagement process: a neglected problem in participant-observation research." *Qualitative Sociology. 3:* pp. 100–122.

Spretnak, Charlene, 1982. *The Politics of Women's Spirituality.* Ed. Charlene Spretnak. Garden City, NY: Anchor Press.

Starhawk, 1979. *The Spiral Dance.* San Francisco: Harper & Row.

Starhawk, 1988. *Dreaming the Dark.* 2nd ed. 1982; rpt. Boston, MA: Beacon Press.

Vernon, G, 1970. *Sociology of Death: An Analysis of Death-Related Behavior.* New York: Ronald Press.

Walker, Barbara, 1985. *The Crone: Woman of Age, Wisdom, and Power.* San Francisco, CA: Harper & Row.

Yinger, Milton, 1957. *Religion, Society, and the Individual.* New York: MacMillan Co.

Turn-Ons for Money

Interactional Strategies
of the Table Dancer

CAROL RAMBO RONAI
and CAROLYN ELLIS

She swayed from side to side above him, her hands on his shoulders, her knee brushing gently against the bulge in his pants. He looked up at the bottom of her breasts, close enough to touch, but subtly forbidden. His breath came in ever shorter gasps.

This is the world of the table dancer—a world where women exchange titillating dances for money. Our study looks at the dynamic processes of interaction that occur in the exchange. Previous studies (Carey et al., 1974; Gonos, 1976; McCaghy and Skipper, 1969, 1972; Salutin, 1971; Skipper and McCaghy, 1970, 1971) have concentrated on "burlesque" or "go-go" dancers, sometimes referring to them more generally as stripteasers. Dancers' interactions with customers were restricted, for the most part, to the stage setting where they danced and received money from customers. Because investigators in these studies occupied positions as researchers or researchers as customers, and relied to a large extent on survey and interview techniques, this work led to a static description of this occupation.

Boles and Garbin (1974) have looked at customer-stripper interaction in a setting where strippers sold drinks in addition to performing stage acts. Although they described interaction, they interpreted it in terms of norms, club motif, and customer goals. They found that the conflict between customers' goals and strippers' goals resulted in "counterfeit intimacy" (Foote, 1954), a situation in which an aura of intimacy masked mutually exploitative interactions.

Although counterfeit intimacy is a structural reality in such contexts, this description created another model of behavior that ignored the interactive, dynamic nature of the exchanges and set up in its place stiff caricatures behaving in an unbending, cardboard

C. R. Ronai and C. Ellis. *Journal of Contemporary Ethnography,* Vol. 18 No. 3, October 1989 271–298
© 1989 Sage Publications, Inc. Reprinted by permission of Sage Publications, Inc.

manner. As actors get caught up in dialogue, they exchange symbols, extract meanings, and modify expectations of what goals they can reasonably expect to reach. Interaction has a tentative quality (Blumer, 1969; Turner, 1962); goals are in a constant state of flux.

The nature of selling and performing table dances that we describe yields more opportunity for interaction between customer and dancer than in previous studies. A table dancer must be a charming and sexy companion, keep the customer interested and turned on, make him feel special, and be a good reader of character and a successful salesperson; at the same time, she must deal with her own negative feelings about the customer or herself, negotiate limits, and then keep him under control to avoid getting fired by management.

Much of the early research literature has described stripping as a deviant occupation. Later, Prus and Irini (1980) looked at stripping as conforming to the norms of a bar subculture. Demystifying this "deviant" activity even further, we show that bargaining strategies in the bar actually mirror "respectable" negotiations in mainstream culture.

We begin by discussing the methods we used to elicit in-depth understanding of strategies used by table dancers. After describing the dance club setting, we turn to a description and analysis of particular tactics used on the stage, at the tables between stage acts, and then during the table dances in the pits. Our conclusion analyzes how this exchange reflects buying and selling in service occupations as well as the negotiation of gender relationships in mainstream society.

Methods

Our study approaches stripping from the point of view of dancers and the dancer as researcher, the people with the most access to the thoughts, feelings, and strategies of exotic dancers. Dancers concentrate on manipulating men as they pursue money in exchange for a turn-on. In order for their strategies to work, they must understand and coordinate them with the games of men.

Our information comes primarily from the experiences of the first author who danced during 1984 and 1985 to pay her way through school. As a "complete-member-researcher" (Adler and Adler, 1987), she conducted opportunistic research (Riemer, 1977), that is, she studied a setting in which she was already a member. She interviewed dancers to find out how and why they began this occupation and kept a journal of events that happened while dancing. Later, she reconstructed, in chronological field notes, a retrospective account of her own dancing history, paying special attention to strategies, emotion work, and identity issues. She used "systematic sociological introspection" (Ellis, forthcoming) to put herself mentally and emotionally back into her experiences and record what she remembered (see Bulmer's, 1982, concept of "retrospective participant observation").

In May 1987, the first author danced in one strip bar for the explicit purpose of gathering data for a master's thesis, chaired by the second author. With approval of bar management, but without the knowledge of other dancers, she acted in the dual capacity of researcher and dancer. This time her primary identity was that of researcher, although as a complete member-researcher she attempted to "become the phenomenon" (Adler and Adler, 1987; Jorgensen, 1989; Mehan and Wood, 1975). When she danced, she took on the identity of a dancer, suffered identity conflicts similar to those she had experienced during earlier dancing, and shared a common set of experiences and feelings with other dancers. She kept field notes of events, which were buttressed by "interactive introspection" (Ellis, 1988), whereas the second author talked her through her experiences, probing at and recording her feelings and thoughts. She conducted informal interviews in the dressing room with dancers and on the floor with customers. Sometimes she revealed her dual role to customers as a strategy to keep them interested in spending more money and to get them to introspect about their own motives for being in the bar.

Because this article is concerned with describing dancers' subtle manipulation strategies that occurred semiprivately, we pulled much of our material from episodes engaged in by the first author, in which process was most easily observed. Because we believe that sociologists should acknowledge the role of their own introspection in their research (Ellis, forthcoming), the first author reveals which of the experiences in the article are hers. Throughout this article, we refer to the first author by her dancer name, Sabrina.

We realize the bias inherent in using introspection primarily from one source. For example, Sabrina, more than most dancers, tended to attract customers interested in mental stimulation as well as physical turn-on. Yet we could not have gained an in-depth understanding of intimate exchange, for example during table dances, in any other way. To understand this bias, we compared Sabrina's strategies and experiences with those of other dancers we observed and other bar participants with whom we talked. Later in 1987, we conducted interviews with four strippers, eight customers, four managers, three bar owners, and a law officer. This article then uses a triangulated method (Denzin, 1978; Webb et al., 1965) to present typical responses from field work and in-depth ones from current and retrospective introspection.

Setting

An exotic dance club located in the Tampa Bay area of Florida provided the setting for this study. Since liquor was served, full nudity was prohibited by state law. Appearing individually in full costume on stage, each stripper gradually removed her clothing during a dance routine. By the end of the act, the dancer wore pasties that concealed her nipples and panties that covered genitals, pubic hair, and the cheeks of her derriere. Men handed out tips to dancers during performances.

Between acts, dancers strolled around the floor, making themselves available to spend time with customers. They made money if customers bought them drinks. However, the main attraction and source of income in this bar was the table dance.

A dancer "sold" dances in a complicated negotiation process through which she convinced the client that he was turned on to her and/or that she was turned on to him. At the same time, she controlled the situation so that she was not caught disobeying "house" rules, many of which corresponded to what county authorities considered illegal. For example, since "charging" for a table dance was considered soliciting, the dancer, using word games similar to those used by the masseuse studied by Rasmussen and Kuhn (1976), suggested that there was "generally a contribution of $5."

After a dancer successfully sold a dance, she led her customer to one of the two elevated corners of the bar, known generically as the "The Pit," and affectionately nicknamed by customers as "Horny Holler" and "The Passion Pit." Railings and dim lights offered an artificial boundary between this area and the rest of the bar. Clothed in a bralike top and full panties or other revealing costume the dancer leaned over a seated patron, her legs inside his, and swayed suggestively in rhythm to the music playing in the bar. Theoretically, customers were allowed to touch only the hips, waist, back, and outside of a dancer's legs. Many men tried and some succeeded in doing more. Disobeying rules prohibiting direct sexual stimulation or touching meant more money for dancers, but it also meant risking that management might reprimand them or that a "customer" would turn out to be an undercover officer or a representative looking for infractions on behalf of club management.

Elements of Strategy

On the Stage

A dancer used symbols that appealed to her audience. At the same time, these symbols distanced her from customers and denoted that the stage was a performance frame (Goffman, 1974; Mullen, 1985). Her appearance, eye contact, manner, and choice of music made up her main expressive equipment.

Having a "centerfold" figure was an obvious asset for dancers. But the best looking woman did not always make the most money. A dancer's presentation of self was also a crucial factor in a customer's decision to tip her. Similar to strippers described by Gonos (1976) and Robboy (1985), women often portrayed exaggerated stereotypes through their clothing style and movement. . . . Others had a "gimmick." For example, one woman was an acrobat; another stood on her head while twirling her large breasts. In contrast, a more sensual dancer dressed in sexy bedroom clothing such as a corset and garters or a teddy, and displayed subtle sensual behavior such as slow undulation of the hips.

A dancer chose symbols that drew a certain type of customer to her. Dressing the part of the vamp, for example, reflected an extroverted attitude that attracted customers out to have a good time. Overtly sexual dancers were more likely to perform sexual favors in the bar or meet a man for sex outside the bar. The sensual presentation of self attracted customers who were interested in a "serious," private interaction. Customers interpreted each dancer's symbols as cues to what it might be like to interact with her or, specifically, to have sex with her. . . .

Most dancers used eye contact to "feel out" a patron. Managing frequent eye contact while dancing on stage usually meant a tip for the dancer and made a customer feel as if a dancer was specifically interested in him.

A dancer's first close contact with a customer often occurred while accepting a tip. During the exchange, the dancer formed impressions about how the customer was reacting to her, and the customer decided whether he was attracted to the woman. The customer stood at the side of the stage holding currency, which signaled the dancer that he wanted to tip her. The dancer greeted him while accepting the tip in her garter and said "thanks," perhaps giving him a "special" look.

At this point, a dancer might choose from several courses of action, such as "coming on" to a customer, doting on a customer, and using humor. When dancers "came on" to customers, they grinned, wiggled their breasts, spread their legs, struck their buttocks, suggestively sucked their fingers, talked dirty, or French kissed.

Others, such as the sensual dancer, doted on a customer for a few seconds. She caressed his arm, wrapped her arms around his neck, and smiled while he tipped her. If she felt confident of his interest, typical comments she might make were: "I would love a chance to get to know you," or "I look forward to sitting with you," which meant accompanying him to his table after her stage performance.

Humor was an effective and safe tool for generating a good impression while accepting a tip on stage. Customers generally construed a funny statement made by a dancer as friendly and spontaneous. Often it made a nervous client more at ease. Sabrina noted lines she used: "What's a nice guy like you doing in a dump like this?" or "I bet you'd look better up here than I do."

Familiar with the usual "acts" of dancers, such as coming on and showing phony interest, customers were pleased when they thought a woman had "dropped the routine." Often this meant only that she had staged a less frequently displayed one. A dancer had to be careful not to use the same line more than once on the same person, or let a customer overhear it being used on another man. No matter a customer's taste, he wanted a sincere performance.

• • •

A dancer's music affected how a customer viewed her. This was reflected in Tim's comment about Jessica: "That girl has a great body, but every time I hear her music [heavy metal] I get the creeps thinking about what she must be like." While most women danced to top-40 music, some used other music to attract a tip from a particular kind of client. Mae, an older dancer in her late thirties, played country music and presented herself as a country woman. Bikers and blue-collar workers were loyal to Mae, expressing sentiments like: "She's the only *real* woman in the bar."

On the Floor

Offstage, interaction was even more complex. Between stage performances, a dancer circulated among customers and offered her company. Body language, expressions, and general appearance helped define each customer's interest in her and the difficulty of being with him. Once a dancer located an interested customer and introduced herself, or followed up on a contact made while performing on stage, she then had to convince him that he wanted to spend time with her. Ordinarily, her eventual goal was to sell a table dance.

Choosing a Customer

The ideal customer had a pleasant disposition, was good looking, had time and money to spend, and was sitting at one of the tables on the floor. Most customers did not meet all these criteria. Dancers weighed these features for each customer and also compared them against the circumstances of the evening. Sabrina often asked herself: "What do I want more right now? Money or someone nonthreatening to sit with?" Her answer was different depending upon time of night, how much money she had made already, and how she felt at the moment. Other dancers made the same calculations. For example, three hours before the bar closed one night, Naomi said, "I know this guy I'm sitting with doesn't have a lot of money, but I've made my hundred for the night so I can afford to take it easy." Another time, Vicky said, "God! I know I should be out there hustling instead of drinking with Jim, but I just can't get into it. I guess I'll just get fucked-up and blow it off today." Darcy displayed a more typical attitude, "It's twelve thirty already and I haven't made shit! This guy I'm sitting with better cough it up or I'm taking off." Negotiations with oneself and with the customer were always in process. Throughout the interaction, each participant tried to ascertain what she or he was willing to give and how much could be acquired from the other.

Attractive customers appeared, at first, more appealing. They were pleasant to look at and the dancer could pretend to be on a date while sitting with them. But these men seemed to know they were more desirable than others in the bar and were more likely to bargain with those resources. . . .

Sometimes customers who were old, heavy, unattractive, or otherwise weak in social resources came into the bar. Many women avoided these men, while others, like Sabrina, realized unattractive men were eager for company and tended to treat a dancer better and spend more money than their more attractive competitors would. With the right strategies, dancers could control these men. For example, a dancer might corner a customer into treating her as he would his granddaughter by acting polite and addressing him as "sir." This insinuated that, of course, he would never act inappropriately. Some accepted the role to such an extent that they acted like grandfathers. One man told Scarlet that she was cute, tweaked her cheek, and compared her to his granddaughter.

When scanning the bar and deciding whom to approach first, a dancer tried to find the man who appeared to have the most money. Logically, the better a customer was dressed, the more likely he was to have money. However, he also had a higher probability of already being in the company of another dancer.

Making sure a customer was not spoken for by another dancer was important. It was considered dangerous (one could get into an argument) and rude to sit with another dancer's customer. Some regular customers, for instance, visited the bar to see particular dancers. These customers often turned down another dancer's offer of company by saying they were "waiting for someone." When a dancer entered the bar, she immediately scanned the room, paying particular attention to which women were seated with which customers. If she noticed later that a woman had left a table for a long period of time, she then asked her if it was okay to sit with that customer. This served the dual purpose of following tacit rules (i.e., being polite) and gave the dancer an opportunity to gather information about the customer in question.

Sabrina was warned about a customer in this manner. Upon asking Debbie if she was finished with "the old man in the corner wearing a hat," Debbie replied, "Sure, you can have him. That's 'Merv the perv.' He has lots of money, but he'll want to stick his finger up your asshole for twenty bucks a feel."

A dancer might ignore all other customers to sit with one of her "regulars." When two or more of her regulars were in the bar, she had to juggle them, first sitting with one and then the other. It was difficult to table dance for both of them and still portray "special attachment." Eventually, she had to offer an account (Scott and Lyman, 1968) to one of them. One excuse was to appeal to the principle of fairness: "I really want to be with you, but he came in first and now I have to be with him." Or she might appeal to higher loyalties (Sykes and Matza, 1957), insinuating that the decision was out of her control: "I have to go sit with another customer now. My bosses know I avoid him and they're watching me."

Time in the bar correlated with decreased spending. If a customer had been spending for a while, it was fair to assume that he would run out of money or would soon decide to leave, that is, unless he was intoxicated and freely using a credit card. Dancers in this situation risked having to deal with and control a problematic person who did not remember or pay for the correct number of dances purchased. On the other hand, a dancer might convince a drunk credit card customer to pay for more dances than he actually bought.

A customer's location in the bar indicated his attitude toward female company. In this club, sitting at the bar meant little interest in interacting with dancers. Patrons near the stage wanted to see the show. Being seated at one of the tables in the floor area was conducive to interaction with dancers and to inquiries about table dances.

At the Tables

Once a customer accepted an offer of company, a dancer sat with him and introduced herself. Her overall goal remained fairly consistent—money with no hassle. Many women also enjoyed the attention they received and got an exhibitionist thrill out of being desired and told how beautiful they were. Others believed the compliments were just part of the game. Some liked the feeling of conquering and being in control. Others felt degraded and out of control.

The customer's manifest goal was impersonal, sexual turn-ons for money; a close examination showed other objectives that shadowboxed with and sometimes transcended this more obvious goal. Although most customers initially focused on the pursuit of sex in or outside the bar, they also came looking for a party, to feel good about themselves, to find a friend or companion, or to develop a relationship. A dancer's strategies varied depending on her personality and her perception of the customer.

Some women said nothing. A customer who wanted passive indifference from an attractive female willing to turn him on liked this approach. Sex, not conversation, was his goal. The dancer did not have to initiate activity nor get to know the customer. Her role was to respond as a sexual nonperson by allowing him to kiss and fondle her body. Verbal interaction potentially endangered the continuance of the exchange.

Most customers wanted a dancer to interact with them. Seduction rhetoric (Rasmussen and Kuhn, 1976) became part of the dancer's sexual foreplay before the table dance as well as a vehicle for the customer to persuade the dancer to see him outside the bar. By talking "dirty" and acting "like a whore"—for example, telling stories about kinky sex in her life outside the bar—a dancer could keep a customer "going," eager to buy the next dance, ready to believe the dancer might have sex with him later.

If a customer wanted a prostitute, he dropped hints such as, "Do you do work on the side?" or "Where does a guy go for a good time around here?" or "Do you date?" Sometimes he propositioned outright: "Will you go to bed with me for a hundred dollars?" The more blatant proposals told the dancer that the customer was not a police officer; all of the requests informed her he had money to spend and opened up the possibility of using strategies to extract it.

• • •

Similar to the strippers discussed by Prus and Irini (1980), a few women used the bar setting as a place to make contacts for their prostitution careers, while many more had sex occasionally outside the bar to augment their incomes. Before accepting an offer, a woman usually asked other dancers about the customer or spent time getting to know him. Interacting with him then gave her an opportunity to make money table dancing. Most women claimed they had sex "only for the money." A few, such as

Sasha, seemed to enjoy sexual contact in and out of the bar. Sasha's enthusiasm—"I'm so horny, I want a cock tonight"—was deemed deviant by the other dancers, who ostracized her—usually avoided her and talked behind her back—for her overt enjoyment.

• • •

If customers were in the bar "to party" (to be entertained) in groups, such as bachelor parties, a dancer wasted no time on interaction. She asked immediately if they wanted a dance. These men interacted mostly with each other, requiring dancers to be lively and entertaining hostesses while treating them like sex objects. Often they commented on her body—her big tits, nice ass, or ugly face—as though she were not there. Party groups purchased dances with the same attitude and frequency as they bought rounds of drinks.

Most men who came to the bar seemed to want to find a friend or companion, or in some other way be treated as a special person. One of Sabrina's customers left the bar twice during an evening to change shirts, just to see if she recognized him when he returned. . . .

Most successful dancers were able to hold conversations with these men. Asking his name, where he lived, occupation, and what he did with his spare time provided initial interaction. Finding common ground helped conversation run smoothly. Asking questions at a leisurely pace, making comments, and showing interest both verbally and nonverbally afforded a semblance of credibility to the conversational process. This dialogue helped the dancer to "check out" (Rasmussen and Kuhn, 1976) the customer to make sure he was not a police officer, determine how much money he had to spend and which of her interactional strategies might make him willing to part with it. Giving the customer an opportunity to talk about himself and to demonstrate whatever expertise he had made him feel good about himself. A customer pleased with his presentation of self was more apt to spend money. . . .

The best way for a dancer to convince a customer that she found him appealing and unique was to find a likable characteristic about the customer and continually tell him how impressed she was with him and with that trait. For example, some men liked to be praised for their appearance, success, intelligence, sexual desirability, trustworthiness, or sensitivity. The dancer had to convey to him directly that she preferred his company to others in the bar, or indirectly through such statements as "You're not as vulgar as the rest of these guys in here"; "You're more intelligent than most men I meet in here"; "You're not just another one of these assholes," or "I appreciate your spending time with me. When I'm sitting with you I'm safe from those animals out there." The message was that because of his specialness, she could be "straight" with him, be who she really was, instead of putting on one of her usual acts.

This tactic worked best with customers the dancer liked and enjoyed talking to; otherwise, it was difficult to muster up and maintain the sincerity necessary for a believable performance. When this strategy worked, the dancer had close to total control of the interaction. Then the customer tried hard to meet the dancer's expectations, spending money and treating her like a date or friend to avoid disappointing her. If he stopped spending money, the dancer might say, and sometimes mean, "I'll see you later. Don't get angry with me. I know you understand that I have to make money, although I would rather spend time with you. If I don't find anything, I'll come back and visit." Sometimes the customer responded by spending more money to keep the dancer around. If not, he was forced to "understand" her leaving because he and the dancer had an honest relationship and she had been "straight" with him about the nature of her job. This strategy was an effective way to cultivate regular customers.

• • •

Some regular customers acted as if they were involved in a long-term, serious relationship with a dancer. They bought her expensive gifts such as diamonds, minks, cars, and flowers. These customers seemed to forget the businesslike nature of the bar setting.

Dancers in these interactions appeared involved with the customers. However, most did not take the relationship outside the bar, since this would have cut off a source of income. But they tried to convince the men of their desire to leave the bar scene and be saved by them, even though it was impossible now. Sabrina, for example, had many offers from men who wanted to rescue her from the bar. She developed a routine to solicit this desire from men—it usually meant more money for her in the bar—but that allowed her to reject their proposals without causing anger. She explained:

> I presented myself as attractive and intelligent, but helpless, trapped by circumstances. When they asked me to leave the bar, I told them I had to work to pay for school. When they suggested setting me up in a place of my own, I told them I was independent and wanted to do it on my own. This put them off, but kept them interested and earned their respect.

• • •

Closing the Sale

A dancer rapidly closed a sale on a table dance to a man who wanted sexual favors in the bar. But since these men often violated rules regarding touching and sexual stimulation, some dancers did not feel that they were worth the trouble. For example, one night Annette came into the dressing room and announced, "I just left this old geezer who wanted me to rub him off with my knee. I'm not into it. If someone else wants to, go for it."

The same problems existed after a quick sale to men in the bar for a party. In this situation, a dancer had to concentrate on not acting offended long enough to perform table dances and collect her money. For some dancers, the money was not worth the degradation. As a result, they avoided the bachelor parties.

The customer who wanted to be treated as special took more time. Questioning allowed time for the dancer to convince him that he wanted a table dance from her. It was important that she not appear pushy, yet she needed to determine quickly whether she could make money from this person. Would he buy table dances? Did he want to spend time getting to know a dancer or go directly to a dance? Answers to such questions guided the dancer in constructing her behavior toward the customer.

If a customer purchased a drink for a dancer, she then knew that he was interested enough to spend some time with her. Some customers, however, bought drinks for dancers but refused to purchase table dances, claiming table dances got them "worked up for nothing." If a customer acknowledged that right away, a dancer then had to make a decision about staying or leaving based on the availability of other money-making opportunities in the bar. If the action in the club was slow, she might stay with him since she made $1 on every drink he bought for her. . . . Often a dancer gave the waitress a secret signal indicating that no liquor should be put in her glass. The waitress brought the drink in a special glass, placed a dollar under the dancer's napkin and the drink on top of it.

Most women closed on a dance after the first drink had arrived and it was apparent that the customer liked her. If the customer said no, most dancers left fairly quickly. But in rare cases a customer paid $50–$100 for a dancer to sit with him for a while. This guaranteed the dancer money without trouble and bought the customer companionship. . . .

Even when a dancer was not paid for her company, it was not always a good idea for her to leave immediately when a man refused a table dance. As a rare and novel routine, staying made the dancer appear sincere in her interest and less concerned about making money. Sabrina occasionally used this approach:

"Why are you still sitting here?" the customer asked immediately after he had turned me down for a table dance.

"I'm finishing my drink," I replied.

"Then you are leaving?" he asked.

"Oh, sir, I had no idea you wanted me to go. You must be waiting for someone. Forgive me for being so rude," I said tongue in cheek. I stood to leave.

"Hold it, hold it. Sit back down. I don't necessarily want you to leave. The girls always leave after you say no to a dance. You must be new here. You really should leave when customers say no. You won't make any money this way." During this exchange he was clutching my arm. He loosened his grip. "Wouldn't that be rude to just up and walk off?" I asked incredulously. He stares at me a minute, and then smiles. "Lady," he says. "You are a card. I want a table dance." He bought four.

In the Pits

• • •

Once in the pit, a woman sat close to the man. Often she put her hand on his leg, draped an arm on his shoulder, or swung a leg over his lap. Some girls necked with their customers, French kissing with a frenzied passion. Other dancers allowed kisses only on the cheek.

If a customer tried to French kiss when a dancer did not want it, she had several "routines" to control him. Leveling a questioning look at the customer and then backing away from him was enough to stop most men. When a client voiced dissatisfaction over the limitation—"What did you do that for?" or "What's your problem? Why are you so cold?"—it usually indicated an aggressive and potentially problematic customer. Sabrina's response to this was, "Imagine if I kissed every guy in the bar like that before I kissed you. Would that be a turn-on for you?" Most customers backed off then with comments such as, "You're absolutely right. I never thought of that before." By their continuous attempts, however, it was apparent that some were being insincere, assuming, like the dancer, that if they moved more slowly, they would get more of what they wanted. But sometimes the restriction reflected positively on the customer's impression of the dancer. One customer stated to Sabrina after she used this routine: "You have a lot of respect for yourself. I like that."

While some women danced immediately, many waited one or two songs before actually starting a table dance. Sabrina noted that she rarely danced on the first available song because it gave off the impression that she was just interested in making money quickly. She preferred to sit with a customer for a while, talk, drink, and get to know him better. This created a sexual or intimate atmosphere and convinced him that she liked spending time with him. Often this cultivated customers who were likely to buy a greater number of dances, and return to visit her later.

At the beginning of a new song, a dancer might say: "Would you like that table dance now?" or "Let's go for it, baby," depending on the type of interaction in which they were involved. Sexually oriented behavior on the part of the customer called for aggressive behavior from the dancer; less sexually overt actions required more subtle requests.

Table Dances

Strategy became important during a table dance; close quarters meant a dancer's presentation could be difficult to maintain and a customer hard to control. Normally, a dancer attempted to maintain eye contact with a patron, operating on the premise that it demonstrated interest and that if he had his eyes on her, he wouldn't have his hands on her as much. Sabrina hypothesized that a customer confronting a dancer's eyes was forced to acknowledge her "personhood," and that he then was less likely to violate it. Another impression given off (Goffman, 1959) by the dancer's body language was that the intimate exchange demonstrated by this eye contact might be impinged upon by the customer's groping at her body. Sometimes eye contact was difficult if a customer caused the dancer to laugh or feel disgusted (for example, if he was ugly or panting). In this situation, a dancer could turn away from him and make an impersonal shaking of her derriere part of her dance.

Sexual activity was illegal during table dances, but it sometimes occurred. Customers and dancers acknowledged that "hand jobs," oral sex, and intercourse happened, although infrequently. . . .

More common were body-to-penis friction and masturbation. The most frequent form consisted of the customer sliding down to the end of his seat, spreading his legs, and pulling the dancer in close to him where she could then use her knees discreetly to rub his genitals while she danced. Customers sometimes wore shorts without underwear to allow their genitals to hang out the side, or they unzipped their pants to bare their genitals, or masturbated themselves by hand while watching the dancer.

If a customer insisted on violating rules—putting his fingers inside the dancer's briefs or touching her breasts—a dancer might dance much faster than normal, or sway quickly side to side, to escape the wandering hands. If he was insistent, a dancer might grab his wrists teasingly, but firmly, and say, "No, no," addressing him as if he were a misbehaving child.

These attempts to control the customer could not be too aggressive at the outset, or the customer would be turned off. A subtle game was being played: The customer attempted to get the dancer to go as far as she would, and bend the rules, without antagonizing her so much that she stopped dancing; the dancer attempted to keep him in line, but in such a way that he still wanted to buy dances from her. A particularly good strategy at this point was for the dancer to make it look as if she was interested in what he wanted to do, but, because of management, was unable to oblige him: "Look, this would be fine, but I'm going to get in trouble with management. They're going to catch us if you keep acting like this." This disclaimer (Hewitt and Stokes, 1975) shifted the focus of the patron's annoyance to management and away from her and reasserted the idea that this was a respectable occupation with rules (see Hong et al., 1975).

If a man continued to act inappropriately, the dancer most likely lost her money and the negotiation process broke down. If the customer did not pay after the dance, the dancer had no recourse. Her only power was her seductiveness or ability to persuade the customer subtly that he "owed" it to her. Fights between customers and dancers started occasionally because a man did not want to pay a woman who "didn't give him a good dance." Management quickly squelched these and fired or fined dancers who were involved.

• • •

After a table dance had been completed, the next goal was to keep the interaction going so that the customer would buy more dances. If a customer continued to hold onto a dancer after the song ended, it usually signaled that he wanted her to dance through the next song. If he let her go, a dancer might look inquisitively at the customer and ask, "Is that all for now? Do you want to continue?" or "Will you want a dance later?" The questions asked depended on the dancer's impression of how involved the customer was with the dance. At the least, she encouraged him to look her up the next time he returned to the bar.

• • •

References

Adler, P. A. and P. Adler (1987) *Membership Roles in Field Research.* Newbury Park, CA: Sage.

Bigus, O. (1972) "The milkman and his customer: a cultivated relationship." *Urban Life and Culture 1:* 131–165.

Blumer, H. (1969) *Symbolic Interactionism: Perspective and Method.* Englewood Cliffs, NJ: Prentice-Hall.

Boles, J. and A. P. Garbin (1974) "The strip club and customer-stripper patterns of interaction." *Sociology and Social Research 58:* 136–144.

Browne, J. (1973) *The Used-Car Game: A Sociology of the Bargain.* Lexington, MA: Lexington Books.

Bulmer, M. (1982) "When is disguise justified? Alternatives to covert participant-observations." *Qualitative Sociology 5:* 251–264.

Carey, S. H., R. A. Peterson, and L. K. Sharpe (1974) "A study of recruitment and socialization in two deviant female occupations." *Soc. Symposium 11:* 11–24.

Chernin, K. (1982) *The Obsession: Reflections on the Tyranny of Slenderness.* New York: Harper Collophon.

Davis, F. (1959) "The cab driver and his fare: facets of a fleeting relationship." *Amer. J. of Sociology 65:* 158–165.

Denzin, N. K. (1978) *The Research Act.* New York: McGraw-Hill.

Ellis, C. (1988) "Keeping emotions in the sociology of emotions." University of South Florida. (unpublished)

Ellis, C. (forthcoming) "Sociological introspection and emotional experience." *Symbolic Interaction 13.*

Foote, N. N. (1954) "Sex as play." *Social Problems 1:* 159–163.

Goffman, E. (1959) *The Presentation of Self In Everyday Life.* Garden City, NY: Doubleday.

Goffman, E. (1974) *Frame Analysis: An Essay on the Organization of Experience.* Cambridge, MA: Harvard Univ. Press.

Gonos, G. (1976) "Go-Go dancing: a comparative frame analysis." *Urban Life 9:* 189–219.

Gouldner, A. (1960) "The norm of reciprocity." *Amer. Soc. Rev. 25:* 161–178.

Henslin, J. (1968) "Trust and the cab driver," pp. 138–155 in M. Truzzi (ed.) *Sociology and Everyday Life.* Englewood Cliffs, NJ: Prentice-Hall.

Hewitt, J. and R. Stokes (1975) "Disclaimers." *Amer. Soc. Rev. 40:* 1–11.

Hochschild, A. (1983) *The Managed Heart: Commercialization of Human Feeling.* Berkeley, CA: Univ. of California Press.

Hong, L. K., W. Darrough and A. Duff (1975) "The sensuous rip-off: consumer fraud turns blue." *Urban Life and Culture 3:* 464–470.

Jorgensen, D. L. (1989) *Participant Observation.* Newbury Park, CA: Sage.

Katovich, M. A. and R. L. Diamond (1986) "Selling time: situated transactions in a noninstitutional environment." *Soc. Q. 27:* 253–271.

Lasch, C. (1977) *Haven in a Heartless World.* New York: Basic Books.

Lipman-Blumen, J. (1984) *Gender Roles and Power.* Englewood Cliffs, NJ: Prentice-Hall.

Luckenbill, D. F. (1984) "Dynamics of the sale." *Deviant Behavior 5:* 337–353.

McCaghy, C. H. and J. K. Skipper (1969) "Lesbian behavior as an adaptation to the occupation of stripping." *Social Problems 17:* 262–270.

McCaghy, C. H. and J. K. Skipper (1972) "Stripping: anatomy of a deviant life style," pp. 362–373 in S. D. Feldman and G. W. Thielbar (eds.) *Life Styles: Diversity in American Society.* Boston: Little, Brown.

Mehan, H. and H. Wood (1975) *The Reality of Ethnomethodology.* New York: John Wiley.

Mullen, K. (1985) "The impure performance frame of the public house entertainer." *Urban Life 14:* 181–203.

Prus, R. (1987) "Developing loyalty: fostering purchasing relationships in the marketplace." *Urban Life 15:* 331–366.

Prus, R. and S. Irini (1980) *Hookers, Rounders, and Desk Clerks: The Social Organization of the Hotel Community.* Salem, WI: Sheffield.

Rambo [Ronai], C. (1987) "Negotiation strategies and emotion work of the stripper." University of South Florida. (unpublished)

Rasmussen, P. and L. Kuhn (1976) "The new masseuse: play for pay." *Urban Life 5:* 271–292.

Riemer, J. W. (1977) "Varieties of opportunistic research." *Urban Life 5:* 467–477.

Robboy, H. (1985) "Emotional labor and sexual exploitation in an occupational role." Presented at the annual meetings of the Mid South Sociological Society, Little Rock, AR.

Safilios-Rothschild, C. (1977) *Love, Sex, and Sex Roles.* Englewood Cliffs, NJ: Prentice-Hall.

Salutin, M. (1971) "Stripper morality." *Transaction 8:* 12–22.

Scott, M. B. and S. M. Lyman (1968) "Accounts." *Amer. Soc. Rev. 33:* 46–62.

Skipper, J. K. and C. H. McCaghy (1970) "Stripteasers: the anatomy and career contingencies of a deviant occupation." *Social Problems 17:* 391–405.

Skipper, J. K. and C. H. McCaghy (1971) "Stripteasing: a sex oriented occupation," pp. 275–296 in J. Henslin (ed.) *The Sociology of Sex.* New York: Appleton Century Crofts.

Sykes, G. and D. Matza (1957) "Techniques of neutralization: a theory of delinquency." *Amer. Soc. Rev. 22:* 664–670.

Turner, R. (1962) "Role-taking: process versus conformity," pp. 20–40 in A. M. Rose (ed.) *Human Behavior and Social Process.* Boston: Houghton Mifflin.

Webb, E. J., D. T. Campbell, R. D. Schwartz, and L. Sechrest (1965) *Unobtrusive Measures.* Chicago: Rand McNally.

Weinstein, E. A., and P. Deutschberger (1963) "Some dimensions of altercasting." *Sociometry 26:* 454–466.

Nonmainstream Body Modification

Genital Piercing, Branding, Burning, and Cutting

JAMES MYERS

The term *body modification* properly includes cosmetics, coiffure, ornamentation, adornment, tattooing, scarification, piercing, cutting, branding, and other procedures done mostly for aesthetic reasons. It is a phenomenon possibly as old as genus *Homo,* or at least as ancient as when an intelligent being looked down at some clay on the ground, daubed a patch of it on each cheek, and caught the pleasing reflection on the surface of a pond. . . .

At the outset, it is important to distinguish between the two main types of body modification: permanent (or irreversible) and temporary. Permanent modifications, such as tattooing, branding, scarification, and piercing result in indelible markings on the surface of the body. With the exception of branding, these marks involve the application of sharp instruments to the skin. Dental alterations, skull modeling, and modern plastic surgery are also forms of permanent body modification. Temporary modifications include body painting, cosmetics, hair styling, costume, ornamentation, and any other alteration that can be washed off, dusted away, or simply lifted off the body. This article focuses on permanent body modifications in contemporary United States, especially genital piercing, branding, and cutting.

The literature of anthropology abounds with descriptive and analytical accounts of body modification among humans, but almost all of it emanates from people living or who had lived in the non-Western traditional societies of the world. From Mayan tongue piercing to Mandan flesh skewering, Ubangi lip stretching to Tiv scarification, there is a vast and incredibly varied body of literature that seeks to explain it all—anthropologically, psychologically, sociologically, and biologically. Curiously, very little research has been done on contemporary, nonmainstream

James Myers. *Journal of Contemporary Ethnography,* Vol. 21 No. 3, October 1992 267–306. © 1992 Sage Publications, Inc. Reprinted by permission of Sage Publications, Inc.

American body modification. When one considers the huge amount of literature devoted to the subject among traditional non-Western peoples, this paucity of data becomes glaringly evident. For example, one of the best recent sources on body modification is Rubin's (1988) *Marks of Civilization,* but even in this excellent publication, most of the articles deal with tattoos and cicatrization and none are devoted to such contemporary Euro-American practices as multiple piercing, scarification, cutting, and branding.

That a tattoo renaissance has been occurring in the United States since the late 1960s is now quite evident in the popular media and to a growing extent in scholarly publications and papers presented at professional conferences (see especially Govenar 1977; Rubin 1988; Sanders 1986, 1988a, 1988b, 1989; St. Clair and Govenar 1981). This void in the literature is probably due more to a simple lack of awareness of the practice than it is a lack of interest, as the population of people involved in multiple piercing, scarification, branding, and cutting is minuscule compared to tattooing. In addition, because the modification and/or jewelry involved typically creates even greater revulsion in the general public's eye than tattoos, much of the work is kept secret among recipients and their intimates.

• • •

This article contains four major sections. First, I discuss the methods used and the population involved in the study. This section also includes some thoughts on the pleasures and problems of conducting fieldwork with nonmainstream body modifiers. Following this is a presentation of the ethnographic data, the largest portion of which is devoted to a description of my participant observation work with four different body modification workshops in San Francisco, California. The next section explores the motivation and rationale behind those who participate in body modification despite the physical pain involved and the stigma that American society attaches to the behavior. Finally, I conclude with some observations on the conventionality of the individuals in the study, an assessment that runs counter to the prevailing medical literature on the subject and the views held by the general American public. I also relate nonmainstream body modification to the worldwide practice of rites and passage and the rich body of ritual symbolism accompanying such rites.

Method and Population

My original plan was to concentrate my research efforts on tattooing, but 4 months into the 24-month study period, I shifted my focus almost entirely to piercing, cutting, burning, and branding. The change was brought about by my increasing awareness of the growing popularity of nonmainstream modification other than tattoos and the realization that research on the subject was scant. I was also intrigued by the deep feelings of revulsion and resentment held by mainstream American society against these forms of body modifications.

Using participant observation and interviews as primary data-gathering techniques, I involved myself in six workshops organized especially for the San Francisco SM (sadomasochist) community by Powerhouse (fictitious name), a San Francisco Bay Area SM organization. Tattoo and piercing studios were also a rich source of data, as was the 5th Annual Living in Leather Convention held in Portland, Oregon in October 1990. I gathered additional data from a small but dedicated group of nonmainstream body modifiers at my university and the city in which it is located. Interviews with several medical specialists and an examination of pertinent medical literature provided an important perspective, as did solicited and unsolicited commentary from hundreds of mainstream society individuals who viewed my body modification slides and/or heard me lecture on the topic. Finally, chance encounters with devotees served to broaden my awareness and understanding of the various forms of nonmainstream body modification.

Entree to the workshops was of paramount importance to the study; thus early in the fieldwork, I contacted the primary organizer of Powerhouse and introduced myself as a straight, male anthropologist interested in attending the workshops in order to gather data on nonmainstream body modification for use in my university classroom and publication in a scholarly journal. Her response was immediate:

Good God, yes! You're welcome to come. We need people to see that just because we're kinky doesn't mean we're crazy, too. You'll see people here with all kinds of sexual interests. We learn from each other and have a heckuva lot of fun while we're at it.

As is true for most ethnographic participant observation situations, the largest amount of my data from the workshops were gathered from observation. I participated in the true sense of the word on two occasions, once during a play piercing demonstration and again during a playing with fire demonstration. The rest of my participation involved such typical "interested involvement" as mingling, asking questions as an audience member, introducing myself around, helping arrange chairs, setting up demonstration paraphernalia, taking photographs, conducting interviews, and generally lending a hand whenever possible. At the Living in Leather Convention in Portland, I was able to expand my involvement by showing my body modification slides to several people, attending parties, and helping out at the host organization's hospitality suite.

The population of body modifiers in my study included males and females, heterosexuals and homosexuals (lesbians and gays), bisexuals, and SMers. It is important to note that the single largest group was composed of SM homosexuals and bisexuals. Although this skewing likely resulted from my extended contact with the Powerhouse workshops and several SM body modifiers who I interviewed at the Living in Leather Convention in Portland, it is supported by a 1985 piercing profile of subscribers to *Piercing Fans International Quarterly* (Nichols 1985). The survey determined that 37% of the group was gay, 15% bisexual, and 57% involved in dominant-submissive play, a keystone of SM activity. Also of interest from the *PFIQ* profile, 83% had attended college, 24% had college degrees, and 33% had undertaken postgraduate study. Caucasians represented 93% of the survey.

Like any fieldwork, this research had its pleasant and difficult aspects. On the positive side was the subject matter itself. Body modification is inherently fascinating to human beings. In addition, there was the relative ease with which I was able to gather empirical data on the topic. The people I interviewed and observed were for the most part, barely subdued exhibtionists who took joy in displaying and discussing their body and its alterations. This was especially true when a group was together and a sense of trust pervaded the room. On such occasions, an exuberant "show and tell" was the order of the day. To fieldworkers accustomed to tight-lipped, monosyllabic responses and other forms of "informant lockjaw" from people they are studying, and who have been advised on occasion what they could do with their camera, it should be understandable why it was a pleasure to work with this uninhibited, communicative population.

Such rapport presupposes that an element of trust has been achieved between the field-worker and the individuals or group being studied. Many people whom I interviewed were keenly aware that because mainstream society regarded them as deviants, there was a high probability that harm to themselves or their life-style was never far away. Thus interaction between the field-worker and the individuals being studied must occur early to establish the trust necessary to conduct a worthwhile study.

Naturally, there were dilemmas and problems, of which photography loomed the largest. Photography is a must in any discipline where the recording and analysis of visual data is important, but unfortunately it also has the capability of violating the personal world of those being studied. The agonizing dilemma in my use of the camera at workshops and with individual informants quickly became apparent to me. Body modification is a visually charged phenomenon that is by its very nature designed to be seen. The richest written description of a tattoo or piercing when compared to a photograph can only pale. I was always plagued by the nagging question, "Should I or shouldn't I?" Fortunately, many subjects made it easy for me by volunteering, "Would you like to take a picture?" Others queried me regarding the use of the photos and their concerns that they might appear in a newspaper or magazine. Some of them flatly said no, often with an apology and some such clarifying comment as "My family lives in the area and they'd die if they knew what kind of scene I was into."

I always asked permission to take photos and tried to use common sense in determining whether or not a particular situation was appropriate for photography. For example, I did not take pictures during actual workshop demonstrations but did so only while people were socializing before and after each session.

I believe that, overall, my camera helped to reduce barriers between myself and my informants. Indeed, many people requested, and received from me, copies of photographs I had taken of them. This exchange served as a type of "cultural brokerage" and enhanced my rapport with several individuals. Still, I must confess that although I took hundreds of pictures during the fieldwork, I was never quite able to shake the uncomfortable feeling that I was intruding in someone's very personal life.

As always in fieldwork, there was the problem of assessing informant reliability. In the case of my SM body modifiers, this problem reached new heights for me because of their devotion to fantasy, imagination, and role-playing. For example, although role-playing in an SM relationship is usually reserved for a specific "scene," on a few occasions I encountered informants who cleverly remained in their contrived roles throughout my interview. If not detected, the ethnographic perils inherent in such a maneuver can be devastating. For example, I am reminded that it took me 2 weeks to discover that one Wolfgang Muller, who wore a heavy, shin-length Wehrmacht coat and spoke English with a thick German accent during my interview, was actually an American accountant from Oregon and not, as he led me to believe, an expatriated East German border guard who had recently immigrated to the United States after the Berlin Wall was razed.

Another difficult aspect of my research was continually having to affirm the legitimacy of my topic to campus colleagues. There were welcome exceptions, but most seemed to view my work as a thinly disguised voyeuristic adventure. I fared better within my own department, but even these culturally aware stalwarts were often incredulous and jokingly referred to me by such cute sobriquets as Dr. Kink or Professor Sleaze. For the most part, students were enthralled with the topic and, with mouths agape, viewed my slides with a mixture of curiosity and astonishment. However, some were less enthusiastic. During a one-semester period, the dean of my college received formal complaints from two students to the effect that I was showing pornography in class. In addition, a colleague for whom I guest-lectured was graced with a particularly nasty written assessment of my presentation. Of interest here is the zero number of complaints registered to me or anyone during my 30-year period of discussing, semester after semester, similar forms of body modification in non-Western cultures. After listening to me ruminate on this problem, one of my anthropology graduate students offered a provocative observation, "As long as the tits and pricks being pierced are brown, OK—but if they're white, no way!"

Most of the ethnographic data in my study were derived from the body modification SM workshops I observed and the contacts I made while in attendance. These workshops were part of a series of continuing programs sponsored by Powerhouse and were designed to "enhance the SM experience." Taught by individuals who were regarded as professional practitioners of various nonmainstream body modifications, the workshops were limited to a top enrollment of 50 people. The six workshops I attended were on male piercing, female piercing, branding and burning, cutting, play piercing, and playing with fire. The audience at each workshop was markedly homogeneous. With the exception of myself and perhaps a half-dozen others, each session was typically attended by SM-oriented lesbians, gays, and bisexuals. Participants ranged in age from their late teens to their late 50s, with most attendees in their mid-20s and 30s. Leather was predominant—jackets, trousers, skirts, chaps, trucker's caps, gloves, boots, arm bands, wrist bands, and gauntlets. Heavily laden key rings, hunting knives in leather scabbards, slave collars, and T-shirts with sexual preference messages were also omnipresent. Tattoos, lip and nasal septum piercings, and multiple pierced ears were quickly visible, whereas more intimate piercings, such as nipple, navel, and genital would become evident as the workshops proceeded. It is fair to say that the groups would have attracted some attention were they to have gathered in a suburban shopping mall.

The four workshops described here were held on Saturday afternoons in an upstairs room of a liberal church in San Francisco. Two other workshops I attended but do not describe in this article were conducted in a small room above a popular San Francisco gay bar.

Male Piercing

The first workshop in the series was on male piercing. Jim Ward, the teacher, was the president of Gauntlet, Inc., one of the few firms in the world that manufactures nonmainstream piercewear. Recognized as a "master piercer," Ward has been piercing since the mid-1970s and has estimated that he has done 15,000 piercings in the 14 years between 1975 and 1989. He is also the editor and publisher of *Piercing Fans International Quarterly (PFIQ)*, a successful glossy publication devoted exclusively to the subject of piercing. . . .

Ward arrived at the workshop early to set up his piercing equipment and a massage table that would serve as a piercing couch. He was wearing Levi's, a studded belt, black boots, and a black T-shirt that had the logo "Modern Primitives" (see Vale and Juno 1989) printed above 12 white-bordered rectangles, each of which contained a graphic drawing of one of the most popular genital piercings. Ward's lover and assistant set out several jewelry display cases and arranged chairs for the audience. He had multiple ear piercings, a bonelike tusk in his nasal septum, and a Gauntlet button on his T-shirt that proclaimed "We've got what it takes to fill your hole."

Ward's popularity and fame were evident as several arrivees paid their respect by shaking his hand or hugging and kissing him. Even though the workshop was on male piercing, one third of the audience was women, a crossing-over evident at each of the workshops regardless of the gender-specific body modification being highlighted. Ward welcomed the group, confirmed that his prearranged volunteers were present, and began his discussion of male piercing. It was evident that he had been through the routine many times, which he had, both before live audiences and in his continuing series in *PFIQ,* "Piercing With a Pro." His presentation was divided into halves, the first of which was a general discussion of the topic, or as he said, "the ins and outs of piercings," and the second consisting of actual demonstrations. As was true of each of the Powerhouse workshops, there was much emphasis on safety, cleanliness, sterilization, and proper hygiene after the procedure. Assuming that most of his audience was already involved in or at least aware of piercing, Ward dispensed without definition such esoteric piercing terminology as ampallang, dydoe, frenum, Prince

Albert, guiche, and so on. Questions were asked about autoclave temperatures, rubber gloves, anesthetics, antiseptics, play piercing versus permanent piercing, the dangers of AIDS and hepatitis, body rejection, jewelry selection, and the like.

During the break, I asked Ward about his own piercings:

Well, you can see them in my ear lobe and tragus, but I also have a Prince Albert in my cock and a nipple ring on each tit. Oh, I've got a guiche with a piece of cord in it, too. I'm wearing all that stuff right now. I've been piercing myself for 20 years, but I don't wear jewelry in most of the holes. I travel all over the country, and I can tell you it's a real mind-fuck to get on an airplane and sit next to some hunk knowing you've got all this sexy stuff on.

I also talked with an audience member who was not interested in getting pierced but wanted to see what the attraction was for his pierced friends:

I don't feel the need to get pierced. Actually, I'm deathly afraid of needles. I don't think I have to look like a pin cushion in order to look sexy. When I'm out cruising I might stuff my balls through a couple cock rings. Gives me a great feeling and enough basket to turn a few heads. Best of all, no artificial holes in my body to get infected.

Ward's first volunteer after the break was a leather-clad male who wanted his left nipple repierced. He sat shirtless on the table as his companion offered him a reassuring hug. Ward examined the nipple and told the group the scar tissue from the previous piercing would make this one more difficult. He also took advantage of the audience's concern to note the difference between pain and sensation in piercing and that he preferred the latter term to best describe the feeling. The volunteer's facial expression gave the impression that he had some doubts about Ward's evaluation. Before starting the piercing, Ward summoned his second volunteer and explained to the group that before he did the nipple job he needed to prep Number 2 for his forthcoming Prince Albert, a procedure that requires the application of a local anesthetic because the needle pierces the urethra, a particularly sensitive area. Number 2 dropped his leather trousers to his ankles, and Ward casually tamped a xylacane-coated cotton swab into the urethra about 1 inch. A male in the audience teased, "I bet he wishes there wasn't any anesthetic on that Q-tip®." Laughter. Ward directed the volunteer to step over to one side of the room and wait for the anesthetic to numb the area. The volunteer, leather trousers still at his ankles and undershorts dropped below his knees, hopped over to the wall where he wafted patiently, with the Q-tip® jauntily protruding from the tip of his penis.

Ward returned to the first volunteer and spent several moments discussing different types of male nipples and the particular piercing technique warranted by each. Then he scrubbed the volunteer's nipple with Hibiclens and Betadine, marked each side of the nipple with a dot to guide the needle path, clamped a Pennington forceps on the nipple to keep it from retracting and to afford better manageability, and expertly pushed a needle through the guide dots. An audible sharp gasp and a rigid tensing of the volunteer's body confirmed Ward's earlier comment about the likelihood of tougher tissue in repiercings. There was an immediate sigh of relief from the group accompanied by applause and congratulatory whoops. One end of the jewelry was used to push the needle the rest of the way through the nipple, thus resulting in the needle being expulsed and the jewelry attached in one continuous movement. The entire procedure had taken less than 3 minutes.

The second volunteer was invited back to the table, Q-tip® still in place as he waddled across the room. Ward had him sit on the table, then decided that it would be better if he stood on the table. There was some concern in the group about this stance, as the volunteer was visibly trembling, a circumstance that was all the more worrisome because the table itself began to shake. It was not clear whether the bare-legged volunteer was simply cold or whether he was suffering from pre-op jitters. Nevertheless, Number 2 balanced precariously atop the uncertain table while Ward, who had now gained an eye-level view of his work site, examined the about-to-be-pierced penis with his eyes and his fingers. As he worked, Ward maintained a running commentary on the history of the Prince Albert, noting that "it was originally designed to tether the penis to either the right or left pant leg for a neater looking appearance, but now it's strictly erotic." After completing the usual prepping around the piercing area, he deftly pushed the needle into the underside of the penis just behind the head, into the urethra, up toward the tip of the penis and the still lodged Q-tip®. As he pushed, the Q-tip® suddenly popped out of the urethra—"a sure sign I'm on course"—followed by the tip of the gleaming needle. The volunteer gazed warily down at the sight while being steadied by a friend. Applause and cheers. The jewelry was attached and Number 2 was eased down from the table. Still shaking, he pulled up his shorts and trousers. Ward peeled off his rubber gloves and disposed of them while discussing his thoughts on abstinence during the healing process.

The third volunteer was to receive a dydoe, a piercing that would pass through both sides of the upper edge of the glans. This volunteer, in his late 40s, removed his trousers and undershorts and stretched out calmly on the table. With more than 2 hours of discussion and demonstrations behind him, Ward was now much quieter. The usual preliminaries were undertaken while the volunteer chattered about his piercing history. The group was only mildly interested in the disclosures, but full attention resumed when Ward began the actual piercing. As with the first two volunteers, this one emitted a controlled but audible gasp, then relaxed. The jewelry was attached and the volunteer hopped off the table and dressed while the group applauded. Later, this person expressed his feelings about piercing to me:

> I like the jewelry very much, but the real turn-on comes from having my body penetrated. Everytime I see that sharp, shiny needle heading towards my flesh I know I'm going to get either a dick orgasm or a head orgasm or maybe both.

Several of the audience congratulated the new piercees and expressed their appreciation to Jim Ward. The first workshop was over.

Branding and Burning

The second workshop of the series was devoted to branding and burning and was taught by Fakir Musafer. Musafer, who pierced his own penis at age 13, was 58 years old at the time of the workshop. Recognized by many as the doyen of "modern primitivism" in the United States, there is little in the practice of body modification and "body play" that he has not experienced on his own body. . . .

Musafer arrived 30 minutes before the start of the workshop. He was wearing a black T-shirt and baggy khaki cotton trousers with large flapped mid-leg pockets. Puffing on a cigarette, his hair dyed sable brown, and bereft of any visible piercing jewelry, he looked like any other middle-aged ad executive enjoying his weekend. I volunteered to help him unload his van. The contents of the box I carried up the stairs vaguely hinted of his workshop's topic—acetylene torch, metal snips, needle-nose pliers, wire, matches, incense sticks, candles, several strips of copper and tin, mirror, two potatoes, and various other oddities.

Like Jim Ward at the previous workshop, Musafer was hugged and kissed by many arrivees. And, as in all the workshops, a spirit of *bon homie* prevailed as arriving couples and singles of both sexes hugged and kissed acquaintances chatted amiably with others, and shared their latest body art. A few moments before the starting time, Musafer shed his T-shirt, revealing a small ring in each nipple. He removed the rings and deftly replaced them with hollow metal tubes, each, according to his admission, 7/8 of an inch in diameter by 1 inch in length. Then he quickly inserted white teflon tubes through the holes on each side of his chest that had been created several years earlier for his Sun Dance hooks. Each tube was about the size of a king-sized cigarette and ran vertically through the flesh behind each nipple. Finally he reached into a pocket and pulled out a large nasal septum ring, which, with the aid of an audience member, was installed in his nose. He pulled his T-shirt back on and commented, "A-h-h, that's more like it!" Now, with open arms he welcomed everyone.

"The Fakir" as he frequently refers to himself, is an old pro at this sort of presentation and glibly but knowledgeably discussed his first topic of the day: branding. With the aid of an easel and predrawn charts, we learned about technique "Don't go too deep, you're not doing a 'Mighty Dog' brand"), patterns ("The simpler the better"), important reminders ("Remember, each mark in the final scar will be two to four times thicker than the original imprint"), desirable locations ("The flatter the surface the better. Try to stick with the chest, back, tummy, thighs, butt, leg, upper arm"), and tools and materials and where to get them.

A prearranged volunteer indicated a preference for a 2-inch skull to be branded on the calf of her left leg. She reclined on the table with her skirt pulled up over her knees and her left leg extended toward Musafer's work site. A previously drawn pattern was transferred onto her left calf. As we watched, he fashioned the skull shape out of a strip of metal cut from a coffee can and showed us how to heat and apply the brand. Holding the brand in his needle-nosed pliers, he heated it in the acetylene torch until it was red hot, then quickly applied it to a piece of cardboard to check the design's appearance. Musafer also cut a potato in half and applied the reheated brand to the cut surface, noting that this was a good way for beginners to practice depth control before doing the real thing on human skin. The volunteer, a professional piercer and cutter in her early 30s, laughed with the audience as the potato hissed and smoked from Musafer's strike. "The Fakir" was now ready and alerted his client. The brand was heated, precisely positioned over the desired part of the pattern, and struck. There was an immediate hiss and a crackling sound, followed by a wisp of smoke and the odor of scorched flesh. The volunteer scarcely twitched. Musafer examined his first strike and proceeded to do six more to finish the skull, complete with stylized eyes, mouth, and teeth. The only time the volunteer reacted to the hot brand, and intensively so, was when Musafer inadvertently brushed the edge of her left foot with a "cooled" brand as he returned it to the torch for renewed heating. Musafer rubbed some Vaseline on the brand and the foot burn, and the volunteer sat up and put her low-cut boot back on. The audience applauded.

Musafer's next demonstration was on burning. Displaying a row of seven or eight self-imposed circular burns on the front of his right thigh, each about the size of a penny and resembling inoculation scars, he discussed different types of burnings ("Cigarette burns are nasty but nice"), and techniques to cause them ("I prefer incense sticks because they work real well and smell so delightful during the burn"). There was no prearranged volunteer for burning, but a woman in her early 20s volunteered from the audience. Her friends cheered her as she removed her Levi's and sat on the table. Musafer touched her gently on the legs and softly said, 'Your are giving your flesh to the gods." He also instructed her on the importance of deep breathing and visualization as he glued a 3-inch length of incense stick to her left thigh and lit it. Within 4 or 5 minutes, the stick had burned down to skin level and extinguished itself. Although the stick was slightly less than a pencil in diameter, the circular burn mark quickly expanded to the penny sized marks I had viewed earlier on Musafer's thigh. Throughout the burning, the volunteer kept her eyes tightly closed and followed Musafer's instructions on deep breathing. She now opened her eyes and the audience applauded. Several of the audience members came up to where she was sitting and examined the burn, while one of her friends asked Musafer for some extra incense sticks to take home. Musafer doled out some sticks and jokingly admonished, "Watch it, this stuff is catching!" Many chuckles. Musafer responded to several last-minute questions while packing up his paraphernalia. This workshop had ended.

Female Piercing

The female piercing workshop was taught by Raelynn Gallina, a woman recognized throughout the Bay Area as a professional "total body" piercer. In addition to her popularity as a piercer and cutter (some of her clients glowingly refer to has as "Queen of the Blood Sports"), Raelynn is a successful designer and manufacturer of jewelry. Although she pierces males ("above the navel only"), the greatest proportion of her clientele is female, most of whom are, like herself, lesbian. She had been piercing for 7 years at the time of the workshop. Two thirds of the workshop's audience of 45 people were women, all but a few of whom were lesbians involved in sadomasochism. Most of the men present were gay SMers. Raelynn announced that she had four volunteers for the afternoon and would pierce a nipple, a clitoris hood, an inner labia, and a nasal septum.

The first half of the workshop was devoted to a "do it yourself" clinic on technique, tools, antiseptics, and various do's and don'ts and ended with the admonition that it was safer and better to be pierced by a pro:

> *I get a lot of people who want me to fix up their bungled piercings. Usually turns out they were heavy into a torrid scene when someone says, "Heh! Wouldn't it be hot if we pierced each other!" All I'm saying is if you do get carried away, make sure you know what you're doing.*

After the break, Raelynn's spiritual-psychological bent revealed itself as she emphasized the importance of centering, grounding, visualization, client-practitioner compatibility, and the relationship between individual personality and type of piercing jewelry to be worn. She later commented to me:

> *Piercing is really a rite of passage. Maybe a woman is an incest victim and wants to reclaim her body. Maybe she just wants to validate some important time in her life. That's why I like to have a ceremony to go along with my piercing and why I do it in a temple—my home. Most of my clientele are bright, sensitive women. It's not as if a bunch of "diesel dykes" are busting into my place to prove how tough they are by getting their boobs punched through with needles.*

Raelynn's first volunteer was an achondroplastic dwarf in her 30s. Dressed in leather trousers and field boots, it was obvious that she was extremely popular with many in the group. At least three different women lifted her up and danced merrily around with her in their arms during the break, while numerous others bent down to kiss her on the cheeks or lips. As Raelynn described the nipple piercing she was about to perform, the volunteer peeled off her blouse and climbed up on a long-legged director's chair. Clearly visible across her left breast in what appeared to be a recent cutting were the words "The bottom from Hell." There was much laughter, expressions of encouragement, and joking about anticipated pain, needles, second doubts, and the like. Raelynn scrubbed the volunteer's left breast and nipple with Hibiclens, applied a good coating of Betadine, and clamped a Pennington forcep on the nipple. The exact penetration and exit points for the needle were marked with a pen, and

Raelynn quickly and expertly forced a needle through the nipple and into a small cork at the exit point. The forceps were removed, and a gold ring was inserted in the place of the needle. The only sign of pain from the volunteer was a short gasp as the needle pierced the nipple. As in the previous piercing procedures, there was a collective sigh of relief from the group, followed by applause and various congratulatory remarks. The volunteer climbed down from her perch and hugged Raelynn around the hips. Raelynn scooped her up, returned the hug, and kissed her.

By the time the first volunteer had put her blouse back on, the second volunteer had already removed her jeans and underpants and was sitting on the chair. In her mid 20s, this volunteer would receive a clitoris hood piercing and jewelry. During most of the procedure, she held a hand mirror over her pubic area to better monitor the procedure. Raelynn advised the client to close her eyes and visualize the process. The piercing and jewelry attachment was completed within 3 minutes, again with the client showing minimal reaction to the actual piercing. As the volunteer pulled her tight jeans on, Raelynn reminded the group that it was important to wear loose-fitting clothes when getting a genital piercing.

The third volunteer, in her mid-20s, had spent the first half of the workshop curled up in the laps of three different women. She removed her cotton skirt and hopped onto the chair. Pantyless and clean-shaven, two labia rings and a clitoris hood ring were easily visible. Raelynn announced that this client would be getting a third labia ring today and with a theatrical leer, added, "And she has asked me to do it real-l-l slow and with a twist." The audience responded with mock moaning and various teasing expressions. While Raelynn talked about genital piercing in general, the client sat spread-legged and observed with the hand mirror her present labia piercings and jewelry. Raelynn noted that a clamp was not usually needed for labia piercings and started the procedure. An audible intake of air and a slight tensing of the body were the only signs that the needle had pierced the flesh. The jewelry was quickly attached and the usual applause delivered.

I was unable to remain for the last piercing of the session, a nasal septum procedure through the nose of the first volunteer.

Cutting

Raelynn was also the teacher for the workshop on cutting. She had arrived in the room an hour before the scheduled starting time to set up her equipment and a videocamera. As people entered the room, she greeted them, occasionally examining a piercing or cutting that she had apparently performed at a previous occasion. By the starting time, 43 people had arrived and there was the usual happy buzz of chatter. Three fourths of the group were women, most of whom were wearing leather. As in the other workshops, the majority of the group members were gay and lesbian. Couples held hands, snuggled, kissed, and engaged in animated conversations. Raelynn sat on a table with knees crossed and officially greeted everyone. Although she welcomed the group by saying "Hello fellow blood sluts," and there was a button attached to her equipment case that read "I'm hungry for your blood," she quickly stated she does her cutting for aesthetic reasons and not just for the joy of blood. Some of the audience responded in unison, "O-h-h, su-u-re!" She told the group she had been cutting for approximately 8 years and that she got her start while "caught up in some heavy SM scenes."

During the 2½ hour workshop, she discussed where cuttings should be done on the body ("Fleshy areas like the butt, thighs, back—not on the neck, joints, places where there are veins"), cleanliness ("Cutting is a clean procedure, not a sterile one"), use of rubber gloves, and concern about AIDS and hepatitis, depth of cut, design, tools, and various other bits of information regarding her subject. She also distinguished between her style of cutting and the types of scarification and cicatrization done in several preliterate populations of the world.

After a short break, Rosie, a prearranged volunteer in her 40s, stripped to the waist to receive her cutting. She and Raelynn had decided earlier on a design that consisted of a pattern of stylized animal scales in a triangular shape. The design was large and would be cut into the upper left area of the back near the should blade. Raelynn scrubbed Rosie's back with the usual antiseptics, dried it off, and covered the area with stick deodorant to facilitate the transfer of the design. Using a No. 15 disposable scalpel ("Toss it after it's been used"), she started her first incision. As she cut, she explained that cutting was not really a painful procedure because of the sharp scalpel and the shallow cuts. Someone in the group wondered aloud, "is it bleeding yet?" to which someone else reported, "I certainly hope so!" Raelynn also urged would-be cutters to remember to start cutting at the bottom of the design so that the dripping blood would not wash away the uncut design. Both the cutter and the client were obviously moved by the procedure. Daubing away some blood, Raelynn told the group, "Once you start cutting someone, you get a very high, heady experience." Rosie, her eyes closed and mouth sensuously open, emitted several soft sighs during the 10-minute procedure. At one point, Rosie squeezed her companion's hand and whispered, "This is intense, wonderfully intense."

When the cutting was completed, Raelynn blotted the design several times to soak up the still bleeding incisions. Rosie was alerted to brace herself for the alcohol rinsings, which were done several times over the cutting. A towel around Rosie's waist kept the alcohol from dribbling further down her body. Raelynn then ignited a fresh rinsing of alcohol with her cigarette lighter. Aloud poof was heard, and a bluish flame danced across the entire left side of Rosie's back. The flame was quickly doused as Raelynn announced, "Rosie asked me to do that because she's into fire." Referred to as "slash and burn" by Raelynn, the fire event was repeated two more times as the audience oohed and aahed. Finally, Raelynn rubbed black ink over the entire design and the wound was covered with a protective surgical wrap. In a few days, the excess ink would be scrubbed away, leaving the lines of the cutting colored black.

Kay, the second prearranged volunteer, wanted the fish cutting already on her back touched up. The original cutting had been done by Raelynn 9 months earlier, and although the design was still easily discernible, Kay liked the idea of having it redone. Raelynn prepared the area, unpackaged a new scalpel, and recut the design in less than 10 minutes. No ink was rubbed into the wound as Kay preferred the natural look.

Raelynn ended the workshop with a discussion of different body reactions to cutting, explaining that some people scarred nicely, well enough that there was no evidence of any cutting, whereas some keloided into large amorphous bumps.

While people were socializing after the session, I talked with a woman I recognized from earlier workshops. She told me Raelynn had pierced her labia, navel, and both nipples. She also compared Fakir Musafer and Jim Ward unfavorably with Raelynn:

> Those guys are out on the edge! They're an embarrassment. I mean, bones through the noses, the branding, the fleshhooks, the pain. You heard them—"If a client is in pain, you just keep on pushing and jabbing. It'll be over before you know it." Raelynn is great because she is gentle and looks for any special aspects of your personality that will help her do a better piercing or cutting.

Motivation and Rationale

Why do certain people in American society involve themselves in nonmainstream body modification? Considering the physical pain and the stigma attached to the behavior, what is the lure? Seeking answers to why people involve themselves in a given behavior is the life blood of the social sciences, but I learned early in my fieldwork that introducing the "why" question was a turn-off for some people and as such threatened rapport. As one person explained to me,

> I get tired of people asking me why I do it. They always get that dumb creaked-out look on their face when they see someone with a nose ring, or maybe they've heard that the office receptionist had her clit pierced and they can hardly wait to ask her why. Unless you've thought seriously of doing it, don't come around and ask why we do it.

Armed with this cautionary advice, I let people choose their own moment to express their thoughts on what motivated them. Fortunately, most of my informants volunteered their feelings without my having to ask them. Not surprising, there are no clear-cut, monolithic answers to the question. The reasons why people are motivated to have their bodies altered are extremely diverse as are the attempts of scholars to account for the behavior.

The responses I received allowed me to construct several categories of individuals based on their stated motivation and rationale for being attracted to nonmainstream body modification. A brief analytical commentary follows each category.

Sexual Enhancement

• • •

Sexual enhancement proved to be one of the most compelling reasons behind people's desire to alter their bodies. Even though sexual enhancement is presented here as a discrete motive, it cut across and joined with all eight categories. Thus whatever the motivational category, there was typically a sexual interest lurking somewhere behind the individuals' decisions to alter their bodies.

Although the high number of sadomasochists in the study population may be a skewing factor (one doesn't have to be around SMers long before realizing that sex is an all-consuming interest), it is clear that sexual enhancement was also a primary motive for the "vanillas" (non-SMers).

• • •

The most commonly expressed belief about the sexual value of genital piercings and erotic jewelry is that they provide the wearer constant stimulation. Sheree Rose, a Los Angeles photographer active in West Coast tattoo and piercing communities, offered her feelings on the subject in Vale and Juno's (1989) *Modern Primitives*:

> *You feel stimulation all the time. Those of us who like vibrators find it's incredible because you put the vibrator on the metal and the metal starts vibrating and—it just blows you away. (p. 110)*

A married, heterosexual female in her mid-30s told me,

> *They feel wonderful. Just the feeling of that metal in my skin keeps me constantly aroused. It's like a little buzz in my body all the time.*

In referring to the sexual value of his "ball weights" (not a piercing but stainless steel rings through which one pushes his scrotum so that the weight on the rings press down on the testicles), British body modifier Genesis P-Orridge observed in *Modern Primitives* (Vale and Juno 1989),

> *[O]nce it's on, it feels like having your balls licked and sucked and being played with by someone's hand. . . . If someone pulls up on your cock, this weight pulls down on your balls, so you get this incredible interplay of up-and-down. You tend to have a semi-hard-on all the time when you wear them. (p. 177)*

In addition to the basic "turn on" of simply having the piercing and jewelry in place, myriad manipulations and tricks are available to resourceful individuals and their partners. For example, depending on the type of jewelry and its location, it may be tugged, stroked, rotated, pushed, or bedecked with sundry devices of either an ornamental or functional nature. Certain piercings and jewelry may be used as tethering points for bondage enthusiasts. A chain or cord connected to one or several pieces of piercing jewelry presents numerous erotic possibilities: A strategic chain tug during sex may intensify pleasure or delay orgasm; a continuous network of delicate chains may interconnect several piercings on an individual (e.g., ears, nipples, navel, and labia), thus maximizing the number of erogenous zones that may be stimulated with a single pull; in an SM scene, a chain or cord may be attached to a slave's penis piercing or labia ring, allowing the master to "take the reins."

There is much discussion (and often spirited disagreement) among genital piercers as to which partner derives benefit during intercourse from a given piercing. Ostensibly, the ampallang (horizontal piercing through the penis head) favors the insertee; the apadravya (similar to ampallang, but the piercing runs vertically through the penis head) is commonly believed to increase sensation for both partners during intercourse; the Prince Albert (piercing through the urethra at the base of the penis head) is said to enhance pleasure for the wearer; labia and clitoris piercings are regarded as primarily beneficial to the wearer but also capable of intensifying a partner's pleasure.

Some individuals opt for piercings and jewelry that temporarily prohibit sex. A ring through the foreskin or a ring connecting the labia majora are examples of contemporary piercings that prevent sexual intercourse. Although most "chastity" piercings in the United States today are done for fantasy and/or erotic reasons, Jim Ward's exotic jewelry firm, Gauntlet, does a brisk business in manufacturing two types of rustless locks designed for fitting on genitalia: a purely decorative model called "The Imposter" and a functional version that requires a key. For the serious chastity-minded individual, a device called a Franey cage is available. The Franey cage involves two piercings, one at the base of the penis and the other through frenum, the effect of which even prohibits masturbation.

Piercing devotees believe that one's imagination and resourcefulness are the only limitations to the various sexual pleasures that may be derived from piercing.

Pain

• • •

Cross-cultural ethnographic literature has long recognized pain as an essential element in rites of passage (e.g., Brain 1979; Brown 1963; Ebin 1979; Gould 1968; Trigger 1969; Van Gennep 1960). Recognizing the process of inflicting and receiving pain in public as part and parcel of a rite of passage ceremony, Bilmes and Howard (1980) concluded that such ceremonies represent ingeniously constructed cultural dramas involving three classes of participants—inflictor, victim (initiate), and audience. Although Bilmes and Howard supported their argument with non-Western examples of ritual pain infliction, their rite-of-passage-as-cultural-drama thesis is particularly relevant to understanding the role of pain in body modification in contemporary United States. For example, all three classes of participants were evident in the piercing, branding, burning, and cutting events I observed. The inflictor reigned supreme during a given body modification drama, not only as the skilled practitioner who performed the modification but as a model representative of the cadre of people who already possess some form of nonmainstream modification. The victim (or initiate) was the sine qua non of each event, having decided to endure the pain in order to become incorporated into the aspired ranks of body modifiers. As in all rites of passage, the initiate's comportment while undergoing pain is of paramount importance. The third class of participants, the audience, is also critical in the drama. Because a change of status frequently underlies a rite of passage ceremony, it is important that the drama be acknowledged by others. Sanders (1988b) observed that 69% of the tattooees in his study received their first tattoo with an audience of family or friends. Having witnesses enhances and validates one's transformation into the desired status, either as a first-timer or a repeating enthusiast. . . .

Thus pain, like sexual enhancement, was an underlying theme that was never far from the minds of those involved in the process. Although only a few individuals in the study stated that pain was a primary motive, everyone, SM or not, recognized its inevitability and importance, and greeted it with a gamut of emotions that ranged from eager anticipation to trembling fear, with most people simply registering a stoic acceptance of the fact.

Affiliation

It's not that we're sheep, getting pierced or cut just because everyone else is. I like to think it's because we're a very special group and we like doing something that sets us off from others . . . You see all the guys at the bar and you know they are pierced and tattooed, and it gives you a good feeling to know you're one of them . . . Happiness is standing in line at a cafeteria and detecting that the straight-looking babe in front of you has her nipples pierced. I don't really care what her sexual orientation is, I can relate to her.

Potential nonmainstream body modifiers frequently decide to alter their bodies because of a desire to identify themselves with a group of people they have deemed significantly important (for the importance of the tattoo as a mark of affiliation, see Sanders 1988b). Through the acquisition of a genital piercing or a brand for instance, individuals obtain a badge of admission—a visible record that affiliates them with others of similar interests and beliefs. Cross-culturally, clothing and hairstyles are the most obvious identifying mediums, and although important to the body modifiers in the study, neither carry the emotional wallop of the irreversible body mark. Whether one wishes to announce affiliation with the Hell's Angels, the Army or Navy, a youth gang, or any specific group, such body marks visually proclaim a sense of camaraderie to others so marked.

Although affiliation with a desired group is typically a primary motivation for nonmainstream body modifiers, some individuals become involved because of the attendant disaffiliation from mainstream society. Similar to the tattooees in Sanders's (1988b) study, these individuals revel in the stigmatic power of their alterations. . . .

Aesthetic

God made my nipples beautiful, but my piercings made them even more so . . . A brand on someone's thigh is very attractive, but so is any kind of mark that shows the person likes to play with his body . . . My cutting is like a piece of fine art . . . The brand I have now is on my back, but the next one I get will be on my arm so I can enjoy it all day.

The old adage "beauty is in the eye of the beholder" is particularly relevant to this motive, as the vast majority of people in the study regarded their alterations as well as those of others as an extraordinarily appealing addition to their bodies. As one devotee explained while examining the newly installed white gold circular barbell on her labia:

Each time I get a piercing my boyfriend accuses me of gilding the lily, but I think my jewelry magically transforms a piece of flesh into a work of art.

• • •

Whether the alteration was a piercing, branding, cutting, or burn mark, everyone involved in the process regarded the new decoration as a piece of art. Thus the recipients, the practitioners, and the audience graced the particular embellishment with such aesthetically descriptive words as gorgeous, elegant, lovely, magnificent, stunning, delicate, and exquisite.

Trust/Loyalty

It meant a lot to me when Nathan fulfilled my wish that he get a Prince Albert . . . Every slave I've had knew damn well he would have to prove his loyalty to me by getting pierced or branded. A good master would expect no less . . . I was always afraid to get pierced because I knew it would hurt. But when Mistress told me it would reflect my trust and love for her, I did it.

Trust and loyalty was an especially important motive for the SM body modifiers in the study. Because SM play ranges from gentle to rough, with some scenes becoming potentially lifethreatening, there is constant talk about trust. No wonder, then, that the achievement of trust, and its companion, loyalty, are regarded by many SMers as the ultimate aphrodisiacs:

> *SM is the anniversary when your lover has a gold ring put through your labia (and no anesthesia); then she holds you and says you're hers forever; and you'd do anything for her. (Miesen 1988, 37)*

The irreversibility of a permanent body modification may be frightening to some people, but others find the prospects terribly appealing. Thus many couples, SM or non-SM, may regard a piercing or a branding as a love token, at once a test and a lasting symbol of trust and loyalty to each other. An interviewee expressed her feelings about the relationship between trust and her piercings this way:

> *The whole thing boils down to who do you trust? Do you think I trust my supervisor not to fire me if he learned about this stuff? Come on! My life-style can only exist on trust. When I find myself in a promising rela- tionship, a mutual piercing with some distinctive jewelry pumps up the trust level.*

Religious/Mystic

• • •

It was not unusual to hear both the practitioners and the recipients of body alter- ations use religious/mystic reasons to account for their involvement in the process. . . .

Fakir Musafer typically couches his "body play" activities in religious/mystic terms. Certainly, his flesh-skewering Sun Dance, his constant intertwining of perma- nent body alterations with talk of shamanic journeys, altered states, primal urges, East- ern religions, and so on serve as examples.

To many contemporary body modifiers, intentional body marks serve as a sa- cred chronicle to the individual's spiritual commitment. As Victor Turner (1987) aptly concluded,

> *It is clear that the body, whether clad or unclad, painted or unpainted, smooth or scarred, is never religiously neutral: it is always and everywhere a complex signifier of spirit, society, self, and cosmos. (pp. 274–75)*

Shock Value

> *I love it when they stare at me and their eyes scream "Deviant!" . . . Half the fun is walking down Powell with a big bone through my nose and watching those straight fuckers' jaws drop . . . Frankly, the*

biggest kick for me is watching my friends' faces when I casually tell them my cock's got a ring through it . . . Some of my so-called cool acquaintances try to look calm while we're talking, but I can tell they're blown away when I'm wearing my monster 4-gauge septum ring. I love it.

There were several opinions expressed regarding one's body modifications and the degree of shock they caused when viewed by others. No one professed that shock value was the primary motive for their involvement, but almost everyone had an observation or story about the reaction their alterations caused in one person or another.

Sanders (1988b) noted that tattooees gauged the reactions of strangers or casual associates in order to categorize them as compatible or noncompatible. Multiple piercers and branders use their body marks or piercings in a similar fashion.

Depending on the degree of association or the context of the encounter, some body modifiers were genuinely tickled when someone registered shock, whereas others were embarrassed. Among strangers, a few brandished their marks and accoutrements like a feisty porcupine, purposely inviting a gawk, leer, or odious comment. Yet in the company of friends or other body modifiers, someone with outlandish "jumbo jewelry" or a particularly salacious tattoo would garner admiring glances and appreciative comments.

Conclusions

Taken as a whole, the responses from my informants portray a group of individuals who for a variety of reasons enthusiastically involve themselves in nonmainstream body modification. They readily admit that their body modification interests are statistically outside the average range, but none transfer this conclusion to a statement regarding a deficiency in mental health. The medical literature on the topic presents a picture of deeply disturbed individuals engaging in self-mutilation for various psychopathological reasons (for an understanding of the medical interpretation of self-mutilation, see American Psychiatric Association 1987; Eckert 1977; Greilsheimer and Grover 1979; Pao 1969; Phillips and Muzaffer 1961; Tsunenari et al. 1981). This view is supported by the general nonparticipating public. My empirical observations lead me to disagree with the latter assessment. The overwhelming number of people in my study appeared to be remarkably conventional sane individuals. Informed, educated, and employed in good jobs, they are functional and successful by social standards.

Given the motivations and rationale for body modification provided by the respondents, and their awareness of the ceremonial nature surrounding the bestowal and receiving of such nonmainstream alterations as branding, cutting, and genital piercing, it is possible to generate some conclusions regarding the phenomenon in contemporary United States. The worldwide practice of rites of passage, the rich body of ritual symbolism accompanying such rites, and the use of body ornamentation as a symbolic language provide the basis for such conclusions.

• • •

The number of contemporary Americans who have become involved with nonmainstream body modification is presently small. However, it is important to remember that the practices discussed in this article are a relatively new phenomenon in this culture. Each year, American society is bombarded with new body alterations, many of which are quickly assessed as unacceptable for one reason or another and fail to enter mainstream society. However, recent history also shows that some initially rejected alterations may take hold in a subculture and eventually catapult their way into the larger society. For example, ear piercing in American moved from nonmainstream to mainstream society in less than a decade and multiple ear piercing among both males and females is now relatively common. Lip and nose piercing is increasingly tolerated, but whether nipple piercing will follow suit remains to be seen.

A growing number of people in American culture believe that the penis and the clitoris are just as deserving of gilding as are earlobes. These individuals, like the style setters in earlier times who defied American society's strictures on body alteration by experimenting with such daring embellishments as lipstick, rouge, painted nails, eye makeup, and radical hairstyles, join human beings around the world in using their bodies to express a symbolic language that reveals their sentiments, dispositions, and desired alliances. Through adornment, the naked skin moves one from the biological world to the cultural world. As David Lévi-Strauss observed in Vale and Juno's (1989) book,

The unmarked body is a raw, inarticulate, mute body. It is only when the body acquires the "Marks of Civilization" that it begins to communicate and becomes an active part of the social body. (p. 158)

References

American Psychiatric Association. 1987. *Diagnostic and statistical manual of mental disorders.* 3d ed. Washington, DC: American Psychiatric Association.

Baumeister, R. 1988. Masochism as escape from self. *Journal of Sex Research* 25:29.

Bilmes, J., and A. Howard. 1980. Pain as cultural drama. *Anthropology and Humanism Quarterly* 5:10–12.

Brain, D. 1979. *The decorated body.* New York: Harper & Row.

Brown, J. 1963. A cross-cultural study of female initiation rites. *American Anthropologist* 65:837–53.

Califia. P. 1987. A personal view of the history of the lesbian community and movement in San Francisco. In *Samois: Coming to power,* 243–87. Boston, MA: Alyson.

Cawte, J. 1973. Why we slit the penis. In *The psychology of aboriginal Australians,* edited by G. E. Kearney, P. R. deLacy, and G. R. Davidson, 390. New York: Wiley.

Ebin, V. 1979. *The body decorated.* London: Thames & Hudson.

Eckert, G. 1977. The pathology of self-mutilation and destructive acts: A forensic study and review. *Journal of Forensic Sciences* 22:54.

Gebhard, R. 1969. Fetishism and sadomasochism. In *Dynamics of deviant sexuality,* edited by J. H. Masserman, 71–80. New York: Grune & Stratton.

Gould, R. 1968. Masculinity and mutilation in a primitive society. *Medical Opinion and Review* 4:59–75.

Gollwitzer, P. 1986. Striving for specific identities: The social reality of self-symbolizing, In *Public self and private self,* edited by R. Baumeister, 143–59. New York: Springer-Verlag.

Govenar, A. 1977. The acquisition of tattooing competence: An introduction. *Folklore Annual of the University Folklore Association* 7 and 8.

Greilsheimer, H., and J. Grover. 1979. Male genital self-mutilation. *Archives of General Psychiatry* 36:441.

Lévi-Strauss, C. 1970. *The raw and the cooked.* New York: Harper.

Mains, G. 1984. *Urban aboriginals.* San Francisco, CA: Gay Sunshine Press.

Miesen, D. 1988. SM: A view of sadomasochism. *Sandmutopia Guardian and Dungeon Journal* 3:37.

Nichols, M. 1985. The piercing profile evaluated. *Piercing Fans International Quarterly* 24:14–15.

Pao, P. 1969. The syndrome of delicate self-cutting. *British Journal of Medical Psychiatry* 42:195.

Phillips, R., and A. Muzaffer. 1961. Aspects of self-mutilation in the population of a large psychiatric hospital. *Psychiatric Quarterly* 35:421.

Reik, T. 1957. *Masochism in modern man.* New York: Grove.

Rubin, A. 1988. *Marks of civilization.* Los Angeles: Museum of Cultural History.

Sanders, C. 1986. Tattooing as fine art and client work: The art work of Carl (Shotsie) Gorman. *Appearances* 12:12–13.

———. 1988a. Drill and fill: Client choice, client typologies and interactional control in commercial tattoo settings. In *Marks of civilization,* edited by A. Rubin, 219–31. Los Angeles, CA: Museum of Cultural History.

———. 1988b. Marks of mischief: Becoming and being tattooed. *Journal of Contemporary Ethnography* 16:395–432.

———. 1989. *Customizing the body. The art and culture of tattooing.* Philadelphia, PA: Temple University Press.

Seeger, A. 1975. The meaning of body ornaments: A Suya example. *Ethnology* 14:211–23.

St. Clair, L., and A. Govenar. 1981. *Stoney knows how: Life as a tattoo artist.* Lexington, KY: University Press of Kentucky.

Tonkinson, R. 1978. *The Mardudjara aborigines: Living the dream in Australia's desert.* New York: Holt, Rinehart & Winston.

Townsend, L. 1983. *The leatherman's handbook 2.* New York: Modernismo.

Trigger, B. 1969. *The Huron: Farmers of the north.* New York: Holt, Rinehart & Winston.

Truscott, C. 1989. Interview with a sexologist: Dr. Charles Moser. *Sandmutopia Guardian and Dungeon Journal* 4:23–24.

Tsunenari, S., et al. 1981. Self-mutilation: Plastic spherules in penile skin in *yakuza,* Japan's racketeers. *American Journal of Forensic Medical Pathology* 2:203.

Turner, T. 1969. Cosmetics: The language of bodily adornment. In *Conformity and conflict: Readings in cultural anthropology, 5th ed.,* edited by J. Spradley and D. McCurdy, 98–107. Boston, MA: Little, Brown.

Turner, V. 1976. *The forest of symbols: Aspects of Ndemburitual.* Ithaca, NY. Cornell University Press.

———. 1987. Bodily marks. *In Encyclopedia of religion,* edited by M. Eliade, 2:274–75. New York: Macmillan.

Vale, V., and A. Juno. 1989. *Modern primitives.* San Francisco, CA: Re/Search.

Van Gennep, A. 1960. *The rites of passage.* Chicago, IL: University of Chicago Press.

Warner, W. L. 1964. *A black civilization. A study of an Australian tribe.* New York: Harper.

Weinberg, T. 1987. Sadomasochism in the United States: A review of recent sociological literature. *Journal of Sex Research* 23:50–69.

Wicklund, R., and R. Gollwitzer. 1982. *Symbolic self-completion.* Hillsdale, NJ: Lawrence Erlbaum.

Conclusion

The first section of this reader defined and advocated the use of alternative qualitative methods, and the second section addressed aspects of the qualitative research process (entry and rapport) that are vital to the successful execution of extreme designs. This section illustrates actual research applications of these methods and successful examples of entry and rapport. The extremes to which researchers are willing to go in order to examine topics becomes apparent.

Note that it is not just the topics studied (exotic dancing, narcotics dealing, and outlaw motorcycle gangs) that are extreme, but also the research strategies that were used to study them. The activities and events that transpire within these circles are virtually invisible to the traditional social science community. Traditional research designs that do address these and similar criminal and deviant topics are almost always "after-the-fact" examinations. Only by being there during the event and observing the dynamics of group actions can we fully begin to understand what transpires in the clandestine world within the immediacy of crime.

Questions for Discussion

1. Could Ronai and Ellis or Miller and Selva have studied their respective topics without such extreme measures? At what cost to the data acquired?

2. Do you agree with the argument that the end justifies the mean in the contexts of some research?

3. Did Hopper and Moore become so immersed in their study that all objectivity was lost? Did they go too far in terms of legal risk or morality?

4. To what extremes should a researcher be willing to go to obtain new data? What should the limits be?

Section 4

Stigma, Danger, and Ethics: Problems in Extreme Methods

R esearchers who practice extreme methods often face a number of difficulties and obstacles that researchers using traditional approaches usually do not encounter. Many of the topics that are studied with extreme methods are activities and types of people/communities that some no doubt find distasteful, irritating, embarrassing, or simply something that brings a negative light to those associated with the topic. Hence, when a researcher devotes time, energy, resources, and/or their career to advancing understandings and explanations for such types of activities, the research may come to be viewed as unsavory or disreputable. In other cases, when a researcher is working with (or in) communities that are rife with danger or that do not necessarily want to be studied and exposed, there is the chance that such persons may react to a researcher's presence with anger and/or violence. Or, sometimes the communities into which an extreme methods research must venture can be dangerous in their own right. Simply being present in some situations can be dangerous, if not physically dangerous, then certainly dangerous for one's reputation and standing in the community. Or, for many (if not most) researchers who have employed extreme methods, or studied extreme groups, there are likely to be situations in which the course of appropriate action may be less than clear. When faced with a situation where what is right might not be what one is being pressured to do, the stress can be immense. However, in all these types of situations, as we will see in the four articles in this section, knowing that trouble might be encountered and having at least some idea of how to handle a troublesome situation can be the best one can hope for.

In the first article, Kirby and Corzine present a classic argument about how researchers studying "odd" or extreme groups and communities may be seen by others (including other researchers) as sharing the "oddities" of the people being studied. Extreme methods researchers are often viewed by both other researchers and society in general as "different" and marginal to the scientific community. As this article points out, what happens for those who study extreme groups, and especially for those who study extreme groups using extreme methods, is that these researchers are given what Goffman called a courtesy stigma. This is the idea of "guilt by association"; it is assumed that the only people who would want to study and hang around with "those types of persons" are others who are also "those types." In short, as Kirby and Corzine show, researchers who take an extreme methods approach to their work need to carefully consider not only how they will manage relations and interactions with research participants, but also how they will manage relations and interactions with personal and professional colleagues.

The idea of stigmatization of researchers is viewed from a different angle in Sonenschein's article. In this article, we see how the mere fact that a researcher takes an extreme methods approach to a marginal topic can have not only serious personal consequences, but legal ramifications as well. Official sanctions—such as having one's research materials seized or one's being arrested—can occur for some researchers. Such outcomes do not have to come from the legal community's intervention in one's research; as Sonnenschein points out there are also other responses researchers can take, such as siding with law enforcement officials, in essence acting as an undercover agent (not a researcher). However, such situations raise clear and significant ethical questions.

The themes of ethical questions and danger to researchers is common throughout the remaining three articles of this section. The dangers that researchers using extreme methods may encounter are even more clearly outlined in the second article by Williams, Dunlap, Johnson, and Hamid. In this direct and frank discussion of dangerous, frightening, and intimidating situations that these extreme methods researchers have faced, we get personal insights to the stresses that many extreme methods researchers might expect. However, even more important in the writing of these authors is the practical advice they give about how to handle such situations. Although they argue that some personal concessions and compromises may be necessary to ensure that a project can be completed, the most important thing to keep in mind is how to protect oneself. Although the research is certainly (usually) important, keeping oneself safe is always more important.

In the third article, Goode discusses the ethics of research based on placing false personal advertisements and studying the responses to these ads. The argument that runs throughout this article is that first of all there is no alternative, valid way to study such persons, and second, that no harm comes from such an approach. As an interesting piece to this article, Goode reports the reactions of colleagues and students whom he queried about the ethics of his approach. Only a small percentage of people familiar with the study actually saw it as ethically questionable. However, one of the questions that we must contend with is whether even a small number of observers finding something unethical means that the research is ill-advised. What is the threshold for deciding that a research project is "too extreme"?

Finally, the issues of stigmatization, danger, and ethics are brought together in the fourth article by Scarce. In this reflective piece, the author discusses his own legal struggles involved in protecting the confidentiality of his research participants and upholding a code of professional ethical standards. Throughout this discussion the tension between personal beliefs, personal safety, professional responsibilities, and legal pressures are shown as nearly universal. Although it may not be common to have law enforcement officials demand disclosure of data or the identities of research participants, the potential conflict of beliefs, safety concerns, professional expectations and possible legal interventions is something to be considered for researchers who use extreme methods. Although this article presents what many would believe is an extreme example, it is fairly easy to see how similar types of situations might have arisen for many of the other researchers whose work is included in this book.

What this all means is that extreme methods are important, useful, sometimes exciting, and sometimes stigmatizing, dangerous, or (by some people's standards) ethically questionable approaches to social science research. This is not to suggest that extreme methods should be used in all situations or by all researchers. Rather, what the articles in this section suggest is that extreme methods should be employed only after careful consideration of both the positive and negative consequences of such actions.

Questions to Consider

1. Why would a researcher put him/herself at risk (physically or legally) in a research role?

2. To what degree does a researcher have a responsibility to put him/herself at risk so as to protect those they study?

3. What are types of risks that extreme methods researchers encounter in conducting their research?

On Having One's Research Seized

DAVID SONENSCHEIN

To my knowledge, Ernest Borneman (1984) is the only one thus far to have made any mention of being arrested in the course of conducting research on children's sexuality or adult-child sexual relationships. Actual arrest of researchers is rare in the history of sexology, although ridicule, harassment, job loss, and violence have been all too common. Some recently documented examples include that of psychologist John Watson, who was purged from Johns Hopkins for his "unorthodox" sex research (Magoun, 1981), and of Max Meyer, whose career at the University of Missouri was ruined by academic officials and inflamatory news reports (Esper, 1967; Magoun).

The difficulties experienced by Kinsey and his associates which were brought on by colleagues, legislators, and the press are well known. I have also learned that in the mid-1950s, the FBI approached Kinsey wanting him to reveal to them his sources of sexually explicit materials. Kinsey and Wardell Pomeroy resisted, and, in turn, pressed the agency to share its holdings with the Institute for research, causing great indignation at the Bureau. Internal memos indicate that the FBI continued to monitor Kinsey's "intrepid band" (as the agency referred to them), particularly because they were afraid the research would lead to an increase in "permissiveness" and "sexual deviancy." Further, the FBI condemned the Rockefeller Foundation's funding of the Institute, feeling that continued research in Kinsey's direction would corrupt and endanger the nation's children. A May 19, 1959, memo says that the foundations have "a stranglehold on the training ground of youth," but goes on to say that "no better instance of a reputable name being lent to enhance an unsavory cause can be found than that offered by the Rockefeller Foundation's support of the Kinsey sex studies." The agency was very upset by Kinsey's "revelation" that sex between adults and children can "contribute favorably to their later sociosexual development."

It appears that 30 years after Kinsey's day, we are again in the midst of a renewed effort to discredit and damage critical sex research. This environment brought Myers (1981) to urge the scientific countering of conservative and religious myths such as those then being promoted through *Medical Aspects of Human Sexuality* and the

David Sonenschein is an independant scholar.

Journal of the American Medical Association. Constantine and Martinson (1981) warned about the risks of research on children's sexuality, incest, and pedophilia. Baker (1984) called attention to the ongoing flow of religious and pseudo-scientific nonsense, especially the Vatican's pronouncement that masturbation "is a seriously and intrinsically disordered act."

The histories of sex education testify well to this assault. Even though the punitive intervention of the state into sexual populations or artifacts is consistent and almost predictable (Gilbert & Barkun, 1981), and the increasing "criminalization of sex" (Money, 1985) is an extension of those politics, it has been very easy—even *necessary* from those same political premises—to attack the projects and lives of researchers and educators, especially when they offer newer subject matter, methods, viewpoints, or activism.

At the 1985 Annual Meeting of the Society for the Scientific Study of Sex, Betty Brooks alluded to her 1982 suspension from California State University at Long Beach (CSULB) after being accused of "promoting lesbianism." A more sensational instance at the same time and the same university involved Barry Singer, who was suspended and felt pressed to resign amidst charges by the same conservative and religious groups of "promoting homosexuality," "immoral conduct," and "taunting license" (the latter by George Will, 1982). The police-like seizure by CSULB officials of Singer's instructional materials aroused no such indignation, however, on the part of news commentators. Included in the confiscated material was a videotape of one of his lectures, not on sex at all, but one critical of academia and "higher education." Lastly, Roger Libby was denied tenure at the University of Massachusetts allegedly because of the content of his sexuality courses; Richburg (1985) included relevant comments by John Money, Lynn Atwater, Ira Reiss, and Larry Constantine.

Most vulnerable, however, are nonacademics. The numbers of unaffiliated researchers have grown considerably since the late 1960s, and particularly when combined with progressive elements of gay liberation and feminism, thinking and research on gender and sex has had their most original and important sources beyond university endeavors. Such investigators and writers, on the other hand, lack the insulations of professions and institutions that have traditionally helped define credibility and deflect attack. More importantly, as the professions and popular media continually advertise a monolithic view of child-adult sex, accounts that are carefully edited to hint of the professional controversy, the projects of independent workers threaten to produce data severely qualifying or contradicting official views of desire, relationships, and artifacts.

In this regard, there have been a number of arrests and seizures that are pertinent to the history of sex research and crucial for the issues they raise for all researchers trying to work under erotophobic constraints. In February, 1984, independent researcher Patrick LaFollette was entrapped and arrested by Los Angeles police during the course of his inquiry into child "pornography" and pedophilia. His defense was based on his right to do research and the misdemeanor charge of exchanging "pornography" was dismissed (P. LaFollette, personal communication, 1985; Stewart, 1985). Al Katz, a State University of New York law professor, was similarly arrested in May,

1985, and all of his research materials on child "pornography" have been seized; the case is still in process (A. Katz, personal communication, 1985).

In April, 1985, the personal papers and research files of Gerald Jones were seized by the FBI using an "open warrant," a document of questionable Constitutional validity that allows the seizure of materials deemed seditious or blasphemous by the state without requiring anything other than possession. No charges have been filed against Jones, and as of this writing (mid-1986), his papers are still in the hands of the state. In a total misreading of the situation, Southern California Civil Liberties Counsel Susan McGreivy refused assistance, asserting the Southern California Civil Liberties Union did not "support pedophila" (G. Jones, personal communication, 1985, 1986). Ironically, it was McGreivy who defended Betty Brooks against charges of "advocating homosexuality." An educational psychologist, Jones is known to sex researchers for his background work on pederasty (Jones, 1982); he is also the first to take legal resistance by filing suit against the FBI and others for violation of his Constitutional rights.

In a move with some uncomfortable similarities to the 1933 Nazi raid on Hirschfeld's sexological institute, San Diego police forces seized the entire library of the lay research and educational organization, The Child Sensuality Circle, in June, 1984. It was over half a year before most, though not all, of the nearly 300 books, articles, and other documents on children's liberation were returned. No charges were filed against the group's leader, 84-year-old Valida Davila, a long-time progressive political activist. The news media participated with police in depicting her Reichian-influenced group as a "sex ring," and police fabricated reports of finding "kiddie porn" in the seizures (V. Davila, personal communication, 1984, 1985).

In January, 1986, Terry Morris, a research pyschologist, was arrested and sentenced to 10 years in federal prison for receiving child "pornography" in the mail during the course of his research; the court has also ordered psychiatric counseling. I know of three other cases of arrest and seizure but cannot detail them because the individuals do not care to be publicly identified.

Finally, in September, 1984, my own 4-year accumulation of research on pedophilia and children's sexuality was seized. At this writing, nearly 2 years later, the materials (including illegally seized legal files and personal and political writings) are still held; it was over 7 months before American Civil Liberties Union lawyers and I were able to inventory the documents. The news media again helped directly in promoting the project as a "ring," and I was charged with "sexual performance of [sic] a child" for photocopying photographs from commercial "kiddie porn" magazines for content analysis. I have been fined $5,000 and sentenced to 10 years in prison.

The content analysis was not completed, and the project, an ethnographic study of child-adult sexual relationships, has been destroyed. Fragments will appear if materials are returned; only one historiographic paper has been published (Sonenschein, 1984). Comments by arresting officer Sgt. John Russell may be of interest to other investigators: "Your research is through. Your research is over. I have finished your research for you. You can research anything but this."

These events raise a number of issues in two major areas. One is, of course, the right to do research, to conduct critical inquiry into areas of one's choice, without having that choice defined or restrained by the state. Corollary issues entail having the rights of access to and possession of materials necessary for that research, and the freedom to present publicly documents, findings, and opinions for open consideration. At issue is the right of *any* citizen to inquire into the validity of "expert" claims, to have access to materials and voices supporting or denying any given position, and to speak or write critically of official views without fear of arrest or exploitation and abuse by the news media.

More than half-a-dozen states now have laws against the mere possession of visual representations of children and sex, and a similar federal law is now being considered, one which also recommends the legal age of a child be raised from 18 to 21 for such depictions. Some states do have exemptions for research, but the burden of proof, after arrest and seizure, falls upon the investigator. More crucial are the laws which require the reporting of individuals (both the adults and the minors) known or merely suspected of engaging in adult-child sexual activity. There are not now, nor have there ever been, exemptions for researchers, although the ethical guidelines of the professional organizations call for the confidentiality of study participants. Therefore, because of the risks involved in collecting data and contacting participants, it is imperative that study design in current research on pedophilia, "pornography," and children's sexuality incorporate adequate protections against seizure and destruction of data by the state. Laws passed in the heat of phobic hysteria, whether against anarchists, communists, Jews, nonwhites, homosexuals, or pedophiles, nearly always violate Constitutional protections. Further, these laws tend to stay on the books for use at the state's determination. . . .

The second general area of concern is more serious. It has to do with professional support and participation in increasing the state's powers of surveillance and control over sexual behavior, representations, and thought. In the relative absence of dissenting voices, such behavior has, again, contributed to a historically continuing breakdown of professional and scientific integrity. I want to mention briefly three ways in which this has been happening while reserving more detailed discussion and documentation for a later work.

The first is perhaps the most astounding and involves the direct and conscious abandonment of science itself. In an article that helped set sexology back 100 years, David Finkelhor (1979) returns research and analysis to an exclusively ideological basis. By asserting his personal belief that children inherently cannot consent to sex with adults, Finkelhor says he deliberately "puts the argument on a moral, rather than empirical footing" (1979, p. 695). This opinion is of such a high order that Finkelhor, now a consulting editor for *The Journal of Sex Research,* further insists that any empirical evidence to the contrary is irrelevant and is to be totally discounted.

More incredible that such a statement could appear in a professional publication in the late 20th century is the fact that not only was so little notice taken of it by way of protest, but that it has come to be accepted as a "scientific fact.". . .

A second professional failure is that personal attack has come to replace scientific debate. The idea that evidence contrary to a position must be discounted is extended into the practice of discrediting those who present conflicting data. Fraser (1981) and Russell (1984) indicate that those who do critical research do so because they have "a self-evident interest." Russell, a featured speaker at the 1985 SSSS Annual Meeting, also censures those who contest the image of adult-child sex solely as abuse because she feels the data would "reduce society's inhibitions" against such relationships, a position remarkably similar to that taken by the FBI against Kinsey. Russell, in fact, pejoratively cites Kinsey's term "contact" as opposed to "abuse" as an example (1984, p. 248).

Like Fraser (1981), Russell (1984) suggests that such people—those discovering the varied and complex range of relationships, including positive and productive ones—are nothing more than "would-be participants" (p. 248). These accusations are easily made and accepted now because there is is a triple supportive resonance with popular prejudices, with an earlier rhetoric which included terms like "sympathizer" or "fellow traveler," and with an ongoing institutional inquisition against sexual dissidents by psychiatrists, clinical psychologists, and social workers.

Consequences of this ideological position include not only extensive disfigurement of data but the support of a climate tending to suppress critical views. Martinson's early book (1973) was rejected by 29 publishers because of the topic, its findings, or its "marketability" (F. Martinson, personal communication, 1985). In another example, the editor of the *International Journal of Law and Psychiatry* refused for 4 years to publish a solicited article by Edward Brongersma commenting on the cultural scapegoating of pedophiles. The editor indicated the reason was that Brongersma "needed to be protected from criticism." The paper, well received by the World Congress of Law and Psychiatry in 1981, was published only after a coeditor threatened to resign if the invited paper continued to be suppressed (Brongersma, 1984, personal communication, 1985).

The third area of irresponsibility is especially crucial because it involves the direct collaboration of professionals with the state in justifying and expanding its powers of ideological and behavioral control. There is a clear symbiosis between those who selectively provide theory and data for the administrative apparatus and the latter which, in turn, expands to accommodate and encourage an uncritical intensification and physical enforcement of the current science-*cum*-morality.

Further, there are instances of academics and others who are actively participating with the state in the identification, surveillance, and arrest of pedophiles simply as a *class* of individuals. I have one report of an investigator passing data and identities to the FBI, an organization famous for its criminal activities and punitive erotophobia (cf. Bullough, 1985). As another example, a book by Ann Burgess (1984), promoted as a scientific study of child "pornography" and "sex rings," includes a chapter by an FBI agent and an appendix on "fighting" to eliminate sexually explicit material. The political intent of such work is very clear and overriding of any purported scientific affiliation.

These positions are not without historical precedent, and it has been argued that medicine, psychiatry, and sexology have, in fact, been largely oriented toward the rhetorical and surgical promotion of social control. Be that as it may, the "moral" ideologies mentioned here have supported, if not originated, two major actions which continue to gather strength and efficiency. They run parallel to contemporary purity movements and a resurgent homophobia as well as relating to the ever-popular sentiments of mysogyny and ageism.

One is the most intense antisexual terrorist campaign against children since the professionally managed antimasturbation frenzies of the 19th century; the other is a movement against pedophiles reaching to predatory levels. The former is fairly obvious and easily documented, but the latter is very recent. Now, it is largely out of the hands of researchers and under the guidance of theraputic and legal agents who, like Finkelhor, consider the matter closed empirically and morally. Ideologically oriented researchers and the news media have provided the scientific and popular authorization the state needs to justify its moves toward arrest and detention of individuals on the basis of sexual interest alone. There was in late 1985 and early 1986 similar planning for "irresponsible" gays triggered by the AIDS issues. I have not yet seen the transcripts of the November, 1985 Miami hearings of the Meese Pornography Commission, but reports forwarded to me by observers indicate that it was a strategy session for prosecutors and police rather than fact-finding on pedophilia. The phrase "predisposed to crime"—a delightful essentialist expression—was added to the forensic inventory of what pedophiles are supposed to be like, and one prosecutor claimed to have a list of 5,000 pedophiles, apparently awaiting passage of appropriate laws to begin arrests. Beyond sexual interest, Bullough (1985) has documented the outrageous instance of his being targeted for arrest and detention by the FBI ("in case of national emergency") because he had the double stigma of being a sex researcher and a rights activist for sexual minorities.

At the 1985 Annual Meeting of SSSS, I heard one young professional while speaking of pedophila remark, "It's a shame such populations have to exist." The phrasing of the sentiment is rather striking. Clearly, some are doing what they can to find a solution to "the pedophile question," a solution which also seems to call for the erasure of data and researchers at variance with the state's purposes.

References

Baker, J. (1984). Sexuality, science, and social responsibility: The Georgetown scandal. *The Journal of Sex Research, 20,* 210–212.

Borneman, E. (1984). Progress in empirical research on children's sexuality. In R. Seagraves & E. Haeberle (Eds.), *Emerging dimensions of sexology* (pp. 77–90). New York: Praeger.

Brongersma, E. (1984). Aggression against pedophiles. *International Journal of Law and Psychiatry, 7,* 79–87.

Bullough, V. (1985). Problems of research on a delicate topic: A personal view. *The Journal of Sex Research, 21,* 375–386.

Burgess, A. (1984). *Child pornography and sex rings.* Lexington, MA: Lexington Books.

Constantine, L., & Martinson, F. (Eds.). (1981). *Children and sex: New findings, new perspectives.* Boston, MA: Little, Brown.

Esper, E. (1967). Max Meyer in America. *Journal of the History of the Behavioral Sciences, 3,* 107–131.

Finkelhor, D. (1979). What's wrong with sex between adults and children? *American Journal of Orthopsychiatry, 49,* 692–697.

Fraser, M. (1981). The child. In B. Taylor (Ed.), *Perspectives on pedophilia* (pp. 41–58). London: Batsford.

Gilbert, A., & Barkun, M. (1981). Disaster and sexuality. *The Journal of Sex Research, 17,* 288–299.

Jones, G. (1982). The social study of pederasty: In search of a literature base. *Journal of Homosexuality, 8,* 61–95.

Magoun, H. (1981). John B. Watson and the study of human sexual behavior. *The Journal of Sex Research, 17,* 368–378.

Martinson, F. (1973). *Infant and child sexuality: A sociological perspective.* St. Peter, MN: Book Mark (Gustavus Adolphus College).

Money, J. (1985). The conceptual neutrality of gender and the criminalization of sex. *Archives of Sexual Behavior, 14,* 279–290.

Myers, L. (1981). Sex researchers and sex myths: A challenge to activism. *The Journal of Sex Research, 17,* 84–89.

Richburg, K. (1985, September 17). Classroom sexology is study in controversy. *Washington Post,* p. A11.

Russell, D. (1984). *Sexual exploitation: Rape, child sexual abuse, and workplace harassment.* Beverly Hills, CA: Sage.

Sonenschein, D. (1984). Breaking the taboo of sex and adolescence: Children, sex, and the media. In R. Browne (Ed.), *Taboos and tabooism in culture* (pp. 111–132). Bowling Green, OH: Popular Press.

Stewart, R. (1985, March 2). Man cleared of child exploitation count. *Los Angeles Times.*

Will, G. (1982, May 27). Sex in Long Beach: Academic extremism invites popular extremism. *Los Angeles Times,* p. II-11.

Personal Safety
in Dangerous Places

TERRY WILLIAMS, ELOISE DUNLAP,
BRUCE D. JOHNSON, and ANSLEY HAMID

Personal safety during fieldwork is seldom addressed directly in the
literature. Drawing from many prior years of ethnographic research
and from field experience while studying crack distributors in New
York City, the authors provide a variety of strategies by which
ethnographic research can be safely conducted in dangerous settings. By projecting an appropriate demeanor, ethnographers can
seek others for protector and locator roles, routinely create a safety
zone in the field, and establish compatible field roles with potential
subjects. The article also provides strategies on avoiding or handling sexual approaches, common law crimes, fights, drive-by
shootings, and contacts with the police. When integrated with other
standard qualitative methods, ethnographic strategies help to ensure
that no physical harm comes to the field-worker and other staff
members. Moreover, the presence of researchers may actually reduce (and not increase) potential and actual violence among crack
distributors/abusers or others present in the field setting.

A serious problem confronting many social scientists is assuring the physical safety
of ethnographers and other staff conducting research among potentially violent
persons who are active in dangerous settings. Of equal concern is attempting to assure
the personal safety of potential research subjects. Even when extensive ethnographic
experience shows that physical violence against ethnographers has rarely occurred,
researchers may have considerable difficulty convincing others (including colleagues
and family members) that they can safely conduct fieldwork.

Some ethnographic research may be a dangerous enterprise. Howell's (1990) discussion of safety offered an extensive discussion of common law crimes (robbery, theft,
rape) in the field. Field-workers have encountered illness, injury, or death in the course

Terry Williams et al. *Journal of Contemporary Ethnography*, Vol. 21 No. 3, October 1992 343–374.
© 1992 Sage Publications, Inc. Reprinted by permission of Sage Publications, Inc.

of fieldwork due to natural and criminal causes. It is often unclear whether the field-workers were harmed by research subjects and other members of the social networks or whether they were merely victimized like any other citizen (Howell 1990).

The question of personal safety is rarely addressed as a methodological issue in its own right (Howell 1990; Sluka 1990), particularly in regard to the social milieu in which ethnographers carry out their work. There is relatively little discussion about how to minimize risks and dangers that ethnographers may face in the field, with suggestions to help ensure their personal safety. Some hints about safety may be gleaned from the extensive methodological literature in ethnography (Agar 1980; Fetterman 1989) that deals with such topics as gaining access and recruiting subjects (Johnson 1990), striking a research bargain (Carey 1972), entering the field, making observations (Broadhead and Fox 1990), selecting roles to pursue in the field (Adler and Adler 1987), building and maintaining rapport (Dunlap et al. 1990; Rose 1990), conducting interviews (McCracken 1988), and writing field notes (Fetterman 1989). In practice, paying attention to the personal safety of ethnographers goes hand in hand with learning and applying skills in these areas.

The lack of good guidelines and methodological strategies for conducting safe ethnographic fieldwork in potentially violent social settings is especially noteworthy. In one of the few articles addressing safety issues, Sluka (1990) provided a systematic discussion of the risks and dangers facing ethnographers in a politically charged, potentially violent setting by studying supporters of the Irish Republican Army in Belfast. His suggestions are strikingly relevant for ethnographers in the substance abuse field and for those who study street- and upper-level crack dealers. Sluka called for "foresight, planning, skillful maneuver, and a conscious effort at impression management" (p. 115) to minimize personal risk and danger in potentially violent settings. He further suggested that field-workers become well acquainted in the community, cultivate well-respected persons who vouch for them, avoid contacts with police, be truthful about the purpose of the research, identify potentially dangerous locales and topics, and be flexible concerning research objectives. He proposed that successful fieldwork in dangerous settings "can be done by recognizing how people are likely to define you, avoiding acting in ways that might reinforce these suspicions, and being as honest and straightforward as possible about who you really are and what you are really doing" (p. 121).

. . . In this article we will conceptually extend and apply his and others' (e.g., Adler and Adler 1987; Denzin 1970; Douglas 1972) ideas to ethnographic research in inner-city settings. We focus on issues of personal safety while conducting fieldwork in potentially dangerous settings. Closely related ethnographic issues—rapport, recruiting subjects, ethnographer roles, reciprocity, personal experiences with contacts, and so on—are briefly included in the discussion. While recognizing that ours is but one approach to doing ethnographic research, we contribute to the literature on ethnographic methods by underscoring themes and practices for personal safety that may be of interest to all ethnographers and staff conducting research in dangerous settings—or even in "safe" settings.

Method

This article emerges from the authors' many years of experience in conducting both quantitative (Johnson 1973; Johnson, Elmoghazy, and Dunlap 1990; Johnson et al. 1985, 1988) and qualitative (Carpenter et al. 1988; Dunlap 1988; Dunlap et al. 1990; Hamid 1979, 1990, 1992; Johnson, Hamid, and Sanabria 1991; Williams 1978, 1989, 1991; Williams and Kornblum 1985) research among abusers and sellers of marijuana, heroin, cocaine, and crack. All of the authors have done much of their work among low-income and minority populations (Dunlap et al. 1990; Hamid 1990; Johnson et al. 1985; Johnson, Williams, et al. 1990; Williams 1989, 1991; Williams and Kornblum 1985). These professional ethnographers (Dunlap, Hamid, Sanabria, and Williams) have extensive experience in qualitative field research on drug-related issues and other topics in New York City, Latin America, and the Caribbean. Four staff members (Arnold, Beddoe, Randolf, and Miller) are ex-drug users and/or ex-dealers who developed wide networks among upper-level dealers. Collectively, the staff has many years of experience working in or researching various aspects of drug use and dealing. The authors are professional researchers and ethnographers whose primary careers are built around research funded by grants. . . .

Building on this experience, we systematically trained staff members on issues of personal safety during an ongoing study called "Natural History of Crack Distribution." This was a qualitative study about the structure and functioning of crack distribution, including the careers of dealers in New York City (Johnson, Williams, et al. 1990; Johnson et al. 1991). During the fieldwork phase of this study, November 1989–March 1991, the ethnographic staff spent an average of 15–20 hours per week in several of New York City's most dangerous locales interacting with numerous street people. Staff members conducted intensive fieldwork in four New York City neighborhoods (Harlem, Washington Heights, Brownsville, and Williamsburg). They wrote field notes that contain observations and references to over 300 different crack distributors. They also conducted open-ended life history interviews (5–15 hours long) with 80 distributors. Fifteen of these were upper-level dealers buying and selling kilograms of cocaine; the remainder were independent sellers. To obtain this information, they conducted three or more sessions with most dealers. All interviews were recorded and transcribed. Our data and analyses rely on the strategies and experiences of ourselves and our ethnographic staff for maintaining their own personal safety as well as on specific experiences reported by other ethnographers in the drug abuse field.

Laypeople and ethnographers anticipate and are fearful about several potential sources of physical danger associated with the use and sale of crack (Brownstein and

Goldstein 1990a, 1990b; Goldstein 1985; Goldstein et al. 1990, 1991a, 1991b; *New York Newsday* 1990; *New York Times* 1990a, 1990b; *Washington Post* 1990): Crack abusers may be paranoid and behave "irrationally"; dealers routinely use violence and may threaten subjects who talk to ethnographers; use of guns leads to "random" shootings; researchers may be robbed or have articles stolen. The mass media typically feature the most violent and extreme activities of crack distributors (Reinarman and Levine 1989), so laypersons are led to believe that severe violence occurs all the time in this business. Despite these fears, ethnographic research in dangerous settings has been safely conducted for years. Our staff and many other researchers (Adler 1985; Biernacki 1988; Feldman 1974; Goldstein et al. 1990; Hanson et al. 1985; Spunt 1988; Morales 1989; Smith and Kornblum 1991) have met, talked with, and interviewed many potentially violent persons over long periods and have never been physically assaulted.

Styles of Safety

Researchers can create "safety zones" in which to conduct research in dangerous settings so as to protect themselves and the persons with whom they are interacting from physical harm or violence during the research endeavor. The following sections are organized according to conceptual themes regarding styles of safety that emphasize demeanor, protector roles, safety zones, neutrality, and common sense during fieldwork.

Style and Demeanor

Style and demeanor are central to safety. First impressions are very important. Wearing clothes appropriate to the setting prevents drawing undue attention and exhibits a sense of belonging in the setting. Researchers' attire can be viewed as an extension and manifestation of their personalities as well as a willingness to fit into the social setting. As ethnographers enter and attempt to establish a presence in the field, they explain the purpose of research, exhibit personal interest in others, and avoid drug use or sales (Adler and Adler 1987; Agar 1980; Horowitz 1986; Johnson 1990). Failure to establish this presence, and especially being perceived as a victim, by those in the drug business for instance, may greatly increase personal dangers of theft/robbery and difficulty in establishing rapport with potential subjects. Although various roles have been employed by ethnographers in a variety of settings (Becker 1960; Adler and Adler 1987), those conducting field research among drug abusers generally employ a variation of friendly stranger (Agar 1980) or friendly outsider. This role is partially mandated by a professional code of ethics forbidding illegal behavior and institutional requirements to obtain informed consent from research subjects.

Purpose and Access. Once accepted as an ordinary person in the area, initial conversations are the first step in seeking persons with whom to develop rapport. Williams has been conducting research among cocaine users since 1974. During a 17-year career, he has visited hundreds of after-hours clubs, base houses, crack houses (Williams 1978, 1989, 1991), number holes, and other settings where illegal and legal activities occur. Williams explained several strategies for gaining entry into such locales:

> *Initially I prefer to be taken into a crack house or dealing location by someone who is known there. They vouch that I'm OK and no cop. When initially approaching a crack house without someone to introduce me, I'll claim to be sent by someone they may know, like Robby, KeeKay, or someone else with a common street name. When I get inside, I may explain that I'm writing a book on crack houses (or another topic). I usually have a copy of a book I've written to show people. This approach goes a long way toward convincing skeptical persons that I'm an author and serious about my intentions.*

After gaining initial entry and some rapport with one or more persons in the setting, Dunlap found it necessary to arrange a meeting with one or more drug dealers to explain herself, to seek their permission and informed consent to conduct long life history interviews, and to strike the research bargain (see Carey 1972). The dealers can also examine the project's Certificate of Confidentiality. Dunlap explained:

> *I begin by telling them about myself, my life, and why I'm interested in them. I spend much time explaining how their identity will be concealed and how our interviews will be protected and never be available to police or law enforcement agencies. I explain the risks and benefits of the research to them in terms of their participation and obtain their informed consent. Even after these lengthy explanations, most subjects tend to remain tense and somewhat terse in their answers. Only during and after the first session of the in-depth interview do they begin to relax and talk openly about themselves. Such conversations would not even begin, however, without the assurances of confidentiality and the promise of benefits.*

The end result is that ethnographers have built substantial rapport with one or more persons, carefully explained the purpose of the research, provided assurances of protection and safety, and obtained informed consent from persons who will become potential research subjects. Of course, the ethnographer must continue to meet with and show a genuine personal interest and friendliness to such persons. Such further conversations and interactions help build strong rapport with subjects.

The "Victim" Role. As ethnographers, we need a "mind set" that assumes safety and does not lead to fearful behavior. Street people act on their intuitions and are experts in reading behavior. Dunlap expressed the critical importance of not being perceived as a victim ("vic"):

> *The ethnographer's state of mind on entering the field must not include fear about studying violent people; at least such fears must not be at the front of one's mind. Overconcern about violence may cause ethnographers to appear afraid or react inappropriately to common street situations and dangers that do not involve themselves. Fearful behavior is easily inferred by violent persons from the way one walks and the way one interacts with others. Fearful behavior may place an ethnographer in the "vic" category to be targeted by others as a true victim of crimes like robbery and assault.*

Not exhibiting fearful behavior does not mean abandoning choices about a sensible course of action. Rather, the mindset we have found appropriate is cautious, friendly, understanding, and open. This mindset emphasizes a degree of determination and self-confidence that does not leave room for ethnographers to be labeled as "vics." Likewise, *not* using or selling drugs is also important for avoiding the "vic" role. If potential subjects observe ethnographers buying or selling illicit drugs, they may be suspected of being undercover agents, or expect them to be potential customers, or people who will share or provide drugs. Further decisions about whether to enter specific locales or meet certain persons must be made deliberately and based on the other themes discussed below.

Locator and Protector Roles

Two roles are especially important in conducting research among upper-level and in many instances among lower-level drug sellers. The roles of *locator* and *protector* are vital to the safety of persons working within the illicit drug industry. Locating individuals who can perform these roles can be critical to ethnographers' safety with and access to upper-level dealers. The ethnographic literature (Agar 1980; Johnson 1990; Liebow 1967; Whyte 1955, 1984) provides advice about finding one or more key informants who can provide access to others in the setting and who give much information about the phenomena being studied. . . .

Crack sellers and upper-level dealers, however, have very good reasons to insulate their identities, locales, and illegal activities from everyone (excepting their trusted co-workers). They are concerned with avoiding detection and arrest and with preventing robbery or injury by other street persons. They systematically evade conversations that may build close relationships (Adler 1985). Yet to conduct their business safely, they must rely on others who perform a variety of roles such as steerers, touts, guards, lookouts, connections, runners, and muscle men (Johnson,

Williams, et al. 1990; Johnson et al. 1991). Approaching a crack dealer directly (without an intermediary) threatens the dealer, as it proves his identity is known or suspected. Ethnographers will always be suspected initially of being a "cop" or an "informer," thus elevating the probability of personal risk and possible harm from the dealer or his associates.

Ethnographers can seek access to drug dealers through someone performing a *locator role* and rely on others to play a *protector role* as access is gained. Experience has indicated that access to crack dealers was most successful when ethnographers worked with a highly trusted former associate of the dealer who performed both the locator and the protector roles. The same person, however, need not perform both roles.

Critical in studies with drug dealers is someone who will perform the locator role of introducing the ethnographers into a setting where dealers are present. Recovered substance abusers who have had management roles in drug-selling organizations or have been incarcerated for several years for drug distribution crimes are particularly valuable in such roles. These ex-dealers typically have a large network of current sellers and dealers, know how to negotiate with active dealers, and can be trained to assist with fieldwork. They can locate and introduce ethnographers to several dealers (the locator role), provide protection in dangerous settings (the protector role), become systematic observers and interviewers (field-worker or interviewer role), and explain many of the informally understood norms to a professional ethnographer (the "expert" role).

Proper Introductions. At the early stages of fieldwork among crack sellers, ethnographers generally do not attempt to enter a setting alone. Someone familiar with the locale is recruited or hired to assist in arranging "proper introductions" of the ethnographers to dealers as well as to provide protection. As a paraprofessional staff member, Arnold contacted several dealers and helped arrange interviews with our ethnographers. He stated that "the contact person has a major affect for the ethnographer upon people in the setting." From his network of acquaintances, he had initial contacts and helped persuade dealers to talk with the ethnographer.

Another paraprofessional, Beddoe, explained why and how proper introductions occur among street dealers:

> *They [good contact persons] tend to have contact across time in the given area. Most street dealers are middle men. They will continue to work together and routinely rely on each other. Introductions by one dealer who vouches to other dealers that someone is "right" and "not a cop" is a vital part of street life and everyday dealing hustles. If an ethnographer gets a positive reference from a dealer, another dealer will still be a little suspicious. They study how you handle yourself in the field and then decide whether to talk more.*

Having the appropriate person provide an introduction to a dealer is vital. Group members respond according to the reputation of the individual who provides the introduction. If that person is not trusted, the ethnographer will not be trusted. Dunlap's field notes recorded why she was unable to gain access to several dealers in one Harlem block:

> My early contact on this block was Chief, a female who worked for several dealers, mainly as a "fill-in seller" at the street level. Chief had committed some act which had deemed her untrustworthy to most of her suppliers. She was only trusted to sell small portions of drugs at a time, never large amounts. When she attempted to introduce me to one of her bosses, it was disastrous. The dealer refused to even meet me. Seeing this, other street sellers whom I had informally met at the same time ceased interacting with me. From this and other experiences, I learned that lower-level crack users/dealers can seldom provide good introductions to their bosses or suppliers.

When a respected and trusted former dealer provided the introduction to other dealers only a few blocks away, several meetings and interviews were the outcome. Arnold reported:

> I contacted several dealers who trusted me because we had done prison time for drug sales. After explaining the study to them, they were willing to attend a meeting. I set up the meetings and got them there, so that she [Dunlap] could explain it in more detail and build some relationship with them. This resulted in several interviews.

The Protector. Ethnographers usually assume that they do not need protection from persons in a social setting. In the context of the drug business, this usual assumption is false; everyone must arrange protection to assure their personal safety. Once ethnographers are properly introduced into a setting, finding someone to perform the protector role is usually not difficult. Everyone in a drug dealer's network is expected to "watch backs" (i.e., help each other avoid possible dangers). Even freelance sellers competing for customers on the same block quickly reach agreement to "divide up" the territory and to "watch backs" for each other in case of physical danger (Johnson et al. 1991). Williams reported:

> In every field setting, some person always appears to perform a protector role and "watches the back" of the ethnographer; he discourages violence among others in the setting "because the Man [ethnographer] is here." If I leave the street for a month, it feels like a year. I need to maintain regular visits. Because I rely on them for protection, my best

protectors in the street are enemies of the police: drug dealers, con men, robbers.

After gaining experience in similar settings, ethnographers can enter another site and expect to rapidly encounter someone who will perform the protector role. Usually, the protector will be among the first to speak to the ethnographer. In the event that a protector does not emerge or cannot be found (see "safety zone" next), or if a feeling of safety is lacking (see "sixth sense" below), researchers are encouraged to leave that setting.

Field Roles. Ethnographers have an anomalous position that potential contacts may find unfamiliar or unclear. While conducting field research, they occupy roles that are "betwixt and between" (Jackson 1990) their own professional roles and the roles enacted by potential subjects in the field setting. The dual role of observer and participant (Adler and Adler 1987) played by the friendly outsider (Agar 1980) is unfamiliar to most subjects. Rather, subjects tend to project familiar roles onto ethnographers.

In fact, field roles are fluid and changing during a typical day and during the course of the field research (Denzin 1970; Spradley 1980). In conversation and interaction with individual subjects and with groups, ethnographers can listen closely for the roles that others assign to them. This is helpful in designing one or more field roles that are compatible with the research, yet understood by subjects and protectors. During this study, several subjects referred to Dunlap as "auntie," "mom," "sister," or other fictive kin; Williams was perceived as a "book author" and a "sharp dude"; Hamid and Curtis (1990) were "voyeurs" when conducting research in a "freak-house" (where crack use and sexual activity occur). These subject-assigned roles were effective because they permitted access to the setting, were used by the protector to briefly explain the ethnographer's presence, and permitted informal conversation, questioning, and direct observations to occur—without suspicion that the ethnographer was a cop or a police informer.

As a single female living in a crack dealing neighborhood, Dunlap did not want research subjects to know where she lived, but she had to return home during early morning hours when only drug dealers and street people were awake. Dunlap described how she created and maintained a "right citizen" role with five regular crack dealers who helped assure her safety when she returned home very late:

I first observed who had the most respect from others and who appeared to have control over various situations—this was usually crack dealers. Then I walked by and said, "How you doing?" and engaged in "nonsensical" conversations about such things as the music on the street, street language, the drunk leaning against a fire hydrant. We avoided conversations about what they were doing or about what I did. I also avoided talking to the drug users. By being friendly with the drug dealers, they quickly accepted me as someone who would do them no harm. In return, they protected me in little ways. For example, one night after speaking briefly to my local dealer, a crack user began to approach me for some money; the dealer told her to "move on" and not to bother me. If some threatening situation were to arise, I feel certain they would act to protect me or intervene if necessary.

Dunlap also practiced this role in other research settings when interacting with persons who were not to be approached as research subjects.

During the past 6 years, many ethnographers and paraprofessionals have assumed the role of health worker doing outreach on AIDS prevention projects (e.g., Broadhead and Fox 1990). The "AIDS outreach worker" is an effective street role for ethnographers; it has become well known and respected among street people in several communities. The AIDS outreach worker role clearly "sides" with subjects and potential subjects and provides a basis for interaction with a variety of persons. Such persons express concern about subjects' health, facilitate referrals to other health service agencies, and help ethnographers to avoid being seen in a law enforcement role.

Safety Zones. When conducting research in settings that may be dangerous, or among persons who may be suspicious or hostile toward researchers, a first order of business is to create and maintain a physical and social environment in which ethnographers and potential subjects accept each other's presence.

In settings where many persons are present, effort should be made to include several persons as protectors in a safety zone. This is conceptualized as a physical area extending a few feet around the researcher, in which researchers and other persons within this area feel comfortable. The safety zone has three major components. First, researchers must have a feeling of a "psychological safety"; that is, they must not feel endangered, they must experience some degree of acceptance by others, and they must be willing to stay in the location (see "sixth sense"). Second, other persons in this zone should accept ethnographers' presence, trusting that they are "right" and "not a cop." Third, the physical environment must not be hazardous (e.g., the floors should not be likely to collapse; the ceiling should not be likely to fall).

When entering a locale, ethnographers can quickly scan the physical environment for obvious signs of danger. They should test steps and flooring, especially in abandoned buildings, and be cognizant of all exits. By introducing ethnographers to others at the site, the protector can facilitate social acceptance. Ethnographers must then establish their own right to be present in the locale during subsequent conversation with others. Such interaction typically brings about an implicit (and sometimes explicit) agreement, thus creating a shared sense of psychological acceptance or a "safety zone."

During the initial visit to a setting, ethnographers can state plans to return in the future and attempt to judge how others in the locale feel about this. If a good relationship has been developed with a key person at the site (apartment resident, owner/manager of crack house, street dealer), ethnographers can return to the location without the initial contact and rely on people in the setting to provide protection and to help maintain the safety zone. Beddoe suggested,

> *Look how they talk with each other, and how they deal with each other, and try to copy their style. This will help you get to other people in the social circle. Any conversation is generally better than none.*

When entering a new setting, Dunlap generally located potential exits and figured out who was in charge:

> *This is accomplished in a subtle and gradual way in order not to cause suspicion or make anyone feel they are being watched. I call this getting the feeling of the place, people, and conditions. Try to fit in by taking a comfortable stance, giving the impression of familiarity with various situations or scenarios.*

Williams usually created the safety zone by paying careful attention to the setting and people's activities:

> *Use your own style and smooth approach. Usually don't be aggressive. Try to figure who is available for a conversation and talk to them when [they're] ready; otherwise wait. They communicate with each other via certain physical gestures which can be learned, especially when "thirsty" for smoke [crack]. Let them know that you really want to talk to other people and meet others.*
>
> *You don't want to create enemies out in the field. You have to be constantly improvisational in the setting. Don't overstay your welcome. Three to 4 hours in one place is too long, so move on. You have to be aware of who you are [a researcher] and where you are at. This is not a recreational place; it is a place where you are conducting research but others are buying and selling illegal cocaine. One should follow the rules of the street—which is surviving.*

As rapport with persons in such settings is increased, a safety zone is created among those present. Norms usually include strong expectations of reciprocity. Dunlap described how she responded to these, expectations:

> *Be counted on to "do the right thing" for them personally, even though [you're] not taking part in what is happening (you do not sell or smoke crack). I was always prepared to participate in ethically appropriate exchanges. I would accept a cigarette but more frequently provided them to those present. I would provide food or coffee that was shared by all or help a person read something. On the other hand, I avoided sharing drugs and declined to chip in to buy drugs.*

This safety zone is a short-term agreement among persons in a concrete locale about the right of other persons to be present. Such temporary agreements do not imply that the potential subjects present have provided ethnographers with informed consent, acceptance, rapport, or a willingness to be interviewed. The safety zone only provides a locale and time during which ethnographers can begin to obtain further cooperation from some of those present.

Humor and Neutrality

Even when ethnographers function within a safety zone, a variety of tense interactions and situations may arise in specific locales. The effective use of humor and neutrality in these settings by ethnographers may also have important benefits for persons in these settings.

Ethnographers' neutrality in tense social situations is well described (Fetterman 1989; Agar 1980; Adler and Adler 1987), but it is sometimes a source of tension between their subjects and themselves (Broadhead and Fox 1990). Humor can defuse such tense situations and build solidarity among group members (Seckman and Couch 1989). Less well documented is the way in which humor and neutrality may help in dangerous situations (Carpenter et al. 1988).

Crack houses and drug-dealing locales are characterized by high levels of mistrust, paranoia, and potential violence. At the same time, these locales are at least partially organized to reduce violence and informally control persons (*New York Times* 1991) who act aggressively. Hamid described the dangers:

> *In crack houses, users constantly argue and accuse others of using too much or hiding or stealing crack or money. Street sellers face frequent arguments about money, the quality of crack or other drugs, threats of robbery, and other topics. Usually these arguments are resolved by the disputants reaching some kind of agreement, but other persons (guards, boss, owner) may occasionally intervene if the argument begins to escalate to physical violence.*

After establishing a safety zone and acquiring protectors, ethnographers in a crack house or crack sale location may introduce an element of stability and safety. Ethnographers are not under the influence of drugs or alcohol and can think swiftly and clearly. They do not want to buy crack or sell drugs or to be used for such purposes. They are neutral in the various disputes between persons and attempt to maintain communication with all. They have requested and generally been granted protection and safety while in the location. Moreover, ethnographers are sophisticated in interpersonal relationships and can deal with tense situations. Hamid described how he sometimes intervenes:

> *When two crackheads are arguing about who got the most crack or stole it [the truth is, they've both used it up], and the dispute is heading*

toward a physical fight, I begin telling an outrageously funny story that has nothing to do with the conflict. The disputants are distracted from their conflict, they laugh and separate; usually the dispute is forgotten. Humor is a major way that tense arguments between crackheads or distributors may be resolved without blows and without any loss of face by either party.

Williams also noted that

a humorous remark, well-timed comment, or casual-appearing interruption by the ethnographer may distract persons who are headed toward violent confrontations. Bring humor into a very tense situation; get them laughing with the ethnographer and with each other. The gift of gab will get you [and them] out of all kinds of difficult situations.

Dunlap explained how she has deliberate conversations with crack users while they are "straight" to reduce the potential for subsequent violence:

Many crack users try to convince themselves and others that the drug does not affect them. They claim their behavior remains the same after they smoke crack as it is before they smoke crack. I always bring this discussion up when the individual is sober, before he of she has ingested any drug. When their behavior begins to change after smoking, I can usually bring them back to normal behavior by remarking that they are acting differently by smoking crack. Persons will try to prove that the drug does not affect them in various ways, and that they can handle the drug. While restating these claims, they generally abandon various kinds of behavior associated with crack intoxication. Also, I never take sides in any disagreement. Let the situation work itself out. If I feel the situation is becoming too dangerous, I leave.

Williams also noted,

In crack houses or similar settings, the ethnographers' presence can help reduce the risk of violence among people who argue and fight over drugs. People respect ethnographers and choose not to express overt violence in their presence. Local norms that are tolerant of threats and violence are set aside, and temporary norms prohibiting such threats are accepted.

By remaining neutral but interested parties, ethnographers gain respect from people in these settings. In many potentially violent situations, ethnographers may be the only "neutral" person who is not high and may become a mediator between individuals and groups. Such neutrality involves not engaging in personal (especially sexual) relationships with subjects during the study as well as avoiding alignment with only one group. Ethnographers' personal "safety zone" is frequently extended to protect subjects and potential subjects from the possible dangers that their own behavior and willingness to use violence may bring about. Thus the presence of ethnographers probably reduces the risk of violence among crack users and sellers in crack houses and dealing locations rather than increasing the potential for violence.

"Sixth Sense" and Common Sense

Not all conflicts and issues in dangerous settings can be resolved by neutrality and humor. Ethnographers need to be prepared to respond effectively in a variety of potentially dangerous circumstances (paranoia, sexual approaches, robbery, theft, shootings, police raids, and arrests) that actually occur infrequently but are a major fear among nonethnographers. Reliance on prudence, common sense, and a "sixth sense" can help reduce physical violence to a minimum. Different kinds of potentially dangerous situations can be handled by evasion and movement away from the danger, controlled confrontation, or rapid departure from the setting. The ability to handle a variety of situations requires both a "sixth sense" for danger and skill in moving away from and evading physical harm. Dunlap provided an illustration:

> Acting from the "sixth sense" is relatively easy. We use it all the time in everyday life when we walk into new situations. There is an uneasiness, an inability to verbalize what is wrong. You may be able to explain everything that is taking place, do not see anything out of the ordinary, but still feel uncomfortable. This is a warning that something may go wrong. When such discomfort occurs, leave as soon as possible. For example, I had planned to hang around Ross and his family on a particular weekend. Each time I made preparations to leave, this uneasy feeling arose—I did not want to go and could not explain it, so I did not see him until the following week. Upon arrival, Ross reported that one of his partners had been shot and killed. If I had gone that weekend, I might have been next to Ross, who was sitting beside his drug-selling partner when the latter was shot by the father of a crack customer.

When and if ethnographers get a feeling of discomfort without reason, they will be safer by leaving the setting and returning another time—even though they may fail to gather some data and violence may not actually occur. But if their "sixth sense" has extracted them from the locale, they will not be harmed during those rare occasions when serious violence does occur.

Crack-Related Paranoia. Cocaine and crack induce a short-term paranoia in which users are very suspicious of others around them. They may believe others are enemies out to arrest or harm them. If challenged, pushed, or threatened, they may become unreasonably aggressive or violent. Yet crack users opt for avoidance and non-confrontation to handle such short-term paranoia exhibited by other crack users. Williams has dealt with crack-induced paranoia in many settings:

> When people are smoking crack, they go through different stages, one of which is paranoia. The crackhead may comment, 'I don't like to be around people who don't get high" or "Why are you watching me?" This person may even be your sponsor or protector but is no longer the rational person you came with. The easy solution is to move away and not watch. Above all else, don't confront or challenge them. Usually you can find another person who is in a talkative stage where they want to talk. After a while, the first person's paranoia will subside and the person is open to conversation again—with no or little recollection of his comments or implicit threats while high.

Sexual Approaches. While using crack, a person may express a desire for physical closeness or sexual intimacy and approach others (including the ethnographer) for satisfaction. Williams explained how he responded to various levels of physical closeness:

> There are touchers; persons who seek affection while they ingest drugs and smoke crack. They seek such affection and closeness when they get high, just before the effect wears off. Usually, I just move away or shift to conversation with someone else. What do you do when sexually approached? Be forceful and let them know that your aren't available for sex play; they usually will not pursue it further.

Several female ethnographers have had their fieldwork severely constrained or have had to terminate it completely (Horowitz 1986; Adler and Adler 1987; Howell 1990; Warren 1989) due to the sexual expectations and demands of subjects or other males in the research setting. The threat of sexual assault or rape is a real concern for most female ethnographers and staff members. As a woman, Dunlap followed several strategies to reduce vulnerability to sexual approaches:

> Smoking crack causes many individuals to be stimulated sexually. Yet when first developing rapport, potential subjects frequently assign a fictive-kin role. I may seem like a sister, cousin, mother, or aunt to them. Assuming such roles leads individuals to become "close friends" and share many behaviors they would not otherwise exhibit. When projecting such roles to me, they place me "off limits" for sexual

approaches and affairs. Enough crack-using women are available for sexual affairs; neither male nor female subjects need me for sex and usually agree to protect me from advances by others. The crack-sex link focuses on the sexual act, not personal relationships. Even women who routinely exchange sex for crack or money will refuse sexual foreplay and intimacy for short periods during their crack consumption cycles; both men and women leave them alone at those times.

The value of the protector role was evident one evening while Dunlap was observing several prostitutes with whom she had established good rapport:

I was standing on the sidewalk talking with Lisa (a prostitute who used crack), when a John (customer) drove up and starting talking dirty to us. Lisa talked back to him while I listened. When Lisa said she wants $20 for a blowjob, the man replied, "I don't want you. How much is she [referring to me]?" Lisa exploded: "She ain't one of us. You leave her alone and keep your fuck'n hands off her." She started kicking and pounding the car. The man looked surprised and drove off quickly.

Abandoned Buildings and Other Dangerous Locales. Most ethnographic research is conducted where the physical environment is structurally safe. Assuming such safety can be dangerous when researchers are studying crack dealers. Crack dealers may set booby traps to slow police or potential robbers. The sale and use of crack often occurs in abandoned buildings, run-down tenements, and hidden locations (e.g., under bridges or tunnels). Such locations are best approached only with a protector who knows it well. Even then, visits should occur only when the ethnographer feels comfortable. Dunlap recalled her trepidations:

A street contact said, "Let's go to a place where a friend lives. I'm doing this as a favor to you." She took me into an abandoned building where her friend gave us a back room. I could have been robbed. But nothing happened. The interview went well but the place was unheated and filthy. On other occasions, I have rented apartments or hotel rooms for interviews because I didn't want to go into particularly bad abandoned buildings where subjects lived. If I enter an abandoned building (most have serious structural defects like broken steps or holes in floor), I do so only with people who know their way around defects that could cause serious harm.

The presence of a protector who can vouch for the safety of the premises and serves as a guide around several obstacles is critical in deciding whether to go into abandoned buildings or outdoor locales that researchers perceive as dangerous.

Typically, ethnographers and subjects prefer more neutral settings like a coffee shop, restaurant, storefront, or apartment of a friend (which usually have comfortable chairs, heat, and some privacy).

Crimes and Threats Involving Money. Robbery, burglary, and theft from field staff are uncommon but do occur (Spunt 1988). In fact, many crack distributors are frequent and proficient robbers, burglars, and thieves (Johnson, Elmoghazy, and Dunlap 1990). Furthermore, crack users are constantly broke and in need of money. Thus we have developed strategies to minimize criminal victimization and monetary losses. Ethnographers and field staff can expect to be constantly approached for money, "loans," and "advances" (Johnson et al. 1985, 205–6). When these are not provided, implicit threats may be made. Dunlap defused threats by trying to provide balanced reciprocation:

> *While declining to provide cash to the "kitty" towards the next purchase of drugs, providing cigarettes, candy, food, drinks, and refreshments will usually satisfy one's social obligation to contribute to shared group activities in a crack house or among drug sellers.*

Usually, persons in protector roles will prevent threats from becoming robbery attempts. Johnson described one simple precaution that may reduce the magnitude of monetary losses if a robbery or theft occurs:

> *While in the field, wear clothing with a lot of pockets. Distribute the money into different pockets and keep $10 in a shoe for emergencies. While in the field, only take money from one pocket—conveying the impression that all my money is in that pocket. If someone observes and actually attempts a hold-up [which has not happened yet], give the contents from only that one pocket. When money in that pocket gets low, go to a private place (e.g., a bathroom) and transfer money to the spending pocket.*

In prior or concurrent research projects (Johnson 1990; Johnson et al. 1985; Goldstein et al. 1990), some staff members have been robbed, and in one case, a physical assault without serious injury (Spunt 1988) occurred. When crimes occur, staff members usually report them to police to indicate that such violations will have consequences. Several thefts of tape recorders and minor personal possessions were not reported, due mainly to lack of police interest.

Fights. A physical fight or show of weapons may break out without warning so that ethnographers have little chance to use humor and neutrality to prevent it. Almost always, such weapons and fights have nothing to do with the ethnographers' presence. Rather, they are linked to disputes with other crack abusers in the locale. Williams followed several strategies for dealing with such occurrences:

Sometimes knives or guns appear, more frequently as a display of possessions (like gold chains or sneakers) than as a means of threatening persons. If they seek approval for their new possession, I may comment about how nice it is, but add "Guns aren't my favorite thing. Could you put it away?" I've been in hundreds of crack houses and dealing locations where weapons were widely evident, but I've never been present when guns were used in a threatening manner. If such an event were to occur, I'd leave as soon as possible, and not get involved as an intermediary.

Stickup Men and Drive-by Shooting. Perhaps the most dangerous situation is a "rip off." This occurs when robbers surprise the occupants at a crack-dealing locale with the clear intention of taking all cash and drugs present. Likewise, when two or more drug dealer groups are competing for a good selling location, they may try to "warn" others by street shootouts. These are not situations for mediation or humor, only for getting out of the way or following orders. Beddoe noted:

Stickup men have usually cased the location and are quite certain who is present before coming in. They want money and drugs. Keep quiet and provide what they want.

Williams noted that ethnographers who have good rapport with dealers may be relatively safe:

How do you know a territorial dispute is going on? Generally, someone will let you know so you can stay out of the way 'til some order has been reestablished. You have more warning of trouble than ordinary citizens in the contested area. Your contacts can provide information later—without your being present.

Violence and shooting in the drug culture/business is unpredictable and without warning because surprise is frequently a major element in its use. But most violence by crack dealers is intentionally directed at specific persons and occurs in a concealed setting (so no witnesses are present). Drive-by shooting/machine-gunning of people on street corners and "stray bullets" that kill children remain the exception in drug-related violence, even though they are a major feature of sensationalizing mass media coverage (*Daily News* 1990; *New York Newsday* 1990; *New York Times* 1990a, 1990b).

Contacts with the Police. Since 1983, police task forces directed against dealers have frequently engaged in surprise raids against dealers and crack houses. Despite concerns about police action and fear of arrest, ethnographers who avoid using and selling drugs themselves are rarely involved with the police. The police are authorized to use force only when a person resists physically, so ethnographers contacted by police are rarely arrested (Bourgois 1990). Particularly in street settings, ethnographers must be careful in dealings with police. Informal conversations with police should be avoided so that subjects and potential subjects do not have a basis for be-lieving that the ethnographer is talking to or "informing" the police. When the police behave unprofessionally toward subjects, ethnographers who are observed to "stand up" to police gain respect in the eyes of potential subjects. Williams reported one such incident:

> One night I was on the streets with a white ethnographer in a copping area. One police officer came up and asked, "Say, white boy, why don't you buy drugs in your own neighborhood?" and pushed him against the squad car to search him. After producing identification showing that he lived within a couple of blocks, he got off with no further has-sle. People in the community saw this as harassment by police and concluded that the ethnographer was not a police officer.

Dunlap's field notes recorded the following incident:

> One afternoon I was with two female subjects who were going to cop some drugs inside an abandoned building. While they copped, I went to the store to buy sodas. When I came out, two male cops had the two subjects against the wall and were patting them down. One of the cops was verbally degrading a subject. I inquired what happened and ob-served the police action. Not finding any drugs (only a crack stem), they let the subjects go. The women believed that my inquiry had saved them from arrest and that the cops were trying to "shake them down" for money. They felt that my presence had deterred the police from carrying out any adverse actions.

Despite many hours and days spent with crack dealers in crack sales locations where police were observed several times a day, our research staff have never been present when "busts" occurred. During a parallel study of sex-for-crack in Miami in 1989, however, Inciardi (personal communication) walked through the back door of a crack house as a police raid came through the front door. He and others present were taken to detention where he was held for 5 hours; he was released at booking without formal arrest following the procedures outline below. He did not, however, return to that crack house or others in its general vicinity.

On a parallel research project evaluating the impact of Tactical Narcotics Teams (TNT), ethnographers at Vera Institute (in cooperation with the New York City police) have been instructed about appropriate procedures to follow in the event of being caught in a police sweep or raid. The ethnographers are not to resist arrest nor attempt to talk to police officers at the arrest location. Rather, they are to follow instructions, let police gain control, and allow themselves to be handcuffed and taken to the station house. At the point of booking, ethnographers should present identification as a researcher working for a nonprofit organization and ask the booking sergeant to call the principal investigator or let the researcher make such a call. If possible, staff members try to arrange the researchers' release at booking, without formal arrest charges. Otherwise, senior staff or a lawyer will be present at arraignment and will attempt to persuade the judge to drop charges or provide bail money. Subsequent efforts will be made to have charges dismissed or the conviction overturned. To date, researchers at Vera Institute or Narcotic and Drug Research, Inc. have not been arrested while conducting research during the 1980s. Narcotic and Drug Research, Inc. now retains a lawyer to act quickly to represent staff, both ethnographers and paraprofessionals, arrested during fieldwork or AIDS outreach activities.

Conclusion

In this article, we have drawn on concrete experiences with a wide range of dangerous situations and subjects we encountered in conducting field research. The approaches described here have evolved over more than 25 years of ethnographic research successfully conducted by ourselves and others among users and sellers of heroin and crack in some of America's most dangerous social settings (see Broadhead and Fox 1990; Feldman 1974; Goldstein et al. 1990; Johnson et al. 1985; Preble and Casey 1969). Yet after spending 2 years involved in direct research among crack distributors and many other years of research with robbers, burglars, murderers, and heroin sellers, none of our professional ethnographers or paraprofessional staff (ex-dealers, ex-drug users) has ever been physically injured; few, in fact, have been robbed or burglarized while performing their research roles. If violence in the drug culture truly occurred on a random basis, then several ethnographers should have been harmed. This is not to suggest that the participation and activities of ethnographers is inherently less dangerous than those employing survey or archival methods. Yet recognizing the potential dangers, it is still possible for ethnographers to choose their field of study with a clear awareness, preparation for, and avoidance of the risks involved.

References

Adler, P. A. 1985. *Wheeling and dealing.* New York: Columbia University Press.
Adler, P. A., and P. Adler. 1987. *Membership roles in field research.* Newbury Park, CA: Sage.
Agar, M. H. 1980. *The professional stranger.* New York: Academic Press.
Becker, H. 1960. Participant observation: The analysis of qualitative field data. In *Human Organization research: Field relations and techniques,* edited by R. N. Adams and J. J. Preiss, 267–89. Homewood, IL: Dorsey.
Biernacki, R 1988. *Pathways heroin addiction.* Philadelphia, PA: Temple University Press.
Bourgois, P. 1990. In search of Horatio Alger: Culture and ideology in the crack economy. *Contemporary Drug Problems* 16:619–50.

Broadhead, R. S., and K. J. Fox. 1990. Takin' it to the streets: AIDS outreach as ethnography. *Journal of Contemporary Ethnography,* 19:322–48.

Brownstein, H. H., and P. J. Goldstein. 1990a. A typology of drug related homicides. In *Drugs, crime and the criminal justice system,* edited by Ralph Weisheit. 171–92. Cincinnati, OH: Anderson.

———. 1990b. Research and the development of public policy. The case of drugs and violent crime. *Journal of Applied Sociology,* 7:77–92.

Carey, J. T. 1972. Problems of access and risk in observing drug scenes. *In Research on deviance,* edited by Jack D. Douglas, 71–92. New York: Random House.

Carpenter, C., B. Glassner, B. D. Johnson, and J. Loughlin. 1988. *Kids, drugs, and crime.* Lexington, MA: Lexington Books.

Daily News. 1990. *Slaughter of the innocents.* October 19:1.

Denzin, N. K. 1970. *The research act.* Chicago, IL: Aldine.

Douglas, J. D., ed. 1972. *Research on deviance.* New York: Random House.

Dunlap, E. 1988. Male-female relations and the black family. Ph.D. diss., University of California, Berkeley.

Dunlap, E., B. D. Johnson, H. Sanabria, et al. 1990. Studying crack users and their criminal careers: The scientific and artistic aspects of locating hard-to-reach subjects and interviewing them about sensitive topics. *Contemporary Drug Problems.* 17:121–44.

Feldman, H. 1974. *Street status and the drug researcher: Issues in participant observation.* Washington, DC: Drug Abuse Council.

Feldman, H. W., M. H. Agar, and G. M. Beschner. 1979. *Angel dust: An ethnographic study of PCP users.* Lexington, MA: Lexington Books.

Fetterman, D. M. 1989. *Ethnography: Step by step.* Newbury Park, CA: Sage.

Goldstein, P. J. 1985. The drugs/violence nexus: A tripartite conceptual model. *Journal of Drug Issues* 15:493–506.

Goldstein, P. J., B. Spunt, T. Miller, and P. A. Bellucci. 1990. Ethnographic field stations. In *The collection and interpretation of data from hidden populations,* edited by Elizabeth Lambert, 80–95, Research Monograph 98. Rockville, MD: National Institute on Drug Abuse.

Goldstein, P. J., P. A. Bellucci, B. Spunt, and T. Miller. 1991a. Volume of cocaine use and violence: A comparison between men and women. *Journal of Drug Issues,* 21:345–68.

———. 1991b. *Frequency of cocaine use and violence: A comparison between men and women.* Rockville, MD: National Institute on Drug Abuse.

Hamid, A. 1979. *Ganja in Granada.* Ph.D. diss. Teachers College, New York.

———. 1990. The political economy of crack-related violence. *Contemporary Drug Problems* 17:31–78.

———. 1992. *The political economy of drugs.* New York: Plenum.

Hamid, A., and R. Curtis. 1990. Beaming up: Contexts for smoking cocaine and sex-for-drugs in the inner-city and what they mean. Manuscript, John Jay College, New York.

Hanson, B., G. Beschner, J. Walters, and E. Bovelle, eds. 1985. *Life with heroin: Voices from the inner city.* Lexington, MA: Lexington Books.

Howell, N., ad. 1990. *Surviving fieldwork. A report of the Advisory Panel on Health and Safety in Fieldwork.* Washington, DC: American Anthropological Association.

Horowitz, R. 1986. Remaining an outsider: Membership as a threat to research rapport. *Urban Life* 14:409–30.

Jackson, J. E. 1990. Deja entendu: The criminal qualities of anthropological fieldnotes. *Journal of Contemporary Ethnography* 19:8–43.

Johnson, B. D. 1973. *Marihuana users and drug subcultures.* New York: Wiley.

Johnson, B. D., E. Elmoghazy, and E. Dunlap. 1990. *Crack abusers and noncrack drug abusers: A comparison of drug use, drug sales, and nondrug criminality.* New York: Narcotic and Drug Research, Inc.

Johnson, B. D., B. Frank, J. Schmeidler, R. Morel, M. Maranda, and C. Gillman. 1988. Illicit substance use among adults in New York State's transient population. *Statewide Household Survey of Substance Abuse, 1986.* New York: Division of Substance Abuse Services.

Johnson, B. D., P. J. Goldstein, E. Preble, J. Schmeidler, D. S. Lipton, B. Spunt, and T. Miller. 1985. *Taking care of business: The economics of crime by heroin abusers.* Lexington, MA: Lexington Books.

Johnson, B. D., A. Hamid, and H. Sanabria. 1991. Emerging models of crack distribution. *In Drugs and crime: A reader,* edited by Tom Mieczkowski, 56–78. Boston, MA: Allyn & Bacon.

Johnson, B. D., T. Williams, K. Dei, and H. Sanabria. 1990. Drug abuse in the inner city: Impact on hard drug users and the community. *In Drugs and crime,* edited by Michael Tonry and James Q. Wilson, 9–67. Chicago, IL: University of Chicago Press.

Johnson, J. C. 1990. *Selecting ethnographic informants.* Newbury Park, CA: Sage.

Liebow, E. 1967. *Tally's Corner: A study of Negro streetcorner men.* Boston, MA: Little, Brown.

McCracken, G. 1988. *The long interview.* Newbury Park, CA: Sage.

Morales, E. 1989. *Cocaine: White gold rush in Peru.* Tucson, AZ: University of Arizona Press.

New York Newsday. 1990. Stray bullets kill 7 in New York in 1990. December 28:4.

New York Times. 1989. Drug wars don't pause to spare the innocent. January 22:25.

———. 1990a. Woman is killed in Bronx drive-by shooting. October 7:40.

———. 1990b. Record year for killings jolts officials in New York. December 31:25.

———. 1991. In a crack house: Dinner and drugs on the stove. April 6:1, 24.

Preble, E. J., and J. J. Casey. 1969. Taking care of business: The heroin user's life an the street. *International Journal of Addictions,* 4(1):1–24.

Reinarman, C., and H. G. Levine. 1989. Crack in context: Politics and media in the making of a drug scare. *Contemporary Drug Problems,* 16:535–78.

Rose, D. 1990. *Living the ethnographic life.* Newbury Park, CA: Sage.

Seckman, M. A., and C. J. Couch. 1989. Jocularity, sarcasm, and relationships. *Journal of Contemporary Ethnography,* 18:327–34.

Sluka, J. A. 1990. Participant observation in violent social contexts. *Human Organization.* 49(2):114–26.

Smith, C., and W. Kornblum, eds. 1991. *In the field: Readings on the field research experience.* Westport, CT: Praeger.

Spradley, J. P. 1980. *Participant observation.* New York: Holt, Rinehart & Winston.

Spunt, B. 1988. Backstage at an ethnographic field station. Paper presented at the annual meeting of the American Society of Criminology, Chicago.

Washington Post. 1990. Violence in the '90s: Drugs deadly residue. October 14: A1, A12.

Warren, C. 1989. *Gender issues in field research.* Newbury Park, CA: Sage.

Whyte, W. P. 1955. *Street corner society.* 2d ed. Chicago, IL: University of Chicago Press.

————. 1984. *Learning from the field: A guide from experience.* Beverly Hills, CA: Sage.

Williams, T. 1978. The cocaine culture in after hours clubs. Ph.D. diss., City University of New York.

————. 1989. *The cocaine kids.* New York: Addison-Wesley.

————. 1991. *The crack house.* New York: Addison-Wesley.

Williams, T. and W. Kornblum, 1985. *Growing up poor.* Lexington, MA: Lexington Books.

The Ethics of Deception in Social Research: A Case Study

ERICH GOODE

. . . Certain kinds of deception are necessary to gather certain data in certain settings. I placed bogus ads in a personal column to obtain, and analyze responses. The data would have remained inaccessible—indeed, many of the responses would not have existed in the first place—without some measure of deception. While deception was used, no risk whatsoever was posed to respondents. I further argue that several of Erikson's criteria of risk do not separate ethical from empirical questions; informants use very different criteria in evaluating the risk of harm to them posed by social research that sociologists use. The question of exploitation is more complex, since it has to be weighed against how much of an effort my respondents made and hence, what it is exactly that I took from them. A "panel of judges" decided that most of my male (but not my female) respondents would not have gotten dates with my hypothetical ad placers, and that the research method I used was not especially unethical.

In a classic essay, Kai Erikson (1967) argues that the use of disguised observation in social research should be regarded as unethical. It is unethical Erikson suggests, "for a sociologist to *deliberately misrepresent* his [or her] identity for the purpose of entering a private domain to *which he [or she] is not otherwise eligible*"; second, he argues, "it is unethical for a sociologist to *deliberately misrepresent* the character of the research in which he [or she] is engaged" (1967: 373).

Erikson maintains four objections to disguised observation in social research. The first is that the research can harm actors in the social scene under study in ways that cannot be anticipated; in disguised observation, the researcher "does not know which of his [or her] actions are apt to hurt other people and it is presumptuous of him [or her] to act as if he [or she] does—particularly when, as is ordinarily the case, he [or she] has elected to wear a disguise exactly because he [or she] is entering a social sphere so far from his [or her] experience" (1967: 368).

Second, Erikson says, disguised observation and other forms of deception are likely to "damage the reputation of sociology in the larger society and close off promising areas of research for future investigators" (1967: 369).

Third, if graduate students are involved in research based on deception, the sociologist is forcing into morally ambiguous contexts persons who are not yet prepared to make painful and difficult ethical choices.

And fourth, which Erikson sees as the most important, in disguised observation, the sociologist has betrayed the complexity and subtlety of the social structure under observation. It seems "a little irresponsible," Erikson says, "for a sociologist to assume that he [or she] can enter social life in any masquerade that suits his [or her] purpose without seriously disrupting the scene he [or she] hopes to study" (1967: 370).

Perhaps the research project conducted over the past generation or two by a sociologist that has attracted the harshest criticism for employing what was (and still is) regarded by many observers as unethical research methods is Laud Humphreys' *Tearoom Trade* (1970, 1975). Interestingly, the most controversial feature of Humphrey's research was not his observing, and serving as a lookout for, men who were engaged in sex in public urinals. Rather, it was Humphreys' strategy of writing down the license plate numbers of the cars parked on a road adjacent to the parks where the urinals were located, then, a year or so later, tracking these men down and interviewing them by claiming to be conducting a "public health survey." On this, Humphrey claims to be guilty of the sin of omission ("less than full representation"), not commission ("false representation"). After all, loosely construed, he *was* conducting a "public health survey"—just not the sort any of his interviewees could have imagined they were participating in (1970: 177). But a decade after the research was conducted, Humphreys decided that his critics may have been right on at least one point. However, the problem was not deception, he said, but risk. "It seemed that I was interviewing subjects in the least disturbing and least dangerous manner possible. I now think my reasoning was faulty and that my respondents were placed in greater danger than deemed plausible at the time" (1975: 230). Instead of taking down license plate numbers, he says, he should have interviewed a number of "willing respondents." By doing this, he admits, the sample of participants would not have been as representative as in the original study, but the data would have been richer. And his respondents would not have been exposed to the risk of arrest or stigma (1975: 231).

A sizeable literature has accumulated on the issue of the ethics of disguised observation and other forms of deception in social research. It should be sufficient here to stress the fact that the field is ambivalent on the question. An "unofficial reading" of the sort Erikson suggested has in fact been taken; however, its answer to his question is less than clear-cut. In a survey based on a random sample of names that appeared in the American Sociological Association membership list, Long and Dorn (1983) found that a high proportion of sociologists "tend, in principle, to condone deception in research if confessed and explained" (1983: 297). Six out of ten of Long and Dorn's sample disagreed with the statement: "It is ethically acceptable for sociologists to deceive research subjects and to expose them to temporary 'harm' so long as care is taken to eliminate long-term post-research effects." (Over a quarter agreed, however.) And four-fifths agreed with, "If a research subject has been deceived, the sociologist must provide full and detailed explanation to the subject of what has been done and the reasons for doing it" (1993: 295). According to Long and Dorn, sociologists favored neither "restrictions in research in the name of ethics, nor did they favor unrestricted research—an apparent inconsistency" (1983: 295). What are sociologists "willing to do" about ethics? Long and Dorn's data suggest "not too much" (1983:297)—except write and talk about the subject.

The same ambivalence toward covert research methods tapped by Long and Dorn is reflected in the writings of sociologists on the subject. Adler, Adler and Rochford (1986) summarize the field's split on the issue by contrasting the classic Chicago School/symbolic interactionist approach, which rejects the deceptive, disguised, or covert role for fieldworker, and the existential, interpretive, and phenomenological school's more radical "conflict" approach, which condones it. To the Chicago sociologists (and their neo-Chicagoan descendants, including Kai Erikson), deception is wrong because it disrespects the intricate subtleties of the scene under investigation, it disrespects the integrity of one's informants, subjects, or respondents, and it compromises the researcher by assigning him or her to a specific insider role rather than permitting a more neutral, detached, or objective stance.

In contrast, existential sociologists, adopting a conflict paradigm, recognize that people hide crucial information from outsiders—or distort it even when they do reveal it. The researcher must therefore "dig behind people's superficial self-presentations and discover the truth about their attitudes and behavior" (Adler, Adler, & Rochford, 1986: 367). One way to do this is to make use of the covert role, "in which the researcher disguises the purpose and interest behind his or her participation in the scene" (1986: 367). Fieldworkers should not be restrained by an absolutist ethic which is binding in any and all research situations; instead, existential sociologists feel that researchers "should be given the freedom to struggle individually with the moral and legal problems they encounter in each research situation" (1986: 368). According to Jack Douglas (1976), a major proponent of the existential "conflict" research style (or the "investigative" paradigm), the Chicago-style researchers engage in something of the "unholy alliance" (1976: 43) with the members of the group under study: If you let me into your world—as an overt, upfront researcher—I will promise only to report your socially acceptable side. I will never reveal—even if I am allowed to discover them—your deepest, ugliest secrets. Above all, I promise not to tell the whole truth about you! "Conflict" methodology argues that such a research strategy is impotent to counteract the inevitable problems of facades, evasions, and lies. The solution? Deceptive research practices. While deception should not be the sociologist's primary mode of research—in most settings, it is not even necessary—Douglas argues that it should not be ruled out as a strategy because for many scenes, it may be the only way to get at the facts of the case.

I agree with Humphreys (1970), most emphatically, when he says that protecting our respondents from harm is the researcher's *primary* interest. However, I also agree with him when he says that the ethics of social research must inevitably be situation ethics; even social scientists who proclaim absolutes betray them in actual practice. Exceptions and contingencies abound, and often derail even the most reasonable-sounding general formulations. Here, I intend to argue against Erikson's position on disguised observation and deception in research. More specifically, I intend to argue that it *is* ethical to engage in *certain kinds* of deception of the sort Erikson *rules out* of our legitimate research domain. I will insist that the ethics of disguised observation be evaluated on a situational, case-by-case basis, and that the ethics of a particular strategy cannot be determined in a blanket fashion. In *specific* social settings, some kinds of deception should be seen as entirely consistent with good ethics. I agree with Douglas: The facts of the case, in many instances, demand deception.

According to some of the criteria Erikson spelled out, I have been involved in an unethical research project. I used deception to gain unwarranted access to a set of research materials; I deliberately misrepresented what I was doing in order to get my hands on it. I obtained information under false pretenses; I wore a kind of disguise, pretending to be someone I was not. In fact, had I not been engaged in deception, not only would I not have gained access to that material, *it would not have existed in the first place;* it was my deception that *created* the material. Moreover, I did not, as Long and Dorn's respondents advise, "provide full and detailed explanation" (1983: 295) to deceived subjects of what I did and why I did it. Here, I wish to argue that what *seems to be*—to some observers—an unethical research strategy should be regarded as entirely consistent with good ethics. . . .

Research on Personal Advertisements

Hundreds, possibly thousands, of periodicals in North America, and probably at least as many in other countries around the world, carry a column in which advertisers request replies from potential dating or romantic partners. Although advertisers, and their respondents, are extremely varied as to motive and characteristics, *most* personal ads are written by heterosexual singles between the ages of 22 and 65 who at least claim to seek a long-term, marriage-oriented relationship.

The procedure for using personal ads as a means of meeting dating partners is essentially the same for all periodicals carrying such a column. The publication prints a series of ads, written by advertisers. Typically, the ads describe the characteristics (or putative characteristics) of the advertiser and describe one or more qualities or characteristics sought by the advertiser in a responder, that is, in a potential or ideal dating partner. Sometimes, the nature of the relationship desired will also be spelled out in the ad. Each ad includes a post office box number, which is held by the publication carrying the ad and/or a telephone code, again, controlled by the ad-bearing publication. (Home phone number and addresses are almost never published directly in personal ads.) The letters and/or calls will be forwarded to the subscriber, who then makes a decision as to which responses will be answered, if any. (Today, in most personal columns, voice mail is more likely to be used than written responses.) . . .

Personals-initiated courtship has one foot in public and one foot in private behavior. Thus, it does not fully qualify for Erikson's strictures, since he objected to deception for the purpose of "entering a private domain" (1967: 373). The *initial* stage of this process—placing or reading the personal ad itself—is distinctly *public* activity. It is a stage that anyone capable of paying a fairly moderate fee can enter. And once an ad is placed, literally any literate human within the catchment area of a journal can inspect the ad's declaration of preferences in a partner and claims as to the writer's own qualities. But once the replies arrive, the locus of the courtship process shifts sharply from the public to the private domain. . . .

A substantial sociological and social-psychological literature exists which examines personal advertisements (or similar "formal intermediaries" or "mediated channels") for dating and mate seeking. Many, probably most, of the writings that deal with personal advertisements are based on a content analysis of the ads themselves. . . . One team of researchers took this process a step further and requested from the advertising journal a tally of the number of replies each ad received (Lynn & Shergot, 1984). To my knowledge, to date, only three social science research teams wrote directly to individuals who placed personal ads concerning the replies they received. In one of these studies, only 19 percent of ad placers responded to the questionnaire (Austromi & Kanel, 1983); in a second, the response rate was 45 percent for women and 36 percent for men (Rajecki, Bledsoe, & Rasmussen, 1991). A third, relying on less formal research methods, did not tally the response rate, but relied on a somewhat more daring research strategy: The researchers placed and answered personal ads themselves (Daren & Koski, 1988). One of the two researchers involved in this study responded to ads, placed several ads, receiving a number of replies—she answered a score of them—and talked with and even met in person several dating parties. All this activity was described as having been "conducted in good faith" (1988: 384), that is, presumably, it was at least partly for the purpose of meeting dating partners. The methodology of this research team is described as "ethnographic" (1988: 383); no systematic quantitative tabulations emerged from this study.

Prior to the research endeavor on which this paper is based, I requested information on replies to ads from the editors of a local newsletter specializing in publishing personal ads; I received no reply to my inquiries. At that point, I sent requests to individuals who placed ads in a particular personals column for information about replies they had received; my response rate was under 10 percent. The dismal results of my efforts led to the percent study.

While these past studies of personals-based courtship have taught us valuable lessons concerning one particular mode of dating and courtship, and possibly some aspects of dating and courtship in general, the researcher must feel constrained by the limitations of their methodologies. Examining personal advertisements is a completely unobtrusive technique; it is "naturalistic" behavior in which "subjects are not aware that they are being studied" (Lynn & Bolig, 1985: 379). On the other hand, one must wonder about the other actors in this scene who have not left permanent traces, specifically in the form of a newspaper or magazine ad. Are ad placers and responders complementary and reciprocal in crucial ways? Are they the same people, do they have similar characteristics, are they engaged in the same sort of partner-seeking activity, do they have the same motives? Requesting information from ad placers gives us a glimpse into a data source that might supply some answers to these questions, but it suffers from a possible problem of bias: Are the 20, 30, or 40 (or unknown) percent who answer the researcher's request for information similar in crucial ways to the 60, 70, or 90 percent who do not? Even participating in personal ad-based dating "in good faith" vitiates getting a broad cross-sectional view: Are partners one has chosen to date because of their appeal to us representative of participants in this scene generally?

Moreover, the endeavor of receiving information on responses to ads negates the value of file ads as unobtrusive instruments, since the avenue we must use to obtain this information may influence the answers we receive. (For instance, how many ad placers who received a humiliating zero responses to a particular advertisement will report that fact to an interviewer?) If we rely on information supplied by the venue in which the ads appear, how complete and detailed can we expect that information to be? So far, social science researchers have requested only fairly simple tallies from the ad-bearing journals. . . .

• • •

Methods

Frustrated by the limitations of the currently available research techniques . . . I decided to place bogus ads in several journals which carry personal columns. I reasoned that, if they were realistic enough, they would attract responses that were representative, reflective of responses to genuine ads, and uncontaminated by the method by which I generated them. Since the most commonly-verified generalization in the literature is that ads placed by men *seek* women who are attractive and *offer* financial success, while ads placed by women *seek* financially successful males and *offer* attractiveness (for instance, Hirschman, 1987), I decided to use this angle as a point of entry. (I focused exclusively on heterosexual ads, reasoning that the dimension of sexual orientation would have introduced more complexity into the research than I was willing to grapple with at present.)

I placed four ads in four different periodicals, published in separate geographical locales, which carry personal advertisements; hence, a total of 16 ads appeared. The wording in the four ads was almost identical except for the two crucial variables. (I did vary the wording very slightly to avoid arousing the suspicion of responders.) One ad referred to a beautiful waitress; she was intended to present to ad readers and responders a potential date who ranked high on physical attractiveness and low on financial success. Another ad referred to a successful female lawyer who was "average" in appearance, that is, a woman who ranks considerably lower in attractiveness, but considerably higher in economic success, than the waitress. A third ad referred to a handsome taxicab driver, who ranked high in attractiveness and low in success. And the fourth ad referred to an average-looking male lawyer, who ranked lower in looks and higher in success than the cab driver. I decided to request written replies rather than voice mail because the former represent a permanent record; written replies are easier to examine, consult, and handle. In addition, photographs (which were not requested) can accompany written responses, but not telephone messages. I present the findings of this study, and a justification of the ads, in another publication.

There were, of course, no actual persons behind these ads; I placed them myself for the purpose of studying the responses they elicited. Hence, deception was involved in this study.

Is Placing a Bogus Personal Ad Unethical?

Erikson (1967) argues that, as a general rule, research based on access to a particular scene through the use of deception, as well as misrepresentation of that research to the subjects of study, should be regarded as unethical. Addressing specifically the issue of research on personal ads, Lynn and Bolig speculate that "investigators may place ads and evaluate the responses that they receive" (1985: 382); however, they add, "such a research strategy" is generally unethical. . . . People who respond to these ads expect to be evaluated by a potential partner. Placing personal ads for research purposes violates these expectations and imposes numerous costs on unwilling subjects" (1985: 383). They mention handling fees that some publications charge for answering personal ads; since I purposely did not place an ad in any publications charging such a fee, this cost is not relevant here. Lynn and Bolig also mention postage costs (at the time of the research, a 29-cent stamp) and writing time. In discussing the drawbacks of this strategy, Lynn and Bolig also claim, without presenting their reasoning, that its utility is "limited," and that the similar wording of parallel ads is likely to arouse suspicion. Judging by their replies, the suspicion of none of the nearly 1,000 responders was aroused—although ad readers who were suspicious might simply not have responded. (Two men did express strong doubts that, given that she relied on personal ads to find a date, the waitress really was as beautiful as she claimed.). . .

As I see it, there are several separate issues to consider when discussing the question of the ethics of disguised or deceptive methods in social research; I would like to discuss two: *risk* and *exploitation*. (A third issue, the *uses* to which the results of the study will be put, while important, is not unique to research techniques which rely on deception or disguised observation.) In addition, and in conjunction with risk, I discuss the question of violating the integrity of a particular scene and offending our informants, issues Erikson deems crucial.

Risk

Erikson distinguishes risk to informants, risk to graduate student researchers, and risk to the profession. He is both wrong and right in his discussion of risk to informants. Insofar as nothing in life is predictable, by definition, the researcher *can* "injure people in ways we can neither anticipate in advance nor compensate for afterward" (1967: 368). On the other hand, any knowledgeable participant observer in every group or setting has some notion of the possible consequences of his or her actions. We ought to know that certain consequences to specific actions are highly likely and others are extremely unlikely. All of us have read textbooks and manuals on field methods and participant observation. All of us have some sense of the social and cultural texture of the groups and scenes we are investigating. Do we expose our subjects to some measure of risk simply by interacting with them, by nosing around their everyday affairs? Of course we do; as Humphreys says, "any conceivable [research] method . . . has at least some potential for harming others" (1970: 169). Whenever humans interact with one another, some measure of risk is involved. Are the risks that flow from pretending to be something one is not qualitatively different from those entailed by the behavior we enact in our own circles, in everyday life? I suspect the *reverse* is the case. It is entirely possible that deep, primary, genuine first-hand involvement with a scene lends a certain confidence to social actors that permit them to involve others in risk. In contrast, adopting a bogus membership in a scene is likely to generate a measure of timidity that mitigates *against* taking certain actions as excessively risky. While not all risks can be predicted many can, and the wise covert fieldworker is not likely to take the worst of them. In any case, this is an empirical question, isn't it? Why should our feelings about the *ethics* of fieldwork get rolled up into our predictions of the *empirical likelihood* of risk? Moreover, it seems to me that Erikson is not discussing ethics so much as sociological incompetence. Any damn fool who does not know enough about the scene under investigation to avoid serious risk—again, statistically, not absolutely, speaking—to his or her subjects does not belong in the field of sociology.

But the interface of ethics and risk cuts both ways (if I may be permitted a mixed metaphor). The very same action which is seen as ethical in one circle may seem unethical in another. It is arrogant for sociologists to assume that *our* (that is, sociological) ethics are identical with our *subjects'* ethics. It is, in fact, entirely possible, in insisting on being *sociologically* ethical, we may harm our subjects by doing something they consider, if not unethical, then either just plain stupid or risky for their own values. During 1982–1983, Mario Brajuha, then a graduate student in sociology, worked as a waiter in a restaurant to earn his way through school. During this time, he took field notes as a participant observer, intending to write his doctoral dissertation on "the dining experience." In March, 1983, a fire of suspicious origin destroyed the restaurant. The Suffolk County District Attorney's office, believing that the owners had arranged to torch the building to collect the insurance money, demanded that Brajuha surrender his field notes. He refused, insisting that he had promised to protect the identity of his informants. Brajuha was forced to go to trial, first in a county case and later in a federal case, to keep his field notes from the gaze of authorities. These cases dragged on for nearly two years before the charges were eventually dropped.

Ironically, Brajuha's refusal to give up his field notes to the authorities may have had an unintended impact on the very individuals he sought to protect, that is, his informants. Because the investigation was based on suspected arson, the insurance company refused to pay the owner's claim. Consequently, the owners could not rebuild the restaurant. As a result, the employees who worked for the restaurant were either unemployed or had to seek work in less desirable, less remunerative jobs. Far from appreciating his efforts, the restaurant's former employees, its owners, and their financial partners deeply resented Brajuha's stubbornness. They felt that his refusal to turn over his field notes was based on trivial, academic, and esoteric notions. As a result, after being a trusted insider for so long, he became an outsider, a "problem person," a persona non grata. Moreover, because he found himself shunned socially within the restaurant business, he found it extremely difficult to get another waiting job during the two years he spent defending his case (Brajuha & Hallowell, 1986). This is not a case of disguised observation, of course, nor is it a question of an outsider faking the accouterments of a particular scene. What we have here is a case of harm being inflicted on subjects as a consequence of a conflict between sociological ethics and local ethics. Brajuha could have foreseen the consequences of his participation in a particular setting, but it was *not* because he employed deception, and it was *not* because he lacked an insider's knowledge of the scene; it was because he followed *sociological* ethics—and, in so doing, violated local ethics.

Are we really talking about the likelihood of harm when we discuss risk? If we are, in my study—unlike Humphreys'—there was no conceivable possibility of harm. No respondent could have been arrested or faced the risk of any of the more serious forms of harm we can imagine that might result from social research in certain scenes by being unwittingly dragged into my research project. On the other hand, what about less serious forms of harm? Specially, what about the risk of exposure and the possibility of embarrassment and humiliation? What if, as a result of answering one of my ads, persons whom one of my respondents knew found out he or she was seeking a date through personal advertisements? What embarrassing revelations were exposed in his or her letter, meant only for the eyes of the (in reality, fictive) advertiser? What about the married respondents who sought "discreet" afternoon liasons? Of course, I read all the letters and notes; this was unavoidable. By the very nature of the research, my knowledge of their participation and revelations was inevitable. In addition, several graduate and undergraduate research assistants coded a number of these letters; and the members of my "panel of judges," to be explained shortly, read the letters. I did take one precaution: When I handed the members of the panel the letters to read, I had blocked out key identifying details—name, address, telephone numbers, etc. I did not do this for my coders, however.

Whenever I could, I minimized the risk of exposure by having members of my panel of judges who live in one venue reading letters that were generated by journals which were published in a different venue. All the female members of my panel of judges lived in venue number one, while all (but a few) of the male responders to the female ads whose letters the female panel read lived in venues three and four; hence, they were extremely unlikely to have been acquainted with them. I was not able to do this with the female letters, however. (And I did not attempt to do this venue juggling at all, obviously, for my research assistants.) Ethically, this is the only aspect of the research about which I feel in the slightest bit uncomfortable. In any case, no research assistant said that he or she knew any of the responders; one member of my panel of judges stated that he thought one of the respondents looked familiar. Was the privacy of my respondents violated? Yes and no. A small number of individuals, including myself, read their notes and letters—which were intended for someone else, and for an entirely different purpose. On the other hand, none of us (with one possible exception) was personally acquainted with the subjects and no one was therefore able to link up what they said in their responses with a real person in the concrete world. Thus, their anonymity—and, I am satisfied, their essential privacy—was preserved.

Violating the Integrity of a Scene

Did I violate the integrity of this scene? It seems to me that Erikson is really discussing a philosophical and esthetic issue, not one of empirical physical or social harm to informants. Erikson seems to believe that groups, scenes, and subcultures in this society are so isolated and radically different from the mainstream culture that they constitute altogether different social worlds, worlds whose values, norms, and lifeways are hidden even from the gaze of the inquisitive fieldworker. And that these lifeways are so deeply ingrained that they cannot be convincingly faked. Erikson's model adheres to the view that being a member of one of these scenes entails something of a full-time commitment. For most sociological scenes—certainly not all—I question Erikson's characterization. In fact, most scenes are *not* made up of participants who are devoted full-time to it. In many—perhaps most—sociological scenes we're likely to study, participants flit in and out, devoting only a segment of their lives to the scene. Most sociological scenes are not like small tribal societies half-way around the world from us. Most participants in the worlds we are likely to study have one foot in the social and cultural mainstream and the other in a scene that bears major similarities to the cultural mainstream. (This is both all empirical question and a matter of degree, of course.) In most cases, we *can* fake the trappings of the scene because it isn't that different from the ones in which we are already involved.

In learning about particular scenes, all participant observers confirm gaffes and blunders; it is one way we learn the configurations of the scene under study. Thus, even the mistakes Erikson claims that disguised observers are likely to make can be productive in that they represent a learning experience. Still, much covert work in groups in which the intruder is not a genuine member demonstrates that evidence of membership *can* be successfully reproduced. Undercover agents, spies, and investigative journalists manage to fake participation convincingly in many scenes without arousing suspicion. . . . The ethical question of whether we have the same *right* to do this as these shady operators do is, again, a completely separate issue. Moreover, most scenes permit the role of neophyte, learner, or convert, who is permitted mistakes. Once again, Erikson has attempted to smuggle empirical questions into an essentially ethical issue. Can insider membership and participation be faked? With varying degrees of success, of course they can! Is this a violation of the integrity of the scene under study? I can't answer that; it's a matter of opinion. . . .

Consider the scene in which I have been interested. For a period of roughly three years in the late 1970's and early 1980s, I was an active and genuine participant in a scene in which dating and courtship was made possible as a consequence of reading, answering, and placing personal advertisements. During this period of time, I answered perhaps three dozen ads, and placed one; I had at least one date with some two dozen women as a result of my participation in the personal ads. In fact, it was partly a result of my participation in personal ads that led to my interest, a decade later, in studying it as a form of dating and courtship. I did not "wear a disguise exactly because" I was entering a social sphere "so far from" my own experience (Erikson, 1967: 368). In fact, the reverse was true: I was successful at wearing a particular disguise which enabled me to enter a social sphere precisely *because* I had been intimate with that social sphere, because it was part of my own personal experience 10 or more years earlier. My particular form of "imitation" was successful; as I said above, judging from the evidence in the nearly one thousand letters I received, little or no "subliminal suspicion" seems to have been aroused. Again, this scene was not the sort of social circle that demands full-time, lifelong membership. Participants continually enter and leave it; in fact, they enter it *in order to* leave it and re-enter the mainstream. My *genuine* participation in it gave me enough insider's information so that I was *capable* of engaging in a form of disguised observation.

Offending Informants

It seems to me that Erikson and other blanket opponents of disguised observation are mixing up genuine risk of physical and social damage to our subjects with *offending* them. Erikson tells us that fraud is "painful to the people who are misled"; it can "cause discomfort" and "distress" (1967: 368). Does that mean that social researchers are ethically obliged to avoid doing anything that causes "distress" and "discomfort" to the people they study? . . .There is no way within the boundaries of legitimate social research to produce results that all or even most subjects will be happy with. It is the ethical researcher who is forced to cause distress to his or her subjects, who will almost always dislike the portrait that is drawn of them.

• • •

Complex portrayals of real people in the real world offer a view most subjects are likely to experience as betrayal—betrayal not so much because details of the portrait are empirically false as a "warts and all" image is the last thing the subject wants presented to the reading public. . . . Please note: the subject wants to read a flattering portrayal, not an accurate one. A research report's lack of flattery is what is most likely to cause pain and discomfort, not the practice of deception the researcher may have used to gather information.

Indeed, it is mainly *because* portrayal is less than completely complimentary *that deception becomes an issue in the first place.* Deception is experienced as offensive *specifically* because the researcher has discovered—again, empirically accurate—facts the subject does not wish to be conveyed to the public. Even when *technical* deception is not employed, complete honesty of necessity represents a kind of deception in that a *contract of dishonesty is implied in intimacy.* If informants let a researcher—or, for that matter, a friend or acquaintance—into their lives, it is *implicitly understood* that he or she will not report certain discrediting information. The issue of unwarranted access cannot be separated from the implicit contract understood by all intimates. The honest sociologist *must* betray informants.

Exploitation

Anyone interested in the ethics of disguised observation must grapple with the issue of exploitation. Here, we are concerned with the question of cost (as opposed to danger or risk). That is, should we condone having our informants on the cheap? Have we asked them to expend resources—an action they otherwise would have been reluctant to undertake—which will result in no recompense to themselves? Much social research demands time and other resources from informants, of course, with little or no payoff to them, other than the gratification of participating in a study or, much later on, reading about a scene in which they are involved. . . . But deception demands that informants expend those resources under false pretenses. In most interview, questionnaire, experimental, or field situations, respondents know they will not compensated. Disguised observation either does not make that clear or even (as with mine) seems to extend an offer which will not be forthcoming. As Lynn and Bolig (1985: 383) point out, answering a bogus personal ad places "costs" on responders; they spend the time and effort answering an ad with no possible chance of actually getting a date. How serious are these costs? How much of an investment do personal ad responders make to get a date? And what is the likely reward in responding to a personal ad?

To begin with, a date is far from certain even when answering a genuine personal advertisement. Rajecki, Bledsoe, and Rasmussen (1991) sent a questionnaire to ad placers to inquire about the responses they received. Women reported an average of 26 replies; men said that they received an average of 15 replies. . . . As a result of each advertisement, ad placers actually ended up going out on a total of slightly less than two dates for both women and men (1991: 464). Hence, the odds that a given response resulted in a date were 7 percent for women and 13 percent for men. . . . Thus, my ruse lowered the respondent's odds, in this effort, from a bit more than one in 10 to zero.

Moreover, something of a quota system operates here; this is true for both ad placers and ad responders. It is not the number of (potential) *dates* that is relevant here, but the number of *acceptable* dates. Ad placers "rank-order incoming replies. Meetings are then arranged with a few respondents who have the highest apparent potential" (1991: 467). If one or more of these meetings proved to be successful, contacts with other parties are not arranged "because the writer's short-term social needs are met" (1991: 467). On the other hand, if these meetings produce no viable dating partners, little further effort will be made, since "the writer is already disappointed by the best candidates" (1991: 467). . . .

It would be instructive to consider the question of the amount of time that responders invested in the endeavor of writing replies to these ads. I operationalized the concept of "minimalism"—a respondent putting an absolute minimal effort into answering an ad—as engaging in one of five actions. Minimalism is defined as sending to the advertiser: (a) a sheet of memo paper with nothing more than a name (first only or first and last) and a telephone number and/or an address and/or a post office box, (b) a business card; (c) a Xerox copy of a generic all-purpose letter not written in response to the ad or ads in question; (d) a computer-generated generic, all-purpose letter; or (e) a hand-written note containing 25 words or less. If a note or letter of more than 25 words was attached or added to or written on any of (a) through (d), it did not qualify as a minimalist effort. Only 11 of the 79 women (or, more properly, as we'll see shortly, responses) who answered my male ads, or 14 percent, were minimalists: They sent in responses that were other than, and in fact, considerably less than, personal letters. In contrast, 79 out of the 240 responses to the female lawyer all (or 33 percent) and 171 of the 668 responses to the waitress ad (26 percent) were minimalist in nature—overall, twice the frequency as the men (28 versus 14 percent). While the overwhelming majority of the women, and a clear majority of the men, put in more than a minimal effort to answer my ads, a substantial minority of the men at least, did not,

All manuals instructing placers of personal ads warn that minimalists are likely to be "blitzers"—that is, someone who puts in a minimal effort in responding to a personal ad is highly likely to send out many replies on an indiscriminate basis rather than a few on a selective, discriminating basis (Foxman, 1982; Block, 1984; Beker & Rosenwald, 1985). Since each of my sets of ads contained two that were strikingly different, I made the assumption that any responder who answered both was a "blitzer," that is, sent responses to a number of ads in addition to the two I placed. (Foxman, 1982: 104, Block, 1984: 113, and Beker & Rosenwald, 1985: 52–53, all make this assumption.) According to the criterion of sending a response to both the cabdriver and the lawyer ads, only three of the women who replied were blitzers (4 percent); thus, the 79 responses represent 76 women. In contrast, 104 of the male responders sent in responses to both the waitress and the lawyer; this means that our 908 male responses represent 805 responders, of whom 13 percent were "blitzers." Even if most of our 800-plus men wrote individually crafted letters, enough of them sent a multiple replies for us to conclude that a significant minority did not give much thought or feeling to their responses.

The Panel of Judges

How many of the replies I received were sent by persons who *should* have sent them in the first place? How many were *realistic* partners of my hypothetical ad placers? Were these individuals engaged in reasonable, practical, rational courtship, or were they acting out a fantasy courtship with someone who, in reality, would not even have considered dating them? How many were doing the same thing with other, highly desirable parties? If they had little or no chance of getting a date from my hypothetical ad placers, what exactly was I taking from them? Should they have responded in the first place?

To address these questions, I assembled a "panel of judges" (a kind of "convenience" or "opportunity" sample) of 20 persons to determine whether the ad placers would be likely to respond to the individuals who answered their ads. Half the members of this panel were women and half were men; half were professionals or professionals in training, half were non-professionals. All the professionals or professionals in training were college graduates; none of the non-professionals were college graduates. Their ages fell five years on either side of the ages of the ad placers (which were 30 for the women, 32 for the men), that is, 25 to 35 for the women, 27 to 37 for the men. I showed each member of the panel the two same-sex ads and a file of opposite-sex respondents' letters or notes and photographs; each panel member was shown a file of 10 responses. Women panel members were shown male responses to female ads, men members were shown female responses to male ads. The male responses were selected randomly anew for each female panel member. (Half had been sent to the waitress ad and half to the lawyer ad.) In contrast, the female responses were the only 10 I received with a clear color photograph accompanying the letter or note; hence, while each woman panel member reviewed a random shuffle of male responses, all male panel members reviewed the same 10 female responses. As I said above, I blocked out all names, addresses, telephone numbers, and other specific identifying information.

Evaluation of Respondents as Dates

All panel members were informed as to the bogus nature of the ad. Each was asked to read the ad placed by the two parties of their own sex. They were then asked the following question: "Try to picture what he/she is like and what sort of woman/man he/she is probably advertising for and wants to go out on a date with. Now, imagine that he/she receives a number of replies. Let's say that one of the replies he/she receives is from *this* woman/man. Here's her/his photograph and here's her/his letter. Now, what do you think the chances are that the man/woman who placed the ad you read would want to go out with this woman/man? Why do you think this is the case?" I asked each female panel member to rate this likelihood for responses to both the waitress and the female lawyer ads. (I tallied these responses separately.) Eight of the women's responses were written to the male lawyer ad, and two were sent to the cabdriver ad. I divided panelists' judgments into three categories—the hypothetical ad placer would *probably* get in touch with the responder, that is, there was more than a 50/50 chance; there was roughly a 50/50 chance of this happening; and getting a date was not very likely, that is, there was less than a 50/50 chance.

Only one-third of the judgements made by the female panelists . . . assessing whether the hypothetical ad placer would make an effort to date the respondents who wrote to their ad—33 percent for the waitress, 38 percent for the lawyer—answered in the affirmative. In contrast, the male panelists were much more sanguine about the male respondent's chances of getting a date with the fictive ad placer: Eight out of ten of the judgments concerning the respondents' chance of getting a date with the cabdriver were positive (80 percent), and over half (56 percent) of the judgements on the respondents' getting a date with the male lawyer were positive. In short, in only a *minority* of the time, female panel members say that the female ad placers have a better than 50/50 chance of making an effort to date the male respondents who answered the ads. In contrast, female respondents were said to have a better chance; more than half of my male panelists said that there was a 50/50 chance that the male ad placers would make an attempt to go out with the female respondents. In no case did a specific respondent elicit universal agreement among all 10 of any opposite-sex panel member that a date with the ad placer was certain or even probable.

The point is, of course, that getting a date with someone who placed an ad is far from a guarantee. To judge from my panel members, in the case of women who place ads, getting a date is something of a long shot; only one out of three men who responded to my ads were judged *worthy* of dating the women who, supposedly, placed the ads. Were the men who responded plausible candidates for the women to whom they wrote? In the view of my panelists, in most instances, no. . . .

Ethical Judgments

In addition to asking my panel members to evaluate responders to the ads as potential dates for the men and women described in those ads. I also asked them about the ethics of my research endeavor. I asked two questions: "Do you think that deception in social research is unethical?" And: "Do you think the methods I used in this study were unethical?"

Only two of my 20 panel members of both sexes said, without qualification, that my study was unethical. One 34-year-old professional woman said. "I feel bad for the people who wrote. Because, even though they don't get responses from many people, each no response has an effect." The others divided evenly between those who said the research methods I used were clearly *not* unethical (9 panelists) and, those who were ambivalent about the issue (9 panelists).

Those who were ambivalent expressed both positive and negative aspects to the research; for the most part, they couched their views in terms of situation ethics: In the abstract, deception is undesirable, but if no harm comes to the respondents, and some benefit results in the form of an addition to knowledge, then a study does more good then harm. In the case of this study, to these respondents, the risk seems small and the pay-off, they assumed, worthwhile. Another 34-year-old professional woman explained her views in the following words: "You don't really affect their lives all that much. . . . Maybe being unethical sometimes is OK. Well, yeah, it's unethical—I mean, you're lying—but it's OK. As I'm thinking through it, yeah, it's totally unethical, but it's OK. It's an acceptable thing to do. You're doing research, you're trying to gather information. You're not really hurting anybody. Besides, how else could you do it? You really couldn't get this information any other way. . . . You're trying to look into human nature and learn about people."

The remaining panel members expressed the view, without qualification, that the study was not unethical; they denied that harm was a realistic possibility and saw only benefits from the study. Some justified their position by stating that certain *other* methods would *definitely* be unethical, but not this one. For instance, if I were to actually set up or got out on dates with the respondents and study their behavior in some way, this would be unacceptable; in comparison, this study's methodology they said, was positively pristine. A 35-year-old mail sorter and deliverer told me: "do I think that what you're doing is unethical? No, not really. . . . I assume it's a bona fide study. But if you were to answer these ads and go out with these women and, just as you're walking down the aisle, you say, oh, by the way, I'm married, I'm just doing a study—*that* would be unethical." Several other panelists stated that answering ads to gather information would definitely be unethical.

Some panel members justified the study's methods by pointing to the world of dating by means of singles ads; it is, by its very nature, a world of deception and chance-taking; no one is assured of a date by writing a response to an ad, some said, nor that the contents of the ad are truthful. The ads are not very revealing or communicative, several panel members added: how could such uncommunicative ads generate realistic hope in any respondents? Said a 30-year-old professional woman: "If these ads were more, communicative, I might think it was unethical. But the, fact that the ads are so uncommunicative and nondescript, so generic, means that it's hard to imagine someone having his heart set on who's behind this particular ad. But these ads could be almost anybody." These panelists did not dismiss the issue of harm to research subjects generally as trivial. All either admitted that deception in social research posed a genuine problem whose harm and benefits had to be weighed carefully—or segued directly from the general question to a consideration of this particular study. But this study, they argued, posed no risk of harm to my respondents. "No harm, no foul," seemed to be their refrain.

Coda

Did I corrupt any graduate students by involving them in the research, either as a researcher assistant or as a member of the panel of judges? Were they placed in an ethically compromising position by engaging in coding or judging the quality of the responders as dates? Life, generally and social research specifically inevitably entail making judgements in morally ambiguous situations. To pretend otherwise is naive. In all phases of this research, I told graduate students that I'm doing what I think is best; it's their choice as to whether they wish to collude in an endeavor they may have reservations about. Moreover, everyone associated with this study was able to make a distinction between involvement in one or another phase of this study and approval of my research strategy. In fact, of the graduate students I talked to, one particular research assistant, who was the most involved in various phases of the research, expressed the most critical views concerning the ethics of the research. My position on the matter and his involvement in the project did not alter his judgement one whit: Even though he worked for me and knew my position on the issue, he nonetheless regarded deception in social research to be unethical. Graduate assistants are capable of thinking for themselves, and my experience with this demonstrates that fact.

$$\cdot\ \cdot\ \cdot$$

Did I place any ongoing or future sociological research—either on personal advertisements or in general—in jeopardy by engaging in deceptive practices? I hope not. It is a troubling question for me. I strongly believe every society *deserves* a skeptical, inquiring, tough-minded, challenging sociological community. It is one of the *obligations* of such a society to nurture such a community and to tolerate occasional intrusions by its members into the private lives of its citizens. . . . When one of these intrusions takes place, its citizens may become resentful and make later sociological research more difficult. I have no problem with the *ethics* of the occasional deceptive prying and intruding that some sociologists do. I approve of it as long as no one's safety is threatened. My problem is a *tactical* and *empirical* one: Does this make further prying and intruding problematic?

I don't think any of us can answer this question, but I do not believe that one sociologist's research should be foreclosed because it has the potential for making another sociologist's possible future research more difficult. If this is a criterion for the viability of a specific line of research, then we must consider additional possible sources of public and official antagonism to sociological research: the religious right's opposition to studies on sexual attitudes and behavior, leftish views which hold that even engaging in certain inquiries is politically incorrect, hostility by the police, to an investigation of brutality and corruption in their ranks, and so on. Can it be that *certain* reasons which pose a possible threat to future research meet with our approval while others do not? Would any among us expect a sociologist of sex to avoid doing a study which is likely to draw controversial conclusions because it might antagonize the public and endanger the work of future sociologists on the subject? (And of what value would that work be if it avoided controversy?) I certainly do not want to make any colleagues' future research more difficult, but I do not wish to close down my research endeavors because they may object to my violating an article of ethics they believe in but I don't.

References

Adler, P. A., Adler, P., & Rochford, E. B., Jr. (1986). The Politics of Participation in Field Research. *Urban Life, 14,* 363–376.

Austrom, D., & Hanel, K. (1983). Looking for Companionship in the Classified Section. North York, Ontario: York University, Unpublished manuscript.

Beker, G., & Rosenwald, C. (1985). *The Personals: The Safe Way to Mate and Date.* New York: Zebra Books.

Berger, P. L. (1963). *Invitation to Sociology: A Humanistic Perpsective.* Garden City, N. Y.: Doubleday Anchor.

Block, S. (1984). *Advertising for Love: How to Play the Personals.* New York: Quill.

Bolig, R., Stein, P. J., & McHenry, P. C. (1984). The Self-Advertisement Approach to Dating: Male-Female Differences. *Family Relations, 33,* 587–592.

Brajuha, M., Hallowell, L. (1986). Legal Intrusion and the Politics of Fieldwork: The Impact of the Brajuha Case, *Urban Life, 14,* 457–478.

Darden, D. K., & Koski, P. R. (1988). Using the Personal Ads: A Deviant Activity? *Deviant Behavior, 9,* 383–400.

Deaux, K., & Hanna R. (1984). Courtship in the Personal Column: The Influence of Gender and Sexual Orientation, *Sex Roles, 11,* 363–375.

Douglas, J. D. (1976). *Investigative Social Research.* Beverly Hills, CA: Sage.

Erikson, K. (1967). A Comment on Disguised Observation in Sociology. *Social Problems, 14,* 366–373.

Foxman, S. (1982). *Classified Love: A Guide to the Personals.* New York: McGraw-Hill.

Hilbert, R. A. (1980). Covert Participant Observation: On its Nature and Practice. *Urban Life, 9,* 51–78.

Hirschman, E. (1987). People as Products: Analysis of a Complex Marketing Exchange. *Journal of Marketing, 51,* 98–108.

Humphreys, L. (1970). *Tearoom Trade: Impersonal Sex in Public Places.* Chicago: Aldine.

Humphreys, L. (1970). *Tearoom Trade: Impersonal Sex in Public Places* (expanded ed.). Chicago, IL: Aldine.

Long, G. L. & Dorn, D. S. (1983). Sociologists' Attitudes Toward Ethical Issues: The Management of an Impression. *Sociologial and Social Research, 67,* 288–300.

Lynn, M., and Bolig, R. (1985). Personal Advertisements: Sources of Data About Relationships. *Journal of Social and Personal Relationships, 2,* 377–383.

Lynn, M., & Shurgot, B. A. (1984). Responses to Lonely Hearts Advertisements: Effects of Reported Physical Attractiveness, Physique, and Coloration. *Personality and Social Psychology Bulletin, 10,* 349–357.

Malcolm, J. (1990). *The Journalist and the Murderer.* New York: Vintage Books.

Montini, T., and Ovrebo, B. (1990). Personal Relationship Ads: An Informal Balancing Act. *Sociological Perspectives, 3,* 327–339.

Rajecki, D. W., Bledsoe, S., & Rasmussen, J. L. (1991). Successful Personal Ads: Gender Differences and Similarities in Offers, Stipulations, and Outcomes. *Basic and Applied Social*

Psychology, 12, 457–469.

Scarce, R. (1994). (No) Trial (But) Tribulations. *Journal of Contemporary Ethnography, 23,* 123–149.

Shulman, D. (1994). Dirty Data and Investigative Methods: Some Lessons from Private Detective Work. *Journal of Contemporary Ethnography, 23,* 214–253.

Whyte, W. F. (1955). *Street Corner Society: The Social Structure of an Italian Slum* (enlarged ed.). Chicago, IL: University of Chicago Press.

Scholarly Ethics
and Courtroom Antics:
Where Researchers Stand
in the Eyes of the Law

RIK SCARCE

In 1993 the author, then a Ph.D. candidate in sociology, was jailed
for 159 days after refusing to violate the American Sociological
Association's *Code of Ethics* provisions prohibiting the sharing of
confidential research data with law enforcement authorities. This
article discusses the *Code,* presents the facts of the case, answers
critics of the author's and the ASA's stance, summarizes an attorney's analysis of researcher's rights in the eyes of the law, and
concludes by urging sociologists to seek federal legislation protecting them and their work product from intrusions by public and
private institutions.

This article's five sections present a set of facts and observations that emerged from
my experiences as the first sociologist to be jailed for refusing to violate the American Sociological Association's (ASA) *Code of Ethics,* experiences that are relevant to
everyone in the profession. I begin by discussing the relevant provisions in the ASA's
Code, the second section outlines the facts of my case and the legal wrangling that it
entailed, emphasizing the intersection of the law and the *Code;* the third section examines the arguments made by critics of my position. . . . .

The goals of this paper are several. First, my hope is to make clear the hegemonic
relationship between the state and scholarship—we are not as free to pursue our
research as we would have ourselves believe. Second, my case appears to have given
rise to some second-guessing regarding the *Code,* and I argue that the provision that
directed my behavior should be maintained regardless of its dubious current legal status. Finally, perhaps this article will make clearer that what we as scholars do is terri-

bly important to society—so important that we may be jailed for conducting sociological research. This may be a shocking concept in an era when some even within the profession question the relevancy of it all.

The American Sociological Association's *Code of Ethics*

In 1968 the ASA adopted a code of ethics for its members, sixteen years before the current *Code* was established. However, it was not until 1982 that a study was conducted to assess ASA members' knowledge and perceptions of the *Code*—a study made all the more important because it appears that none other like it has been attempted since (Dean Dorn, personal communication). In reporting the results of their survey, Gary Long and Dean Dorn (Long and Dorn 1982) wrote, "Perhaps the main implication of our data is our respondents' relative ignorance of the *Code of Ethics* and the Committee on Ethics. Even the ethically conscious sociologists seem to be somewhat oblivious" (Long and Dorn 1982: 82). Though 61 percent of the 240 respondents were *aware* of the *Code's* existence, fewer than 26 percent of ASA members claimed to be *familiar* with it (Long and Dorn 1982: 81). . . .

Thus, ASA members appeared to have little concern about their *Code of Ethics*. Perhaps it is not too much of a stretch to assume that they had even less awareness, familiarity, or concern about where they and their research stood in the eyes of the law. My case clarifies those topics. The *Code* may indeed be useful in legal cases but, as the law stands today, it alone is inadequate to protect research subjects from harm arising from their participation in research. To do that, in extreme cases sociologists must be willing to go to jail.

The arguments that I made to the various federal courts in my case as to why I should not be jailed for protecting confidential communications largely hinged upon the *Code*. Section B(7) of the *Code* states, "Confidential information provided by research participants must be treated as such by sociologists, *even when this information enjoys no legal protection or privilege and legal force is applied*" (American Sociological Association 1984: 3; emphasis mine). The ASA is not alone in its stand directing strict adherence to the spirit of confidentiality agreements. For instance, the American Political Science Association's *Code of Professional Conduct* states,

> As citizens, [scholars] have an obligation to cooperate with grand juries, other law enforcement agencies, and institutional officials.
>
> Conversely, scholars also have a professional duty not to divulge the identity of confidential sources of information or data developed in the course of research, whether to governmental or non-governmental officials or bodies, even though in the present state of American law they run the risk of suffering an applicable penalty. (American Political Science Association 1991: 9)

A similar, though more equivocal provision is included in the *Statements on Ethics* of the American Anthropological Association, which states, "Anthropologists' first responsibility is to those whose lives and cultures they study. Should conflicts of interest arise, the interests of these people take precedence over other considerations. . . . The right of those providing information to anthropologists either to remain anonymous or to receive recognition is to be respected *and defended*" (American Anthropological Association [1971] 1990: 1; emphasis mine). In contrast, the American Psychological Association actually appears to allow its members to compromise their promises of confidentiality. Its *Ethical Principles of Psychologists and Code of Conduct* states, "Psychologists disclose confidential information without the consent of the individual only as mandated by law, or where permitted by law for a valid purpose . . . " (American Psychological Association 1992: Standard 5.05).

Ultimately, the *Code* did me little good *legally*. However, morally it was a mainstay of mine. The ASA's ethical guidelines, like those of other professional organizations, establish standards of behavior relative to professional expectations and independent of the law. Below I address critics who say that that independence places sociologists "above the law." For now suffice it to say that ethical codes *restrain* as well as *direct* behavior. Though general in scope, nonetheless they are normative, and as with all norms they emerge from social activity. They have a basis in a certain reality, that of the practicing social researcher (American Sociological Association 1968; Schuler 1969).

Scholarly Ethics and Courtroom Antics

The Raid and the Subpoena

In 1990 I enrolled as a Ph.D. student in sociology at Washington State University (WSU) in Pullman, where I had decided to study because of its strong program in environmental sociology. Shortly after I began coursework that fall my book, *Eco-Warriors: Understanding the Radical Environmental Movement*, was published. I had worked on the book full time for a year prior to its publication. Although I relied upon several sources of data for my book, primary among them were interviews with environmental activists from three groups: Earth First!, the Sea Shepherd Conservation Society, and the Animal Liberation Front. Collectively, this movement is distinguished from nearly all other environmental advocacy groups by its extensive use of "direct action" by grassroots activists—tactics range from letter writing and speech making to street theater, civil disobedience, and property destruction—rather than the lobbying and mass mailing approaches undertaken by better known, highly bureaucratized groups.

My book was the first one of its kind to take an in-depth look at this controversial movement through the eyes of the participating activists. There was little explicit theory or theorizing in the book—my background was in journalism, and I took a reporter's approach to the material, as distinguished from a more academic analysis of the subject matter. However, for my Ph.D. dissertation I hoped to conduct a more scholarly study of the radical environmental movement (REM). . . .

I began my dissertation research on the REM in my first semester at WSU. At that time I was unaware of my university's requirement that all research undertaken to fulfill course or program requirements had to be approved by an Institutional Review Board (IRB). This requirement was not noted in the WSU graduate study bulletin, in the graduate study rules and procedures manual, or in my department's published guidelines for graduate students. My research on the REM was not preapproved by the IRB.

Rod Coronado was one of the activists whom I interviewed for my book. He is intelligent, thoughtful, and somewhat outgoing, with an academic bent—he once told me that he was considering attending college. At that time he was in his mid- or late twenties. He had joined the REM shortly after graduating from high school and my impression was that he had been involved almost continuously ever since. Following my move from California to Washington, Coronado and I remained in contact, and eventually we agreed that he would house sit for me and my family for three weeks during July and August 1991. Prior to confirming that he would house sit, I had not heard from Coronado for some time, and I had asked coworkers on the summer research project I was working on if they would be interested in staying at our place. My primary concern was that someone would be there to take care of our cat. I got no takers other than Coronado.

Late in July we left for the East Coast to visit family and so that I could conduct research; the annual Earth First! "Rendezvous," its equivalent of a national convention, was being held in Vermont that year and it seemed like a good opportunity for me to gather data. Coronado picked us up when we arrived back in Pullman on the evening of August 14. We were tired from a long day's travel, and after arriving home, my family and I went to bed. The next morning I picked up the newspaper from the front step and found an article discussing an Animal Liberation Front (ALF) raid that had occurred on the WSU campus on the evening of August 12–13. Coyotes had been freed to the fields around the research site and mink and mice had been stolen—"liberated" in ALF parlance. I was surprised by the raid. To my knowledge there never had been any antianimal experimentation protests on my campus, and now this. The adults talked about the newspaper report around the breakfast table as any other group might have done that morning. Then my stepson whisked his mother away to go shopping for his ninth birthday that day. Some time after that Coronado left town.

In the months following the raid it was revealed that a press release announcing the raid had been faxed to the Spokane office of a wire service from a nearby Kinko's Copy Center and that police had obtained descriptions of two persons who allegedly sent the fax. Later, Coronado was named as a "person of interest" in the case—a suspect, in other words. Then, late on a Friday afternoon in May 1992, I was summoned to the Washington State University police station by a campus police officer. It was a call that I had been anticipating. My book had made me a somewhat well-known character on campus—I had been invited to present several guest lectures—and I had been interviewed about the raid shortly after it occurred by the region's largest newspaper. Furthermore, I had not hidden Coronado's presence at my home, which was half of a duplex in a residential neighborhood, and I felt he would be tracked there. Waiting for me at the police station was the officer who had phoned me and an agent from the Federal Bureau of Investigation. They talked with me for about an hour, during which I said very little and the police officer seemed oddly ingratiating. Eventually they asked me one or more questions about Coronado, which I refused to answer, and I was handed a subpoena to appear before a federal grand jury meeting the following month in Spokane, 80 miles north of Pullman.

The subpoena frightened me terribly. Though I knew little about grand juries, it was clear to me that they had extraordinary powers and that in a clash with one I would likely have to go to jail rather than discuss aspects of my research that were confidential. It took me nearly two weeks to find an attorney experienced with grand jury procedure, and by then I had lost ten pounds and was getting almost no sleep. Preparation for my preliminary examinations and for a summer school class slowed nearly to a halt. I constantly felt sick to my stomach. In short, I was falling apart.

My attorney, Jeffry Finer of Spokane, was intrigued by the case and almost immediately found an apparent violation of Department of Justice (DOJ) procedures that indefinitely delayed the proceedings. The DOJ requires its prosecutors to go to great lengths to obtain information from other sources before they approach members of the press. Finer later obtained the government's assurance that it would further delay my grand jury appearance until after my prelims in September, and I did not go before the grand jury until November.

Scholars as Members of "The Press"

A brief aside is necessary in this chronological rendering to address the relationship between scholars and "the press." Some have been troubled by the linkages between my case and the press, arguing instead that the issue was how science should be treated in the courts. These sentiments resonate with me, though I do not believe they lead down the best path for protecting scholars from governmental intrusion into their work. Still, an emphasis on sociology as science rather than sociologists as members of the press has its advantages. For one, society vests "science" with substantial prestige and status. Why not take advantage of its position and clarify scientists' unique roles? Second, a not uncommon epithet in the social sciences is to refer to a given piece of research as "mere journalism"—simplistic, untheoretical reportage without analysis. Thus, it is easy to understand why some wish to distinguish between science and journalism. Another, less common but thought-provoking tack is to assert that labeling what sociologists do as equivalent to the work of the press is to cave in to the dominant legal paradigm; instead, we should be carving out science's niche in the law. Ironically, there are legal cases that do precisely that already, so the distance is not so great (for example, see *Dow Chemical v. Allen* 1982).

My case sought to link science and the press. This was based on two factors, the first leading to the second. As scholars and researchers we behave much like members of the institutionalized press (let us exclude from this generalization digging through garbage cans for information and lurid headlines based on shoddy reportage). We conduct thorough, thoughtful exploration into social phenomena. Moreover, the ultimate goal of our efforts is publication, and in the majority of cases publication is sought in public venues: scholarly journals and books. As a former journalist, I recognize the distinctions between newspaper or magazine publication and these other forms. My sense is that scholars may act more in the democratic spirit of a free and open press than even the most respected reporters because of the immense amount of time we spend gathering data and analyzing it prior to publication. Moreover, the concept of the press needs to be interpreted broadly. . . . "The press" is not only *The New York Times* or *The Washington Post;* it is, as well, The Palouse-Clearwater Environmental Institute *Newsletter* and *The Sharon Park Homeowner* and *The American Sociological Review.* And that means that the press is *us,* those of us who seek to investigate or comment about the world around us in ways that illuminate the social world. Our work is time-consuming, well-considered and reviewed anonymously by peers, not rushed through at deadline. As scholars we are members of the press in the highest, most democratic and socially responsible sense.

This leads to the second reason why I relied on the Constitution's first amendment protection of the press as the cornerstone legal basis in my case: given that we scholars have claim to such protection, the existing law is far more advanced than that concerning scientific enterprises. Unlike the press, science is not explicitly recognized in the Constitution (though see below). The existing law may not all be friendly, but it has the advantage of being surveyed territory, if only roughly. The federal court decisions speaking to the value of science to society are important, but they serve as a weak basis for claim of a "scientist's privilege" against compelled grand jury testimony.

Asserting the "Privilege"

It was obvious from the beginning of my ordeal that I could not cooperate with the government if it sought access to my data that was gathered under promises of confidentiality. At no point did I admit or deny interviewing anyone involved in the raid at WSU. My concerns were broader than that, for I felt that the government had no right to tamper with my unpublished, ongoing research. These points emerged from the ASA's *Code* and guided me in all that followed.

On November 4, 1992, I appeared before the grand jury for the first time. Bill Clinton had been elected president the prior evening, but for me it was a somber occasion because earlier on November 3 an animal rights activist had been jailed for contempt of court in the same case, and I felt I might be joining him the next day. My appearance before the twenty-three members of the grand jury was brief. I answered several questions, but on the advice of my attorney I refused to answer two others on the basis of my fifth amendment rights against self incrimination. Why did I "plead the fifth," a tactic that most of us think is only taken by those guilty of a crime or who have something to hide, when I had done nothing wrong and only wished to withhold confidential information and nothing else? The purpose was to force the government to grant me immunity from prosecution to protect me from unfounded prosecution by the government. But it seemed to me that justice had been perverted, like it was a child's game of strategy played by adults: everyone knew one another's move. It was perfectly choreographed—everyone had been through this before but me. After I asserted my fifth amendment rights I was taken before U.S. District Court Judge Fremming Nielsen. The Assistant U.S. Attorney in the case, Frank Wilson, told the judge—who had been forewarned that this might happen and made himself available for the proceedings—what had transpired in the grand jury room and that the government was prepared to grant me immunity. He handed Nielsen the faxed form letter from the DOJ in Washington, D.C. My name and the other pertinent information was typed into the proper places, and the judge summarily signed the letter allowing the game to go on, forcing me to testify or risk jail on a contempt of court charge because the DOJ letter stripped me of my fifth amendment rights in exchange for the grant of immunity.

Then my attorney requested that Nielsen hold a hearing on my asserted "academic privilege" exempting me from grand jury testimony. The judge agreed to hold the hearing, forestalling my grand jury appearance and giving me a ray of hope. After some delays the hearings was held on February 19, 1993. The government told the judge that I was not a suspect in the case, reaffirming a statement first made in a letter to my attorney the prior summer. But the government said it felt that I had information that would assist it in pursuing its investigation of the WSU raid. I was called to the witness stand, and under direct examination by my attorney and cross examination by Wilson, I sought to show Judge Nielsen that I was undertaking legitimate scholarly research on the REM when the raid occurred. This was done to lay the groundwork for my asserted academic or scholar's privilege, and the tactic was taken from the only other case of its kind before mine, that of Mario Brajuha.

In the early 1980s Brajuha was a graduate student at SUNY-Stony Brook. First the state of New York and then the federal government sought information from him as part of their investigations of an arson at a restaurant where Brajuha was working. Brajuha's work there was part of his dissertation research (Hallowell 1985; *In re Grand Jury Subpoena (Brajuha)* 1984); like me, he was not a suspect in the crime being investigated. In his case a federal district court judge established several criteria for weighing assertions of a scholar's privilege and said that those claiming such a privilege should be allowed to present evidence in a judge's chambers and without the government's presence. In my case Judge Nielsen refused to allow this *in camera, ex parte* examination of my testimony and instead forced a hypothetical situation on me that accepted the government's supposition that I had interviewed one or more persons involved in the WSU raid. In my cross-examination I argued that working scholars were entitled to first amendment, free press protection—the first amendment reads, "Congress shall make no law . . . abridging the freedom of speech, or of the press . . ."—and that complete grand jury testimony would violate the letter of the ASA *Code of Ethics.* I was anxious that unethical behavior on my part would prevent me from getting the academic position that I aspired to and that research subjects would view me with disdain.

None of this made any difference to the court, however. It ruled that I had to testify, and the judge went so far as to say that a newspaper reporter in my position would fare no differently.

Inviting Contempt

Two weeks later, on March 2 and 3, I appeared before the grand jury for seven and a-half hours. For part of that time three prosecutors were present, including Bill Hyslop, the U.S. Attorney for eastern Washington, and the head of his criminal division. As if I did not already know it, the message was reinforced; the government was treating my testimony very seriously. I answered all of the prosecutors' questions regarding nonconfidential matters, but I refused to answer thirty-two questions that probed confidential communications. In each case I told the grand jury,

> *Your question calls for information that I have only by virtue of a confidential disclosure given to me in the course of my research activities. I cannot answer the question without actually breaching a confidential communication. Consequently, I decline to answer the question under my ethical obligations as a member of the American Sociological Association and pursuant to any privilege that may extend to journalists, researchers, and writers under the First Amendment. (In re: Grand Jury Investigation and Testimony of James Richard Scarce 1993: 36)*

(As the hours wore on, prosecutor Wilson and I agreed on a shorthand version of this statement.) It was my refusal to answer these questions that led to my jailing. At an April 6 hearing before Judge Nielsen, my attorney was joined by an American Civil Liberties Union lawyer in reasserting my first amendment/ASA *Code* arguments. They added that common law created by the Washington State Supreme Court directed that my status as a member of the press exempted me from compelled grand jury testimony about confidential matters, or at least directed a balancing of free press rights and grand jury obligations. But the court would have none of it, and I was found in contempt of court.

The federal contempt statute permits persons who refuse to answer grand jury questions—"recalcitrant witnesses"—to be jailed for the shorter of 18 months or until the grand jury's term ends (*United States Code,* Title 28, §1826). Though most criminologists and most areas of the law make no distinction between "coercion" and "punishment," this statute does. One cannot be jailed unless he or she has been accused or convicted of a crime, since jail is for punishment. But in a congressional act of legerdemain, a sentence of contempt of court was defined as *mere* coercion, and therefore legal, until a magical and empirically indecipherable time when it becomes punishment and therefore *punitive* and illegal. Those who are held to be "in contempt" of grand jury proceedings are not tried, and since they have not been convicted of a crime, they cannot be punished. However, they can be jailed and denied the rights of citizens in ways no different from those who have been convicted of a crime.

Civil contempt is in a legal nether region between civil litigation and criminal law. It is prospective, not retrospective as in criminal cases. Yet it almost always is brought about because of a criminal trial or a grand jury's criminal investigation and leads to punishment that is no different than that which criminals face (at least in terms of location of incarceration and treatment while there), in contrast to civil law.

I remained free on my own recognizance while my appeal was considered by the Ninth U.S. Circuit Court of Appeals. The appeals court denied oral argument in the case and summarily upheld the district court's ruling on May 6 by a 3–0 vote. Its written decision was supposed to be promptly forthcoming. In the meantime I was jailed on the morning of May 14, 1993, after U.S. Attorney Hyslop made a rare appearance in court to plead for my incarceration. It was one of his last official acts before his resignation took effect.

For the next 159 days I lived as an innocent among convicts and the accused in the high-security Spokane County Jail (and for one week at another jail in eastern Washington during a Spokane jailers' strike). I amassed 265 pages of journal notes—my request to conduct an in-jail ethnographic study was denied by WSU's Institutional Review Board in part because I had not made clear what I would do to ensure the confidentiality of my respondents. I tried to use my time inside well. I read extensively, from pulp fiction to philosophy, and I received more than 550 pieces of mail from seven countries, including about 65 cards and letters from faculty and students around the world and from the president of my undergraduate institution. (Prior to my incarceration the sociology faculty at WSU approved a resolution supporting my stance, as did the graduate and undergraduate student associations.) All of my correspondents supported my stand for academic freedom. The time was hard—agonizingly slow and boring, largely devoid of intellectual stimulation. But I grew to know and respect my fellow inmates for the humanity that was within them, and they accorded me respect for refusing to be a "snitch," for keeping my word. When Judge Nielsen felt that my treatment had crossed the magic boundary and had become punitive he ordered me to be released. Early in the evening of October 19 the men of the Three East wing of the Spokane County Jail stood in a line, outside my cell door to shake my hand and hug me good-bye. I had never seen them do anything like it in all my months inside. Later I held my wife and son for the first time since May.

The Appeals Court Ruling

I was in jail more than four months before I found out the Ninth Circuit panel's reasoning behind upholding my contempt citation. The substance of that ruling should send a chill down all scholars' spines. The appeals court said that, so long as the government has a legitimate reason for demanding cooperation with a grand jury, *no one* has a privilege against the grand jury's power. This was based on the long-standing right of the grand jury to hear evidence from all persons. Not even the press has special status when it comes to federal grand juries. They are the most powerful entity in the Constitution. The three-judge panel wrote,

> *Scarce argues that because that work involves the collection and dissemination of information to the public, he is entitled to the same privileges afforded members of the institutional press under the First Amendment's Freedom of Press Clause. Assuming without deciding that scholarly inquiry enjoys the same freedom of press protections that traditional news gathering does, and that Scarce's contact with his informants was incident to such work, we must nonetheless reject Scarce's argument. Under the circumstances presented by this case, the privilege to which Scarce lays claim by analogy simply does not exist. (In re Grand Jury Proceedings (James Richard Scarce) 1993: 399)*

The court did not elaborate on what "the circumstances" were in my case to warrant its extreme view. In addition, the Ninth Circuit's rendering of the facts came entirely from the government's description of them, and it was in serious error. Most important of these errors was the government's assertion that all conversations that I might have had with Coronado took place in the presence of my wife and therefore could not have taken place in confidence. In my response to the government's brief, I stated that there was a considerable gap in time between when my wife and son went birthday shopping and Coronado's departure. Regrettably, the government's erroneous version of the facts has been reported by some without knowledge of its problematic aspects (Anonymous 1994).

The Ninth Circuit's decision was an interpretation of a 1972 Supreme Court decision in *Branzburg v. Hayes*. That case concerned the rights of reporters to withhold information from grand juries when the reporters were witnesses to illegal acts, so-called "percipient witnesses," and the court ruled that no tenable claim to a free press privilege exists in such circumstances. However, lower courts like the Ninth Circuit have extended *Branzburg's* provisions much farther. This creates chaos in the federal court system.

> *In my own case, and in three others over the last year and perhaps as many as two others per year over the last 20 years, federal courts have*

ruled that writers and scholars may protect sources only when (a) the researcher has not witnessed a crime and (b) when, on balance, protecting the source/subject and disseminating the resulting information yields society more benefits than does solving a crime. This is what the best of the rulings say. And only rarely have court decisions come out on the side of the press. (Scarce 1994: 135)

The *Branzburg* ruling left a confused state of affairs in the lower courts, one which the Supreme Court has not clarified. In my appeal of the Ninth Circuit's ruling to the Supreme Court my attorney wrote,

In the majority of circuits, a qualified confidential-source privilege for non-percipient journalist-witnesses is favored. In other circuits, in particular the Ninth, the privilege is denied any validity. Still others reach no definitive conclusion. The lack of a clear standard has resulted in district courts—even within the same circuit—arbitrarily interpreting Branzburg. *(Petition for Certiorari, Scarce v United States, 1993: 10–11)*

My hope was that the Supreme Court might rule on my case and thereby clarify the ambiguities in *Branzburg*. In January 1994 it refused to hear my appeal.

Why Obey an Ethical Code?

Critics of my position usually took any of three perspectives. The first held that the reason that I had refused to cooperate with the grand jury was that I had something to hide. The second type of objection claimed that my stance improperly affected a legitimate investigation. And the third emphasized the problematical nature of the *Code's* absolute injunction against revealing the content of information obtained by researchers under promises of confidentiality.

Each of these arguments was broached by Murray Comarow, an adjunct professor at American University and "a lawyer and former federal official" (Comarow 1993) who wrote a column about my case published in *The Chronicle of Higher Education*. For an attorney Comarow did a shoddy job of fact finding before penning his column. Regarding the first objection, that I had refused to cooperate with the grand jury because of possibly self-incriminatory evidence, Comarow (1993) wrote, ". . . Mr. Scarce may have refused to testify because he feared prosecution or embarrassment. He may or may not have been doing serious research. We simply don't know." What Comarow did not note and did not take the time to find out was that on at least two occasions federal prosecutors stated that I was not a suspect, and in my sworn testimony I stated that I had no foreknowledge of the ALF raid; I was not fearful of prosecution. Comarow correctly notes that I was granted immunity; if there was incriminating evidence, why wouldn't I have shared that with the grand jury to take advantage of the immunity? I fully answered *all* of the government's questions regarding my personal, nonresearch activities or activities that took place outside of the bounds of confidentiality. I had nothing to hide and I cooperated with the government. As for "embarrassment," from the beginning I was embarrassed by the attention and, moreover, I was anxious and anguished at the looming possibility of going to jail to protect my research subjects. Finally, Comarow fails to note that the District Court ruled that my research was bona fide. That my work was a legitimate scholarly enterprise was never in doubt, though it did not have IRB approval for reasons already stated.

Comarow also condemned my actions as impeding a legitimate governmental investigation. He cites federal court cases that note the cherished role of the grand jury in American jurisprudence and that virtually no social group has been exempted from grand jury testimony. Does that make the judiciary's lopsided rendering of the freedom/order equation correct? It does under the law, but ethical codes often espouse and impose higher standards than the law. The law frequently is unjust and often it is only through individual challenge and subsequent judicial response that change is possible.

That was one of the insights that struck me during my jail time. It had fallen upon me, as it very nearly did upon Mario Brajuha a decade before, to uphold an ethical standard that was not recognized in the law. Yet in discussing my reaction to my time in jail, Comarow stooped to *ad hominem* attacks, accusing me of "whining" about my treatment (Comarow 1993).

My actions were a direct result of my commitment to the ASA's position on confidentiality, and Comarow makes the *Code's* direction on this point the object of his third complaint about my stance. Once again going far out on a weak factual and logical limb, Comarow writes, "The ASA code [sic] is silent on the value of research versus the competing value of disclosure to society. A sociologist who secures confidential information on a planned act of terrorism thus should bravely refuse to reveal that information, even in response to a court order" (Comarow 1993). Clearly, if one were to read the *Code* in this way he or she would set themselves up for a far more serious charge than contempt of court. There is no justification whatsoever for a researcher to remain silent about information he or she has about a crime not yet committed, and Comarow's example is a preposterous one.

As for the question of the value of research versus the value of disclosure, the two are not necessarily at odds. Law enforcement personnel often cite my book as being of value to them as they investigate illegal activities by the REM. Eventual disclosure of a researcher's data is the goal of research, without regard to who has access to that data or how it is used. However, thoughtful consideration of material prior to publication is crucial to science and to the press generally. This is recognized by the courts. . . . Comarow, it appears, would willingly have researchers act as agents of the state by compelling us to betray promises of confidentiality. In conversations with several senior professors in my department and in others, that idea clearly is seen as repugnant. . . .

Within the discipline some questioned less my actions than the *Code's* provisions that prompted them. Lee Clarke wrote, "But just as I'm suspicious of law firms and oil companies using social science for nefarious purposes I can't help but look askance at our own organization, making claims on behalf of its members, asserting, basically, that it knows the public interest" (Clarke 1994). However, there are grounds to argue that, in its uncompromising language, the *Code* is in the spirit of the "public interest" as found in the statute that established human subjects review and which effectively codified the concept *do no harm to research subjects.*

Clarke also wrote, "As a collectivity we are forcing field workers to extend promises to respondents that we can not legally keep. *This* seems to me unethical" (Clarke 1994; emphasis in original). At one level Clarke appears to fall into the same trap as Comarow, arguing that the law always comes before ethics. Such an interpretation misses his crucial point, however. It boils down to a question of power. Clarke wrote, "Perhaps our confidentiality rights should be conferred through a democratic process, not organizational fiat." He reasons that our attempts to secure protection for our respondents through the courts have failed because of the powerlessness of the ASA and its members—a legal powerlessness based in a lack of secure constitutional claim to a first amendment privilege for scholars. Though I differ with Clarke on this point, we end up with the same conclusion: we need federal legislation to protect the scholarly work product. . . .

There is another democratic process that needs to be initiated as well, one that more narrowly focuses on the profession. This should precede any attempt at legislative action. First, we as a profession need to know of the *Code's* provisions. It appears that many of us may be unaware of the *Code's* content and that an educational effort is needed within the profession. Further, the ASA should open a dialogue about the *Code* as it exists now and any proposed changes to it. Let us first have consensus about our ethics before we attempt to chisel morality into law.

Despite the seemingly clear and absolute position of the ASA in interpreting and supporting the *Code's* provisions on confidentiality, my case appears to have precipitated some second-guessing. In a response to Comarow's piece published in *The Chronicle of Higher Education,* ASA Executive Director Felice Levine wrote,

> *Thus, Scarce operated consistently with the ASA Code, first in asserting the confidentiality of his research data when it was sought by the prosecutor and then in urging the district court and the court of appeals not to order disclosure to protect his subjects.*
>
> *However, when Scarce decided not to testify after the district court's order was affirmed on appeal, he was no longer acting under compulsion or suggestion of the Code; he was acting out of his own sense of obligation to his subjects. (Levine 1993)*

Levine later explained her position to me, repeating her statement in the *Chronicle* and adding, "Essentially what that is saying is that the *Code* does not compel or suggest that one should not comply with a court order, although the *Code* is quite clear that confidentiality, when granted, should be maintained and that you were acting consistently with the *Code* in urging that that be done to protect subjects" (Personal communication).

$$\bullet \quad \bullet \quad \bullet$$

Conclusion

Where does this leave sociologists? Some say we need to alter our *Code of Ethics,* and to some extent I agree. The *Code* needs to make clear that unless researchers are prepared to go to jail, they should set limits on the scope of their confidentiality assurances at the outset. Important methodological ramifications will follow from this, however. In some instances explicitly telling respondents that you are not willing to go to jail to protect their identity or the content of your communications with them will affect the quality and quantity of data. There may be other ways of handling this situation—one senior researcher at WSU simply dropped the confidentiality statement from his surveys altogether. However, this may not be as forthright as being completely up front with respondents regarding the limits of confidentiality.

This may not appear to be a particularly vexing problem in the profession; it *will not* sound troubling if attitudes toward the *Code* are no different than they were when Long and Dorn's survey on the ASA's ethical statement and committee was administered. But who is to say what work will not be of interest to inquiring government and private entities? Our first duty is to provide for the well-being of our research subjects, and erring on the side of caution is the only ethically defensible position to take.

If researchers do make absolute assurances of confidentiality, though, they should do so with the complete knowledge of what those assurances portend. This means making a conscious decision to go to jail rather than relent in the face of legal pressure to violate confidentiality agreements. And there needs to be the expectation that the profession will support those who make this terrible sacrifice for us all.

$$\bullet \quad \bullet \quad \bullet$$

This is not a question of one scholar every decade facing the dilemma of jail or unethical behavior. The trend of demanding scholars' data appears to be growing. As recently as the summer of 1994 a University of Maryland professor successfully fended off a subpoena that sought his testimony in a criminal trial (personal communication with Michael Traynor). In the face of such mounting pressure, members of the ASA and other scholarly organizations owe it to themselves, to the public, and most of all to their research subjects to evaluate the profession's ethics, the relation of ethics to method, and whether legal backing for those ethics is needed.

References

American Anthropological Association. [1971] 1990. *Statements on Ethics*. Washington, DC: American Anthropological Association.

American Political Science Association. 1991. *Code of Professional Conduct*. Washington, DC: American Political Science Association.

American Psychological Association. 1992. *Ethical Principles of Psychologists and Code of Conduct*. Washington, DC: American Psychological Association.

American Sociological Association. 1968. "Toward a Code of Ethics for Sociologists." *The American Sociologist*, 3(4): 316–318.

———. 1984. *Code of Ethics*. Washington, DC: American Sociological Association.

Anonymous. 1994. "Researcher Goes to Jail for Refusing to Divulge Details about Research Subject." *Human Research Report*, 9(5): 4–5.

Application of American Tobacco Co. 1987. 880 F. 2d. 1520.

Branzburg v. Hayes. 1971. 408 U.S. 665.

Clarke. Lee. 1994. "Some Questions about Confidentiality." *Footnotes*, 22(3): 8.

Cohen v. Cowles Media Co. 1991. 501 U.S. 663.

Comarow, Murray. 1993. "Are Sociologists above the Law?" *The Chronicle of Higher Education*, 40(17): A44.

Connolly v. Pension Benefit Guaranty Corporation. 1986. 475 U.S. 211.

Dow Chemical Co. v. Allen. 1982. 672 F. 2d 1262 (7th Cir.).

Federal Rules of Evidence, §501.

First National Bank of Boston v. Bellotti. 1978. 435 U.S. 765.

Hallowell, Lyle. 1985. "The Outcome of the Brajuha Case: Legal Implications for Sociologists." *Footnotes*, 13(9): 1ff.

In re: Grand Jury Investigation and Testimony of James Richard Scarce. 1993. Panel 92-1S (Eastern District of Washington).

In re: Grand Jury Proceedings (James Richard Scarce). 1993. 5 F. 3d. 397 (9th Cir.).

In re: Grand Jury Subpoena (Brajuha). 1984. 750 F. 2d. 233 (2nd Cir.).

Levine, Felice. 1993. "Protecting the Confidentiality of Research Subjects." *Chronicle of Higher Education*, January 12: B4.

Long, Gary L and Dean S. Dorn. 1982. "An Assessment of the ASA Code of Ethics and Committee on Ethics." *The American Sociologist*, 17(2): 80–86.

Marshall, Eliot. 1993. "Court Orders 'Sharing' of Data." *Science*, 261 (July 16): 284–286.

Petition for Writ of Certiorari. *Scarce v. United States*. 1993. 93–587.

Reporters Committee for Freedom of the Press. N.d. "Recent Jailed Reporters." Photocopy.

Scarce, Rik. 1990. *Eco-Warriors: Understanding the Radial Environmental Movement*. Chicago: Noble Press.

———. 1994. "(No) Trial (But) Tribulations: When Courts and Ethnography Conflict." *The Journal of Contemporary Ethnography*, 23(2): 123–149.

Schuler, Edgar A. 1969. "Toward a Code of Professional Ethics for Sociologists: A Historical Note." *The American Sociologist*, 4(2): 144–146.

Traynor, Michael. 1993. "Countering the Excessive Subpoena for Scholarly Research." Photocopy.

United States Code, Title 28, §1826.

———. Title 42, §242(a).

United States Code of Federal Regulations, Title 42, §§2a. 1–.8.

Conclusion

As demonstrated in section three, an extreme methodological approach is typically employed in the analysis of clandestine, taboo, and highly dangerous topics. It is usually these characteristics that necessitate the use of an alternative qualitative approach in the first place. The illustrations that are provided in the readings often involved perilous and unpredictable settings, such as drug dealing, sexually deviant, and similar subcultures, demonstrate the extreme measures that carry researchers into situations in which their personal safety is jeopardized and their ethical and moral boundaries challenged. The readings in this last section have examined in more detail these problems that almost always must be confronted by extreme researchers.

Here we have observed strategies for addressing issues of stigma, both for subjects and stigma that can extend to the researcher via guilt by association with deviants and criminals. Strategies were advocated for dealing with a variety of potentially dangerous situations ranging from extreme (e.g., drive-by shootings) to more common occurrences (e.g., unwanted sexual advances, fighting, and encounters with law enforcement authorities). Perhaps a more common problem is the matter of ethics—many situations may call for difficult decisions despite an absence of immediate danger or legal violation. Below are questions that extreme researchers need to seriously consider, although such questions have no clear answers.

Questions for Discussions

1. How is conducting field research on stigmatized groups different from using other methods to study similar groups? What are some consequences of choosing to conduct field research on stigmatized subject groups?

2. Given that researchers' willingness to enter dangerous field settings is consistent with the social science principle of informed consent, should dangerous fieldwork be regulated? If yes, by whom?

3. What would you have done had you been in Ric Scarce's situation? Should relationships between social scientists and their research subjects be afforded the same standards of legal protection as physician/patient or attorney/client relationships?